ADDISON AND STEELE
SELECTIONS FROM
THE TATLER
AND THE SPECTATOR

Second Edition

INTRODUCTION AND NOTES
BY ROBERT J. ALLEN
Williams College

HOLT, RINEHART AND WINSTON, INC.
New York • Chicago • San Francisco • Atlanta
Dallas • Montreal • Toronto • London • Sydney

Introduction, Chronology, and Notes © 1957, 1970 by Robert J. Allen
All Rights Reserved
Library of Congress Catalog Card Number: 79-97857
SBN: 03-080790-5
Printed in the United States of America
1 2 3 4 5 6 7 8 9

INTRODUCTION

In the two literary forms which they themselves considere greatest, epic and tragedy, the English writers of the eigh eenth century made no very remarkable contributions. Ye the age was not without its originality. It saw the beginning of new and extraordinarily fruitful developments in fiction and biography; and it brought to perfection three minor forms, the ballad opera, the letter, and the periodical essay. In the limited and perhaps arbitrary selections from *The Tatler* and *The Spectator* which make up the present volume, it is possible to glimpse some of the new traits that were soon to enter prose fiction and some of the calculated artistry with which eighteenth-century letter writers entertained their correspondents. In addition, these selections provide an opportunity to study in all its variety that subtle and permanently delightful form, the familiar essay.

Although this is not the place to follow the history of the essay form in European literature, it is worth noting that in Addison's time the word "essay" was a relatively new one in English. It had been given currency in France in 1580, when Montaigne's highly personal reflections on men and their behavior were first published as *Essais*. The word had come into English in 1597 with the publication, under the title of *Essayes,* of Francis Bacon's aphoristic generalizations on the human condition. During the seventeenth century two main currents are visible in the development of the essay. One, represented by Abraham Cowley, preserved the intention of Montaigne to convey a moment of personal reflection on whatever subject was uppermost in the author's mind. The other current, derived in part from Bacon, pursued general human truth and sought to enlighten the reader for his moral benefit. Various influences, from the Platonic dialogue to the Theophrastian character, drifted into these currents, but at their confluence in the papers of *The Tatler* and *The Spectator* the two main streams are still apparent, sometimes noticeably distinct, sometimes happily blended. The moral import of their essays is frequently insisted upon by both Addison and Steele. The creation of fictitious authors for the two periodicals, on the other hand, suggests that they recognized the interest to readers of an understood personality engaged in reflections that were in some measure capricious and self-indulgent. In an age when emotional modesty was a part of good manners, the essayists were embarrassed to speak in their own persons, as Steele said plainly in the essay which brought *The Spectator* to a close on December 6, 1712. Yet neither he nor Addison could deny himself the pleasure of Montaigne in recording highly personal impressions.

In method, as well as intention, the originality of *The Tatler* and *The Spectator* consisted in their skillful fusion of the practices of other writers. Much of the vividness and immediacy of the papers resulted from what may be called their dramatic quality. They are full of characters. When Steele wished to comment on the evils of dueling, he was not content merely to describe the inanities of the existing code of honor. He produced in *The Tatler* (No. 25) a letter from a hypothetical gentleman not much used to the ways of the Town who had been insulted in public and could not understand why he should be offered "satisfaction" in the form of an opportunity to get himself run through the body. When Addison wished to present a pedant who prided himself on his knowledge of typography and editions without knowing anything of the contents of books, there appeared in *The Tatler* (No. 158) the portrait of the learned ignoramus Tom Folio. As in the essays of La Bruyère, these fictitious persons are revealed by their speech and actions as well as by what the author says about them in his own person. More than any of their predecessors, however, Steele and Addison managed to endow their characters with an interest that is independent of, at the same time that it contributes to, the statement being made about contemporary manners. Sir Roger de Coverley, Will Wimble, and Sir Andrew Freeport have an almost Chaucerian superiority to the stock roles in which they are cast as Tory baronet, younger son, and influential merchant.

Another factor in the vitality of the essays can only be described as journalistic. As the papers first appeared, they had the format and some of the interest of a newspaper. They came out at regular intervals (*The Tatler* three times a week, *The Spectator* every day except Sunday), they preserved a running title and dateline, and they were printed on both sides of a folio half-sheet just as contemporary newspapers were. Whereas *The Post Man* and *The Flying Post* furnished news of events in England and the various capitals of Europe, *The Tatler* and *The Spectator* supplied news of the Town and the everyday concerns of its people in the realms of manners, morals, literature, and the arts. In the early issues of *The Tatler,* Steele tried to cover all these areas of polite conversation in a single paper with results that can be seen in Nos. 1 and 25. Later, as advertising encroached on the inexorably limited space of the folio half-sheet, a single subject was considered enough for a whole issue and the coverage was maintained by varying the material from paper to paper. Almost always, however, there was a connection between the day's essay and a topic that was, or in the opinion of the authors ought to be, on the tongues of the town — a new play, a military exploit, a specific cause that deserved charitable contributions, a new affectation in dress, a freshly applicable idea of a critic or a philosopher. The more the papers are studied in connection with the day-to-day events of their time, the clearer their journalistic nature becomes.

The principal authors of *The Tatler* and *The Spectator* were admirably suited, both as individuals and as collaborators, to the kind of enterprise on which Steele now embarked. A glance at the chronologies of their lives reveals that they were almost exactly the same age, Steele being, surprisingly, a few weeks the elder. They had met as boys at Charterhouse and had maintained their friendship at Oxford, whence Steele had departed without a degree for a career in the army while Addison settled down at Magdalen as a don. By the time they were thirty-five, the life of each had altered its course. Under the patronage of influential Whig statesmen, Addison had made the grand tour of Europe and had embarked on a diplomatic career. Steele had written three successful comedies and identified himself with the literary world of London. Their collaboration had begun at least as early as 1705, when Addison had helped Steele in revising *The Tender Husband*. It continued after Steele became editor of the government-sponsored *London Gazette* in 1707. Since Addison, by this time, was an undersecretary of state, both men found advantage in working together on the *Gazette,* Addison's private intelligences furnishing the Gazetteer with material not always available to journalists and Steele helping the Government to put its best foot forward in the official news releases. Both men were on easy terms with the great Whig statesmen of the day as well as with their fellow wits, and they were alike in dividing their time between politics and writing except in the matter of emphasis. Addison became primarily a professional stateman, whose surplus energies were devoted to the world of letters. Steele developed into a professional journalist and man of the theater, who also engaged in politics. Thus, when Steele began *The Tatler* in April, 1709, near the beginning of his thirty-eighth year, the collaboration which soon followed was the continuance of a well-established relationship.

Tradition has it that Addison, who had gone to Ireland with Lord Wharton, knew nothing of Steele's journalistic venture until in the sixth number of *The Tatler* he came across a comment on the use of epithets by Virgil and Homer which he remembered having made to Steele years earlier. Pleasant as this story is, it seems quite unlikely. Addison had stood godfather to Steele's daughter Elizabeth on April 6 and had left London on the ninth. The first *Tatler* appeared April 12. Busy though Addison may have been with affairs of state, he could hardly have failed to be consulted on a literary project of this scope. Steele acknowledged more than once that he consulted Swift while the project was taking shape, and since the three were in close touch with each other during the early part of that spring Addison must have known in advance what was afoot.

Before *The Tatler* was two months old, Addison had sent over from Ireland material for three numbers (Nos. 18, 20, and 24.) All through the summer, however, Steele carried on the periodical almost single-handed, and it was not until November, two months after Addison's return from Ireland, that it became in reality a joint enterprise. For about a month, March 30 to April 25, 1710, Addison carried on *The Tatler* with very little help from Steele. (Of the 271 numbers, Steele wrote at least two-thirds and collaborated in many more.) For most of the journal's run, Steele, as editor, was responsible for providing an essay each Tuesday, Thursday, and Saturday if no one else did; and it is no wonder if Steele's papers do not always show the finish of those supplied by Addison. His role as Gazetteer of the Town was a strenuous one.

The popularity of *The Tatler* was immediate and enormous. The Town was already familiar with the name of the supposed author, Isaac Bickerstaff, who had been created by Swift a year earlier in the course of a literary prank, carried on for months at the expense of the almanac-maker, John Partridge. Swift represented Mr. Bickerstaff as a sedate and responsible astrologer who resented the catch-penny publications of quacks like the miserable Partridge. Posing as Mr. Bickerstaff, Swift foretold the death of Partridge and then, in an anonymous pamphlet, announced the accomplishment of Mr. Bickerstaff's prediction. Partridge's protest that he was still alive resulted in a series of replies by Swift and his friends, including Steele, and the game had amused the Town for the better part of a year. Not only did Swift now permit the use of his already popular character, Mr. Bickerstaff, as the fictitious writer of *The Tatler,* but he gave numerous hints for essays and contributed all or part of a dozen or so.

During the weeks following Mr. Bickerstaff's reappearance, the correspondence of ladies and gentlemen residing in London was full of delighted references to the "whimsical new newspaper" and guesses were freely exchanged on the identity of the beaus and coquettes who served anonymously as examples of the social foibles held up to ridicule. The broad appeal of the papers seems to have been due not only to their wit and variety, but also to the editorial position which was soon set up. Along with the easy assurance of a well-educated gentleman of quality, Steele showed a genuine interest in reforming manners that pleased well-to-do middle-class readers. He measured the evils of dueling, the inadequacies of education, the extravagances of dress, and the oppressiveness of current marriage conventions by standards that came not from court society but from common sense and Christian morality. Steele was unwilling to see good manners sacrificed to fine manners, and he was unashamed in his concern for the domestic, middle-class virtues. Thus *The Tatler* had an appeal which went far beyond the limits of the beau monde—as far, indeed, as did the newly arisen sentimental comedy, which Steele did much to popularize. His middle-class readers particularly enjoyed the witty pictures (often satiric) of their social superiors because the moral position from which London manners were viewed was essentially their own.

When Steele brought *The Tatler* to a close on January 2, 1711, after nearly two years, it was not because he and Addison had lost their touch as essayists. It was because their disguise as Isaac Bickerstaff had been penetrated and because the periodical had become involved in party politics.[1] During its course, the Whigs had fallen, Addison had lost his Irish secre-

---

[1] For a more detailed account of political matters with which *The Tatler* became concerned, see Calhoun Winton, *Captain Steele* (Baltimore: The Johns Hopkins Press, 1964), pp. 112-122.

taryship, and Steele had been replaced as Gazetteer. Their witty friend, Jonathan Swift, had stopped giving them materials and "hints" for *The Tatler* and was now writing for the ascendant Tories. Since their journal was subject to frequent attacks from Tory journalists, it was difficult to continue in the role of an unbiased censor of manners, especially after the editors had entered the political arena to the extent of eulogizing one of the great Whigs of the day, the Duke of Marlborough. Altogether it seemed easier to begin a new periodical, with a new fictitious author and a more careful avoidance of party associations. Being out of employment and surrounded by witty friends who were willing to help, they waited only two months before launching their new enterprise, *The Spectator*.

Although Steele was once more the responsible editor, the new work was a joint enterprise to a degree that *The Tatler* never was. Writing later of Addison's contribution, his friend and first editor, Thomas Tickell, made known that "the plan of the *Spectator,* as far as it regards the feigned person of the Author, and of the several characters that compose his club, was projected in concert with Sir *Richard Steele*." Addison wrote the first number, creating Mr. Spectator as the fictitious author. Steele wrote the second, introducing the members of the club, whom Tickell was the first to call the *Dramatis Personae*. The two shared the editorial work, and though Steele wrote and signed the final number, Addison's total contribution comprised almost half of the 555 papers which made up the original run of the periodical.[2]

This time the collaborators managed to keep their journal entirely out of politics and to maintain the editorial policy on which *The Tatler* had been founded. Steele continued to pay court to his lady readers with papers on social and domestic

[2] In the latter half of 1714 *The Spectator* was revived for eighty numbers (Nos. 556-635) by Addison, Eustace Budgell, and Thomas Tickell. The publication and authorship of both series of papers are treated in detail by Donald F. Bond, ed., *The Spectator* (Oxford, 1965), I, xx-xxix, xliii-lix, lxxiii-lxxxiii. See also Calhoun Winton, *Captain Steele,* pp. 112-122.

matters, and Addison was able to repeat his success with witty, satirical portraits of contemporary fops and fools. Although the best of *The Spectator* is perhaps no better than the best of *The Tatler,* the general level of excellence is noticeably higher.

In addition, two important advances were made. In the first place, the recurring characters in *The Spectator* became a sustained device for linking the papers together. Sir Roger, Sir Andrew, and Will Honeycomb, Captain Sentry and the Templar were so persuasively characterized that readers were delighted each time they reappeared. Besides giving an artificial unity to the varied satire, these characters supplied a kind of narrative interest which gave a structure to the periodical as a whole. How well the collaborators were aware of this is revealed by the care they took, in ending *The Spectator,* to let their readers know what became of each member of the club. The treatment of the characters in this respect, as well as their use for satiric purposes and the methods by which they were portrayed, reminds one of Fielding's *Tom Jones.*

A second advance in *The Spectator* can be seen in the subject matter treated in the more serious essays. For some years, if we can believe Thomas Tickell, Addison had been collecting "little hints and minutes" which he now proceeded to turn into groups of essays. Of this sort were the series on true and false wit, on tragedy, on Milton's *Paradise Lost,* and on the pleasures of the imagination. Some of these essays were so brightly written that any reader would have been delighted with them—witness the following passage on puns from No. 61:

But the Age in which *the Punn* chiefly flourished, was the Reign of King *James* the First. That learned Monarch was himself a tolerable Punnster, and made very few Bishops or Privy-Counsellors that had not some time or other signalized themselves by a Clinch, or a *Conundrum*. . . . The Sermons of Bishop *Andrews,* and the Tragedies of *Shakespear,* are full of them. The Sinner was punned into Repentence by the former, as in the latter nothing is more usual than to see a Hero weeping and quibbling for a dozen Lines together.

Here the intention is satiric as well as critical, and the brittle rhythms remind one stylistically of the dialogue in Congreve's comedies. In the essays on tragedy, however, and those on Milton, Addison was serializing a substantial piece of literary criticism, calculated for an audience with a fair amount of literary sophistication. Unwilling to tire his less serious readers, he spaced the eighteen papers on *Paradise Lost* by publishing them on consecutive Saturdays. But the eleven on the pleasures of the imagination were run without interruption (Nos. 411 - 421) as a rather daring experiment. The boldness of the editors in venturing their tea-table popularity to this extent in the interest of improving the critical faculties of their readers suggests the confidence they had gained by three years' experience in delighting a wide public.

So far as the learned world was concerned, the critical essays were less daring. Although Addison's two papers on *Chevy Chase* were vastly influential in arousing interest in the popular ballads, his critical method was the method of his time. He rationalized the emotional impact of *Chevy Chase* by citing its appeal to the sixteenth-century *libertin* Sir Philip Sidney and verified the universality of the ballad by adducing parallel passages from Virgil. The poem was of a sort which had been approved in all times and places, and Addison's defense of it was not particularly advanced in resting its merits on the *consensus gentium,* the common agreement of mankind. The same may be said, less emphatically, of the papers on *Paradise Lost,* which were colored by a kind of mild Aristotelianism and tended to make excuses for Milton when he departed from currently accepted theories of the epic.

In the series of papers on the pleasures of the imagination, Addison was somewhat bolder. It is true that he was concerned with the relative value of learning and genius in the make-up of a poet, a problem which had interested English critics from

Sidney and Jonson to Dryden and Pope. Addison's position, however, was fortified not only by "Longinus on the Sublime" but by the new psychology of John Locke. Much more than Pope he invited readers to consider the impact of poetry on their feelings and their literary sensitivities, to reject nothing out of a prejudice in favor of rigid classicism, and to try to understand how their reactions were evoked.

Of the subsequent periodical ventures of Addison and Steele, *The Guardian* was most nearly in their established vein. Begun by Steele on March 12, 1713, three months after the demise of *The Spectator,* it appeared every weekday for 175 numbers, with Addison contributing more than a third. The fictitious author was Nestor Ironside, an elderly gentleman with a university education, and the satire on contemporary manners was derived from conversations around the tea table of Lady Lizard, in whose family Mr. Ironside had served for years as tutor, adviser, and guardian of her children. The device was a good one, though it lent itself more readily to serious moralizing than to a gay dissection of contemporary manners. It was the heavier emphasis on philosophical and critical subjects and the eventual intrusion of politics that gave *The Guardian* its altered character. In spite of Berkeley's lively contribution (No. 39) on the pineal gland of a free-thinker and Pope's malicious trick (No. 40) in connection with Ambrose Philips's pastorals, *The Guardian* often lacked the sprightliness of its immediate predecessors. None of Steele's later journalistic enterprises matched the success he and Addison had attained in *The Tatler* and *The Spectator.*

In an odd way, the middle-class morality purveyed by Addison and Steele limited the success of the new genre which they had so brilliantly initiated. Their reformative program was such a salable commodity that their imitators could neglect to be amusing. Certain writers for *The Adventurer, The World,* and *The Connoisseur* managed during the 1750s to recapture some of the variety and wit of their models. The countless reprints of *The Tatler* and *The Spectator* during the eighteenth century must be explained, however, in terms of their literary superiority as well as their moral position. Dr. Johnson considered them "to be among the first books by which both sexes are initiated into the elegances of knowledge" and admired them for teaching "the frolick and the gay to unite merriment with decency." But when Johnson came to write periodical essays himself in *The Rambler,* there was little gaiety and little elegance. Lady Mary Wortley Montagu's famous dictum that Johnson followed *The Spectator* "with the same pace a pack-horse would do a hunter" is not altogether fair. Her figure of speech does suggest, however, a recognizable difference in style between the two periodicals and a noticeable tendency in Johnson to emphasize morality at the expense of wit.

Throughout the nineteenth century *The Tatler* and *The Spectator* continued to delight a large public. Their position on moral and social matters was congenial to the humanitarian impulses of the times, and the familiar essay continued to be a practiced literary form. During the past hundred years, however, dueling has ceased to be a problem, witch hunting has subsided into a metaphor, and the state has begun to accept responsibilities for human welfare which Addison and Steele urged charitable individuals to assume. The novelist and the dramatist, meanwhile, have largely taken over the art of propagandizing, leaving more direct efforts to tell people "what to think" to the writers of informative articles and newspaper editorials. The modern reader cannot, then, expect from *The Tatler* and *The Spectator* the kind of experience which many Victorians had—the experience of being addressed on subjects still important, from a position still shared, in a form which had not yet been abandoned.

Far from placing him at a disadvantage, this detachment from Queen Anne's England enables the twentieth-century reader to respond to the essays in ways that the Victorians could not. There is little temptation to re-form the complex of eighteenth-century thought and feeling in our own image, as Thackeray tended to do in writing *Henry Esmond*. Through the essays we enter a world that is so clearly not ours that we can enjoy it and understand it as it is. At the same time, we are equipped with a built-in commentary, which, save for a few specific allusions, makes the intellectual and social milieu self-explanatory. It would be hard to find, in the same compass, a better introduction to the world inhabited by Farquhar and Gay, Swift and Pope, Richardson and Fielding. Meanwhile there is an opportunity to delight in a minor form of literary art, now almost as rare as pastoral poetry, which in the hands of Steele and Addison reached its highest perfection.

R.J.A.

October 1969

CHRONOLOGY

Addison

1672 Born, May 1, at his father's rectory in Wiltshire.

1683 Lancelot Addison, his father, became Dean of Lichfield.

1683-85 At school in Lichfield.

1686-87 At Charterhouse. Became a friend of Steele, who later visited in the Dean's family in Lichfield.

1687-91 At Oxford: undergraduate at Queen's and Magdalen.

1691-98 Tutor at Oxford; M. A. 1693; made the acquaintance of Dryden in London; growing reputation for Latin verse.

Contributed English poems to Tonson's *Miscellany* (1694).

Admitted a Fellow of Magdalen, July 30, 1698.

1699-1703 Granted £ 200, through the influence of leading Whig statesmen, to prepare for a diplomatic career.

Traveled and studied in France, Italy, Switzerland, Austria, Germany, Holland.

Visited the Hanoverian Court.

1703 Met the Whiggish publisher Jacob Tonson and various Whig statesmen in Holland; news of the death of his father.

1704 Returned to England. Renewed his friendship with Steele and the Whig wits.

Published *The Campaign,* a poem on Marlborough's victory at Blenheim.

1705 Aided Steele in revising his comedy, *The Tender Husband.* Published *Remarks on Italy.*

1706 Appointed Undersecretary of State. Accompanied Lord Halifax on a mission to the Court of Hanover.

Wrote the libretto of the opera, *Rosamond,* which was performed March 4, 1707.

1707   Busy with duties as Undersecretary. Lodged with Steele during the summer.

1708   Saw much of Steele and Swift. Appointed Secretary to Lord Wharton, the new Lord Lieutenant of Ireland.

1709   Godfather to Steele's daughter, Elizabeth.

       In Ireland, April to September, with Lord Wharton.

1710   Frequent contributions to *The Tatler.* Elected M. P. for Malmesbury, March 11.

       Published five numbers of *The Whip Examiner* in defense of the tottering Whig government.

       End of the Irish Secretaryship, with the fall of the Whigs.

1711   Collaborated with Steele in *The Spectator.* Cooling of friendship with Swift, who was now allied with the Tories.

1712   Leader of the group of Whig wits, including Steele, who gathered at Button's Coffee-house. Extensive contributions to *The Spectator.*

1713   Bought an estate in Warwickshire. Revised his tragedy, *Cato,* under encouragement of Steele. *Cato* acted, April 14.

       Took over *The Guardian,* July 1 to August 3.

1714   Revived *The Spectator* (Nos. 556 - 635), June 18 to December 20, with the help of Eustace Budgell and Thomas Tickell. Short but distinguished term as Secretary to the Regency and to the Lords Justices, in August and September, following the death of Queen Anne.

       Disappointed at being reappointed to his old position as Secretary of the Irish Government.

1715   Active among the Whig wits at Button's Coffee-house. Appointed to the lucrative post of Commissioner of Trade.

1716   Published *The Freeholder,* begun December 20, 1715. Revised his comedy, *The Drummer,* for production by Steele.

       Married to the Countess of Warwick, August 9.

1717   Appointed to his highest post, Secretary of State.

1718   Ill from overwork; resigned as Secretary of State.

       Visited Bristol for his health.

1719   Daughter, Charlotte, born, January 30. Defended the Peerage
       Bill, in *The Old Whig,* against attacks by Steele.
         Died, June 17, having named Thomas Tickell his literary executor.
1721   Publication of Tickell's edition of Addison's *Works.*

CHRONOLOGY

Steele

1672 Born, March 12, in Dublin near Swift's birthplace.

1677? Death of Steele's father and, soon after, of his mother.

1677-84 Educated in Dublin by his uncle and guardian, Henry Gascoigne.

1684-89 Sent to one of London's most famous schools, the Charterhouse.

1689-94 At Oxford: Christ Church and Merton.

1694-95 Left Oxford without taking a degree and enlisted in the Horse Guards.

1695 Published a poem on the death of Queen Mary, dedicated to his commanding officer, Lord Cutts.

1695-1700 Ensign, then Captain, in the Coldstream Guards, attached to Lord Cutts.

1700 Wrote verses in defense of Addison; wounded Captain Kelly in a duel.

1701 Wrote *The Christian Hero* and his first comedy, *The Funeral, or Grief à la Mode* (acted in 1702).

1703-04 Wrote *The Lying Lover* (acted in December, 1703); stationed near London at Landguard Fort; renewed friendship with Addison and met Whig wits and statemen.

1705 Published *The Tender Husband,* a comedy, first acted April 23. First marriage, to Margaret Stretch.

1706 Became gentleman-waiter to Prince George, the husband of Queen Anne. Death of his first wife.

1707 Contributed poems to *The Muses Mercury.* Appointed Gazetteer, through the influence of his Whig friend, Arthur Maynwaring.

Married Mary Scurlock ("Prue").

1708 The Bickerstaff pamphlets published by Swift.

1709 Published *The Tatler,* beginning April 12.

1710 Made a Commissioner of the Stamp Office, January.

Lost the position of Gazetteer in October upon the fall of the Whig government.

1711 Conclusion of *The Tatler,* January 2. Began *The Spectator,* in close collaboration with Addison, March 1.

1712 Conclusion of *The Spectator,* December 6.

1713 Published *The Guardian,* March 12 to October 1.

Elected M.P. for Stockbridge, August 25.

Published *The Englishman,* October 6 to February 14, 1714.

1714 Published political pamphlets, including *The Crisis,* which attacked the Tories.

Expelled from Parliament, March 18, for writing *The Crisis* and *The Englishman.*

Published *The Lover,* February 25 to May 27, and *The Reader,* April 22 to May 10.

When the death of Queen Anne returned the Whigs to power, August 1, Steele was appointed manager of Drury Lane Theatre (October 18).

1715 Elected to Parliament from Boroughbridge, February 2.

Knighted by George I.

Revived *The Englishman,* July 11 to November 21.

1716 Aided Addison in revising *The Drummer* (acted March 10).

Published *Town Talk,* December 17, 1715, to February 13.

Supported the bill for septennial parliaments.

1717 Journey to Scotland as a Commissioner.

1718 Obtained a royal patent for shipping fish alive in "wellboats."

Second visit to Scotland.

Death of Lady Steele.

1719 Aided in defeating the Peerage Bill by publishing *The Plebeian* and *A Letter to the Earl of O[xfor]d.*

1720   Controversy with Newcastle over Drury Lane. Published *The Theatre*, January 2 to April 5. Managership of Drury Lane terminated by Newcastle.

1721   Managership of Drury Lane restored. Answered Tickell's preface to Addison's *Works* in an apologia prefixed to a new edition of Addison's *The Drummer*.

1722   Elected M. P. for Wendover. Finished *The Conscious Lovers* (acted November 7).

1725-29   Spent his time largely in Wales for reasons of health and economy. Partly paralyzed by a stroke, 1726. Worked on an unfinished comedy.

Died, September 1, 1729.

SELECTED BIBLIOGRAPHY

Complete Texts of THE TATLER AND THE SPECTATOR:

Aitken, G. A., ed. *The Tatler*. 4 Vols.; London: Duckworth & Co., 1898-99.

———, ed. *The Spectator*. 8 Vols.; London: John C. Nimmo, 1898.

Bond, Donald F., ed. *The Spectator*. 5 Vols.; Oxford: Clarendon Press, 1965. [Superior text and critical apparatus.]

Smith, G. Gregory, ed. *The Spectator*. 4 Vols.; London: J. M. Dent & Sons Ltd., 1954 (Everyman Library).

Works on ADDISON and STEELE:

Aitken, G. A. *The Life of Richard Steele*. 2 Vols.; Boston and New York: Houghton, Mifflin and Company, 1889.

Blanchard, Rae, ed. *The Correspondence of Richard Steele*. London: Oxford University Press, 1941.

———, ed. *Tracts and Pamphlets by Richard Steele*. Baltimore: The Johns Hopkins Press, 1944.

Bond, Richmond P., ed. *Studies in the Early English Periodical*. Chapel Hill: The University of North Carolina Press, 1957.

———, ed. *New Letters to the Tatler and Spectator*. Austin: University of Texas Press, 1959.

Connely, Willard. *Sir Richard Steele*. New York: Charles Scribner's Sons, 1934.

Dobrée, Bonamy. "The First Victorian," in *Essays in Biography, 1680-1726*. London: Oxford University Press, 1925.

Gay, Peter. "The Spectator as Actor: Addison in Perspective," *Encounter*, Vol. 29, No. 6, pp. 27-32.

Graham, Walter. *English Literary Periodicals.* New York: Thomas Nelson and Sons, 1930.

———, ed. *The Letters of Joseph Addison.* Oxford: Clarendon Press, 1954.

Loftis, John. *Steele at Drury Lane.* Berkeley and Los Angeles: University of California Press, 1952.

Smithers, Peter. *The Life of Joseph Addison.* Oxford: Clarendon Press, 1968.

Watson, Melvin R. "*The Spectator* Tradition and the Development of the Familiar Essay," *English Literary History,* XIII (1946), 189-215.

Winton, Calhoun. *Captain Steele.* Baltimore: The Johns Hopkins Press, 1964.

For a more exhaustive bibliography of works written since 1926, see *English Literature, 1660-1800: A Bibliography of Modern Studies Compiled for Philological Quarterly by Ronald S. Crane and others.* 4 Vols.; Princeton: Princeton University Press, 1950-62. For works written before 1926, see the bibliography at the end of Walter Graham's *English Literary Periodicals.*

TEXTUAL NOTE

The text of the papers is based on the first *octavo* reprints of the original half-sheets: *The Tatler* (1710-1711), 4 Vols.; *The Spectator* (1712-1715), 8 Vols. Departures from the texts of these editions consist chiefly in minor matters of typography, except for the correction of a few obvious printers' errors.

Addison comments in *The Spectator,* No. 529, on the added status acquired by a single-sheet publication like *The Spectator* when it is reprinted in octavo. Although his remarks are undoubtedly facetious in part, Addison may at the same time be justifying his practice of making liberal corrections in the text of his own essays, both at the single-sheet stage of publication and later when they were being reprinted in the octavo editions.

Under the careful editing of Professor Donald F. Bond a text has been provided that reproduces with extraordinary accuracy the original folio half-sheets. In presenting a text based on the first octavo editions, the present volume will not only avoid duplication; it will, at the same time, offer a later stage in the textual development of the essays reprinted, along with an opportunity to make exploratory comparisons that may throw light on the intentions and methods of the essayists.

SUBJECT INDEX
TO THE ESSAYS

PROSE FICTION

The Tatler, Nos. 107, 181, 249

The Spectator, Nos. 1, 2, 11, 15, 34, 80, 94, 96, 106, 108, 109, 113, 122, 130, 131, 159, 181, 335, 499, 517, 530, 549, 555

(Note: These categories frequently overlap, particularly "manners" and "moral and philosophical climate." Since a number of the papers bear on more than one subject, they are often listed more than once. The following papers involving Sir Roger de Coverley have been included: Nos. 2, 6, 26, 34, 106, 108, 109, 110, 113, 117, 122, 131, 335, 517.)

CONTENTS

THE TATLER

BY ISAAC BICKERSTAFF ESQ;

No. 1   *Tuesday, April* 12, 1709.   [Steele]

Quicquid agunt Homines nostri Farrago Libelli.[1]

Tho' the other Papers which are publish'd for the Use of the good People of ENGLAND *have certainly very wholesom Effects, and are laudable in their particular Kinds, they do not seem to come up to the main Design of such Narrations, which, I humbly presume, should be principally intended for the Use of Politick Persons, who are so publick-spirited as to neglect their own Affairs to look into Transactions of State. Now these Gentlemen, for the most Part, being Persons of strong Zeal and weak Intellects, It is both a Charitable and Necessary Work to offer something, whereby such worthy and well-affected Members of the Commonwealth may be instructed, after their Reading,* WHAT TO THINK: *Which shall be the End and Purpose of this my Paper, wherein I shall from Time to Time Report and Consider all Matters of what Kind soever that shall occur to Me, and publish such my Advices and Reflections every* TUESDAY, THURSDAY, *and* SATURDAY, *in the Week, for the Convenience of the Post. I resolve also to have something which may be of Entertainment to the Fair Sex, in Honour of whom I have invented the Title of this Paper. I therefore earnestly desire all Persons, without Distinction, to take it in for the present* GRATIS, *and hereafter at the Price of one Penny, forbidding all Hawkers to take more for it at their Peril. And I desire all*

---

[1] "All the doings of mankind shall form the motley subject of my page." In the original folio half-sheet edition, this motto was used continuously throughout the first forty numbers.

Persons to consider, that I am at a very great Charge for proper Materials for this Work, as well as that before I resolv'd upon it I had settled a Correspondence in all Parts of the Known and Knowing World. And forasmuch as this Globe is not trodden upon by mere Drudges of Business only, but that Men of Spirit and Genius are justly to be esteem'd as considerable Agents in it, we shall not upon a Dearth of News present you with musty Foreign Edicts, or dull Proclamations, but shall divide our Relation of the Passages which occur in Action or Discourse throughout this Town, as well as elsewhere, under such Dates of Places as may prepare you for the Matter you are to expect, in the following Manner:

All Accounts of GALLANTRY, PLEASURE, *and* ENTERTAINMENT, *shall be under the Article of* WHITE'S CHOCOLATE-HOUSE: POETRY, *under that of* WILL'S COFFEE-HOUSE; LEARNING *under the Title of* GRÆCIAN; FOREIGN *and* DOMESTICK NEWS, *you will have from* ST. JAMES'S COFFEE-HOUSE; *and what else I have to offer on any other Subject, shall be dated from my own* APARTMENT.[2]

I once more desire my Reader to consider, That as I cannot keep an Ingenious Man to go daily to WILL'S, *under Twopence each Day merely for his Charges; to* WHITE'S, *under Sixpence; nor to the* GRÆCIAN, *without allowing him some Plain* SPANISH,[3] *to be as able as others at the Learned Table; and that a good Observer cannot speak with even* KIDNEY[4] *at St.*

---

[2] In dating his news of the town from these well-known coffee-houses, Steele was imitating the practice of contemporary newspapers in dating local and foreign news from London and various foreign cities. White's Chocolate-house and the St. James's Coffee-house, both near the royal palace, were rendezous of those concerned with court society and with the latest political news. Will's, in the theater district, was the haunt of poets and dramatists, and the Grecian of men of learning. As *The Tatler* progressed, more and more of the papers tended to be made up of a single essay, dated "From my own Apartment" or, later, from "Sheer Lane." See note 9.

[3] Snuff.

[4] Kidney was a waiter at St. James's Coffee-house.

James's without clean Linnen: I say, these Considerations will, I hope, make all Persons willing to comply with my Humble Request (when my GRATIS *Stock is exhausted) of a Penny a Piece; especially since they are sure of some Proper Amusement, and that it is impossible for me to want Means to entertain 'em, having, besides the Force of my own Parts, the Power of Divination, and that I can, by casting a Figure, tell you all that will happen before it comes to pass.* [5]

But this last Faculty I shall use very sparingly, and speak but of few Things 'till they are pass'd, for fear of divulging Matters which may offend our Superiors.

White's Chocolate-house, April 7.

The deplorable Condition of a very pretty Gentleman, who walks here at the Hours when Men of Quality first appear, is what is very much lamented. His History is, That on the 9th of *September,* 1705, being in his One and twentieth Year, he was washing his Teeth at a Tavern Window in *Pall-Mall,* when a fine Equipage pass'd by, and in it a young Lady who look'd up at him; away goes the Coach, and the young Gentleman pull'd off his Night-Cap, and instead of rubbing his Gums, as he ought to do, out of the Window, 'till about Four a Clock sits him down, and spoke not a Word 'till Twelve at Night; after which, he began to enquire, If any Body knew the Lady. . . . The Company ask'd, What Lady? But he said no more, 'till they broke up at Six in the Morning. All the ensuing Winter he went from Church to Church every Sunday, and from Play-

[5] A reference to Mr. Bickerstaff's power of seeing the future through astrological calculations, as humorously set forth in *Swift's Predictions for the Year 1708 . . . by Isaac Bickerstaff, Esq.* Mr. Bickerstaff's role as prophet-astrologer is not much emphasized in *The Tatler.*

house to Play-house every Night in the Week, but could never find the Original of the Picture which dwelt in his Bosom. In a Word, his Attention to any Thing, but his Passion, was utterly gone. He has lost all the Money he ever play'd for, and been confuted in every Argument he has enter'd upon since the Moment he first saw her. He is of a Noble Family, has naturally a very good Air, is of a frank, honest Temper: But this Passion has so extreamly maul'd him, that his Features are set and uninform'd, and his whole Visage is deaden'd by a long Absence of Thought. He never appears in an Alacrity, but when rais'd by Wine; at which Time he is sure to come hither, and throw away a great deal of Wit on Fellows, who have no Sense further than just to observe, That our poor Lover has most Understanding when he is drunk, and is least in his Senses when he is sober.

Will's Coffee-house, April 8.

On *Thursday* last was acted, for the Benefit of Mr. *Betterton,*[6] the Celebrated Comedy, call'd *Love for Love.*[7] Those excellent Players, Mrs. *Barry,* Mrs. *Bracegirdle,* and Mr. *Dogget,* tho' not at present concerned in the House, acted on that Occasion. There has not been known so great a Concourse of Persons of Distinction as at that Time; the Stage it self was covered with Gentlemen and Ladies, and when the Curtain was drawn, it discovered even there a very splendid Audience. This unusual Encouragement, which was given to a Play for the Advantage of so great an Actor, gives an undeniable Instance, That the true Relish for Manly Entertainments and Rational Pleasures is not wholly lost. All the Parts were acted

---

[6] The greatest tragic actor of his time. See *The Tatler,* No. 167.
[7] A comedy by William Congreve (1670-1729).

to Perfection; the Actors were careful of their Carriage, and no one was guilty of the Affectation to insert Witticisms of his own, but a due Respect was had to the Audience, for encouraging this accomplish'd Player. It is not now doubted but Plays will revive, and take their usual Place in the Opinion of Persons of Wit and Merit, notwithstanding their late Apostacy in Favour of Dress and Sound. This Place[8] is very much altered since Mr. *Dryden* frequented it; where you used to see *Songs, Epigrams,* and *Satyrs,* in the Hands of every Man you met, you have now only a Pack of Cards; and instead of the Cavils about the Turn of the Expression, the Elegance of the Style, and the like, the Learned now dispute only about the Truth of the Game. But however, the Company is altered, all have shewn a great Respect for Mr. *Betterton.* And the very Gaming Part of this House have been so much touch'd with a Sense of the Uncertainty of Human Affairs, (which alter with themselves every Moment) that in this Gentleman, they pitied *Mark Anthony* of *Rome, Hamlett* of *Denmark, Mithridates* of *Pontus, Theodosius* of *Greece,* and *Henry* the Eighth of *England.* It is well known, he has been in the Condition of each of those illustrious Personages for several Hours together, and behaved himself in those high Stations, in all the Changes of the Scene, with suitable Dignity. For these Reasons, we intend to repeat this Favour to him on a proper Occasion, lest he who can instruct us so well in personating Feigned Sorrows, should be lost to us by suffering under Real Ones. The Town is at present in very great Expectation of seeing a Comedy now in Rehearsal, which is the 25th Production of my Honoured Friend Mr. *Thomas D'Urfey;* who, besides his great Abilities in the Dramatick, has a peculiar Talent in the Lyrick Way of Writing, and that with a Manner wholly new and unknown to the Antient *Greeks* and *Romans,* wherein he is but faintly imitated in the Translations of the Modern *Italian* Opera's.

[8] Will's Coffee-house.

St. James's Coffee-house, April 11.[9]

Letters from the *Hague* of the 16th say, That Major General *Cadogan* was gone to *Brussels,* with Orders to disperse proper Instructions for assembling the whole Force of the Allies in *Flanders* in the Beginning of the next Month. The late Offers concerning Peace, were made in the Style of Persons who think themselves upon equal Terms: But the Allies have so just a Sense of their present Advantages, that they will not admit of a Treaty, except *France* offers what is more suitable to her present Condition. At the same Time we made Preparations, as if we were alarm'd by a greater Force than that which we are carrying into the Field. Thus this Point seems now to be argued Sword in Hand. This was what a Great General alluded to, when being ask'd the Names of those who were to be Pleni-potentiaries for the ensuing Peace; answer'd, with a serious Air, *There are about an Hundred thousand of us.* Mr. *Kidney,* who has the Ear of the greatest Politicians that come hither, tells me, There is a Mail come in to Day with Letters, dated *Hague, April* 19. *N. S.* which say, a Design of bringing Part of our Troops into the Field at the latter End of this Month, is now alter'd to a Resolution of marching towards the Camp about the 20th of the next. There happen'd t'other Day, in the Road of *Scheveling,* an Engagement between a Privateer of *Zealand* and one of *Dunkirk.* The *Dunkirker,* carrying 33 Pieces of Cannon, was taken and brought into the *Texel.* It is said, the Courier of Monsieur *Rouille* is return'd to him from the Court of *France.* Monsieur *Vendosme* being reinstated in the Favour of the Dutchess of *Burgundy,* is to command in *Flanders.*

Mr. *Kidney* added, That there were Letters of the 17th

---

[9] Although Steele's post as Gazeteer gave him access to the latest political news until October, 1710, the dispatches from St. James's Coffee-house appeared infrequently after the first fifty numbers.

from *Ghent,* which give an Account, that the Enemy had form'd a Design to surprize two Battalions of the Allies which lay at *Alost;* but those Battalions receiv'd Advice of their March, and retir'd to *Dendermond.* Lieutenant General *Wood* appear'd on this Occasion at the Head of 5000 Foot, and 1000 Horse, upon which the Enemy withdrew, without making any further Attempt.

From my own Apartment.

I am sorry I am oblig'd to trouble the Publick with so much Discourse upon a Matter which I at the very first mentioned as a Trifle, *viz.* the Death of Mr. *Partridge,* [10] under whose Name there is an *Almanack* come out for the year 1709. In one Page of which it is asserted by the said *John Partridge,* That he is still living, and not only so, but that he was also living some Time before, and even at the instant when I writ of his Death. I have in another Place, and in a Paper by it self, sufficiently convinc'd this Man that he is dead, and if he has any Shame, I don't doubt but that by this Time he owns it to all his Acquaintance; For tho' the Legs and Arms, and whole Body of that Man still appear and perform their animal Functions; yet since, as I have elsewhere observ'd, his Art is gone, the Man is gone. I am, as I said, concern'd, that this little Matter should make so much Noise; but since I am engag'd, I take my self oblig'd in Honour to go on in my Lucubrations, and by the Help of these Arts of which I am Master, as well as my Skill in Astrological Speculations, I shall, as I see Occasion, proceed to confute other dead Men, who pretend to be in Being, that they

[10] The astrologer and almanac maker, whose death, facetiously announced by Swift in *The Accomplishment of the First of Mr. Bickerstaff's Predictions* (1708), had been indignantly denied by Partridge himself.

are actually deceased. I therefore give all Men fair Warning to mend their Manners, for I shall from Time to Time print Bills of Mortality; and I beg the Pardon of all such who shall be named therein, if they who are good for Nothing shall find themselves in the Number of the Deceased.

White's Chocolate-house, May 26.

A Gentleman has writ to me out of the Country a very civil Letter, and said Things which I suppress with great Violence to my Vanity. There are many Terms in my Narratives which he complains want explaining, and has therefore desired, that, for the Benefit of my Country Readers, I would let him know what I mean by a *Gentleman,* a *Pretty Fellow,* a *Toast,* a *Coquet,* a *Critick,* a *Wit,* and all other Appellations of those now in the gayer World who are in Possession of these several Characters; together with an Account of those who unfortunately pretend to 'em. I shall begin with him we usually call a *Gentleman,* or Man of Conversation.

It is generally thought, That Warmth of Imagination, quick Relish of Pleasure, and a Manner of becoming it, are the most essential Qualities for forming this Sort of Man. But any one that is much in Company will observe, That the Height of good Breeding is shown rather in never giving Offence, than in doing obliging Things. Thus, he that never shocks you, though he is seldom entertaining, is more likely to keep your Favour, than he who often entertains, and sometimes displeases you. The most necessary Talent therefore in a Man of Conversation, which is what we ordinarily intend by a Fine Gentleman, is a good Judgment. He that has this in Perfection, is Master of his Companion, without letting him see it; and has the same Advantage over Men of any other Qualifications whatsoever, as one that can see would have over a blind Man of Ten times his Strength.

This is what makes *Sophronius* the Darling of all who converse with him, and the most Powerful with his Acquaintance of any Man in Town. By the Light of this Faculty, he acts with great Ease and Freedom among the Men of Pleasure, and acquits himself with Skill and Dispatch among the Men of Business. All which he performs with such Success, that, with as much Discretion in Life as any Man ever had, he neither is, nor appears, Cunning. But as he does a good Office, if he ever does it, with Readiness and Alacrity; so he denies what he does not care to engage in, in a Manner that convinces you, that you ought not to have asked it. His Judgment is so good and unerring, and accompanied with so chearful a Spirit, that his Conversation is a continual Feast, at which he helps some, and is helped by others, in such a Manner, that the Equality of Society is perfectly kept up, and every Man obliges as much as he is obliged: For it is the greatest and justest Skill in a Man of Superior Understanding, to know how to be on a Level with his Companions. This sweet Disposition runs through all the Actions of *Sophronius,* and makes his Company desired by Women, without being envyed by Men. *Sophronius* would be as just as he is, if there were no Law; and would be as discreet as he is, if there were no such Thing as Calumny.

In Imitation of this agreeable Being, is made that Animal we call a *Pretty Fellow;* who being just able to find out, that what makes *Sophronius* acceptable, is a Natural Behaviour; in order to the same Reputation, makes his own an Artificial one. *Jack Dimple* is his perfect Mimick, whereby he is of Course the most unlike him of all Men living. *Sophronius* just now passed imto the inner Room directly forward: *Jack* comes as fast after as he can for the Right and Left Looking-glass, in which he had but just approved himself by a Nod at each, and marched on. He will meditate within for Half an Hour, 'till he thinks he is not careless enough in his Air, and come back to the Mirror to recollect his Forgetfulness.

Will's Coffee-house, May 27.

This Night was acted the Comedy, called *The Fox;*[1] but I wonder the Modern Writers do not use their Interest in the House to suppress such Representations. A Man that has been at this, will hardly like any other Play during the Season: Therefore I humbly move, That the Writings, as well as Dresses, of the last Age, should give Way to the present Fashion. We are come into a good Method enough (if we were not interrupted in our Mirth by such an Apparition as a Play of *Johnson's*) to be entertained at more Ease, both to the Spectator and the Writer, than in the Days of Old. It is no Difficulty to get Hats, and Swords, and Wigs, and Shoes, and every Thing else, from the Shops in Town, and make a Man show himself by his Habit, without more ado, to be a Counsellor, a Fop, a Courtier, or a Citizen, and not be obliged to make those Characters talk in different Dialects to be distinguished from each other. This is certainly the surest and best Way of Writing: But such a Play as this makes a Man for a Month after over-run with Criticism, and enquire, *What every Man on the Stage said? What had such a one to do to meddle with such a Thing? How came t'other, who was bred after this or that Manner, to speak so like a Man conversant among a different People?* These Questions rob us of all our Pleasure; for at this Rate, no Sentence in a Play should be spoken by any one Character, which could possibly enter into the Head of any other Man represented in it; but every Sentiment should be peculiar to him only who utters it. Laborious *Ben's* Works will bear this Sort of Inquisition; but if the present Writers were thus examin'd, and the Offences against this Rule cut out, few Plays would be long enough for the whole Evening's Entertainment.

But I don't know how they did in those old Times: This

[1] Ben Jonson's *Volpone*.

same *Ben Johnson* has made every one's Passion in this Play be towards Money, and yet not one of them expresses that Desire, or endeavours to obtain it any Way but what is peculiar to him only: One sacrifices his Wife, another his Profession, another his Posterity from the same Motive; but their Characters are kept so skilfully a-part, that it seems prodigious their Discourses should rise from the Invention of the same Author.

But the Poets are a Nest of Hornets, and I'll drive these Thoughts no farther, but must mention some hard Treatment I am like to meet with from my Brother Writers. I am credibly informed, that the Author of a Play, call'd, *Love in a Hollow Tree,* has made some Remarks upon my late Discourse on *The Naked Truth.* I cannot blame a Gentleman for writing against any Error; it is for the Good of the learned World. But I would have the Thing fairly left between us Two, and not under the Protection of Patrons. But my Intelligence is, that he has dedicated his Treatise to the Honourable Mr. *Ed____d H ____rd.*

From my own Apartment, May 27.

To Isaac Bickerstaff, *Esq:*

York, *May* 16, 1709.

SIR,

Being convinc'd, as the whole World is, how infallible your Predictions are, and having the Honour to be your near Relation of the STAFFIAN *Family, I was under great Concern at one of your Predictions relating to your self, wherein you foretold your own Death would happen on the* 17th *Instant, unless it were prevented by the Assistance of well-disposed People: I have therefore prevail'd on my own Modesty to send you a Piece of News, which may serve instead of* GODDARD'S

DROPS.[2] *to keep you alive for Two Days, till Nature be able to recover it self, or till you meet with some better Help from other Hands. Therefore, without further Ceremony, I will go on to relate a singular Adventure just happened in the Place where I am writing, wherein it may be highly useful for the Publick to be inform'd.*

Three young Ladies of our Town were on SATURDAY *last indicted for* WITCHCRAFT. *The Witnesses against the First deposed upon Oath before Justice* BINDOVER, *That she kept Spirits locked up in Vessels, which sometimes appeared in Flames of blue Fire; That she used Magical Herbs, with some of which she drew in Hundreds of Men daily to her, who went out from her Presence all inflamed, their Mouths parched, and a hot Steam issuing from them, attended with a grievous Stench; That many of the said Men were by the Force of that Herb metamorphos'd into Swine, and lay wallowing in the Kennels for Twenty four Hours, before they could reassume their Shapes or their Senses.*

It was proved against the Second, That she cut off by Night the Limbs from dead Bodies that were hang'd, and was seen to dig Holes in the Ground, to mutter some conjuring Words, and bury Pieces of the Flesh, after the usual Manner of Witches.

The Third was accus'd for a notorious Piece of Sorcery, long practiced by Hags, of moulding up Pieces of Dough into the Shapes of Men, Women, and Children, then heating them at a gentle Fire, which had a Sympathetick Power to torment the Bowels of those in the Neighbourhood.

This was the Sum of what was objected against the Three Ladies, who indeed had nothing to say in their own Defence, but downright denying the Facts, which is like to avail very little when they come upon their Tryals.

But the Parson of our Parish, a strange refractory Man, will believe nothing of all this; so that the whole Town cries

---

[2] A well-known remedy concocted by Dr. Jonathan Goddard, physician to Oliver Cromwell and medical professor at Gresham College.

out SHAME! THAT ONE OF HIS COAT SHOULD BE SUCH AN ATHE-
IST! *And design to complain of him to the Bishhop. He goes
about very odly to solve the matter. He supposes, That the
First of these Ladies keeping a Brandy and Tobacco Shop,
the Fellows went out smoaking, and got drunk towards Evening, and made themselves Beasts. He says, The Second is a
Butcher's Daughter, and sometimes brings a Quarter of Mutton from the Slaughter-house over Night against a Market-Day,
and once buried a Bit of Beef in the Ground, as a known Receipt to cure Warts on her Hands. The Parson affirms, That
the Third sells Gingerbread, which, to please the Children,
she is forc'd to stamp with Images before 'tis bak'd; and if it
burns their Guts, 'tis because they eat too much, or do not
drink after it.*

*These are the Answers he gives to solve these wonder-
ful* Phænomena; *upon which I shall not animadvert, but leave
it among Philosophers: And so wishing you all Success in your
Undertakings for the Amendment of the World, I remain,*

Dear Cousin,

Your most Affectionate Kinsman,
and Humble Servant,

Ephraim Bedfast.

P.S. Those who were condemn'd to Death among the
Athenians, were obliged to take a Dose of Poison, which made
them die upwards, seizing first upon their Feet, making them
cold and insensible, and so ascending gradually, till it reach'd
the Vital Parts. I believe your Death, which you foretold would
happen on the 17th Instant, will fall out the same Way, and
that your Distemper hath already seiz'd on you, and makes
Progress daily. The lower Part of you, that is, the *Advertisements,* is dead; and these have risen for these Ten Days last
past, so that they now take up almost a whole Paragraph. Pray,
Sir, do your Endeavour to drive this Distemper as much as
possible to the extreme Parts, and keep it there, as wise Folks
do the Gout; for if it once gets into your Stomach, it will soon
fly up into your Head, and you are a dead Man.

St. James's Coffee-house, May 27.

Our last Advices from the *Hague,* dated *June* the 4th, *N.S.*[3] say, That they expected a Courier from the *French* Court with the Ratification of the Preliminaries that Night or the Day following. His Grace the Duke of *Marlborough* will set out for *Brussels* on *Wednesday* or *Thursday* next, if the Dispatches which are expected from *Paris* don't alter his Resolutions. Letters from *Majorca* confirm the Honourable Capitulation of the Castle of *Alicant,* and also the Death of the Governor Major-General *Richards,* Colonel *Sibourg,* and Major *Vignolles,* who were all buried in the Ruins of that Place by the springing of their Mine, which did, it seems, more Execution than was reported. Monsieur *Torcy* pass'd through *Mons* in his Return, and had there a long Conference with the Elector of *Bavaria;* after which, that Price spoke publickly of the Treatment he had receiv'd from *France* with the utmost Indignation.

Any Person that shall come publickly Abroad in a fantastical Habit, contrary to the present Mode and Fashion, except Don Diego Desmallo, *or any other out of Poverty, shall have his Name and Dress inserted in our next.*

N.B. *Mr.* How'd call *is desired to leave off those Buttons.*

---

[3] "N.S." means the "New Style" of dating events, which had become accepted in seventeenth-century Europe with the adoption of the Gregorian calendar. Until 1752, England officially retained the old Julian calendar, which ran eleven days behind that in use on the continent and began the legal new year March 25 instead of January 1. Thus an event which happened February 22 in France would be dated February 11, 1709-10, in England.

White's Chocolate-house, June 6.

A Letter from a young Lady, written in the most passionate Terms, wherein she laments the Misfortune of a Gentleman, her Lover, who was lately wounded in a Duel, has turned my Thoughts to that Subject, and enclined me to examine into the Causes which precipitate Men into so fatal a Folly. And as it has been proposed to treat of Subjects of Gallantry in the Article from hence, and no one Point in Nature is more proper to be consider'd by the Company who frequent this Place, than that of Duels, it is worth our Consideration to examine into this Chimærical groundless Humour, and to lay every other Thought aside, till we have strip'd it of all its false Pretences to Credit and Reputation amongst Men.

But I must confess, when I consider what I am going about, and run over in my Imagination all the endless Crowd of Men of Honour who will be offended at such a Discourse;[1] I am undertaking, methinks, a Work worthy an invulnerable Hero in Romance, rather than a private Gentleman with a single Rapier: But as I am pretty well acquainted by great Opportunities with the Nature of Man, and know of a Truth, that all Men fight *against their Will,* the Danger vanishes, and Resolution rises upon this Subject. For this Reason I shall talk very freely on a Custom which all Men wish exploded, tho' no Man has Courage enough to resist it.

But there is one unintelligible Word which I fear will ex-

---

[1] Steele, who had fought a duel in 1700, had already incurred some ridicule from his fellow guardsmen by attacking dueling in *The Christian Hero* (1701).

tremely perplex my Dissertation; and I confess to you I find very hard to explain, which is, the Term *Satisfaction*. An honest Country Gentleman had the Misfortune to fall into Company with Two or Three modern Men of Honour, where he happened to be very ill treated; and one of the Company being conscious of his Offence, sends a Note to him in the Morning, and tells him, He was ready to give him Satisfaction. This is fine Doing (says the plain Fellow): Last Night he sent me away cursedly out of Humour, and this Morning he fancies it would be a Satisfaction to be run through the Body.

As the Matter at present stands, it is not to do handsome Actions denominates a Man of Honour; it is enough if he dares to defend ill Ones. Thus you often see a common sharper in Competition with a Gentleman of the first Rank; tho' all Mankind is convinced, that a fighting Gamester is only a Pickpocket, with the Courage of an Highway-Man. One cannot with any Patience reflect on the unaccountable Jumble of Persons and Things in this Town and Nation, which occasions very frequently, that a brave Man falls by a Hand below that of the common Hangman, and yet his Executioner escapes the Clutches of the Hangman for doing it. I shall therefore hereafter consider, how the bravest Men in other Ages and Nations have behaved themselves upon such Incidents as we decide by Combat; and show, from their Practice, that this Resentment neither has its Foundation from true Reason, or solid Fame; but is an Imposture, made up of Cowardice, Falshood, and Want of Understanding. For this Work, a good History of Quarrels would be very edifying to the Publick, and I apply my self to the Town for Particulars and Circumstances within their Knowledge, which may serve to embellish the Dissertation with proper Cuts. Most of the Quarrels I have ever known, have proceeded from some valiant Coxcomb's persisting in the Wrong, to defend some prevailing Folly, and preserve himself from the Ingenuity of owning a Mistake.

By this Means it is called, *Giving a Man Satisfaction,* to urge your Offence against him with your Sword; which puts me in Mind of *Peter's* Order to the Keeper, in *The Tale of a Tub: If you neglect to do all this, damn you and your Generation for ever; and so we bid you heartily farewel.*[2] If the Contradiction in the very Terms of one of our Challenges were as well explained, and turn'd into downright *English,* would it not run after this Manner?

SIR

Your extraordinary Behaviour last Night, and the Liberty you were pleased to take with me, makes me this Morning give you this, to tell you, because you are an ill-bred Puppy, I will meet you in HIDE-*Park an Hour hence; and because you want both Breeding and Humanity, I desire you would come with a Pistol in your Hand, on Horseback, and endeavour to shoot me through the Head; to teach you more Manners. If you fail of doing me this Pleasure, I shall say, You are a Rascal on every Post in Town: And so, Sir, if you will not injure me more, I shall never forgive what you have done already. Pray Sir, do not fail of getting every Thing ready, and you will infinitely oblige,*

Sir,

Your most Obedient,

Humble Servant, &c.

From my own Apartment, June 6.

Among the many Employments I am necessarily put upon by my Friends, that of giving Advice is the most unwelcome to me; and indeed, I am forced to use a little Art in the Matter; for some People will ask Counsel of you, when they have already acted what they tell you is still under Deliberation.

[2] Inaccurately quoted from Swift, *A Tale of a Tub,* Section 4.

I had almost lost a very good Friend t'other Day, who came to know how I lik'd his Design to marry such a Lady. I answered, By no Means; and I must be positive against it, for very solid Reasons, which are not proper to communicate. Not proper to communicate! (said he with a grave Air) I will know the Bottom of this. I saw him moved, and knew from thence he was already determined; therefore evaded it by saying, To tell you the Truth, dear *Frank,* Of all Women living, I would have her my self. *Isaac,* said he, Thou art too late, for we have been both one these two Months. I learned this Caution by a Gentleman's consulting me formerly about his Son. He railed at his damn'd Extravagance, and told me, In a very little Time, he would beggar him by the exorbitant Bills which came from *Oxford* every Quarter. *Make the Rogue bite upon the Bridle,* said I, *pay none of his Bills, it will but encourage him to further Trespasses.* He look'd plaguy sowr at me. His Son soon after sent up a Paper of Verses, forsooth, in Print, on the last Publick Occasion; upon which, he is convinced the Boy has Parts, and a Lad of Spirit is not to be too much cramp'd in his Maintenance, lest he take ill Courses. Neither Father nor Son can ever since endure the Sight of me. These Sort of People ask Opinions, only out of the Fulness of their Heart on the Subject of their Perplexity, and not from a Desire of Information. There is nothing so easy as to find out which Opinion the Person in Doubt has a Mind to; therefore the sure Way is to tell him, that is certainly to be chosen. Then you are to be very clear and positive; leave no Handle for Scruple. Bless me! Sir, there's no Room for a Question. This rivets you into his Heart; for you at once applaud his Wisdom, and gratify his Inclination. However, I had too much Bowels to be insincere to a Man who came Yesterday to know of me, With which of two eminent Men in the City he should place his Son? Their Names are *Paulo* and *Avaro.*[3] This gave me much Debate with my

[3] The identities of two real London merchants of Steele's day are concealed behind these fictitious names.

self, because not only the Fortune of the Youth, but his Virtue also depended upon this Choice. The Men are equally wealthy; but they differ in the Use and Application of their Riches, which you immediately see upon entring their Doors.

The Habitation of *Paulo* has at once the Air of a Nobleman and a Merchant. You see the Servants act with Affection to their Master, and Satisfaction in themselves: The Master meets yo with an open Countenance, full of Benevolence and Integrity: Your Business is dispatched with that Confidence and Welcome which always accompanies honest Minds: His Table is the Image of Plenty and Generosity, supported by Justice and Frugality. After we had dined here, our Affair was to visit *Avaro:* Out comes an aukward Fellow with a careful Countenance; Sir, Would you speak with my Master? May I crave your Name? After the first Preambles, he leads us into a noble Solitude, a great House that seem'd uninhabited; but from the End of the spacious Hall moves towards us *Avaro,* with a suspicious Aspect, as if he believed us Thieves; and as for my Part, I approached him as if I knew him a Cut-purse. We fell into Discourse of his noble Dwelling, and the Great Estate all the World knew he had to enjoy in it: And I, to plague him, fell a commending *Paulo's* Way of Living. *Paulo,* answered *Avaro,* is a very good Man; but we who have smaller Estates, must cut our Coat according to our Cloth. Nay, says I, Every Man knows his own Circumstance best; you are in the Right, if you han't wherewithal. He look'd very sowr; (for it is, you must know, the utmost Vanity of a mean-spirited rich Man to be contradicted, when he calls himself Poor.) But I was resolved to vex him, by consenting to all he said; the main Design of which was, that he would have us find out, he was one of the wealthiest Men in *London,* and lived like a Beggar. We left him, and took a Turn on the Change. My Friend was ravished with *Avaro:* This (said he) is certainly a sure Man. I contradicted him with much Warmth, and summed up their different Characters as well as I could. This *Paulo* (said I) grows wealthy by being a common Good; *Avaro,* by being a general Evil: *Paulo* has the Art, *Avaro* the Craft of Trade. When *Paulo* gains, all Men he deals with are the better: Whenever *Avaro* profits, another certainly loses. In a Word, *Paulo* is a Citizen, and *Avaro* a Cit. I convinced my Friend, and carried the young Gentleman the next Day to *Paulo,* where he will learn the Way both to gain, and enjoy a good Fortune. And though I cannot say, I have, by keeping him from *Avaro,* saved him from the Gallows, I have prevented his deserving it every Day he lives: For with *Paulo* he will be an honest Man, without being so for Fear of the Law; as with *Avaro,* he would have been a Villain within the Protection of it.

St. James's Coffee-house, June 6.

Advices from the *Hague* of the 14th Instant, *N.S.*[4] say, That all Things tended to a vigorous and active Campagne; the Allies having strong Resentments against the late Behaviour of the Court of *France;* and the *French* using all possible Endeavours to animate their Men to defend their Country against a victorious and exasperated Enemy. Monsieur *Rouillé* had passed through *Brussels* without visiting either the Duke of *Marlborough* or Prince *Eugene,* who were both there at that Time. The States have met, and publickly declared their Satisfaction in the Conduct of their Deputies during the whole Treaty. Letters from *France* say, That the Court is resolved to put all to the Issue of the ensuing Campagne. In the mean Time, they have ordered the Preliminary Treaty to be publish'd, with Observation upon each Article, in order to quiet the Minds of the People, and perswade them, that it has not been in the Power of the King to procure a Peace, but to the Diminution

[4] See *The Tatler,* No. 21, n.3.

of his Majesty's Glory, and the Hazard of his Dominions. His Grace the Duke of *Marlborough* and Prince *Eugene* arrived at *Ghent* on *Wednesday* last, where, at an Assembly of all the General Officers, it was thought proper, by Reason of the great Rains which have lately fallen, to defer forming a Camp, or bringing the Troops together; but as soon as the Weather would permit, to march upon the Enemy with all Expedition.

No. 107   Thursday, December 15, 1709.   [Steele]

> . . . *Ah miser,*
> *Quanta laborabas Charybdi*
> *Digne puer meliore flamma?*[1] — Hor.

Sheer Lane, December 14.

About Four this Afternoon, which is the Hour I usually put my self in a Readiness to receive Company, there enter'd a Gentleman who I believed at first came upon some ordinary Question; but as he approached nearer to me, I saw in his Countenance a deep Sorrow, mixed with a certain ingenuous Complacency that gave me a sudden Good-will towards him. He star'd, and betrayed an Absence of Thought as he was going to communicate his Business to me. But at last, recovering himself, he said, with an Air of great Respect, Sir, It would be an Injury to your Knowledge in the Occult Sciences, to tell you what is my Distress; I dare say, you read it in my Countenance: I therefore beg your Advice to the most unhappy of all Men.

Much Experience has made me particularly sagacious in the Discovery of Distempers, and I soon saw that his was Love. I then turned to my Common-place Book, and found his Cafe under the Word *Coquette;* and reading over the Catalogue which I have collected out of this great City of all under that Character, I saw at the Name of *Cynthia* his Fit came upon

---

[1] "Ah, wretched youth, in what a fatal whirlpool art thou caught, boy worthy of a better flame?"

25

him. I repeated the Name thrice after a musing Manner, and immediately perceived his Pulse quicken two Thirds; when his Eyes, instead of the Wildness with which they appeared at his Entrance, looked with all the Gentleness imaginable upon me, not without Tears.

Oh, Sir! (said he) *you know not the unworthy Usage I have met with from the Woman my Soul doats on. I could gaze at her to the End of my Being; yet when I have done so, for some Time past I have found her Eyes fix'd on another. She is now Two and Twenty, in the full Tyranny of her Charms, which she once acknowledg'd she rejoiced in, only as they made her Choice of me, out of a Crowd of Admirers, the more obliging. But in the Midst of this Happiness, so it is Mr.* Bickerstaff, *that young* Quicksett, *who is just come to Town, without any other Recommendation than that of being tolerably handsome, and excessively rich, has won her Heart in so shameless a Manner, that she dies for him. In a Word, I would consult you, how to cure myself of this Passion for an ungrateful Woman, who triumphs in her Falshood, and can make no Man happy, because her own Satisfaction consists chiefly in being capable of giving Distress. I know* Quicksett *is at present considerable with her, for no other Reason but that he can be without her, and feel no Pain in the Loss. Let me therefore desire you, Sir, to fortify my Reason against the Levity of an Inconstant, who ought only be treated with Neglect.*

All this Time I was looking over my Receipts, and asked him, If he had any good Winter Boots—*Boots, Sir!* said my Patient—I went on; You may easily reach *Harwich* in a Day, so as to be there when the Packet goes off.

Sir, (said the Lover) *I find you design me for Travelling; but alas! I have no Language, it will be the same Thing to me as Solitude, to be in a strange Country. I have* (continued he sighing) *been many Years in Love with this Creature, and have almost lost even my* English, *at least to speak such as any body else does. I asked a Tenant of ours, who came up to Town the Other Day with Rent, whether the Flowry Meads near my*

Father's House in the Country had any Shepherd in it. I have called a Cave a Grotto these Three Years, and must keep ordinary Company, and frequent busie People for some Time, before I can recover my common Words. I smiled at his Raillery upon himself, though I well saw it came from an heavy Heart. *You are (said I) acquainted to be sure with some of the General Officers; Suppose you made a Campagne? If I did, (said he) I should venture more than any Man there, for I should be in Danger of starving; my Father is such an untoward old Gentleman, that he would tell me he found it hard enough to pay his Taxes towards the War, without making it more expensive by an Allowance to me. With all this, he is as fond as he is rugged, and I am his only Son.*

I looked upon the young Gentleman with much Tenderness, and not like a Physician, but a Friend; for I talked to him so largely, that if I had parcelled my Discourse into distinct Prescriptions, I am confident I gave him Two Hundred Pounds worth of Advice. He heard me with great Attention, bowing, smiling, and showing all other Instances of that natural good Breeding which ingenuous Tempers pay to those who are elder and wiser than themselves. I entertained him to the following Purpose. I am sorry, Sir, that your Passion is of so long a Date, for Evils are much more curable in their Beginnings; but at the same Time must allow, that you are not to be blamed, since your Youth and Merit has been abused by one of the most charming, but the most unworthy Sort of Women, the Coquets.

A Coquet is a chast Jilt, and differs only from a common One, as a Soldier, who is perfect in Exercise, does from one that is actually in Service. This Grief, like all other, is to be cured only by Time; and although you are convinced this Moment, as much as you will be Ten Years hence, that she ought to be scorned and neglected, you see you must not expect your Remedy from the Force of Reason. The Cure then, is only in Time; and the hastening of the Cure, only in the Manner of employing that Time. You have answered me as to Travel and a Campagne, so that we have only *Great Britain* to avoid her in. Be then your self, and listen to the following Rules, which only can be of Use to you in this unaccountable Distemper, wherein the Patient is often averse even to his Recovery. It has been of Benefit to some to apply themselves to Business; but as that may not lie in your Way, go down to your Estate, mind your Fox-hounds, and venture the Life you are wreary of over every Hedge and Ditch in the Country. These are wholesome Remedies; but if you can have Resolution enough, rather stay in Town, and recover your self even in the Town where she inhabits. Take particular Care to avoid all Places where you may possibly meet her, and shun the Sight of every Thing which may bring her to your Remembrance; there is an Infection in all that relates to her: You'll find, her House, her Chariot, her Domesticks, and her very Lap-Dog, are so many Instruments of Torment. Tell me seriously, Do you think you could bear the Sight of her Fan? He shook his Head at the Question, and said, Ah! Mr. *Bickerstaff,* you must have been a Patient, or you could have not have been so good a Physician. To tell you truly, said I, about the Thirtieth Year of my Age, I received a Wound that has still left a Scar in my Mind, never to be quite worn out by Time or Philosophy.

The Means which I found the most effectual for my Cure, were Reflections upon the ill Usage I had received from the Woman I loved, and the Pleasure I saw her take in my Sufferings.

I considered the Distress she brought upon me, the greatest that could befal an humane Creature, at the same Time that she did not inflict this upon one who was her Enemy, one that had done her an Injury, one that had wished her ill; but on the Man who loved her more than any else loved her, and more than it was possible for him to love any other Person.

In the next Place I took Pains to consider her in all her Imperfections; and that I might be sure to hear of them constantly, kept Company with those her Female Friends who were her dearest and most intimate Acquaintance.

Among her highest Imperfections, I still dwelt upon her

Baseness of Mind and Ingratitude, that made her triumph in the Pain and Anguish of the Man who loved her, and of one who in those Days (without Vanity be it spoken) was thought to deserve her Love.

To shorten my Story, she was married to another, which would have distracted me had he proved a good Husband; but to my great Pleasure, he used her at first with Coldness, and afterwards with Contempt. I hear he still treats her very ill; and am informed, that she often says to her Woman, This is a just Revenge for my Falsehood to my First Love: What a Wretch am I, that might have been married to the famous Mr. *Bickerstaff.*

My Patient looked upon me with a kind of melancholy Pleasure, and told me, He did not think it was possible for a Man to live to the Age I now am of, who in his Thirtieth Year had been tortured with that Passion in its Violence: For my Part, (said he) I can neither eat, drink, nor sleep in it; nor keep Company with any Body, but Two or Three Friends who are in the same Condition.

There (answer I) you are to blame; for as you ought to avoid nothing more than keeping Company with your self, so you ought to be particularly cautious of keeping Company with Men like your self. As long as you do this, you do but indulge your Distemper.

I must not dismiss you without further Instructions. If possible, transfer your Passion from the Woman you are now in Love with, to another; or if you cannot do that, change the Passion it self into some other passion; that is, to speak more plainly, find out some other agreeable Woman: Or if you can't do this, grow covetous, ambitious, litigious; turn your Love of Woman into that of Profit, Preferment, Reputation; and for a Time, give up your self intirely to the Pursuit.

This is a Method we sometimes take in Physick, when we turn a desperate Disease into one we can more easily cure.

He made little Answer to all this, but crying out, Ah, Sir! For his Passion reduced his Discourse to Interjections.

There is one Thing added, which is present Death to a

Man in your Condition, and therefore to be avoided with the greatest Care and Caution: That is, in a Word, to think of your Mistress and Rival together, whether walking, discoursing, dallying—The Devil! (he cried out) Who can bear it? To compose him, for I pitied him very much, the Time will come, said I, when you shall not only bear it, but laugh at it. As a Preparation to it, ride every Morning an Hour at least with the Wind full in your Face. Upon your Return, recollect the several Precepts which I have now given you, and drink upon them a Bottle of *Spaw -Water*. Repeat this every Day for a Month successively, and let me see you at the End of it. He was taking his Leave, with many Thanks, and some Appearance of Consolation in his Countenance, when I called him back to acquaint him, That I had private Information of a Design of the Coquets to buy up all the true *Spaw-Water* in Town: Upon which he took his Leave in haste, with a Resolution to get all Things ready for entring upon his Regimen the next Morning.

No. 108   Saturday, December 17, 1709. [Addison]

Pronaque cum spectant Animalia cætera Terram,
Os Homini sublime dedid, Cœlumque tueri Jussit . . .[1]—Ovid. Met.

Sheer-Lane, December 16.

It is not to be imagined, how great an Effect well-disposed Lights, with proper Forms and Orders in Assemblies, have upon some Tempers. I am sure I feel it in so extraordinary a Manner, that I cannot in a Day or Two get out of my Imagination any very beautiful or disagreeable Impression which I receive on such Occasions. For this Reason I frequently look in at the Play-house, in order to enlarge my Thoughts, and warm my Mind with some new Ideas, that may be serviceable to me in my Lucubrations.

In this Disposition I entered the Theatre the other Day, and placed my self in a Corner of it, very convenient for seeing, without being my self observed. I found the Audience hushed in a very deep Attention, and did not question but some noble Tragedy was just then in its Crisis, or than an Incident was to be unravelled which would determine the Fate of an Hero. While I was in this Suspence, expecting every Moment to see my old Friend Mr. *Betterton* appear in all the Majesty of Distress, to my unspeakable Amazement, there came up a Monster[2] with a Face between his Feet; and as I was look-

[1] "Although other animals face downward and look at the ground, he made man look up towards the heavens."
[2] A "posture-master" or contortionist.

31

ing on, he raised himself on one Leg in such a perpendicular Posture, that the other grew in a direct Line above his Head. It afterwards twisted it self into the Motions and Wreathings of several different Animals, and after great Variety of Shapes and Transformations, went off the Stage in the Figure of an humane Creature. The Admiration, the Applause, the Satisfaction of the Audience, during this strange Entertainment, is not to be expressed. I was very much out of Countenance for my dear Countrymen; and looked about with some Apprehension for fear any Foreigner should be present. Is it possible (thought I) that humane Nature can rejoice in its Disgrace, and take Pleasure in seeing its own Figure turned to Ridicule, and distorted into Forms that raise Horror and Aversion? There is something disingenuous and immoral in the being able to bear such a Sight. Men of elegant and noble Minds, are shocked at seeing the Characters of Persons who deserve Esteem for their Virtue, Knowledge, or Services to their Country, placed in wrong Lights, and by Misrepresentation made the Subject of Buffoonry. Such a nice Abhorrence is not indeed to be found among the Vulgar; but methinks it is wonderful, that these who have nothing but the outward Figure to distinguish them as Men, should delight in seeing it abused, vilified, and disgraced.

I must confess, there is nothing that more pleases me, in all that I read in Books, or see among Mankind, than such Passages as represent humane Nature in its proper Dignity. As Man is a Creature made up of different Extremes, he has something in him very great and very mean: A skilful Artist may draw an excellent Picture of him in either of these Views. The finest Authors of Antiquity have taken him on the more advantagious Side. They cultivate the natural Grandeur of the Soul, raise in her a generous Ambition, feed her with Hopes of Immortality and Perfection, and do all they can to widen the partition between the Virtuous and the Vicious, by making the Difference betwixt them as great as between Gods and Brutes. In short, it is impossible to read a Page in *Plato, Tully,* and a Thousand other ancient Moralists, without being a greater and a better Man for it. On the contrary, I could never read any of our modish *French* Authors, or those of our own Country, who are the Imitators and Admirers of that trifling Nation, without being for some Time out of Humour with my self, and at every Thing about me. Their Business is, to depreciate humane Nature, and consider it under its worst Appearances. They give mean Interpretations and base Motives to the worthiest Actions: They resolve Virtue and Vice into Constitution. In short, they endeavour to make no Distinction between Man and Man, or between the Species of Men and that of Brutes. As an Instance of this kind of Authors, among many others, let any one examine the celebrated *Rochefoucault,* who is the great Philosopher for administring of Consolation to the Idle, the Envious, and worthless Part of Mankind.

I remember a young Gentleman of moderate Understanding, but great Vivacity, who by dipping into many Authors of this Nature, had got a little Smattering of Knowledge, just enough to make an Atheist or a Free-thinker, but not a Philosopher or a Man of Sense. With these Accomplishments, he went to visit his Father in the Country, who was a plain rough, honest Man, and wise, though not learned. The Son, who took all Opportunities to show his Learning, began to establish a new Religion in the Family, and to enlarge the Narrowness of their Country Notions; in which he succeeded so well, that he had seduced the Butler by his Table-Talk, and staggered his eldest Sister. The old Gentleman began to be alarmed at the Schisms that arose among his Children, but did not yet believe his Son's Doctrine to be so pernicious as it really was, 'till one Day talking of his Setting-Dog, the Son said, He did not Question but *Tray* was as immortal as any one of the Family; and in the Heat of the Argument told his Father, That for his own Part, he expected to die like a Dog. Upon which, the old Man starting up in a very great Passion, cried out, Then, Sirrah, you shall live like one; and taking his Cane in his Hand, cudgelled him out of his System. This had so good an Effect upon him, that he took up from that Day, fell to reading good Books, and is now a Bencher in the *Middle-Temple.*

I do not mention this Cudgelling Part of the Story with a Design to engage the secular Arm in Matters of this Nature; but certainly, if it ever exerts it self in Affairs of Opinion and Speculation, it ought to do it on such shallow and despicable Pretenders to Knowledge, who endeavour to give Man dark and uncomfortable Prospects of his Being, and destroy those Principles which are the Support, Happiness, and Glory, of all publick Societies, as well as private Persons.

I think it is one of *Pythagoras*'s Golden Sayings, *That a Man should take Care above all Things to have a due Respect for himself:* And it is certain, that this licentious Sort of Authors, who are for depreciating Mankind, endeavoured to disappoint and undo what the most refined Spirits have been labouring to advance since the Beginning of the World, the very Design of Dress, Good-Breeding, outward Ornaments, and Ceremony, were to lift up humane Nature, and set it off to an Advantage. Architecture, Painting, and Statuary, were invented with the same Design; as indeed every Art and Science contributes to the Embellishment of Life, and to the wearing off or throwing into Shades the mean and low Parts of our Nature. Poetry carries on this great End more than all the rest, as may be seen in the following passage, taken out of Sir *Francis Bacon's Advancement of Learning,* which gives a truer and better Account of this Art than all the Volumes that were ever written upon it.

Poetry, especially Heroical, seems to be raised altogether from a noble Foundation, which makes much for the Dignity of Man's Nature. For seeing this sensible World is in Dignity inferior to the Soul of Man, Poesy seems to endow humane Nature with that which History denies; and to give Satisfaction to the Mind, with at least the Shadow of Things, where the Subsance cannot be had. For if the Matter be thoroughly considered, a strong Argument may be drawn from Poesy, that a more stately Greatness of Things, a more perfect Order, and a more beautiful Variety, delights the Soul of Man, than any Way can be found in Nature since the Fall. Wherefore seeing the Acts and Events, which are the Subjects of true History, are not of that Amplitude as to content the Mind of Man; Poesy is ready at Hand to feign Acts more Heroical. Because true History reports the Successes of Business not proportionable to the Merit of Virtues and Vices, Poesy corrects it, and presents Events and Fortunes according to Desert, and according to the Law of Providence: Because true History, through the frequent Satiety and Simulitude of Things, works a Distast and Misprision in the Mind of Man, Poesy cheareth and refresheth the Soul, chanting Things rare and various, and full of Vicissitudes. So as Poesy serveth and conferreth to Delectation, Magnanimity, and Morality; and therefore it may seem deservedly to have some Participation of Divineness, because it doth raise the Mind, and exalt the Spirit with high Raptures, by proportioning the Shews of Things to the Desires of the Mind; and not submitting the Mind to Things, as Reason and History do. And by these Allurements and Congruities, whereby it cherisheth the Soul of Man, joined also with Consort of Musick, whereby it may more sweetly insinuate it self; it hath won such Access, that it hath been in Estimation even in rude Times, and barbarous Nations, when other Learning stood excluded. [3]

But there is nothing which favours and falls in with this natural Greatness and Dignity of humane Nature so much as Religion, which does not only promise the entire Refinement of the Mind, but the glorifying of the Body, and the Immortality of both.

---

[3] A better version of this passage from *The Advancement of Learning* (Book II, Chapter xiii) is to be found in James Spedding's edition of Bacon's *Works,* IV(1883), 315-316.

No. 111   Saturday, December 24, 1709. [Addison]¹

Procul O! procul este, profani!² — Virg.

Sheer-Lane, December 23

The Watchman, who does me particular Honours, as being the chief Man in the Lane, gave so very great a Thump at my Door last Night, that I awakened at the Knock, and heard my self complimented with the usual Salutation of, *Good morrow* Mr. Bickerstaff, *Good morrow my Masters all.* The Silence and Darkness of the Night, disposed me to be more than ordinarily serious; and as my Attention was not drawn out among exterior Objects, by the Avocations of Sense, my Thoughts naturally fell upon my self. I was considering, amidst the Stilness of the Night, What was the proper Employment of a Thinking Being? What were the Perfections it should propose to it self? And, What the End it should aim at? My Mind is of such a particular Cast, that the Falling of a Shower of Rain, or the Whistling of Wind, at such a Time, is apt to fill my Thoughts with something awful and solemn. I was in this Disposition, when our Bellman began his Midnight Homily (which he has been repeating to us every Winter Night for these Twenty Years) with the usual Exordium.

Oh! mortal Man, thou that art born in Sin!

---

¹ Assisted by Steele.
² "Keep off, whatever is unholy!"
36

Sentiments of this Nature, which are in themselves just and reasonable, however debased by the Circumstances that accompany them, do not fail to produce their natural Effect in a Mind that is not perverted and depraved by wrong Notions of Gallantry, Politeness, and Ridicule. The Temper which I now found my self in, as well as the Time of the Year, put me in Mind of those Lines in *Shakespeare*, wherein, according to his agreeable Wildness of Imagination, he has wrought a Country Tradition into a beautiful Piece of Poetry. In the Tragedy of *Hamlet*, where the Ghost vanishes upon the Cock's Crowing, he takes Occasion to mention its Crowing all Hours of the Night about *Christmas* Time, and to insinuate a Kind of religious Veneration for that Season.

> *It faded on the Crowing of the Cock.*
> *Some say, That ever 'gainst that Season comes*
> *Wherein our Saviour's Birth is celebrated,*
> *The Bird of Dawning singeth all Night long;*
> *And then, say they, no Spirit dares walk Abroad:*
> *The Nights are wholesom, then no Planets strike,*
> *No Fairy takes, no Witch has Power to charm;*
> *So hallowed, and so gracious is the Time.* [3]

This admirable Author, as well as the best and greatest Men of all Ages, and of all Nations, seems to have had his Mind thoroughly seasoned with Religion, as is evident by many Passages in his Plays, that would not be suffered by a modern Audience; and are therefore certain Instances, that the Age he lived in had a much greater Sense of Virtue than the present.

It is indeed a melancholy Reflection to consider, That the *British* Nation, which is now at a greater Height of Glory for its Councils and Conquests than it ever was before, should distinguish it self by a certain Looseness of Principles, and a Falling off from those Schemes of Thinking which conduce

[3] *Hamlet*, 1, i, 157-164.

to the Happiness and Perfection of humane Nature. This Evil comes upon us from the Works of a few solemn Blockheads, that meet together with the Zeal and Seriousness of Apostles, to extirpate common Sense, and propagate Infidelity. These are the Wretches, who, without any Show of Wit, Learning, or Reason, publish their crude Conceptions with an Ambition of appearing more wise than the rest of Mankind, upon no other Pretence, than that of dissenting from them. One gets by Heart a Catalogue of Title Pages and Editions; and immediately to become conspicuous, declares that he is an Unbeliever. Another knows how to write a Receipt, or cut up a Dog, and forthwith argues against the Immortality of the Soul. I have know many a little Wit, in the Ostentation of his Parts, rally the Truth of the Scripture, who was not able to read a Chapter in it. These poor Wretches talk Blasphemy for Want of Discourse, and are rather the Objects of Scorn or Pity, than of our Indignation; but the grave Disputant, that reads and writes, and spends all his Time in convincing himself and the World, that he is no better than a Brute, ought to be whipped out of a Government, as a Blot to a civil Society, and a Defamer of Mankind. I love to consider an Infidel, whether distinguished by the Title of Deist, Atheist, or Free-thinker, in Three different Lights, in his Solitudes, his Afflictions, and his Last Moments.

A wise Man, that lives up to the Principles of Reason and Virtue, if one considers him in his Solitude, as taking in the System of the Universe, observing the mutual Dependance and Harmony, by which the whole Frame of it hangs together, beating down his Passions, or swelling his Thoughts with magnificent Idea's of Providence, makes a nobler Figure in the Eye of an intelligent Being, than the greatest Conqueror amidst all the Pomps and Solemnities of a Triumph. On the contrary, there is not a more ridiculous Animal than an Atheist in his Retirement. His Mind is incapable of Rapture or Elevation: He can only consider himself as an insignificant Figure in a Landskip, and wandring up and down in a Field or a Meadow, under the same Terms as the meanest Animals about him, and as subject to as total a Mortality as they, with this Aggravation, That he is the only one amongst 'em who lies under the Apprehension of it.

In Distresses, he must be of all Creatures the most helpless and forlorn; he feels the whole Pressure of a present Calamity, without being relieved by the Memory of any Thing that is passed, or the Prospect of any Thing that is to come. Annihilation is the greatest Blessing that he proposes to himself, and an Halter or a Pistol the only Refuge he can fly to. But if you would behold one of these Gloomy Miscreants in his poorest Figure, you must consider him under the Terrors, or at the Approach, of Death.

About Thirty Years ago I was a Shipboard with one of these Vermin, when there arose a brisk Gale, which could frighten no Body but himself. Upon the rowling of the Ship he fell upon his Knees, and confessed to the Chaplain, that he had been a vile Atheist, and had denied a Supreme Being ever since he came to his Estate. The good Man was astonished, and a Report immediately ran through the Ship, That there was an Atheist upon the Upper-Deck. Several of the common Seamen, who had never heard the Word before, thought it had been some strange Fish; but they were more surprised when they saw it was a Man, and heard out of his own Mouth, That he never believed till that Day that there was a God. As he lay in the Agonies of Confession, one of the honest Tarrs whispered to the Boatswain, That it would be a good Deed to heave him over Board. But we were now within Sight of Port, when of a sudden the Wind fell, and the Penitent relapsed, begging all of us that were present, as we were Gentlemen, not to say any Thing of what had passed.

He had not been ashore above Two Days, when one of the Company began to rally him upon his Devotion on Shipboard, which the other denied in so high Terms, that it produced the Lie on both Sides, and ended in a Duel. The Atheist was run through the Body, and after some Loss of Blood, became as good a Christian as he was at Sea, till he found that his Wound was not mortal. He is at present one of the Free-Thinkers of the Age, and now writing a Pamphlet against several received Opinions concerning the Existence of Fairies.

As I have taken upon me to censure the Faults of the Age, and Country which I live in, I should have thought my self inexcusable to have passed over this Crying one, which is the Subject of my present Discourse. I shall therefore from Time to Time give my Countrymen particular Cautions against this Distemper of the Mind, that is almost become fashionable, and by that Means more likely to spread. I have somewhere either read or heard a very memorable Sentence, That a Man would be a most insupportable Monster, should he have the Faults that are incident to his Years, Constitution, Profession, Family, Religion, Age, and Country; and yet every Man is in Danger of them all. For this Reason, as I am an old Man, I take particular Care to avoid being covetous, and telling long Stories: As I am Cholerick, I forbear not only Swearing, but all Interjections of Fretting, as Pugh! Pish! and the like. As I am a Layman, I resolve not to conceive an Aversion for a wise and a good Man, because his Coat is of a different Colour from mine. As I am descended of the ancient Family of the *Bickerstaffs,* I never call a Man of Merit an Upstart. As a Protestant, I do not suffer my Zeal so far to transport me, as to name the Pope and the Devil together. As I am fallen into this degenerate Age, I guard my self particularly against the Folly I have been now speaking of. And as I am an *Englishman,* I am very cautious not to hate a Stranger, or despise a poor *Palatine.*

Pars minima est ipsa Puella sui. [1]—Ovid.

Sheer-Lane, January 4.

The Court being prepared for proceeding on the Cause of the Petticoat, I gave Orders to bring in a Criminal who was taken up as she went out of the Puppet-Show about Three Nights ago, and was now standing in the Street with a great Concourse of People about her. Word was brought me, that she had endeavour'd Twice or Thrice to come in, but could not do it by reason of her Petticoat, which was too large for the Entrance of my House, though I had ordered both the Folding-Doors to be thrown open for its Reception. Upon this, I desired the Jury of Matrons, who stood at my Right Hand, to inform themselves of her Condition, and know whether there were any private Reasons why she might not make her Appearance separate from her Petticoat. This was managed with great Discretion, and had such an Effect, that upon the Return of the Verdict from the Bench of Matrons, I issued out an Order forthwith, That the Criminal should be stripped of her Incumbrances, till she became little enough to enter my House. I had before given Directions for an Engine of several Legs, that could contract or open it self like the Top of an Umbrello, in order to place the Petticoat upon it, by which Means I might take a leisurely Survey of it, as it should appear in its proper Dimensions. This was all done accordingly; and forthwith, upon the Closing of the Engine, the Petticoat was brought into Court.

[1] "A woman is the least part of herself."

I then directed the Machine to be set upon the Table, and dilated in such a Manner as to show the Garment in its utmost Circumference; but my great Hall was too narrow for the Experiment; for before it was half unfolded, it described so immoderate a Circle, that the lower Part of it brush'd upon my Face as I sate in my Chair of Judicature. I then enquired for the Person that belonged to the Petticoat; and to my great Surprize, was directed to a very beautiful young Damsel, with so pretty a Face and Shape, that I bid her come out of the Crowd, and seated her upon a little Crock at my Left Hand. "My pretty Maid, (said I) do you own your self to have been the Inhabitant of the Garment before us?" The Girl I found had good Sense, and told me with a Smile, That notwithstanding it was her own Petticoat, she should be very glad to see an Example made of it; and that she wore it for no other Reason, but that she had a Mind to look as big and burly as other Persons of her Quality; That she had kept out of it as long as she could, and till she began to appear little in the Eyes of all her Acquaintance; That if she laid it aside, People would think she was not made like other Women. I always give great Allowances to the Fair Sex upon Account of the Fashion, and therefore was not displeased with the Defence of my pretty Criminal. I then ordered the Vest which stood before us to be drawn up by a Pully to the Top of my great Hall, and afterwards to be spread open by the Engine it was placed upon, in such a Manner, that it formed a very splendid and ample Canopy over our Heads, and covered the whole Court of Judicature with a Kind of Silken Rotunda, in its Form not unlike the Cupolo of St. *Paul's*. I enter'd upon the whole Cause with great Satisfaction as I sate under the Shadow of it.

The Council for the Petticoat was now called in, and ordered to produce what they had to say against the popular Cry which was raised against it. They answered the Objections with great Strength and Solidity of Argument, and expatiated in very florid Harangues, which they did not fail to set off and furbelow (if I may be allowed the Metaphor) with many Periodical Sentences and Turns of Oratory. The chief Arguments for their Client were taken, first, from the great Benefit that might arise to our Woollen Manufactury from this Invention, which was calculated as follows: The common Petticoat has not above Four Yards in the Circumference; whereas this over our Heads had more in the Semi-diameter; so that by allowing it Twenty-four Yards in the Circumference, the Five Millions of Woollen Petticoats, which (according to Sir *William Petty*) supposing what ought to be supposed in a well-governed State, that all Petticoats are made of that Stuff, would amount to Thirty Millions of those of the ancient Mode. A prodigious Improvement of the Woollen Trade! and what could not fail to sink the Power of *France* in a few Years.

To introduce the Second Argument, they begged Leave to read a Petition of the Rope-Makers, wherein it was represented, That the Demand for Cords, and the Price of them, were much risen since this Fashion came up. At this, all the Company who were present lifted up their Eyes into the Vault; and I must confess, we did discover many Traces of Cordage which were interwoven in the Stiffening of the Drapery.

A Third Argument was founded upon a Petition of the *Greenland* Trade, which likewise represented the great Consumption of Whale-bone which would be occasioned by the present Fashion, and the Benefit which would thereby accrue to that Branch of the *British* Trade.

To conclude, they gently touched upon the Weight and Unwieldiness of the Garment, which they insinuated might be of great Use to preserve the Honour of Families.

These Arguments would have wrought very much upon me, (as I then told the Company in a long and elaborate Discourse) had I not considered the great and additional Expence which such Fashions would bring upon Fathers and Husbands; and therefore by no Means to be thought of till some Years after a Peace. I further urg'd, that it would be a Prejudice to the Ladies themselves, who could never expect to have any Money in the Pocket, if they laid out so much on the Petticoat. To this I added, the great Temptation it might give to Virgins, of acting in Security like married Women, and by that Means give a Check to Matrimony, an Institution always encouraged by wise Societies.

At the same Time, in Answer to the several Petitions produced on that Side, I shewed one subscribed by the Women of several Persons of Quality, humbly setting forth, That since the Introduction of this Mode, their respective Ladies had (instead of bestowing on them their Cast-Gowns) cut them into Shreds, and mixed them with the Cordage and Buckram, to compleat the Stiffening of their Under-Petticoats. For which, and sundry other Reasons, I pronounced the Petticoat a Forfeiture: But to shew that I did not make that Judgment for the Sake of filthy Lucre, I ordered it to be folded up, and sent it as a Present to a Widow-Gentlewoman, who has Five Daughters, desiring she would make each of them a Petticoat out of it, and send me back the Remainder, which I design to cut into Stomachers, Caps, Facings of my Wastcoat-Sleeves, and other Garnitures suitable to my Age and Quality.

I would not be understood, that (while I discard this monstrous Invention) I am an Enemy to the proper Ornaments of the Fair Sex. On the contrary, as the Hand of Nature has poured on them such a Profusion of Charms and Graces, and sent them into the World more amiable and finished than the rest of her Works; so I would have them bestow upon themselves all the additional Beauties that Art can supply them with, provided it does not interfere with Disguise, or pervert those of Nature.

I consider Woman as a beautiful Romantick Animal, that may be adorned with Furs and Feathers, Pearls and Diamonds, Ores and Silks. The Lynx shall cast its Skin at her Feet to make her a Tippet; the Peacock, Parrot, and Swan, shall pay Contributions to her Muff; the Sea shall be searched for Shells, and the Rocks for Gems; and every Part of Nature furnish out its Share towards the Embellishment of a Creature that is the most consummate Work of it. All this I shall indulge them in; but as for the Petticoat I have been speaking of, I neither can, nor will allow it.

No. 132   Saturday, February 11, 1709-10.   [Steele]

Habeo Senectuti magnam Gratiam, quae mihi
Sermonis aviditatem auxit, Potionis &
Cibi sustulit.[1] — Tull. *de Sen.*

Sheer-Lane, February 10.

After having applied my Mind with more than ordinary Attention to my Studies, it is my usual Custom to relax and unbend it in the Conversation of such as are rather easy than
shining Companions. This I find particularly necessary for
me before I retire to Rest, in order to draw my Slumbers upon
me by Degrees, and fall asleep insensibly. This is the particular Use I make of a Set of heavy honest Men, with whom I have
passed many Hours with much Indolence, though not with
great Pleasure. Their Conversation is a kind of Preparative
for Sleep: It takes the Mind down from its Abstractions, leads
it into the familiar Traces of Thought, and lulls it into that
State of Tranquility, which is the Condition of a thinking Man
when he is but half awake. After this, my Reader will not be
surprised to hear the Account which I am about to give of a
Club of my own Contemporaries, among whom I pass Two
or Three Hours every Evening. This I look upon as taking my
first Nap before I go to Bed. The Truth of it is, I should think
my self unjust to Posterity, as well as to the Society at the *Trum-*

[1] "I am much beholden to old age, which has increased my eagerness for conversation in proportion as it has lessened my appetites of hunger and thirst."
The abbreviation "Tull." is, of course, for Marcus Tullius Cicero, often referred
to in Steele's time as Tully. See *The Tatler,* No. 167, n.3.

pet,[2] of which I am a Member, did not I in some Part of my Writings give an Account of the Persons among whom I have passed almost a Sixth Part of my Time for these last Forty Years. Our Club consisted originally of Fifteen; but partly by the Severity of the Law in arbitrary Times, and partly by the natural Effects of old Age, we are at present reduced to a Third Part of that Number: In which however we have this Consolation, That the best Company is said to consist of Five Persons. I must confess, besides the afore-mentioned Benefit which I meet with in the Conversation of this select Society, I am not the less pleased with the Company, in that I find my self the greatest Wit among them, and am heard as their Oracle in all Points of Learning and Difficulty.

Sir *Jeoffrey Notch,* who is the oldest of the Club, has been in Possession of the Right-Hand Chair Time out of Mind, and is the only Man among us that has the Liberty of stirring the Fire. This our Foreman is a Gentleman of an ancient Family, that came to a great Estate some Years before he had Discretion, and run it out in Hounds, Horses, and Cock-fighting; for which Reason he looks upon himself as an honest worthy Gentleman who has had Misfortunes in the World, and calls every thriving Man a pitiful Upstart.

Major *Matchlock* is the next Senior, who served in the last Civil Wars, and has all the Battles by Heart. He does not think any Action in *Europe* worth talking of since the Fight of *Marston-Moor*[3] and every Night tells us of his having been knock'd off his Horse at the Rising of the *London* Apprentices[4] for which he is in great Esteem amongst us.

Honest old *Dick Reptile* is the Third of our Society: He is a good-natured indolent Man, who speaks little himself, but

[2] In Shire Lane, near Temple Bar, which divides the City of London from Westminster. The Society here described anticipates the club which provided the framework for *The Spectator.*
[3] A critical defeat of Royalist by Parliamentarian forces, July 2, 1644.
[4] In 1647.

laughs at our Jokes, and brings his young Nephew along with him, a Youth of Eighteen Years old, to show him good Company, and give him a Tast of the World. This young Fellow sits generally silent; but whenever he opens his Mouth, or laughs at any Thing that passes, he is constantly told by his Uncle after a jocular Manner, "Ay, ay, *Jack,* you young Men think us Fools; but we old Men know you are."

The greatest Wit of our Company, next to my self, is a Bencher of the neighbouring Inn, who in his Youth frequented the Ordinaries about *Charing-Cross,* and pretends to have been intimate with *Jack Ogle.* He has about Ten Distichs of *Hudibras* without Book, and never leaves the Club till he has applied them all. If any modern Wit be mentioned, or any Town Frolick spoken of, he shakes his Head at the Dulness of the present Age, and tells us a story of *Jack Ogle.*

For my own Part, I am esteemed among them, because they see I am something respected by others, though at the same Time I understand by their Behaviour, that I am considered by them as a Man of a great deal of Learning, but no Knowledge of the World; insomuch that the Major sometimes, in the Height of his Military Pride, calls me the Philosopher: and Sir *Jeoffrey* no longer ago than last Night, upon a Dispute what Day of the Month it was then in *Holland,*[5] pulled his Pipe out of his Mouth, and cried, What does the Scholar say to it?

Our Club meets precisely at Six a Clock in the Evening; but I did not come last Night till Half an Hour after Seven, by which Means I escaped the Battle of *Naseby,*[6] which the Major usually begins at about Three Quarters after Six; I found also, that my good Friend the Bencher had already spent Three of his Distichs, and only waiting an Opportunity to hear a Sermon spoken of, that he might introduce the Couplet where *a-Stick* rhimes to *Ecclesiastick.*[7] At my Entrance into the Room,

[5] See *The Tatler,* No. 21, n.3.
[6] One of the great battles of the Civil War, June 14, 1645.
[7] From *Hudibras,* a satire on the puritans by Samuel Butler (1612—1680).

they were naming a red Petticoat and a Cloak, by which I found
that the Bencher had been diverting them with a Story of *Jack
Ogle.*

I had no sooner taken my Seat, but Sir *Jeoffrey,* to show
his good Will towards me, gave me a Pipe of his own Tobacco, and stirred up the Fire. I look upon it as a Point of Morality, to be obliged by those who endeavour to oblige me; and
therefore in Requital for his Kindness, and to set the Conversation a going, I took the best Occasion I could to put him upon
telling us the Story of old *Gantlett,* which he always does with
very particular Concern. He traced up his Descent on both
Sides for several Generations, describing his Diet and Manner of Life, with his several Battles, and particularly that in
which he fell. This *Gantlett* was a Game-Cock, upon whose
Head the Knight in his Youth had won Five Hundred Pounds,
and lost Two Thousand. This naturally set the Major upon
the Account of *Edgehill* Fight, and ended in a Duel of *Jack
Ogle's.*

Old *Reptile* was extremely attentive to all that was said,
though it was the same he had heard every Night for these
Twenty Years, and upon all Occasions winked upon his Nephew
to mind what passed.

This many suffice to give the World a Tast of our innocent
Conversation, which we spun out till about Ten of the Clock,
when my Maid came with a Lanthorn to light me Home. I could
not but reflect with my self as I was going out upon the talkative Humour of old Men, and the little Figure which that Part
of Life makes in one who cannot employ this natural Propensity in Discourses which would make him venerable. I must
own, it makes me very melancholy in Company, when I hear
a young Man begin a Story; and have often observed, That
one of a Quarter of an Hour long in a Man of Five and twenty,
gathers Circumstances every Time he tells it, till it grows into
a long *Canterbury* Tale of two Hours by that Time he is Threescore.

The only Way of avoiding such a trifling and frivolous

old Age, is, to lay up in our way to it such Stores of Knowledge and Observation as may make us useful and agreeable in our declining Years. The Mind of Man in a long Life will become a Magazine of Wisdom or Folly, and will consequently discharge it self in something impertinent or improving. For which Reason, as there is nothing more ridiculous than an old trifling Story-Teller, so there is nothing more venerable than one who has turned his Experience to the Entertainment and Advantage of Mankind.

In short, we who are in the last Stage of Life, and are apt to indulge our selves in Talk, ought to consider, if what we speak be worth being heard, and endeavour to make our Discourse like that of *Nestor,* which *Homer* compares to the Flowing of Honey for its Sweetness.

I am afraid I shall be thought guilty of this Excess I am speaking of, when I cannot conclude without observing, that *Milton* certainly thought of this Passage in *Homer,* when in his Description of an eloquent Spirit, he says, *His Tongue drop'd Manna.*[8]

[8] *Paradise Lost,* II, 112-113.

Aliena Negotia curat
Excussus propriis.[1] —Hor.

From my own Apartment, April 5.

There lived some Years since within my Neighbourhood a very grave Person, an Upholsterer, who seemed a Man of more than ordinary Application to Business. He was a very early Riser, and was often abroad Two or Three Hours before any of his Neighbours. He had a particular Carefulness in the knitting of his Brows, and a kind of Impatience in all his Motions, that plainly discover'd he was always intent on Matters of Importance. Upon my Enquiry into his Life and Conversation, I found him to be the greatest Newsmonger in our Quarter; that he rose before Day to read the *Post-Man;* and that he would take Two or Three Turns to the other End of the Town before his Neighbours were up, to see if there were any *Dutch* Mails come in. He had a Wife and several Children; but was much more inquisitive to know what passed in *Poland* than in his own Family, and was in greater Pain and Anxiety of Mind for King *Augustus's* Welfare than that of his nearest Relations. He looked extremely thin in a Dearth of News, and never enjoy'd himself in a Westerly Wind. This indefatigable kind of Life was the Ruin of

---

[1] "He looks after other people's business after having been flung overboard from his own."

50

his Shop; for about the Time that his Favourite Prince left the Crown of *Poland,* he broke[2] and disappear'd.

This Man and his Affairs had been long out of my Mind, till about Three Days ago, as I was walking in St. *James's* Park, I heard some Body at a Distance hemming after me: And who should it be but my old Neighbour the Upholsterer? I saw he was reduc'd to extreme Poverty, by certain shabby Superfluities in his Dress: For notwithstanding that it was a very sultry Day for the Time of the Year, he wore a loose great Coat and a Muff, with a long Campaign-Wig out of Curl; to which he had added the Ornament of a Pair of black Garters buckled under the Knee. Upon his coming up to me, I was going to enquire into his present Circumstances; but was prevented by his asking me, with a Whisper, Whether the last Letters brought any Accounts that one might rely upon from *Bender?* I told him, None that I heard of; and asked him, Whether he had yet married his eldest Daughter? He told me, No. But pray, says he, tell me sincerely, What are your Thoughts of the King of *Sweden?* For though his Wife and Children were starving, I found his chief Concern at present was for this great Monarch. I told him, That I looked upon him as one of the first Heroes of the Age. But pray, says he, do you think there is any Thing in the Story of his Wound? And finding me surprised at the Question, Nay, says he, I only propose it to you. I answer'd, That I thought there was no Reason to doubt of it. But why in the Heel, says he, more than in any other Part of the Body? Because, says I, the Bullet chanced to light there.

This extraordinary Dialogue was no sooner ended, but he began to launch out into a long Dissertation upon the Affairs of the *North;* and after having spent some Time on them, he told me, He was in a great Perplexity how to reconcile the *Supplement* with the *English-Post,* and had been just now examining what the other Papers say upon the same Subject. The *Daily-*

[2] Went bankrupt.

Courant, says he, has these Words, *We have Advices from very good Hands, That a certain Prince has some Matters of great Importance under Consideration.* This is very mysterious; but the *Post Boy* leaves us more in the Dark, for he tells us, *That there are private Intimations of Measures taken by a certain Prince, which Time will bring to Light.* Now the *Post-Man,* says he, who uses to be very clear, refers to the same News in these Words; *The late Conduct of a certain Prince affords great Matter of Speculation.* This certain Prince, says the Upholsterer, whom they are all so cautious of naming, I take to be—Upon which, though there was no body near us, he whisper'd something in my Ear, which I did not hear, or think worth my while to make him repeat.

We were now got to the upper End of the *Mall,* where were Three or Four very odd Fellows sitting together upon the Bench. These I found were all of them Politicians, who us'd to Sun themselves in that Place every Day about Dinnertime. Observing them to be Curiosities in their Kind, and my Friend's Acquaintance, I sat down among them.

The chief Politician of the Bench was a great Asserter of Paradoxes. He told us, with a seeming Concern, That by some News he had lately read from *Muscovy,* it appear'd to him that there was a Storm gathering in the Black Sea, which might in Time do Hurt to the Naval Forces of this Nation. To this he added, That for his Part, he could not wish to see the Turk driven out of *Europe,* which he believ'd could not but be prejudicial to our Woolen Manufacture. He then told us, That he looked upon those extraordinary Revolutions which had lately happen'd in these Parts of the World, to have risen chiefly from Two Persons who were not much talked of; and those, says he, are Prince *Menzikoff,* and the Dutchess of *Mirandola.* He back'd his Assertions with so many broken Hints, and such a Show of Depth and Wisdom, that we gave our selves up to his Opinions.

The Discourse at length fell upon a Point which seldom

escapes a Knot of true-born *Englishmen,* Whether in Case of a Religious War, the Protestants would not be too strong for the Papists? This we unanimously determined on the Protestant Side. One who sat on my Right Hand, and, as I found by his Discourse, had been in the *West-Indies,* assur'd us, That it would be a very easy Matter for the Protestants to beat the Pope at Sea; and added, That whenever such a War does break out, it must turn to the Good of the *Leeward* Islands. Upon this, one who sat at the End of the Bench, and, as I afterwards found, was the Geographer of the Company, said, That in case the Papists should drive the Protestants from these Parts of *Europe,* when the worst came to the worst, it would be impossible to beat them out of *Norway* and *Greenland,* provided the Northern Crowns hold together, and the Czar of *Muscovy* stand Neuter.

He further told us for our Comfort, That there were vast Tracts of Land about the Pole, inhabited neither by Protestants nor Papists, and of greater Extent than all the *Roman* Catholick Dominions in *Europe.*

When we had fully discussed this Point, my Friend the Upholsterer began to exert himself upon the present Negotiations of Peace, in which he depos'd Princes, settled the Bounds of Kingdoms, and ballanced the Power of *Europe,* with great Justice and Impartiality.

I at length took my Leave of the Company, and was going away; but had not been gone Thirty Yards, before the Upholsterer hemm'd again after me. Upon his advancing towards me, with a Whisper, I expected to hear some secret Piece of News, which he had not thought fit to communicate to the Bench; but instead of that, he desired me in my Ear to lend him Half a Crown. In Compassion to so needy a Statesman, and to dissipate the Confusion I found he was in, I told him, if he pleas'd, I would give him Five Shillings, to receive Five Pounds of him when the Great Turk was driven out of *Constantinople;* which he very readily accepted, but not before he had laid down to me the Impossibility of such an Event, as the Affairs of *Europe* now stand.

This Paper I design for the particular Benefit of those worthy Citizens who live more in a Coffee-house than in their Shops, and whose Thoughts are so taken up with the Affairs of the Allies, that they forget their Customers.

No. 158   Thursday, April 13, 1710.   [Addison]

Faciunt næ intelligendo, ut nihil intelligant. [1] — Ter.

From my own Apartment, April 12.

Tom Folio is a Broker in Learning, employ'd to get together
good Editions, and stock the Libraries of great Men. There
is not a Sale of Books begins till *Tom Folio* is seen at the Door.
There is not an Auction where his Name is not heard, and that
too in the very Nick of Time, in the Critical Moment, before
the last decisive Stroke of the Hammer. There is not a Subscription goes forward, in which *Tom* is not privy to the first
rough Draught of the Proposals; [2] nor a Catalogue printed,
that doth not come to him wet from the Press. He is an universal Scholar, so far as the Title-Page of all Authors, knows
the Manuscripts in which they were discover'd, the Editions
through which they have passed, with the Praises or Censures
which they have receiv'd from the several Members of the
Learned World. He has a greater Esteem for *Aldus* and *Elzevir,*
than for *Virgil* and *Horace.* If you talk of *Herodotus,* he breaks
out into a Panegyrick upon *Harry Stephans.* He thinks he gives
you an Account of an Author, when he tells you the Subject
he treats of, the Name of the Editor, and the Year in which
it was printed. Or if you draw him into further Particulars, he

---

[1] "Does not this use of their critical faculty show that they are no critics?"
[2] A description of an expensive book, circulated by its publishers to obtain sub-
scribers in advance of publication. The handsome octavo edition of *The Tatler*
on which the present text is based was published by subscription in 1710 and
1711 at a guinea a volume.

cries up the Goodness of the Paper, extols the Diligence of the Corrector, and is transported with the Beauty of the Letter.[3] This he looks upon to be sound Learning and substantial Criticism. As for those who talk of the Fineness of Style, and the Justness of Thought, or describe the Brightness of any particular Passages; nay, though they write themselves in the Genius and Spirit of the Author they admire, *Tom* looks upon them as Men of superficial Learning, and flashy Parts.

I had Yesterday Morning a Visit from this learned Idiot, (for that is the Light in which I consider every Pedant) when I discover'd in him some little Touches of the Coxcomb, which I had not before observed. Being very full of the Figure which he makes in the Republick of Letters, and wonderfully satisfied with his great Stock of Knowledge, he gave me broad Intimations, that he did not *believe* in all Points as his Forefathers had done. He then communicated to me a Thought of a certain Author upon a Passage of *Virgil's* Account of the Dead, which I made the Subject of a late Paper. This Thought hath taken very much among Men of *Tom's* Pitch and Understanding, though universally exploded by all that know how to construe *Virgil,* or have any Relish of Antiquity. Not to trouble my Reader with it, I found upon the whole, that *Tom* did not believe a future State of Rewards and Punishments, because Æneas, at his leaving the Empire of the Dead, passed through the Gate of Ivory, and not through that of Horn. Knowing that *Tom* had not Sense enough to give up an Opinion which he had once received, that he might avoid wrangling, I told him, That *Virgil* possibly had his Oversights as well as another Author. Ah! Mr. *Bickerstaff,* says he, you would have another Opinion of him, if you would read him in *Daniel Heinsius's* Edition. I have perused him my self several Times in that Edition, continued he; and after the strictest and most malicious Examination, could find but two Faults in him: One of them is in the *Æneids,* where there are two Comma's instead of a Parenthesis;

[3] Typography.

and another in the Third *Georgick,* where you may find a Semi-colon turned upside down. Perhaps, said I, these were not *Virgil's* Thoughts, but those of the Transcriber. I do not design it, says *Tom,* as a Reflection on *Virgil:* On the contrary, I know that all the Manuscripts *reclaim* against such a Punctuation. Oh! Mr. *Bickerstaff,* says he, what would a Man give to see one Simile of *Virgil* writ in his own Hand? I asked him which was the Simile he meant; but was answered, Any Simile in *Virgil.* He then told me all the secret History in the Commonwealth of Learning; of Modern Pieces that had the Names of ancient Authors annex'd to them; of all the Books that were now writing or printing in the several Parts of *Europe;* of many Amendments which are made, and not yet publish'd; and a Thousand other Particulars, which I would not have my Memory burthen'd with for a Vatican.

At length, being fully perswaded that I thoroughly admired him, and looked upon him as a Prodigy of Learning, he took his Leave. I know of several of *Tom's* Class who are professed Admirers of *Tasso* without understanding a Word of *Italian;* and one in particular, that carries a *Pastor-Fido* in his Pocket, in which I am sure he is acquainted with no other Beauty but the Clearness of the Character.

There is another Kind of Pedant, who, with all *Tom Folio's* Impertinencies, hath greater Superstructures and Embellishments of *Greek* and *Latin,* and is still more insupportable than the other, in the same Degree as he is more learned. Of this Kind very often are Editors, Commentators, Interpreters, Scholiasts, and Criticks; and in short, all Men of deep Learning without common Sense. These Persons[4] set a greater Value on themselves for having found out the Meaning of a Passage in *Greek,* than upon the Author for having written it; nay, will allow the Passage it self not to have any Beauty in it, at the same Time that they would be considered as the greatest Men

---

[4] One of "these persons" was Richard Bentley, satirized by Swift in *The Battle of the Books* and *A Tale of a Tub,* and later by Pope in *The Dunciad Variorum* and *Epistle to Dr. Arbuthnot.*

of the Age for having interpreted it. They will look with Contempt upon the most beautiful Poems that have been composed by any of their Contemporaries; but will lock themselves up in their Studies for a Twelvemonth together, to correct, publish, and expound, such Trifles of Antiquity as a modern Author would be contemn'd for. Men of the strictest Morals, severest Lives, and the gravest Professions, will write Volumes upon an idle Sonnet that is originally in *Greek* or *Latin;* give Editions of the most Immoral Authors, and spin out whole Pages upon the various Readings of a lewd Expression. All that can be said in Excuse for them, is, That their Works sufficiently show they have no Tast of their Authors; and that what they do in this Kind, is out of their great Learning, and not out of any Levity or Lasciviousness of Temper.

A Pedant of this Nature is wonderfully well described in Six Lines of *Boileau,*[5] with which I shall conclude his Character:

> Un Pedant enyvré de sa vaine science,
> Tout herissé de Grec, tout bouffi d'arrogance,
> Et qui de mille Auteurs retenus mot pour mot,
> Dans sa tête entassez n'a souvent fait qu'un Sot,
> Croit qu'un Livre fait tout, & que sans Aristote
> La Raison ne voit goute, & le bon Sens radote.

[5] French critic and satirist (1636-1711).

No. 163   Monday, April 25, 1710.   [Addison]

Idem Inficeto est inficetior Rure
Simul Poemata attigit; neque idem unquam
Æque est beatus, ac Poema cum scribit:
Tam gaudet in se, tamque se ipse miratur.
Nimirum idem omnes fallimur; neque est quisquam
Quem non in aliqua re videre Suffenum
Possis. [1] —Catul. *de Suffeno.*

Will's Coffee-house, [2] *April 24.*

I Yesterday came hither about Two Hours before the Company generally make their Appearance, with a Design to read over all the News-Papers; but upon my sitting down, I was accosted by *Ned Softly,* who saw me from a Corner in the other End of the Room, where I found he had been writing something. Mr. *Bickerstaff*, says he, I observe by a late Paper of yours, that you and I are just of a Humour; for you must know, of all Impertinencies, there is nothing which I so much hate as News. I never read a *Gazette* in my Life; and never trouble my Head about our Armies, whether they win or lose, or in what Part of the World they lie encamped. Without giving me Time to reply, he drew a Paper of Verses out of his Pocket, telling me, That he had something which would entertain me

[1] "And at the same time he is never so happy as when he is writing a poem, he delights in himself and admires himself so much. True enough, we are all under the same delusion, and there is no one whom you may not see to be a Suffenus in one thing or another."
[2] See *The Tatler,* No. 1, n.2.

more agreeably, and that he would desire my Judgment upon every Line, for that we had Time enough before us till the Company came in.

Ned Softly is a very pretty Poet, and a great Admirer of easie Lines. *Waller* is his Favourite: And as that admirable Writer has the best and worst Verses of any among our great *English* Poets, *Ned Softly* has got all the bad Ones without Book, which he repeats upon Occasion, to show his Reading, and garnish his Conversation. *Ned* is indeed a true *English* Reader, incapable of relishing the great and masterly Strokes of this Art; but wonderfully pleased with the little *Gothick*[3] Ornaments of Epigrammatical Conceits, Turns, Points, and Quibbles, which are so frequent in the most admired of our *English* Poets, and practiced by those who want Genius and Strength to represent, after the Manner of the Ancients, Simplicity in its natural Beauty and Perfection.

Finding my self unavoidably engaged in such a Conversation, I was resolved to turn my Pain into a Pleasure, and to divert my self as well as I could with so very odd a Fellow. You must understand, says *Ned,* that the Sonnet I am going to read to you was written upon a Lady, who showed me some Verses of her own making, and is perhaps the best Poet of our Age. But you shall hear it. Upon which he begun to read as follows:

To Mira, *on her incomparable Poems.*

1.

When dress'd in Lawrel Wreaths you shine,
And tune your soft melodious Notes,
You seem a Sister of the Nine,
Or Phœbus *self in Petticoats.*

2.

I fancy, when your Song you sing,
(Your Song you sing with so much Art)
Your Pen was pluck'd from Cupid's *Wing;*
For ah! it wounds me like his Dart.

[3] Here, "overelaborate and quaintly out of date."

Why, says I, this is a little Nosegay of Conceits, a very Lump of Salt: Every Verse hath something in it that piques; and then the Dart in the last Line is certainly as pretty a Sting in the Tail of an Epigram (for so I think your Criticks call it) as ever entered into the Thought of a Poet. Dear Mr. *Bickerstaff,* says he, shaking me by the Hand, every Body knows you to be a Judge of these Things; and to tell you truly, I read over *Roscommon's* Translation of *Horace's Art of Poetry* Three several Times, before I sat down to write the Sonnet which I have shown you. But you shall hear it again, and pray observe every Line of it, for not one of them shall pass without your Approbation.

When dress'd in Lawrel Wreaths you shine.

That is, says he, when you have your Garland on; when you are writing Verses. To which I replied, I know your Meaning: A Metaphor! The same, said he, and went on:

And tune your soft melodious Notes.

Pray observe the Gliding of that Verse; there is scarce a Consonant in it: I took Care to make it run upon Liquids. Give me your Opinion of it. Truly, said I, I think it as good as the former. I am very glad to hear you say so, says he; but mind the next:

You seem a Sister of the Nine.

That is, says he, you seem a Sister of the Muses; for if you look into ancient Authors, you will find it was their Opinion, that there were Nine of them. I remember it very well, said I; but pray proceed.

> *Or* Phœbus *self in Petticoats.*

Phœbus, says he, was the God of Poetry. These little instances, Mr. *Bickerstaff,* show a Gentleman's Reading. Then to take off from the Air of Learning, which *Phœbus* and the Muses have given to this first Stanza, you may observe, how it falls all of a sudden into the Familiar; *in Petticoats.*

> *Or* Phœbus *self in Petticoats.*

Let us now, say I, enter upon the Second Stanza. I find the First Line is still a Continuation of the Metaphor.

> *I fancy, when your Song you sing.*

It is very right, says he; but pray observe the Turn of Words in those Two Lines. I was a whole Hour in adjusting of them, and have still a Doubt upon me, Whether in the Second Line it should be, *Your Song you sing;* or, *You sing your Song?* You shall hear them both:

> *I fancy, when your Song you sing,*
> *(Your Song you sing with so much Art.)*

OR

> *I fancy, when your Song you sing,*
> *(You sing your Song with so much Art.)*

Truly, said I, the Turn is so natural either Way, that you have made me almost giddy with it. Dear Sir, said he, grasping me by the Hand, you have a great deal of Patience; but pray what do you think of the next Verse?

Your Pen was pluck'd from Cupid's *Wing.*

Think! says I; I think you have made *Cupid* look like a little Goose. That was my Meaning, says he; I think the Ridicule is well enough hit off. But we now come to the last, which sums up the whole Matter:

For Ah! it wounds me like his Dart.

Pray how do you like that *Ah!* Doth it not make a pretty Figure in that Place? *Ah!* It looks as if I felt the Dart, and cried out at being pricked with it.

For Ah! it wounds me like his Dart.

My Friend *Dick Easy*, continued he, assured me, he would rather have written that *Ah!* than to have been the Author of the *Æneid.* He indeed objected, that I made *Mira's* Pen like a Quill in one of the Lines, and like a Dart in the other. But as to that—Oh! as to that, says I, it is but supposing *Cupid* to be like a Porcupine, and his Quills and Darts will be the same Thing. He was going to embrace me for the Hint; but half a Dozen Criticks coming into the Room, whose Faces he did not like, he conveyed the Sonnet into his Pocket, and whispered me in the Ear, he would show it me again as soon as his Man had written it over fair.

Qui sibi promittit Cives, Urbem, sibi Curæ
Imperium fore, & Italiam, & Delubra Deorum,
Quo Patre sit natus, num ignota Matre inhonestus,
Omnes Mortales curare & quærere cogit.[1]—Hor.

From my own Apartment, April 26.

I have lately been looking over the many Pacquets of Letters which I have received from all Quarters of *Great Britain,* as well as from Foreign Countries, since my entering upon the Office of *Censors,* and indeed am very much surprized to see so great a Number of them, and pleased to think that I have so far encreased the Revenue of the *Post-Office.* As this Collection will grow daily, I have digested it into several Bundles, and made proper Endorsements on each particular Letter, it being my Design, when I lay down the Work that I am now engaged in, to erect a Paper-Office, and give it to the Publick.[2]

I could not but make several Observations upon reading over the Letters of my Correspondents: As first of all, on the different Tasts that reign in the different Parts of this City. I find, by the Approbations which are given me, That I am seldom fa-

[1] "So he who takes it upon himself to look after his fellow-citizens and the city, the empire and Italy, and the temples of the gods, compels all the world to take an interest, and to ask who his father was, and whether he is dishonored through an unknown mother."
[2] As George A. Aitken pointed out in a footnote to this essay, "This idea was carried out in 1725, when Charles Lillie published, by Steele's permission, two volumes of 'Original and genuine Letters sent to the *Tatler* and *Spectator*, during the time those works were publishing. None of which have before been printed.'"

mous on the same Days on both Sides of *Temple-Bar;* and that when I am in the greatest Repute within the Liberties, I dwindle at the Court-End of the Town. Sometimes I sink in both these Places at the same Time; but for my Comfort, my Name hath then been up in the Districts of *Wapping* and *Rotherhithe.* Some of my Correspondents desire me to be always serious, and others to be always merry. Some of them entreat me to go to Bed and fall into a Dream, and like me better when I am asleep than when I am awake: Others advise me to sit all Night upon the Stars, and be more frequent in my Astrological Observations; for that a Vision is not properly a Lucubration. Some of my Readers thank me for filling my Paper with the Flowers of Antiquity, others desire News from *Flanders.* Some approve my Criticisms on the Dead, and others my Censures on the Living. For this Reason, I once resolved in the new Edition of my Works, to range my several Papers under distinct Heads, according as their principal Design was to benefit and instruct the different Capacities of my Readers, and to follow the Example of some very great Authors, by writing at the Head of each Discourse, *Ad Aulam, Ad Academiam, Ad Populum, Ad Clerum.*

There is no Particular in which my Correspondents of all Ages, Conditions, Sexes, and Complexions, universally agree, except only in their Thirst after Scandal. It is impossible to conceive how many have recommended their Neighbours to me upon this Account, or how unmercifully I have been abused by several unknown Hands, for not publishing the secret Histories of Cuckoldom that I have received from almost every Street in Town.

It would indeed be very dangerous for me to read over the many Praises and Eulogiums which come Post to me from all the Corners of the Nation, were they not mix'd with many Checks, Reprimands, Scurrilities, and Reproaches, which several of my good-natured Countrymen cannot forbear sending me, though it often costs them Two-pence or a Groat before they can convey them to my Hands: So that sometimes when

I am put into the best Humour in the World, after having read a Panegyrick upon my Performance, and looked upon my self as a Benefactor to the *British* Nation, the next Letter perhaps I open, begins with, *You old Doting Scoundrel—Are not you a sad Dog—Sirrah, you deserve to have your Nose slit;* and the like ingenious Conceits. These little Mortifications are necessary to suppress that Pride and Vanity which naturally arise in the Mind of a received Author, and enable me to bear the Reputation which my courteous Readers bestow upon me, without becoming a Coxcomb by it. It was for the same Reason, that when a *Roman* General entered the City in the Pomp of a Triumph, the Commonwealth allowed of several little Drawbacks to his Reputation, by conniving at such of the Rabble as repeated Libels and Lampoons upon him within his Hearing, and by that Means engaged his Thoughts upon his Weakness and Imperfections, as well as on the Merits that advanced him to so great Honours. The Conqueror however was not the less esteemed for being a Man in some Particulars, because he appeared as a God in others.

There is another Circumstance in which my Countrymen have dealt very perversely with me; and that is, in Searching not only into my own Life, but also into the Lives of my Ancestors. If there has been a Blot in my Family for these Ten Generations, it hath been discovered by some or other of my Correspondents. In short, I find the ancient Family of the *Bickerstaffs* has suffered very much through the Malice and Prejudice of my Enemies. Some of them twit me in the Teeth with the Conduct of my Aunt *Margery:* Nay, there are some who have been so disingenuous, as to throw *Maud* the Milk-Maid into my Dish, notwithstanding I my self was the first who discovered that Alliance. I reap however many Benefits from the Malice of these my Enemies, as they let me see my own Faults, and give me a View of my self in the worst Light; as they hinder me from being blown up by Flattery and Self-conceit; as they make me keep a watchful Eye over my own Actions, and at the same Time make me cautious how I talk of others, and particularly of my Friends and Relations, or value my self upon the Antiquity of my Family.

But the most formidable Part of my Correspondents are those whole Letters are filled with Threats and Menaces. I have been treated so often after this Manner, that not thinking it sufficient to fence well, in which I am now arrived at the utmost Perfection, and carry Pistols about me, which I have always tuck'd within my Girdle; I several Months since made my Will, settled my Estate, and took Leave of my Friends, looking upon my self as no better than a dead Man. Nay, I went so far as to write a long Letter to the most intimate Acquaintance I have in the World, under the Character of a departed Person, giving him an Account of what brought me to that untimely End, and of the Fortitude with which I met it. This Letter being too long for the present Paper, I intend to print it by it self very suddenly; and at the same Time I must confess, I took my Hint of it from the Behaviour of an old Soldier in the Civil Wars, who was Corporal of a Company in a Regiment of Foot, about the same Time that I my self was a Cadet in the King's Army.

This Gentleman was taken by the Enemy; and the Two Parties were upon such Terms at that Time, that we did not treat each other as Prisoners of War, but as Traitors and Rebels. The poor Corporal being condemned to die, wrote a Letter to his Wife when under Sentence of Execution. He writ on the *Thursday,* and was to be executed on the *Friday:* But considering that the Letter would not come to his Wife's Hands till *Saturday*, the Day after Execution, and being at that Time more scrupulous than ordinary in speaking exact Truth, he formed his Letter rather according to the Posture of his Affairs when she should read it, than as they stood when he sent it: Though it must be confessed, there is a certain Perplexity in the Style of it, which the Reader will easily pardon, considering his Circumstances.

Dear Wife,
Hoping you are in good Health, as I am at this present Writing, This is to let you know, that Yesterday, between the Hours of Eleven and Twelve, I was hanged, drawn, and quartered. I died very penitently, and every Body thought my Case very hard. Remember me kindly to my poor Fatherless Children.

Yours till Death,
W. B.

It so happened, that this honest Fellow was relieved by a Party of his Friends, and had the Satisfaction to see all the Rebels hanged who had been his Enemies. I must omit a Circumstance which exposed him to Raillery his whole Life after. Before the Arrival of the next Post, that would have set all Things clear, his Wife was married to a Second Husband, who lived in the peaceable Possession of her; and the Corporal, who was a Man of plain Understanding did not care to stir in the Matter, as knowing that she had the News of his Death under his own Hand, which she might have produced upon Occasion.

No. 165   Saturday, April 29, 1710.   [Addison] [1]

From my own Apartment, April 28.

It has always been my Endeavour to distinguish between Realities and Appearances, and to separate true Merit from the Pretence to it. As it shall ever be my Study to make Discoveries of this Nature in Humane Life, and to settle the proper Distinctions between the Virtues and Perfections of Mankind, and those false Colours and Resemblances of them that shine alike in the Eyes of the Vulgar; so I shall be more particularly careful to search into the various Merits and Pretences of the learned World. This is the more necessary, because there seems to be a general Combination among the Pedants to extol one another's Labours, and cry up one another's Parts; while Men of Sense, either through that Modesty which is natural to them, or the Scorn they have for such trifling Commendations, enjoy their Stock of Knowledge like a hidden Treasure with Satisfaction and Silence. Pedantry [2] indeed in Learning is like Hypocrisy in Religion, a Form of Knowledge without the Power of it, that attracts the Eyes of the Common People, breaks out in Noise and Show, and finds its Reward not from any inward Pleasure that attends it, but from the Praises and Approbations which it receives from Men.

Of this shallow Species there is not a more importunate, empty, and conceited Animal, than that which is generally known by the Name of a Critick. This, in the common Accep-

---

[1] This number is without a Latin motto in the original folio and the first octavo edition.

[2] Compare the treatment of pedantry in *The Tatler*, No. 158.

tation of the Word, is one that, without entering into the Sense and Soul of an Author, has a few general Rules, which, like mechanical Instruments, he applies to the Works of every Writer, and as they quadrate with them, pronounces the Author perfect or defective. He is Master of a certain Set of Words, as Unity, Style, Fire, Flegm, Easie, Natural, Turn, Sentiment, and the like; which he varies, compounds, divides, and throws together, in every Part of his Discourse, without any Thought or Meaning. The Marks you may know him by are, an elevated Eye, and dogmatical Brow, a positive Voice, and a Contempt for every Thing that comes out, whether he has read it or not. He dwells altogether in Generals. He praises or dispraises in the Lump. He shakes his Head very frequently at the Pedantry of Universities, and bursts into Laughter when you mention an Author that is known at *Will's*. He hath formed his Judgment upon *Homer, Horace,* and *Virgil,* not from their own Works, but from those of *Rapin* and *Bossu.*[3] He knows his own Strength so well, that he never dares praise any Thing in which he has not a *French* Author for his Voucher.

With these extraordinary Talents and Accomplishments, Sir *Timothy Tittle* puts Men in Vogue, or condemns them to Obscurity, and sits as Judge of Life and Death upon every Author that appears in Publick. It is impossible to represent the Pangs, Agonies, and Convulsions, which Sir *Timothy* expresses in every Feature of his Face, and Muscle of his Body, upon the reading of a bad Poet.

About a Week ago I was engaged at a Friend's House of mine in an agreeable Conversation with his Wife and Daughters, when in the Height of our Mirth, Sir *Timothy*, who makes Love to my Friend's eldest Daughter, came in amongst us puffing and blowing, as if he had been very much out of Breath. He

---

[3] René Rapin (1621 - 87) wrote on Virgil, Horace, and Aristotle, and had a considerable influence on English criticism, as did his French compatriots Bossu (1627 - 1704) and Dacier (1651 - 1722). Sir Timothy is being laughed at because his inadequacy with the Latin language forces him to fall back on modern French critics as a substitute for the classical writers themselves.

immediately called for a Chair, and desired Leave to sit down, without any further Ceremony. I asked him, Where he had been? Whether he was out of Order? He only replied, That he was quite spent, and fell a cursing in Soliloquy. I could hear him cry, *A Wicked Rogue—An Execrable Wretch—Was there ever such a Monster—* The young Ladies upon this began to be affrighted, and asked, Whether any one had hurt him? He answered nothing, but still talked to himself. *To lay the first Scene,* says he, *in* St. James's Park, *and the last in* Northamptonshire! Is that all? says I: Then I suppose you have been at the Rehearsal of a Play this Morning. *Been!* says he; I have been at *Northampton,* in the *Park,* in a Lady's Bed Chamber, in a Dining-Room, every where; the Rogue has led me such a Dance—Tho' I could scarce forbear laughing at his Discourse, I told him I was glad it was no worse, and that he was only Metaphorically weary. In short, Sir, says he, the Author has not observed a single Unity in his whole Play; the Scene shifts in every Dialogue; the Villain has hurried me up and down at such a Rate, that I am tired off my Legs. I could not but observe with some Pleasure, that the young Lady whom he made Love to, conceived a very just Aversion towards him, upon seeing him so very passionate in Trifles. And as she had that natural Sense which makes her a better Judge than a Thousand Criticks, she began to rally him upon this foolish Humour. For my Part, says she, I never knew a Play take that was written up to your Rules, as you call them. How Madam! says he, Is that your Opinion? I am sure you have a better Tast. It is a pretty Kind of Magick, says she, the Poets have to transport an Audience from Place to Place without the Help of a Coach and Horses. I could travel round the World at such a Rate. 'Tis such an Entertainment as an Enchantress finds when she fancies her self in a Wood, or upon a Mountain, at a Feast, or a Solemnity; though at the same Time she has never stirred out of her Cottage. Your Simile, Madam, says Sir *Timothy,* is by no Means just. Pray, says she, let my Similes pass without a Criticism. I must confess, continued she, (for I found she was resolved to exasperate him) I laughed very heartily at the last New Comedy which you found so much Fault with. But Madam, says he, you ought not to have laughed; and I defie any one to show me a single Rule that you could laugh by. Ought not to laugh! says she: Pray who should hinder me. Madam, says he, there are such People in the World as *Rapin, Dacier,* and several others, that ought to have spoiled your Mirth. I have heard, says the young Lady, That your great Criticks are always very bad Poets: I fancy there is as much Difference between the Works of one and the other, as there is between the Carriage of a Dancing-Master and a Gentleman. I must confess, continued she, I would not be troubled with so fine a Judgment as yours is; for I find you feel more Vexation in a bad Comedy, than I do in a deep Tragedy. Madam, says Sir *Timothy,* That is not my Fault, they should learn the Art of Writing. For my Part, says the young Lady, I should think the greatest Art in your Writers of Comedies is to please. To please! says Sir *Timothy*; and immediately fell a laughing. Truly, says she, that is my Opinion. Upon this, he composed his Countenance, looked upon his Watch, and took his Leave.

I hear that Sir *Timothy* has not been at my Friend's House since this notable Conference, to the great Satisfaction of the young Lady, who by this Means has got rid of a very impertinent Fop.

I must confess, I could not but observe, with a great deal of Surprize, how this Gentleman, by his ill Nature, Folly and Affectation, hath made himself capable of suffering so many imaginary Pains, and looking with such a senseless Severity upon the common Diversions of Life.

No. 167   Thursday, May 4, 1710.   [Steele]

Segnius irritant Animos dimissa per Aures,
Quam quæ sunt Oculis submissa fidelibus. [1] —Hor.

From my own Apartment, May 2.

Having received Notice, That the famous Actor Mr. *Betterton*[2] was to be interred this Evening in the Cloysters near *Westminster-Abbey,* I was resolved to walk thither, and see the last Office done to a Man whom I had always very much admired, and from whose Action I had received more strong Impressions of what is great and noble in Humane Nature, than from the Arguments of the most solid Philosophers, or the Descriptions of the most charming Poets I had ever read. As the rude and untaught Multitude are no Way wrought upon more effectually than by seeing publick Punishments and Executions; so Men of Letters and Education feel their Humanity most forcibly exercised, when they attend the Obsequies of Men who had arrived at any Perfection in Liberal Accomplishments. Theatrical Action is to be esteemed as such, except it be objected, that we cannot call that an Art which cannot be attained by Art. Voice, Stature, Motion, and other Gifts, must be very bountifully bestowed by Nature, or Labour and Industry will but push the unhappy Endeavourer, in that Way, the further off his Wishes.

[1] "Less vividly is the mind stirred by what finds entrance through the ears than by what is brought before the trusty eyes."
[2] See *The Tatler,* No. 1, n.6.

73

Such an Actor as Mr. *Betterton* ought to be recorded with the same Respect as *Roscius* among the *Romans*. The greatest Orator has thought fit to quote his Judgment, and celebrate his Life. *Roscius* was the Example to all that would form themselves into proper and winning Behaviour. His Action was so well adapted to the Sentiments he expressed, that the Youth of *Rome* thought they wanted only to be virtuous to be as graceful in their Appearance as *Roscius*. The Imagination took a lovely Impression of what was great and good; and they who never thought of setting up for the Art of Imitation, became themselves imitable Characters.

There is no Humane Invention so aptly calculated for the forming of a Free-born People as that of a Theatre. *Tully*[3] reports, That the celebrated Player of whom I am speaking used frequently to say, *The Perfection of an Actor is only to become what he is doing.* Young Men, who are too unattentive to receive Lectures, are irresistibly taken with Performances. Hence it is, that I extremely lament the little Relish the Gentry of his Nation have at present for the just and noble Representations in some of our Tragedies. The Opera's, which are of late introduced, can leave no Trace behind them that can be of Service beyond the present Moment. To sing and to dance, are Accomplishments very few have any Thoughts of practising; but to speak justly, and move gracefully, is what every Man thinks he does perform, or wishes he did.

I have hardly a Notion, that any Performer of Antiquity could surpass the Action of Mr. *Betterton* in any of the Occasions in which he has appeared on our Stage. The wonderful Agony which he appeared in, when he examined the Circumstance of the Handkerchief in *Othello;* the Mixture of Love that intruded upon his Mind upon the innocent Answers *Desdemona* makes, betrayed in his Gesture such a Variety and Vicissitude of Passions, as would admonish a Man to be afraid of

---

[3] Cicero, the "greatest orator" referred to in the preceding paragraph.

his own Heart, and perfectly convince him, that it is to stab it, to admit that worst of Daggers, Jealousy. Whoever reads in his Closet this admirable Scene, will find that he cannot, except he has as warm an Imagination as *Shakespear* himself, find any but dry, incoherent, and broken Sentences: But a Reader that has seen *Betterton* act it, observes there could not be a Word added; that longer Speeches had been unnatural, nay impossible, in *Othello's* Circumstances. The charming Passage in the same Tragedy, where he tells the Manner of winning the Affection of his Mistress, was urged with so moving and graceful an Energy, that while I walked in the Cloysters, I thought of him with the same Concern as if I waited for the Remains of a Person who had in real Life done all that I had seen him represent. The Gloom of the Place, and faint Lights before the Ceremony appeared, contributed to the melancholy Disposition I was in; and I began to be extremely afflicted, that *Brutus* and *Cassius* had any Difference; that *Hotspur's* Gallantry was so unfortunate; and that the Mirth and good Humour of *Falstaff,* could not exempt him from the Grave. Nay, this Occasion in me, who look upon the Distinctions amongst Men to be meerly Scenical, raised Reflections upon the Emptiness of all Humane Perfection and Greatness in general; and I could not but regret, that the Sacred Heads which lie buried in the Neighbourhood of this little Portion of Earth in which my poor old Friend is deposited, are returned to Dust as well as he, and that there is no Difference in the Grave between the Imaginary and the Real Monarch. This made me say of Humane Life it self with *Mackbeth:*

> *To Morrow, to Morrow, and to Morrow,*
> *Creeps in a stealing Pace from Day to Day,*
> *To the last Moment of recorded Time!*
> *And all our Yesterdays have lighted Fools*
> *To their eternal Night! Out, out short Candle*
> *Life's but a walking Shadow, a poor Player*

> *That struts and frets his Hour upon the Stage,*
> *And then is heard no more.* [4]

The mention I have here made of Mr. *Betterton,* for whom I had, as long as I have known any Thing, a very great Esteem and Gratitude for the Pleasure he gave me, can do him no Good; but it may possibly be of Service to the unhappy Woman he has left behind him, to have it known, that this great Tragedian was never in a Scene half so moving, as the Circumstances of his Affairs created at his Departure. His Wife, after the Cohabitation of Forty Years in the strictest Amity, has long pined away with a Sense of his Decay, as well in his Person as his little Fortune; and in Proportion to that, she has her self decayed both in her Health and Reason. Her Husband's Death, added to her Age and Infirmities, would certainly have determined her Life, but that the Greatness of her Distress has been her Relief, by a present Depravation of her Senses. This Absence of Reason is her best Defense against Age, Sorrow, Poverty, and Sickness. I dwell upon this Account so distinctly, in Obedience to a certain great Spirit who hides her Name, and has by Letter applied to me to recommend to her some Object of Compassion, from whom she may be concealed.

This I think, is a proper Occasion for exerting such heroick Generosity; and as there is an ingenuous Shame in those who have known better Fortune to be reduced to receive Obligations, as well as a becoming Pain in the truly Generous to receive Thanks in this Case, both those Delicacies are preserved; for the Person obliged is as incapable of knowing her Benefactress, as her Benefactress is unwilling to be known by her. [5]

---

[4] Steele is quoting, not entirely accurately, from Sir William Davenant's version of *Macbeth* rather than from the current (1709) edition of Shakespeare by Nicholas Rowe.

[5] At the end of this essay Steele inserted an amusing advertisement, which he reprinted in the first octavo edition of *The Tatler.* It is omitted here as unintelligible to anyone who has not read several papers not included in the present selection.

No. 181   Tuesday, June 6, 1710.   [Steele]

Dies, ni fallor, adest, quem semper acerbum,
Semper honoratum; sic, Dii, voluistis, habebo. [1] —Virg.

From my own Apartment, June 5.

There are those among Mankind, who can enjoy no Relish
of their Being, except the World is made acquainted with all
that relates to them, and think every Thing lost that passes
unobserved; but others find a solid Delight in stealing by the
Crowd, and modelling their Life after such a Manner, as is
as much above the Approbation as the Practice of the Vulgar.
Life being too short to give Instances great enough of true
Friendship or Good-Will, some Sages have thought it pious to
preserve a certain Reverence for the Manes of their deceased
Friends, and have withdrawn themselves from the rest of the
World at certain Seasons, to commemorate in their own
Thoughts such of their Acquaintance who have gone before
them out of this Life: And indeed, when we are advanced in
Years, there is not a more pleasing Entertainment, than to recollect in a gloomy Moment the many we have parted with that
have been dear and agreeable to us, and go cast a melancholy
Thought or Two after those with whom, perhaps, we have indulged our selves in whole Nights of Mirth and Jollity. With
such Inclinations in my Heart I went to my Closet Yesterday in
the Evening, and resolved to be sorrowful; upon which Occa-

---

[1] "If I err not, the day is at hand which I shall keep (such, O Gods, was your
will) ever as a day of grief, ever as of honor."

sion, I could not but look with Disdain upon my self, that though all the Reasons which I had to lament the Loss of many of my Friends are now as forcible as at the Moment of their Departure, yet did not my Heart swell with the same Sorrow which I felt at that Time; but I could, without Tears, reflect upon many pleasing Adventures I have had with some who have long been blended with common Earth. Though it is by the Benefit of Nature that Length of Time thus blots out the Violence of Afflictions; yet with Tempers too much given to Pleasure, it is almost necessary to revive the old Places of Grief in our Memory, and ponder Step by Step on past Life, to lead the Mind into that Sobriety of Thought which poises the Heart, and makes it beat with due Time, without being quickened with Desire, or retarded with Despair, from its proper and equal Motion. When we wind up a Clock that is out of Order, to make it go well for the future, we do not immediately set the Hand to the present Instant, but we make it strike the Round of all its Hours, before it can recover the Regularity of its Time. Such, thought I, shall be my Method this Evening; and since it is that Day of the Year which I dedicate to the Memory of such in another Life as I much delighted in when living, an Hour or Two shall be sacred to Sorrow and their Memory, while I run over all the melancholy Circumstances of this Kind which have occurred to me in my whole Life.

The first Sense of Sorrow I ever knew was upon the Death of my Father, at which Time I was not quite Five Years of Age; but was rather amazed at what all the House meant, than possessed with a real Understanding why no Body was willing to play with me. I remember I went into the Room where his Body lay, and my Mother sat weeping alone by it. I had my Battledore in my Hand, and fell a beating the Coffin, and calling Papa; for I know not how I had some slight Idea that he was locked up there. My Mother catched me in her Arms, and transported beyond all Patience of the silent Grief she was before in, she almost smothered me in her Embrace, and told me in a Flood of Tears, Papa could not hear me, and would play with me no more, for they were going to put him under Ground, whence he could never come to us again.[2] She was a very beautiful Woman, of a noble Spirit, and there was a Dignity in her Grief amidst all the Wildness of her Transport, which, methought, struck me with an Instinct of Sorrow, which, before I was sensible of what it was to grieve, seized my very Soul, and has made Pity the Weakness of my Heart ever since. The Mind in Infancy is, methinks, like the Body in Embrio, and receives Impressions so forcible, that they are as hard to be removed by Reason, as any Mark with which a Child is born is to be taken away by any future Application. Hence it is, that Good-Nature in me is no Merit; but having been so frequently over-whelmed with her Tears before I knew the Cause of any Affliction, or could draw Defences from my own Judgment, I imbibed Commiseration, Remorse, and an unmanly Gentleness of Mind, which has since insnared me into Ten Thousand Calamities, and from whence I can reap no Advantage, except it be, that in such an Humour as I am now in, I can the better indulge my self in the Softnesses of Humanity, and enjoy that sweet Anxiety which arises from the Memory of past Afflictions.

We that are very old, are better able to remember Things which befel us in our distant Youth, than the Passages of later Days. For this Reason it is, that the Companions of my strong and vigorous Years present themselves more immediately to me in this Office of Sorrow. Untimely or unhappy Deaths are what we are most apt to lament, so little are we able to make it indifferent when a Thing happens, though we know it must happen. Thus we groan under Life, and bewail those who are relieved from it. Every Object that returns to our Imagination raises different Passions, according to the Circumstance of

[2] This passage was used as a speech by Steele to young Henry Esmond in Thackeray's *Henry Esmond,* Book I, Chapter vi.

their Departure. Who can have lived in an Army, and in a serious Hour reflect upon the many gay and agreeable Men that might long have flourished in the Arts of Peace, and not join with the Imprecations of the Fatherless and Widow on the Tyrant to whose Ambition they fell Sacrifices? But gallant Men, who are cut off by the Sword, move rather our Veneration than our Pity, and we gather Relief enough from their own Contempt of Death, to make it no Evil, which was approached with so much Chearfulness, and attended with so much Honour. But when we turn our Thoughts from the great Parts of Life on such Occasions, and instead of lamenting those who stood ready to give Death to those from whom they had the Fortune to receive it; I say, when we let our Thoughts wander from such noble Objects, and consider the Havock which is made among the Tender and the Innocent, Pity enters with an unmixed Softness, and possesses all our Souls at once.

Here (were there Words to express such Sentiments with proper Tenderness) I should record the Beauty, Innocence, and untimely Death, of the first Object my Eyes ever beheld with Love. The beauteous Virgin! How ignorantly did she charm, how carelessly excel? Oh Death! Thou has Right to the Bold, to the Ambitious, to the High, and to the Haughty; but why this Cruelty to the Humble, to the Meek, to the Undiscerning, to the Thoughtless? Nor Age, nor Business, nor Distress, can erase the dear Image from my Imagination. In the same Week, I saw her dressed for a Ball, and in a Shrowd. How ill did the Habit of Death become the Pretty Trifler? I still behold the smiling Earth—A large Train of Disasters were coming on to my Memory, when my Servant knocked at my Closet Door, and interrupted me with a Letter, attended with a Hamper of Wine, of the same Sort with that which is to be put to Sale on *Thursday* next at Garraway's Coffeehouse. Upon the Receipt of it, I sent for Three of my Friends. We are so intimate, that we can be Company in whatever State of Mind we meet, and can entertain each other without expecting always to rejoice. The Wine we found to be generous and warming, but with such an Heat as moved us rather to be chearful than frolicksome. It revived the Spirits without firing the Blood. We commended it till Two of the Clock this Morning, and having to Day met a little before Dinner we found, that though we drank Two Bottles a Man, we had much more Reason to recollect than forget what had passed the Night before.

No. 224 Thursday, September 14, 1710. [Addison]

Materiam superabat Opus.[1]—Ovid.

From my own Apartment, September 13.

It is my Custom in a Dearth of News, to entertain my self with those Collections of Advertisements that appear at the End of all our publick Prints. These I consider as Accounts of News from the little World, in the same Manner that the foregoing Parts of the Paper are from the great. If in one we hear that a Sovereign Prince is fled from his Capital City, in the other we hear of a Tradesman who hath shut up his Shop, and run away. If in one we find the Victory of a General, in the other we see the Desertion of a private Soldier. I must confess, I have a certain Weakness in my Temper, that is often very much affected by these little Domestick Occurrences, and have frequently been caught with Tears in my Eyes over a melancholy Advertisement.

But to consider this Subject in its most ridiculous Lights, Advertisements are of great Use to the Vulgar: First of all, as they are Instruments of Ambition. A Man that is by no Means big enough for the *Gazette,* may easily creep into the Advertisements; by which Means we often see an Apothecary in the same Paper of News with a Plenipotentiary, or a Running-Footman with an Ambassador. An Advertisement from Pickadilly goes down to Posterity, with an Article from *Madrid;* and *John Bartlett*[2] of *Goodman's Fields* is celebrated in the same Paper with

[1] "The workmanship was more beautiful than the material."
[2] Bartlett's shop sold trusses and orthopedic appliances.

the Emperor of *Germany*. Thus the Fable tells us, That the Wren mounted as high as the Eagle, by getting upon his Back.

A Second Use which this Sort of Writings have been turned to of late Years, has been the Management of Controversy, insomuch that above half the Advertisements one meets with now-a-Days are purely Polemical. The Inventors of *Strops for Razors* have written against one another this Way for several Years, and that with great Bitterness; as the whole Argument *pro* and *con* in the Case of the *Morning Gowns* is still carried on after the same Manner. I need not mention the several Proprietors of Dr. *Anderson's* Pills; nor take Notice of the many Satyrical Works of this Nature so fequently published by Dr. *Clark,*[3] who has had the Confidence to advertise upon that learned Knight, my very worthy Friend, Sir *William Read:*[4] But I shall not interpose in their Quarrel; Sir *William* can give him his own in Advertisements, that, in the Judgment of the Impartial, are as well penned as the Doctor's.

The Third and last Use of these Writings is, to inform the World where they may be furnished with almost every Thing that is necessary for Life. If a Man has Pains in his Head, Cholicks in his Bowels, or Spots in his Clothes, he may here meet with proper Cures and Remedies. If a Man would recover a Wife or a Horse that is stolen or strayed; if he wants new Sermons, Electuaries, Asses Milk, or any Thing else, either for his Body or his Mind, this is the place to look for them in.

The great Art in writing Advertisements, is the finding out a proper Method to catch the Reader's Eye; without which a good Thing may pass over unobserved, or be lost among Commissions of Bankrupt. Asterisks and Hands were formerly of great Use for this Purpose. Of late Years, the *N.B.* has been much in Fashion; as also little Cuts and Figures, the Invention of which we must ascribe to the Author of Spring-Trusses. I must not here omit the blind *Italian* Character, which being

[3] Physician and oculist to Charles II and James II.
[4] Oculist to Queen Anne, who knighted him in 1705.

scarce legible, always fixes and detains the Eye, and gives the curious Reader something like the Satisfaction of prying into a Secret.

But the great Skill in an Advertiser, is chiefly seen in the Style which he makes Use of. He is to mention *the universal Esteem, or general Reputation,* of Things that were never heard of. If he is a Physician or Astrologer, he must change his Lodgings frequently, and (though he never saw any Body in them besides his own Family) give publick Notice of it, *For the Information of the Nobility and Gentry.* Since I am thus usefully employed in writing Criticisms on the Works of these diminutive Authors, I must not pass over in Silence an Advertisement which has lately made its Appearance, and is written altogether in a *Ciceronian* Manner. It was sent to me, with Five Shillings, to be inserted among my Advertisements; but as it is a Pattern of good Writing in this Way, I shall give it a Place in the Body of my Paper.

The highest compounded Spirit of Lavender, the most glorious (if the Expression may be used) enlivening Scent and Flavour that can possibly be, which so raptures the Spirits, delights the Gust, and gives such Airs to the Countenance, as are not to be imagined but by those that have tried it. The meanest Sort of the Thing is admired by most Gentlemen and Ladies; but this far more, as by far it exceeds it, to the gaining among all a more than common Esteem. It is sold (in neat Flint Bottles fit for the Pocket) only at the Golden-Key in Warton's-Court near Holborn-Bars, for 3 s. 6 d. with Directions.

At the same Time that I recommend the several Flowers in which this Spirit of Lavender is wrapped up, (if the Expression may be used) I cannot excuse my Fellow-Labourers for admitting into their Papers several uncleanly Advertisements, not at all proper to appear in the Works of polite Writers. Among these I must reckon the *Carminitive Windexpelling* Pills. If the Doctor had called them only his Carminitive Pills, he had been as cleanly as one could have wished; but the Second Word entirely destroys the Decency of the First. There are other Absurdities of this Nature so very gross, that I dare not mention them; and shall therefore dismiss this Subject, with a publick Admonition to *Michael Parrot.* That he do not presume any more to mention a certain Worm he knows of, which, by the Way, has grown Seven Foot in my Memory; for, if I am not much mistaken, it is the same that was but Nine Foot long about Six Months ago.

By the Remarks I have here made, it plainly appears, that a Collection of Advertisement is a Kind of Miscellany; the Writers of which, contrary to all Authors, except Men of Quality, give Money to the Booksellers who publish their Copies. The Genius of the Bookseller is chiefly shown in his Method of ranging and digesting these little Tracts. The last Paper I took up in my Hands, places them in the following Order:

The true Spanish Blacking for Shoes, *&c.*
The Beautifying Cream for the Face, *&c.*
Pease and Plaisters, *&c.*
Nectar and Ambrosia, *&c.*
Four Freehold Tenements of 15 1. per Annum, *&c.*
***The Present State of England, *&c.*
†††Annotations upon the Tatler, *&c.*
A Commission of Bankrupt being awarded against B. L. Bookseller, *&c.*

No. 229   Tuesday, September 26, 1710.   [Addison]

Quæsitam Meritis sume Superbiam. [1] —Hor.

From my own Apartment, Sept. 25.

The whole Creation preys upon it self: Every living Creature is inhabited. A Flea has a Thousand invisible Insects that teaze him as he jumps from Place to Place, and revenge our Quarrels upon him. A very ordinary Microscope shows us, that a Louse is it self a very lousy Creature. A Whale, besides those Seas and Oceans in the several Vessels of his Body, which are filled with innumerable Shoals of little Animals, carries about it a whole World of Inhabitants; insomuch that, if we believe the Calculations some have made, there are more living Creatures which are too small for the naked Eye to behold about the Leviathan, than there are of visible Creatures upon the Face of the whole Earth. Thus every nobler Creature is as it were the Basis and Support of Multitudes that are his Inferiors.

This Consideration very much comforts me, when I think on those numberless Vermin that feed upon this Paper, and find their Sustenance out of it; I mean, the small Wits and Scribblers that every Day turn a Penny by nibbling at my Lucubrations. This has been so advantageous to this little Species of Writers, that, if they do me Justice, I may expect to have my Statue erected in *Grub-street,* as being a common Benefactor to that Quarter.

They say, when a Fox is very much troubled with Fleas, he

[1] "Accept the proud honor won by thy merits."

goes into the next Pool with a little Lock of Wool in his Mouth, and keeps his Body under Water till the Vermin get into it, after which he quits the Wool, and diving, leaves his Tormentors to shift for themselves, and get their Livelihood where they can. I would have these Gentlemen take Care that I do not serve them after the same Manner; for though I have hitherto kept my Temper pretty well, it is not impossible but I may some Time or other disappear; and what will then become of them? Should I lay down my Paper, What a Famine would there be among the Hawkers, Printers, Booksellers and Authors? It would be like Dr. *B. _____s's*[2] dropping his Cloak, with the whole Congregation hanging upon the Skirts of it. To enumerate some of these my doughty Antagonists, I was threatened to be answered Weekly *Tit* for *Tat:* I was undermined by the *Whisperer,* haunted by *Tom Brown's Ghost,* scolded at by a *Female Tatler*, and slandered by another of the same Character, under the Title of *Atalantis.* I have been *annotated, re-tattled, examined,* and *condoled:* But it being my standing Maxim, Never to speak ill of the Dead; I shall let these Authors rest in Peace, and take great Pleasure in thinking that I have sometimes been the Means of their getting a Belly-full. When I see my self thus surrounded by such formidable Enemies, I often think of the Knight of the *Red Cross* in *Spencer's Den of Error,* who after he has cut off the Dragon's Head, and left it wallowing in a Flood of Ink, sees a Thousand monstrous Reptiles making their Attempts upon him, one with many Heads, another with none, and all of them without Eyes.

The same so sore annoyed has the Knight,
  That well nigh choaked with the deadly Stink,
  His Forces fail, he can no longer fight;
  Whose Courage when the Fiend perceived to shrink,
  She poured forth out of her Hellish Sink
  Her fruitful cursed Spawn of Serpents small,

[2] Dr. Daniel Burgess, a puritan preacher, whose ranting had drawn ridicule from Steele in *The Tatler,* No. 66.

Deformed Monsters, foul, and black as Ink;
Which swarming all about his Legs did crawl,
And him encombred sore, but could not hurt at all.

As gentle Shepherd in sweet Even-tide,
When ruddy PHOEBUS *gins to welk in West,*
High on an Hill, his Flock to viewen wide,
Marks which do bite their hasty Supper best;
A Cloud of combrous Gnats do him molest,
All striving to infix their feeble Stings,
That from their Noyance he no where can rest;
But with his clownish Hands their tender Wings
He brusheth oft, and oft doth mar their Murmurings. [3]

If ever I should want such a Fry[4] of little Authors to attend me, I shall think my Paper in a very decaying Condition. They are like Ivy about an Oak, which adorns the Tree at the same Time that it eats into it; or like a great Man's Equipage, that do Honour to the Person on whom they feed. For my Part, when I see my self thus attacked, I do not consider my Antagonists as malicious, but hungry, and therefore am resolved never to take any Notice of them.

As for those who detract from my Labours without being prompted to it by an empty Stomach, in Return to their Censures I shall take Pains to excel, and never fail to perswade my self, that their Enmity is nothing but their Envy or Ignorance.

Give me Leave to conclude, like an old Man and a Moralist, with a Fable:

The Owls, Bats, and several other Birds of Night, were one Day got together in a thick Shade, where they abused their Neighbours in a very sociable Manner. Their Satyr at last fell upon the Sun, whom they all agreed to be very troublesome,

---

[3] *The Faerie Queene,* I, i, 22-23.
[4] Spawn.

impertinent, and inquisitive. Upon which the Sun, who over-heard them, spoke to them after this Manner: Gentlemen, I wonder how you dare abuse one that you know could in an Instant scorch you up, and burn every Mother's Son of you: But the only Answer I shall give you, or the Revenge I shall take of you, is, to *shine on.*

No. 249   Saturday, November 11, 1710.   [Addison]

Per varios Casus, per tot Discrimina Rerum,
Tendimus. [1] — Virg.

From my own Apartment, November 10.

I was last Night visited by a Friend [2] of mine who has an inexhaustible Fund of Discourse, and never fails to entertain his Company with a Variety of Thoughts and Hints that are altogether new and uncommon. Whether it were in Complaisance to my Way of Living, or his real Opinion, he advanced the following Paradox, That it required much greater Talents to fill up and become a retired Life, than a Life of Business. Upon this Occasion he rallied very agreeably the busie Men of the Age, who only valued themselves for being in Motion, and passing through a Series of trifling and insignificant Actions. In the Heat of his Discourse, seeing a Piece of Money lying on my Table, I defie (says he) any of these active Persons to produce half the Adventures that this Twelvepenny-Piece has been engaged in, were it possible for him to give us an Account of his Life.

My Friends's Talk made so odd an Impression upon my Mind, that soon after I was a-Bed I fell insensibly into a most unaccountable *Reverie,* that had neither Moral nor Design in it, and cannot be so properly called a Dream as a Delirium.

Methought the Shilling that lay upon the Table reared

---

[1] "Through divers mishaps, through so many perilous chances, we fare. . . ."
[2] Swift.

it self upon its Edge, and turning the Face towards me, opened
its Mouth, and in a soft Silver Sound gave me the following
Account of his Life and Adventures:

I was born, says he, on the Side of a Mountain, near a
little Village of *Peru,* and made a Voyage to *England* in an
Ingot, under the Convoy of Sir *Francis Drake.* I was, soon
after my Arrival, taken out of my *Indian* Habit, refined, naturalized, and put into the *British* mode, with the Face of
Queen *Elizabeth* on one Side, and the Arms of the Country on
the other. Being thus equipped, I found in me a wonderful Inclination to ramble, and visit all the Parts of the new World
into which I was brought. The People very much favoured
my natural Disposition, and shifted me so fast from Hand
to Hand, that before I was Five Years old, I had travelled
into almost every Corner of the Nation. But in the Beginning
of my Sixth Year, to my unspeakable Grief, I fell into the
Hands of a miserable old Fellow, who clapped me into an
Iron Chest, where I found Five Hundred more of my own
Quality who lay under the same Confinement. The only Relief
we had, was to be taken out and counted over in the fresh
Air every Morning and Evening. After an Imprisonment of
several Years, we heard some Body knocking at our Chest,
and breaking it open with an Hammer. This we found was the
old Man's Heir, who, as his Father lay a dying, was so good as to
come to our Release: He separated us that very Day. What was
the Fate of my Companions I know not: As for my self, I was
sent to the Apothecary's Shop for a Pint of Sack. The Apothecary gave me to an Herb-Woman, the Herb-Woman to a Butcher, the Butcher to a Brewer, the Brewer to his Wife, who made
a Present of me to a Nonconformist Preacher. After this Manner
I made my Way merrily through the World; for, as I told you
before, we Shillings love nothing so much as travelling. I sometimes fetched in a Shoulder of Mutton, sometimes a Play-Book,
and often had the Satisfaction to treat a Templer at a Twelve-
penny Ordinary, or carry him with Three Friends to *Westminster-Hall.*

In the Midst of this pleasant Progress which I made from Place to Place, I was arrested by a superstitious old Woman, who shut me up in a greazy Purse, in Pursuance of a foolish Saying, That while she kept a Queen *Elizabeth's* Shilling about her, she should never be without Money. I continued here a close Prisoner for many Months, till at last I was exchanged for Eight and Forty Farthings.

I thus rambled from Pocket to Pocket till the Beginning of the Civil Wars, when, to my Shame be it spoken, I was employed in raising Soldiers against the King: For being of a very tempting Breadth, a Serjeant made Use of me to inveigle Country Fellows, and list them in the Service of the Parliament.

As soon as he had made one Man sure, his Way was to oblige him to take a Shilling of a more homely Figure, and then practise the same Trick upon another. Thus I continued doing great Mischief to the Crown, till my Officer chancing one Morning to walk Abroad earlier than ordinary sacrificed me to his Pleasures, and made Use of me to seduce a Milk-Maid. This Wench bent me, and gave me to her Sweetheart, applying more properly than she intended the usual Form of, *To my Love and from my Love.* This ungenerous Gallant marrying her within few Days after, pawned me for a Dram of Brandy, and drinking me out next Day, I was beaten flat with an Hammer, and again set a running.

After many Adventures, which it would be tedious to relate, I was sent to a young Spendthrift, in Company with the Will of his deceased Father. The young Fellow, who I found was very extravagant, gave great Demonstrations of Joy at the receiving the Will; but opening it, he found himself disinherited and cut off from the Possession of a fair Estate, by Vertue of my being made a Present to him. This put him into such a Passion, that after having taken me in his Hand, and cursed me, he squirred me away from him as far as he could fling me. I chanced to light in an unfrequented Place under a dead Wall, where I lay undiscovered and useless, during the Usurpation of *Oliver Cromwell.*

About a Year after the King's Return, a poor cavalier that was awalking there about Dinner-time fortunately cast his Eye upon me, and, to the great Joy of us both, carried me to a Cook's Shop, where he dined upon me, and drank the King's Health. When I came again into the World, I found that I had been happier in my Retirement than I thought, having probably by that Means escaped wearing a monstrous Pair of Breeches.

Being now of great Credit and Antiquity, I was rather looked upon as a Medal than an ordinary Coin; for which Reason a Gamester laid hold of me, and converted me to a Counter, having got together some Dozens of us for that Use. We led a melancholy Life in his Possession, being busy at those Hours wherein Current Coin is at rest, and partaking the Fate of our Master, being in a few Moments valued at a Crown, a Pound, or a Sixpence, according to the Situation in which the Fortune of the Cards placed us. I had at length the good Luck to see my Master break, by which Means I was again sent Abroad under my primitive Denomination of a Shilling.

I shall pass over many other Accidents of less Moment, and hasten to that fatal Catastrophe when I fell into the Hands of an Artist who conveyed me under Ground, and with an unmerciful Pair of Sheers cut off my Titles, clipped my Brims, retrenched my Shape, rubbed me to my inmost Ring, and, in short, so spoiled and pillaged me, that he did not leave me worth a Groat. You may think what a Confusion I was in to see my self thus curtailed and disfigured. I should have been ashamed to have shown my Head, had not all my old Acquaintance been reduced to the same shameful Figure, excepting some few that were punched through the Belly. In the midst of this general Calamity, when every Body thought our Misfortune irretrievable, and our Case desperate, we were thrown into the Furnace together, and (as it often happens with Cities rising out of a Fire) appeared with greater Beauty and Lustre than we could ever boast of before. What has happened to me since this Change of Sex which you now see, I shall take some other

Opportunity to relate. In the mean Time I shall only repeat Two Adventures, as being very extraordinary, and neither of them having ever happened to me above once in my Life. The First was, my being in a Poet's Pocket, who was so taken with the Brightness and Novelty of my Appearance, that it gave Occasion to the finest Burlesque Poem in the *British* Language, entituled from me, *The Splendid Shilling.*[3] The Second Adventure, which I must not omit, happened to me in the Year 1703, when I was given away in Charity to a blind Man; but indeed this was by a Mistake, the Person who gave me having heedlessly thrown me into the Hat among a Pennyworth of Farthings.

[3] By John Philips (1676-1709).

No. 271   Tuesday, January 2, 1710-11.   [Steele]

The Printer having informed me, that there are as many of these Papers printed as will make Four Volumes, I am now come to the End of my Ambition in this Matter, and have nothing further to say to the World under the Character of *Isaac Bickerstaff.* This Work has indeed for some Time been disagreeable to me, and the Purpose of it wholly lost by my being so long understood as the Author. I never designed in it to give any Man any secret Wound by my Concealment, but spoke in the Character of an old Man, a Philosopher, an Humorist, an Astrologer, and a Censor, to allure my Reader with the Variety of my Subjects, and insinuate, if I could, the Weight of Reason with the Agreeableness of Wit. The general Purpose of the whole has been to recommend Truth, Innocence, Honour, and Virtue, as the chief Ornaments of Life; but I considered, that Severity of Manners was absolutely necessary to him who would censure others, and for that Reason, and that only, chose to talk in a Mask. I shall not carry my Humility so far as to call my self a vicious Man; but at the same Time must confess, my Life is at best but pardonable. And with no greater Character than this, a Man would make but an indifferent Progress in attacking prevailing and fashionable Vices, which Mr. *Bickerstaff* has done with a Freedom of Spirit that would have lost both its Beauty and Efficacy, had it been pretended to by Mr. *Steele.*

As to the Work it self, the Acceptance it has met with is the best Proof of its Value; but I should err against that Candour which an honest Man should always carry about him, if I did not own, that the most approved Pieces in it were written by others, and those which have been most excepted against[1]

[1] Objected to.

by my self. The Hand[2] that has assisted me in those noble Discourses upon the Immortality of the Soul, the glorious Prospects of another Life, and the most sublime Idea's of Religion and Virtue, is a Person who is too fondly my Friend ever to own them; but I should little deserve to be his, if I usurped the Glory of them. I must acknowledge at the same Time, that I think the finest Strokes of Wit and Humour in all Mr. *Bickerstaff's* Lucubrations are those for which he is also beholden to him.

As for the Satyrical Parts of these Writings, those against the Gentlemen who profess Gaming are the most licentious; but the main of them I take to come from losing Gamesters, as Invectives against the Fortunate; for in very many of them I was very little else but the Transcriber. If any have been more particularly marked at, such Persons may impute it to their own Behaviour, (before they were touched upon) in publickly speaking their Resentment against the Author, and professing they would support any Man who should insult him. When I mention this Subject, I hope Major-General *Davenport,* Brigadier *Bisset,* and my Lord *Forbes,*[3] will accept of my Thanks for their frequent good Offices, in professing their Readiness to partake any Danger that should befal me in so just an Undertaking, as the Endeavour to banish Fraud and Couzenage from the Presence and Conversation of Gentlemen.

But what I find is the least excusable Part of all this Work, is, That I have, in some Places in it, touched upon Matters which concern both the Church and State. All I shall say for this is, That the Points I alluded to are such as concerned every Christian and Freeholder in *England;* and I could not be cold enough to conceal my Opinion on Subjects which related to either of those Characters. But Politicks apart. I must confess, it has been a most exquisite Pleasure to me to frame Characters of Domestick Life, and put those Parts of it which are least observed into an agreeable View; to enquire into the Seeds

---

[2] Addison's.
[3] Three friends of Steele who publicly faced down a group of cardsharpers who threatened Steele for his attacks.

of Vanity and Affectation, to lay before my Readers the Emptiness of Ambition: In a Word, to trace Humane Life through all its Mazes and Recesses, and show much shorter Methods than Men ordinarily practice, to be happy, agreeable, and great.

But to enquire into Men's Faults and Weaknesses has something in it so unwelcome, that I have often seen People in Pain to act before me, whose Modesty only make them think themselves liable to Censure. This, and a Thousand other nameless Things have made it an irksome Task to me to personate Mr. *Bickerstaff* any longer; and I believe it does not often happen, that the Reader is delighted where the Author is displeased.

All I can now do for the further Gratification of the Town, is to give them a faithful Index and Explication of Passages and Allusions, and sometimes of Persons intended in the several scattered Parts of the Work. At the same Time, the succeeding Volumes shall discover which of the whole have been written by me, and which by others, and by whom, as far as I am able, or permitted.

Thus I have voluntarily done what I think all Authors should do when call'd upon. I have published my Name to my Writings, and given my self up to the Mercy of the Town (as *Shakespear* expresses it) with all my Imperfections on my Head. The indulgent Reader's

> *Most Obliged,*
> *Most Obedient*
> *Humble Servant,*
> Richard Steele.

THE SPECTATOR

No. 1   Thursday, March 1, 1710-11.   [Addison]

Non fumum ex fulgore, sed ex fumo dare lucem
Cogitat, ut speciosa dehinc miracula promat.[1]—Hor.

I have observed, that a Reader seldom peruses a Book with Pleasure, 'till he knows whether the Writer of it be a black or a fair Man, of a mild or cholerick Disposition, Married or a Bachelor, with other Particulars of the like nature, that conduce very much to the right understanding of an Author. To gratifie this Curiosity, which is so natural to a Reader, I design this Paper, and my next, as Prefatory Discourses to my following Writings, and shall give some Account in them of the several Persons that are engaged in this Work. As the chief Trouble of Compiling, Digesting, and Correcting will fall to my Share, I must do myself the Justice to open the Work with my own History.

I was born to a small Hereditary Estate, which, according to the Tradition of the Village where it lies, was bounded by the same Hedges and Ditches in *William* the Conqueror's Time that it is at present, and has been delivered down from Father to Son whole and entire, without the Loss or Acquisition of a single Field or Meadow, during the Space of six hundred Years. There runs a Story in the Family, that when my Mother was gone with Child of me about three Months, she dreamt that she was brought to Bed of a Judge: Whether this might proceed from a Law-Suit which was then depending in the Family, or my Father's being a Justice of the Peace, I

[1] "Not smoke after flame does he plan to give, but after smoke the light, that he may set forth striking and wondrous tales."

cannot determine; for I am not so vain as to think it presaged any Dignity that I should arrive at in my future Life, though that was the Interpretation which the Neighbourhood put upon it. The Gravity of my Behaviour at my very first Appearance in the World, and all the Time that I sucked, seemed to favour my Mother's Dream: For, as she has often told me, I threw away my Rattle before I was two Months old, and would not make use of my Coral 'til they had taken away the Bells from it.

As for the rest of my Infancy, there being nothing in it remarkable, I shall pass it over in Silence. I find, that, during my Nonage, I had the Reputation of a very sullen Youth, but was always a Favourite of my School-master, who used to say, *that my Parts were solid and would wear well.* I had not been long at the University, before I distinguished my self by a most profound Silence: For during the Space of eight Years, excepting in the publick Exercises of the College, I scarce uttered the Quantity of an hundred Words; and indeed do not remember that I ever spoke three Sentences together in my whole Life. Whilst I was in this Learned Body I applied myself with so much Diligence to my Studies, that there are very few celebrated Books, either in the Learned or the Modern Tongues, which I am not acquainted with.

Upon the Death of my Father I was resolved to travel into Foreign Countries, and therefore left the University, with the Character of an odd unaccountable Fellow, that had a great deal of Learning, if I would but show it. An insatiable Thirst after Knowledge carried me into all the Countries of *Europe,* in which there was any thing new or strange to be seen; nay, to such a Degree was my Curiosity raised, that having read the Controversies of some great Men concerning the Antiquities of *Egypt,* I made a Voyage to *Grand Cairo,* on purpose to take the Measure of a Pyramid; and as soon as I had set my self right in that Particular, returned to my Native Country with great Satisfaction.

I have passed my latter Years in this City, where I am frequently seen in most Publick Places, tho' there are not above half a dozen of my select Friends that know me; of whom my next Paper shall give a more particular Account. There is no place of general Resort, wherein I do not often make my Appearance; sometimes I am seen thrusting my Head into a Round of Politicians at *Will's*,[2] and listning with great Attention to the Narratives that are made in those little Circular Audiences. Sometimes I smoak a Pipe at *Child's;*[3] and whilst I seem attentive to nothing but the *Post-Man,* over-hear the Conversation of every Table in the Room. I appear on *Sunday* nights at St. *James's* Coffee-House, and sometimes join the little Committee of Politicks in the Inner-Room, as one who comes there to hear and improve. My Face is likewise very well known at the *Grecian,* the *Cocoa-Tree,*[4] and in the Theatres both of *Drury-Lane* and the *Hay-Market.* I have been taken for a Merchant upon the *Exchange* for above these ten Years, and sometimes pass for a *Jew* in the Assembly of Stock-Jobbers at *Jonathan's.* In short, where-ever I see a Cluster of People I always mix with them, though I never open my Lips but in my own Club.

Thus I live in the World, rather as a Spectator of Mankind, than as one of the Species; by which means I have made my self a Speculative Statesman, Soldier, Merchant and Artizan, without ever medling with any Practical Part in Life. I am very well versed in the Theory of an Husband, or a Father, and can discern the Errors in the Oeconomy, Business and Diversion of others, better than those who are engaged in them; as Standers-by discover Blots, which are apt to escape those who are in the Game. I never espoused any Party with Violence, and am resolved to observe an exact Neutrality between the Whigs and Tories, unless I shall be forced to declare my-self by the Hostilities of either Side. In short, I have acted in

[2] See *The Tatler,* No. 1, n.2.
[3] Child's Coffee-house, in St. Paul's Churchyard, was frequented by clergymen and physicians.
[4] A Tory chocolate-house.

all the Parts of my Life as a Looker-on, which is the Character I intend to preserve in this Paper.

I have given the Reader just so much of my History and Character, as to let him see I am not altogether unqualfied for the Business I have undertaken. As for other Particulars in my Life and Adventures, I shall insert them in following Papers, as I shall see occasion. In the mean time, when I consider how much I have seen, read and heard, I begin to blame my own Taciturnity; and since I have neither Time nor Inclination to communicate the Fulness of my Heart in Speech, I am resolved to do it in Writing; and to Print my self out, if possible, before I Die. I have been often told by my Friends, that it is Pity so many useful Discoveries which I have made, should be in the Possession of a Silent Man. For this Reason therefore, I shall publish a Sheet-full of Thoughts every Morning, for the Benefit of my Contemporaries; and if I can any way contribute to the Diversion or Improvement of the Country in which I live, I shall leave it, when I am summoned out of it, with the secret Satisfaction of thinking that I have not Lived in vain.

There are three very material Points which I have not spoken to in this Paper, and which, for several important Reasons, I must keep to my self, at least for some Time: I mean, an Account of my Name, my Age, and my Lodgings. I must confess I would gratifie my Reader in any thing that is reasonable; but as for these three Particulars, though I am sensible they might tend very much to the Embellishment of my Paper, I cannot yet come to a Resolution of communicating them to the Publick. They would indeed draw me out of that Obscurity which I have enjoyed for many Years, and expose me in Publick Places to several Salutes and Civilities, which have been always very disagreeable to me; for the greatest Pain I can suffer, is the being talked to, and being stared at. It is for this Reason likewise, that I keep my Complexion and Dress as very great Secrets; tho' it is not impossible but I may make

Discoveries of both, in the Progress of the Work I have undertaken.

After having been thus particular upon my self, I shall in to-Morrow's Paper give an Account of those Gentlemen who are concerned with me in this Work. For, as I have before intimated, a Plan of it is laid and concerted (as all other Matters of Importance are) in a Club. However, as my Friends have engaged me to stand in the Front, those who have a mind to correspond with me, may direct their Letters *To the* SPECTATOR, at Mr. *Buckley's* in *Little Britain*. For I must further acquaint the Reader, that tho' our Club meets only on *Tuesdays* and *Thursdays,* we have appointed a Committee to sit every Night, for the Inspection of all such Papers as may contribute to the Advancement of the Publick Weal.

... *Haec Alii sex*
Vel plures uno conclamant ore.[1] —Juv.

The first of our Society is a Gentleman of *Worcestershire,* of antient Descent, a Baronet, his Name Sir ROGER DE COVERLY.[2] His great Grandfather was Inventor of that famous Country-Dance which is call'd after him. All who know that Shire, are very well acquainted with the Parts and Merits of Sir ROGER. He is a Gentleman that is very singular in his Behaviour, but his Singularities proceed from his good Sense, and are Contradictions to the Manners of the World, only as he thinks the World is in the wrong. However, this Humour creates him no Enemies, for he does nothing with Sourness or Obstinacy; and his being unconfined to Modes and Forms, makes him but the readier and more capable to please and oblige all who know him. When he is in town he lives in *Soho-Square:* It is said, he keeps himself a Batchelor by reason he was crossed in Love, by a perverse beautiful Widow of the next County to him. Before this Disappointment, Sir ROGER was what you call a fine Gentleman, had often supped with my Lord *Rochester,*[3] and Sir *George Etherege,*[4] fought a Duel upon his first coming

---

[1] "So cry half a dozen or more of our sophists in one breath."

[2] The original of Sir Roger de Coverley was long thought to be Sir John Packington (1671-1721). More recently Sir Roger's devotion to the "perverse widow" has led to his identification with the critic, poet, and Worcestershire country gentleman William Walsh (1663-1708), who for years paid unsuccessful court to Mrs. Catherine Bovey of Gloucestershire.

[3] John Wilmot, Earl of Rochester (1648-1680), who was distinguished as a poet and notorious as a rake about the time of Steele's birth.

[4] A dramatist and wit; friend of Lord Rochester.

to Town, and kick'd Bully *Dawson* in a publick Coffee-house for calling him Youngster. But being ill used by the above-mentioned Widow, he was very serious for a Year and a half; and though, his Temper being naturally jovial, he at last got over it, he grew careless of himself, and never dressed afterwards; he continues to wear a Coat and Doublet of the same Cut that were in Fashion at the Time of his Repulse, which, in his merry Humours, he tells us, has been in and out twelve Times since he first wore it. 'Tis said Sir ROGER grew humble in his Desires after he had forgot this cruel Beauty, insomuch that it is reported he has frequently offended in Point of Chastity with Beggars and Gypsies: But this is look'd upon by his Friends rather as Matter of Raillery than Truth. He is now in his Fifty sixth Year, chearful, gay, and hearty, keeps a good House both in Town and Country; a great Lover of Mankind; but there is such a mirthful Cast in his Behaviour, that he is rather beloved than esteemed: His Tenants grow rich, his Servants look satisfied, all the young Women profess Love to him, and the young Men are glad of his Company: When he comes into a House he calls the Servants by their Names, and talks all the way up Stairs to a Visit. I must not omit that Sir ROGER is a Justice of the *Quorum;* that he fills the chair at a Quarter-Session with great Abilities, and three Months ago gain'd universal Applause by explaining a Passage in the Game-Act.

The Gentleman next in Esteem and Authority among us, is another Batchelor, who is a Member of the *Inner-Temple;* a Man of great Probity, Wit, and Understanding; but he has chosen his Place of Residence rather to obey the Direction of an old humoursome Father, than in Pursuit of his own Inclinations. He was placed there to study the Laws of the Land, and is the most learned of any of the House in those of the Stage. *Aristotle* and *Longinus* are much better understood by him than *Littleton* or *Cooke.*[5] The Father sends up every Post Questions relating to Marriage-Articles, Leases, and Tenures, in

[5] Two famous justices.

the Neighborhood; all which Questions he agrees with an Attorney to answer and take care of in the Lump: He is studying the Passions themselves, when he should be inquiring into the Debates among Men which arise from them. He knows the Argument of each of the Orations of *Demosthenes* and *Tully,* but not one Case in the Reports of our own Courts. No one ever took him for a Fool, but none, except his intimate Friends, know he has a great deal of Wit. This Turn makes him at once both disinterested and agreeable: As few of his Thoughts are drawn from Business, they are most of them fit for Conversation. His Taste of Books is a little too just for the Age he lives in; he has read all, but approves of very few. His Familiarity with the Customs, Manners, Actions, and Writings of the Antients, makes him a very delicate Observer of what occurs to him in the present World. He is an excellent Critick, and the Time of the Play is his Hour of Business; exactly at five he passes thro' *New-Inn,* crosses thro' *Russel-Court,* and takes a turn at *Will's* 'till the play begins; he has his Shooes rubbed and his Perriwig powder'd at the Barber's as you go into the *Rose.*[6] It is for the Good of the Audience when he is at a Play, for the Actors have an Ambition to please him.

The Person of next Consideration, is Sir ANDREW FREEPORT, a Merchant of great Eminence in the City of *London.* A Person of indefatigable Industry, strong Reason, and great Experience. His Notions of Trade are noble and generous, and (as every rich Man has usually some sly Way of Jesting, which would make no great Figure were he not a rich Man) he calls the Sea the *British Common.* He is acquainted with Commerce in all its Parts, and will tell you that it is a stupid and barbarous Way to extend Dominion by Arms; for true Power is to be got by Arts and Industry. He will often argue, that if this Part of our Trade were well cultivated, we should gain from one Nation; and if another from another. I have heard him prove, that Diligence makes more lasting Acquisitions than Valour,

---

[6] A tavern adjoining the Drury Lane Theatre.

and that Sloth has ruined more Nations than the Sword. He abounds in several frugal Maxims, among which the greatest Favourite is, 'a Penny saved is a Penny got.' A General Trader of good Sense, is pleasanter company than a general Scholar; and Sir ANDREW having a natural unaffected Eloquence, the Perspicuity of his Discourse gives the same Pleasure that Wit would in another Man. He has made his Fortunes himself; and says that *England* may be richer than other Kingdoms, by as plain Methods as he himself is richer than other men; tho' at the same Time I can say this of him, that there is not a point in the Compass but blows home a Ship in which he is an Owner.

Next to Sir ANDREW in the Club-room sits Captain SENTRY, a Gentleman of great Courage, good Understanding, but invincible Modesty. He is one of those that deserve very well, but are very awkward at putting their Talents within the Observation of such as should take Notice of them. He was some Years a Captain, and behaved himself with great Gallantry in several Engagements and at several Sieges; but having a small Estate of his own, and being next Heir to Sir ROGER, he has quitted a Way of Life in which no Man can rise suitably to his Merit, who is not something of a Courtier as well as a Soldier. I have heard him often lament, that in a Profession where Merit is placed in so conspicuous a View, Impudence should get the better of Modesty. When he has talked to this Purpose I never heard him make a sour Expression, but frankly confess that he left the World, because he was not fit for it. A strict Honesty and an even regular Behaviour, are in themselves Obstacles to him that must press through Crowds, who endeavour at the same End with himself, the Favour of a Commander. He will however in his way of Talk excuse Generals, for not disposing according to Men's Desert, or enquiring into it: For, says he, that great Man who has a Mind to help me, has as many to break through to come at me, as I have to come at him: Therefore he will conclude, that the Man who would make a Figure, especially in a military Way, must get over all false Modesty, and assist his Patron against the Importunity of other Pretenders, by a proper Assurance in his own Vindication. He says it is a civil Cowardice to be backward in asserting what you ought to expect, as it is a military Fear to be slow in attacking when it is your Duty. With this Candour does the Gentleman speak of himself and others. The same Frankness runs through all his Conversation. The military Part of his Life has furnish'd him with many Adventures, in the Relation of which he is very agreeable to the Company; for he is never over-bearing, though accustomed to command Men in the utmost Degree below him; nor ever too obsequious, from an Habit of obeying Men highly above him.

But that our Society may not appear a Set of Humourists unacquainted with the Gallantries and Pleasures of the Age, we have among us the gallant WILL. HONEYCOMB, a Gentleman who according to his Years should be in the Decline of his Life, but having ever been very careful of his Person, and always had a very easie Fortune, Time has made but very little Impression, either by Wrinkles on his Forehead, or Traces in his Brain. His Person is well turn'd, of a good Height. He is very ready at that sort of Discourse with which Men usually entertain Women. He has all his Life dressed very well, and remembers Habits as others do Men. He can smile when one speaks to him, and laughs easily. He knows the History of every Mode, and can inform you from which of the *French* King's Wenches our Wives and Daughters had this Manner of curling their Hair, that Way of placing their Hoods; whose Frailty was covered by such a Sort of Petticoat, and whose Vanity to shew her Foot made that Part of the Dress so short in such a Year. In a Word, all his Conversation and Knowledge has been in the female World: As other Men of his Age will take Notice to you what such a Minister said upon such and such an Occasion, he will tell you when the Duke of *Monmouth*[7] danced at Court such a Woman was then smitten, another was taken with him at the Head of his Troop in the *Park*. In

[7] Son of Charles II and Lucy Walters.

all these important Relations, he has ever about the same Time received a kind Glance or a Blow of a Fan from some celebrated Beauty, Mother of the present Lord such-a-one. If you speak of a young Commoner that said a lively thing in the House, he starts up, 'He has good Blood in his Veins, *Tom Mirabell* begot him, the Rogue cheated me in that affair; that young Fellow's Mother used me more like a Dog than any Woman I ever made Advances to.' This way of Talking of his very much enlivens the Conversation among us of a more sedate Turn; and I find there is not one of the Company, but my self, who rarely speak at all, but speaks of him as of that Sort of Man who is usually called a well-bred fine Gentleman. To conclude his Character, where Women are not concern'd, he is an honest worthy Man.

I cannot tell whether I am to account him whom I am next to speak of, as one of our Company; for he visits us but seldom, but when he does it adds to every Man else a new Enjoyment of himself. He is a Clergyman, a very philosophick Man, of general Learning, great Sanctity of Life, and the most exact good Breeding. He has the Misfortune to be of a very weak Constitution, and consequently cannot accept of such Cares and Business as Preferments in his Function would oblige him to: He is therefore among Divines what a Chamber-Counsellor is among Lawyers. The Probity of his Mind, and the Integrity of his Life, create him Followers, as being eloquent or loud advances others. He seldom introduces the Subject he speaks upon; but we are so far gone in Years, that he observes, when he is among us, an Earnestness to have him fall on some divine Topick, which he always treats with much Authority, as one who has no Interests in this World, as one who is hastening to the Object of all his Wishes, and conceives Hope from his Decays and Infirmities. These are my ordinary Companions.

No. 6   Wednesday, March 7, 1710-11.   [Steele]

Credebant hoc grande Nefas, & Morte piandum,
Si Juvenis Vetulo non assurrexerat . . .[1]—Juv.

I know no Evil under the Sun so great as the Abuse of the Understanding, and yet there is no one Vice more common. It has diffus'd it self through both Sexes and all Qualities of Mankind; and there is hardly that Person to be found, who is not more concern'd for the Reputation of Wit and Sense, than Honesty and Virtue. But this unhappy Affectation of being Wise rather than Honest, Witty than Good-natur'd, is the Source of most of the ill Habits of Life. Such false Impressions are owing to the abandon'd Writings of Men of Wit, and the awkward Imitation of the rest of Mankind.

For this Reason, Sir ROGER was saying last Night, That he was of Opinion none but Men of fine Parts deserve to be hanged. The Reflections of such Men are so delicate upon all Occurrences which they are concerned in, that they should be exposed to more than ordinary Infamy and Punishment, for offending against such quick Admonitions as their own Souls give them, and blunting the fine Edge of their Minds in such a Manner, that they are no more shocked at Vice and Folly, than Men of slower Capacities. There is no greater Monster in Being, than a very ill Man of great Parts: He lives like a Man in a Palsy, with one Side of him dead. While perhaps he enjoys the Satisfaction of Luxury, of Wealth, of Ambition, he has lost the Taste of Good-will, of Friendship, of Innocence.

---

[1] "Men deemed it a heinous sin, worthy of death, if a youth did not rise before his elders."

112

Scarecrow, the Beggar in *Lincoln's-Inn-Fields,* who disabled himself in his Right Leg, and asks Alms all Day to get himself a warm Supper and a Trull at Night, is not half so despicable a Wretch as such a Man of Sense. The Beggar has no Relish above Sensations; he finds Rest more agreeable than Motion; and while he has a warm Fire and his Doxy, never reflects that he deserves to be whipped. Every Man who terminates his Satisfactions and Enjoyments within the Supply of his own Necessities and Passions, is, says Sir ROGER, in my Eye as poor a Rogue as *Scarecrow.* But, continued he, for the Loss of publick and private Virtue, we are beholden to your Men of Parts forsooth; it is with them no matter what is done, so it is done with an Air. But to me, who am so whimsical in a corrupt Age as to act according to Nature and Reason, a selfish Man, in the most shining Circumstance and Equipage, appears in the same Condition with the Fellow above-mentioned, but more contemptible, in Proportion to what more he robs the Public of and enjoys above him. I lay it down therefore for a Rule, That the whole Man is to move together; that every Action of any Importance is to have a Prospect of publick Good;[2] and that the general Tendency of our indifferent Actions ought to be agreeable to the Dictates of Reason, of Religion, of good Breeding; without this, a Man, as I before have hinted, is hopping instead of walking, he is not in his entire and proper motion.

While the honest Knight was thus bewildering himself in good Starts, I look'd intentively upon him, which made him, I thought, collect his Mind a little. What I aim at, says he, is to represent, That I am of Opinion, to polish our Understandings and neglect our Manners, is of all things the most inexcusable. Reason should govern Passion, but instead of that, you see, it is often subservient to it; and as unaccountable as one would think it, a wise Man is not always a good Man. This

---

[2] Steele's moral position, as here stated, had already been set forth in *The Christian Hero* (1701).

Degeneracy is not only the Guilt of particular Persons, but also at some times of a whole People; and perhaps it may appear upon Examination, that the most polite Ages are the least virtuous. This may be attributed to the Folly of admitting Wit and Learning as Merit in themselves, without considering the Application of them. By this Means it becomes a Rule, not so much to regard what we do, as how we do it. But this false Beauty will not pass upon Men of honest Minds and true Taste: Sir *Richard Blackmore*[3] says, with as much good Sense as Virtue, *It is a mighty Dishonour and Shame to employ excellent Faculties and abundance of Wit, to humour and please Men in their Vices and Follies. The great Enemy of Mankind, notwithstanding his Wit and Angelick Faculties, is the most odious Being in the whole Creation.* He goes on soon after to say very generously, That he undertook the writing of his Poem to *rescue the Muses out of the Hands of Ravishers, to restore them to their sweet and chaste Mansions, and to engage them in an Employment suitable to their Dignity.* This certainly ought to be the Purpose of every Man who appears in Publick; and whoever does not proceed upon that Foundation, injures his Country as fast as he succeeds in his Studies. When Modesty ceases to be the Chief Ornament of one Sex, and Integrity of the other, Society is upon a wrong Basis, and we shall be ever after without Rules to guide our Judgment in what is really becoming and ornamental. Nature and Reason direct one thing, Passion and Humour another: To follow the Dictates of the two latter, is going into a Road that is both endless and intricate; when we pursue the other, our Passage is delightful, and what we aim at easily attainable.

I do not doubt but *England* is at present as polite a Nation as any in the World; but any Man who thinks can easily see, that the Affectation of being Gay and in Fashion, has very near eaten up our good Sense and our Religion. Is there anything so just, as that Mode and Gallantry should be built upon

[3] Whig physician (d.1729) and author of *Prince Arthur,* from the preface to which Steele is here quoting.

exerting our selves in what is proper and agreeable to the Institutions of Justice and Piety among us? And yet is there any thing more common, than that we run in perfect Contradiction to them? All which is supported by no other Pretension, than that it is done with what we call a good Grace.

Nothing ought to be held laudable or becoming, but what Nature it self should prompt us to think so. Respect to all kind of Superiors is founded, methinks, upon Instinct; and yet what is so ridiculous as Age? I make this abrupt Transition to the Mention of this Vice more than any other, in order to introduce a little Story, which I think a pretty Instance that the most polite Age is in danger of being the most vicious.

'It happen'd at *Athens,* during a publick Representation of some Play exhibited in Honour of the Commonwealth, that an old Gentleman came too late for a Place suitable to his Age and Quality. Many of the young Gentlemen who observed the Difficulty and Confusion he was in, made Signs to him that they would accommodate him if he came where they sate: The good Man bustled through the Crowd accordingly; but when he came to the Seats to which he was invited, the Jest was to sit close, and expose him, as he stood out of Countenance, to the whole Audience. The Frolick went round all the *Athenian* Benches. But on those Occasions there were also particular Places assigned for Foreigners: When the good Man skulked towards the Boxes appointed for the *Lacedemonians,* that honest People, more virtuous than polite, rose up all to a Man, and with the greatest Respect received him among them. The *Athenians* being suddenly touch'd with a Sense of the *Spartan* Virtue and their own Degeneracy, gave a Thunder of Applause; and the old Man cried out, *The* Athenians *understand what is good, but the* Lacedemonians *practise it.'*

No. 10   Monday, March 12, 1710-11.   [Addison]

Non aliter quam qui adverso vix flumine lembum
Remigiis subigit: si brachia forte remisit,
Atque illum præceps prono rapit alveus amni.[1]—Virg.

It is with much Satisfaction that I hear this great City inquiring Day by Day after these my Papers, and receiving my Morning Lectures with a becoming Seriousness and Attention. My Publisher tells me, that there are already Three Thousand of them distributed every Day: So that if I allow Twenty Readers to every Paper, which I look upon as a modest Computation, I may reckon about Threescore Thousand Disciples[2] in *London* and *Westminster,* who I hope will take care to distinguish themselves from the thoughtless Herd of their ignorant and unattentive Brethren. Since I have raised to my self so great an Audience, I shall spare no Pains to make their Instruction agreeable, and their Diversion useful. For which Reasons I shall endeavour to enliven Morality with Wit, and to temper Wit with Morality, that my Readers may, if possible, both Ways find their Account in the Speculation of the Day. And to the End that their Virtue and Discretion may not be short, transient, intermitting Starts of Thought, I have resolved to refresh their Memories from Day to Day, till I have recovered them out of that desperate State of Vice and Folly into which the Age is fallen. The Mind that lies fallow but a single Day, sprouts

[1] "Even as if one, whose oars can scarce force his skiff against the stream, should by chance slacken his arms, and lo! headlong down the current the boat sweeps him along."
[2] Although Addison's reckoning is probably excessive, there is no question about the phenomenal success of the *The Spectator.*

116

up in Follies that are only to be killed by a constant and assiduous Culture. It was said of *Socrates,* that he brought Philosophy down from Heaven, to inhabit among Men; and I shall be ambitious to have it said of me, that I have brought Philosophy out of Closets and Libraries, Schools and Colleges, to dwell in Clubs and Assemblies, at Tea-Tables and in Coffee-Houses.

I would therefore in a very particular Manner recommend these my Speculations to all well regulated Families, that set apart an Hour in every Morning for Tea and Bread and Butter; and would earnestly advise them for their Good to order this Paper to be punctually served up, and to be looked upon as a Part of the Tea Equipage.

Sir *Francis Bacon* observes, that a well-written Book, compared with its Rivals and Antagonists, is like *Moses's* Serpent, that immediately swallow'd up and devoured those of the *Ægyptians.* I shall not be so vain as to think, that where the SPECTATOR appears, the other publick Prints will vanish; but shall leave it to my Reader's Consideration, whether, Is it not much better to be let into the Knowledge of ones self, than to hear what passes in *Muscovy* or *Poland;* and to amuse our selves with such Writings as tend to the wearing out of Ignorance, Passion, and Prejudice, than such as naturally conduce to inflame Hatreds, and make Enmities irreconcileable?

In the next Place, I would recommend this Paper to the daily Perusal of those Gentlemen whom I cannot but consider as my good Brothers and Allies, I mean the Fraternity of Spectators who live in the World without having any thing to do in it; and either by the Affluence of their Fortunes, or Laziness of their Dispositions, have no other Business with the rest of Mankind, but to look upon them. Under this Class of Men are comprehended all contemplative Tradesmen, titular Physicians, Fellows of the Royal Society, Templers that are not given to be contentious, and Statesmen that are out of Business; in short, every one that considers the World as a Theatre, and desires to form a right Judgment of those who are the Actors on it.

There is another Set of Men that I must likewise lay a Claim to, whom I have lately called the Blanks of Society, as being altogether unfurnish'd with Ideas, till the Business and Conversation of the Day has supplied them. I have often consider'd these poor Souls with an Eye of great Commiseration, when I have heard them asking the first Man they have met with, whether there was any News stirring? and by that Means gathering together Materials for thinking. These needy Persons do not know what to talk of, 'till about twelve a Clock in the Morning; for by that Time they are pretty good Judges of the Wheather, know which Way the Wind sits, and whether the *Dutch* Mail be come in. As they lie at the Mercy of the first Man they meet, and are grave or impertinent all the Day long, according to the Notions which they have imbibed in the Morning, I would earnestly intreat them not to stir out of their Chambers till they have read this Paper, and do promise them that I will daily instill into them such sound and wholesom Sentiments, as shall have a good Effect on their Conversation for the ensuing twelve Hours.

But there are none to whom this Paper will be more useful, than to the Female World. I have often thought there has not been sufficient Pains taken in finding out proper Employments and Diversions for the Fair Ones. Their Amusements seem contrived for them rather as they are Women, than as they are reasonable Creatures; and are more adapted to the Sex than to the Species. The Toilet is their great Scene of Business, and the right adjusting of their Hair the principal Employment of their Lives. The sorting of a Suit of Ribbons, is reckon'd a very good Morning's Work; and if they make an Excursion to a Mercer's or a Toy-shop, so great a Fatigue makes them unfit for any thing else all the Day after. Their more serious Occupations are Sowing and Embroidery, and their greatest Drudgery the Preparation of Jellies and Sweetmeats. This, I say, is the State of ordinary Women; tho' I know there are multitudes of those of a more elevated Life and Conversation, that move in an exalted Sphere of Knowledge and Virtue, that join all the Beauties of the Mind to the Ornaments of Dress, and inspire a kind of Awe and Respect, as well as Love, into their Male-Beholders. I hope to encrease the Number of these by Publishing this daily Paper, which I shall always endeavour to make an innocent if not an improving Entertainment, and by that Means at least divert the Minds of my Female Readers from greater Trifles. At the same Time, as I would fain give some finishing Touches to those which are already the most beautiful Pieces in human Nature, I shall endeavour to point out all those Imperfections that are the Blemishes, as well as those Virtues which are the Embelishments of the Sex: In the mean while I hope these my gentle Readers, who have so much Time on their Hands, will not grudge throwing away a Quarter of an Hour in a Day on this Paper, since they may do it without any Hindrance to Business.

I know several of my Friends and Well-wishers are in great Pain for me, lest I should not be able to keep up the Spirit of a Paper which I oblige my self to furnish every Day: But to make them easie in this Particular, I will promise them faithfully to give it over as soon as I grow dull. This I know will be Matter of great Raillery to the small Wits; who will frequently put me in mind of my Promise, desire me to keep my Word, assure me that it is high Time to give over, with many other little Pleasantries of the like Nature, which Men of a little smart Genius cannot forbear throwing out against their best Friends, when they have such a Handle given them of being witty. But let them remember that I do hereby enter my Caveat against this Piece of Raillery.

Dat veniam corvis, vexat censuræ columbas. [1]—Juv.

Arietta is visited by all Persons of both Sexes, who have any
Pretence to Wit and Gallantry. She is in that time of Life which
is neither affected with the Follies of Youth, or Infirmities
of Age; and her Conversation is so mixed with Gaiety and Prudence, that she is agreeable both to the Young and the Old.
Her Behaviour is very frank, without being in the least blame-
able; and as she is out of the Tract of any amorous or ambitious Pursuits of her own, her Visitants entertain her with Accounts of themselves very freely, whether they concern their
Passions or their Interests. I made her a Visit this Afternoon,
having been formerly introduced to the Honour of her Acquaintance, by my Friend WILL. HONEYCOMB, who has prevailed
upon her to admit me sometimes into her Assembly, as a civil
inoffensive Man. I found her accompanied with one Person
only, a Common-Place Talker, who, upon my Entrance, rose,
and after a very slight Civility sat down again; then turning
to *Arietta,* pursued his Discourse, which I found was upon
the old Topick, of Constancy in Love. He went on with great
Facility in repeating what he talks every Day of his Life; and,
with the Ornaments of insignificant Laughs and Gestures, en-
forced his Arguments by Quotations out of Plays and Songs,
which allude to the Perjuries of the Fair, and the general Levity of Women. Methought he strove to shine more than ordinarily in his Talkative Way, that he might insult my Silence,
and distinguish himself before a Woman of *Arietta's* Taste

[1] "He forgives the crows and censures the pigeons."

and Understanding. She had often an Inclination to interrupt him, but could find no Opportunity, till the Larum ceased of it self; which it did not 'till he had repeated and murdered the celebrated Story of the *Ephesian* Matron.

Arietta seemed to regard this Piece of Raillery as an Outrage done to her Sex; as indeed I have always observed that Women, whether out of a nicer Regard to their Honour, or what other Reason I cannot tell, are more sensibly touched with those general Aspersions which are cast upon their Sex, than Men are by what is said of theirs.

When she had a little recovered her self from the serious Anger she was in, she replied in the following manner.

SIR, When I consider how perfectly new all you have said on this Subject is, and that the Story you have given us is not quite Two thousand Years old, I cannot but think it a Piece of Presumption to dispute with you: But your Quotations put me in Mind of the Fable of the Lion and the Man. The Man walking with that noble Animal, shewed him, in the Ostentation of Human Superiority, a Sign of a Man killing a Lion. Upon which the Lion said very justly, *We Lions are none of us Painters, else we could shew a hundred Men killed by Lions, for one Lion killed by a Man.* You Men are Writers, and can represent us Women as Unbecoming as you please in your Works, while we are unable to return the Injury. You have twice or thrice observed in your Discourse, that Hypocrisie is very Foundation of our Education; and that an Ability to dissemble our Affections, is a professed Part of our Breeding. These, and such other Reflections, are sprinkled up and down the Writings of all Ages, by Authors, who leave behind them Memorials of their Resentment against the Scorn of particular Women, in Invectives against the whole Sex. Such a Writer, I doubt not, was the celebrated *Petronius,* who invented the pleasant Aggravations of the Frailty of the *Ephesian* Lady[2]; but when we consider this Question between the Sexes, which

[2] A tale told by Eumolpus in the *Satyricon* of Petronius about an easily consoled widow.

has been either a Point of Dispute or Raillery ever since there were Men and Women, let us take Facts from plain People, and from such as have not either Ambition or Capacity to embellish their Narrations with any Beauties of Imagination. I was the other Day amusing my self with *Ligon's* Account of *Barbadoes;*[3] and, in Answer to your well-wrought Tale, I will give you (as it dwells upon my Memory) out of that honest Traveller, in his fifty fifth Page, the History of *Inkle* and *Yarico*.

Mr. *Thomas Inkle,* of *London,* aged twenty Years, embarked in the *Downs* on the good Ship called the *Achilles*, bound for the *West-Indies,* on the 16th of *June,* 1647, in order to improve his Fortune by Trade and Merchandize. Our Adventurer was the third Son of an eminent Citizen, who had taken particular Care to instill into his Mind an early Love of Gain, by making him a perfect Master of Numbers, and consequently giving him a quick View of Loss and Advantage, and preventing the natural Impulses of his Passions, by Prepossession towards his Interests. With a Mind thus turned, young *Inkle* had a Person every way agreeable, a ruddy Vigour in his Countenance, Strength in his Limbs, with Ringlets of fair Hair loosely flowing on his Shoulders. It happened, in the Course of the Voyage, that the *Achilles*, in some Distress, put into a Creek on the Main of *America*, in Search of Provisions: The Youth, who is the Hero of my Story, among others, went ashore on this Occasion. From their first Landing they were observed by a Party of *Indians,* who hid themselves in the Woods for that Purpose. The *English* unadvisedly marched a great distance from the Shore into the Country, and were intercepted by the Natives, who slew the greatest Number of them. Our Adventurer escaped among others, by flying into a Forest. Upon his coming into a remote and pathless Part of the Wood, he threw himself, tired and breathless, on a little Hillock, when an *Indian* Maid rushed from a Thicket behind

---

[3] Richard Ligon's *True and Exact History of the Island of Barbados* had been published in 1657. Steele's version of the story became very popular during the eighteenth century.

him: After the first Surprize, they appeared mutually agree-able to each other. If the *European* was highly Charmed with the Limbs, Features, and wild Graces of the Naked *American;* the *American* was no less taken with the Dress, Complexion, and Shape of an *European,* covered from Head to Foot. The *Indian* grew immediately enamoured of him, and consequently sollicitous for his Preservation: She therefore conveyed him to a Cave, where she gave him a delicious Repast of Fruits, and led him to a Stream to slake his Thirst. In the midst of these good Offices, she would sometimes play with his Hair, and delight in the Opposition of its Colour to that of her Fingers: Then open his Bosom, then laugh at him for covering it. She was, it seems, a Person of Distinction, for she every Day came to him in a different Dress, of the most beautiful Shells, Bugles, and Bredes. She likewise brought him a great many Spoils, which her other Lovers had presented to her; so that his Cave was richly adorned with all the spotted Skins of Beasts, and most Party-coloured Feathers of Fowls, which that World af-forded. To make his Confinement more tolerable, she would carry him in the Dusk of the Evening, or by the favour of Moon-light, to unfrequented Groves and Solitudes, and shew him where to lye down in Safety, and sleep amidst the Falls of Waters, and Melody of Nightingales. Her Part was to watch and hold him awake in her Arms, for fear of her Country-men, and wake him on Occasions to consult his Safety. In this manner did the Lovers pass away their Time, till they had learn'd a Lan-guage of their own, in which the Voyager communicated to his Mistress, how happy he should be to have her in his Coun-try, where she should be Cloathed in such Silks as his Waste-coat was made of, and be carried in Houses drawn by Horses, without being exposed to Wind or Weather. All this he prom-ised her the Enjoyment of, without such Fears and Alarms as they were there tormented with. In this tender Correspondence these Lovers lived for several Months, when *Yarico,* instruct-ed by her Lover, discovered a Vessel on the Coast, to which she made Signals; and in the Night, with the utmost Joy and

Satisfaction, accompanied him to a Ship's-Crew of his Countrymen, bound for *Barbadoes*. When a Vessel from the Main arrives in that Island, it seems the Planters come down to the Shoar, where there is an immediate Market of the *Indians* and other Slaves, as with us of Horses and Oxen.

To be short, Mr. *Thomas Inkle,* now coming into *English* Territories, began seriously to reflect upon his loss of Time, and to weigh with himself how many Days Interest of his Mony he had lost during his Stay with *Yarico*. This Thought made the young Man very pensive, and careful what Account he should be able to give his Friends of his Voyage. Upon which Considerations, the prudent and frugal young Man sold *Yarico* to a *Barbadian* Merchant; notwithstanding that the poor Girl, to incline him to commiserate her Condition, told him that she was with Child by him: But he only made use of that Information, to rise in his Demands upon the Purchaser.

I was so touch'd with this Story (which I think should be always a Counterpart to the *Ephesian* Matron) that I left the Room with Tears in my Eyes; which a Woman of *Arietta's* good Sense, did, I am sure, take for greater Applause, than any Compliments I could make her.

Parva leves capiunt animos. . . . [1]—Ovid

When I was in *France,* I used to gaze with great Astonishment at the Splendid Equipages, and Party-coloured Habits, of that Fantastick Nation. I was one Day in particular contemplating a Lady, that sate in a Coach adorned with gilded *Cupids,* and finely painted with the Loves of *Venus* and *Adonis.* The Coach was drawn by six milk-white Horses, and loaden behind with the same Number of powder'd Footmen. Just before the Lady were a Couple of beautiful Pages, that were stuck among the Harness, and, by their gay Dresses and smiling Features, looked like the elder Brothers of the little Boys that were carved and painted in every corner of the Coach.

The Lady was the unfortunate *Cleanthe,* who afterwards gave an Occasion to a pretty melancholy Novel. She had, for several Years, received the Addresses of a Gentleman, whom, after a long and intimate Acquaintance she forsook, upon the Account of this shining Equipage, which had been offered to her by one of Great Riches, but a Crazy Constitution. The Circumstances in which I saw her, were, it seems, the Disguises only of a broken Heart, and a kind of Pageantry to cover Distress; for in two Months after she was carried to her Grave with the same Pomp and Magnificence; being sent thither partly by the Loss of one Lover, and partly by the Possession of another.

I have often reflected with my self on this unaccountable Humour in Woman-kind, of being smitten with every thing

[1] "Little things occupy light minds."

125

that is showy and superficial; and on the numberless Evils that befal the Sex, from this light, fantastical Disposition. I my self remember a young Lady, that was very warmly sollicited by a Couple of importunate Rivals, who for several Months together did all they could to recommend themselves, by Complacency of Behaviour, and Agreeableness of Conversation. At length, when the Competition was doubtful, and the Lady undetermined in her Choice, one of the young Lovers very luckily bethought himself of adding a supernumerary Lace to his Liveries, which had so good an Effect that he Married her the very Week after.

The usual Conversation of ordinary Women[2] very much cherishes this natural Weakness of being taken with Outside and Appearance. Talk of a new-married Couple, and you immediately hear whether they keep their Coach and six, or eat in Plate: Mention the Name of an absent Lady, and it is ten to one but you learn something of her Gown and Petticoat. A Ball is a great Help to Discourse, and a Birth-Day furnishes Conversation for a Twelve-month after. A Furbelow of precious Stones, an Hat buttoned with a Diamond, a Brocade Waistcoat or Petticoat, are standing Topicks. In short, they consider only the Drapery of the Species, and never cast away a Thought on those Ornaments of the Mind, that make Persons Illustrious in themselves, and Useful to others. When Women are thus perpetually dazzling one another's Imaginations, and filling their Heads with nothing but Colours, it is no Wonder that they are more attentive to the superficial Parts of Life, than the solid and substantial Blessings of it. A Girl, who has been trained up in this kind of Conversation, is in danger of every Embroidered Coat that comes in her Way. A Pair of fringed Gloves may be her Ruin. In a word, Lace and Ribbons, Silver and Gold Galloons,[3] with the like glittering Gew-gaws, are so many Lures to Women of weak Minds or low Educations,

[2] Compare the situation of Belinda in *The Rape of the Lock*, I, 95 - 102.
[3] Trimming made of gold or silver braid.

and when artificially displayed, are able to fetch down the most airy Coquet from the wildest of her Flights and Rambles.

True Happiness is of a retired Nature, and an Enemy to Pomp and Noise; it arises, in the first place, from the Enjoyment of one's self; and, in the next, from the Friendship and Conversation of a few select Companions. It loves Shade and Solitude, and naturally haunts Groves and Fountains, Fields and Meadows: In short, it feels every thing it wants within it self, and receives no Addition from Multitudes of Witnesses and Spectators. On the contrary, false Happiness loves to be in a Crowd, and to draw the Eyes of the World upon her. She does not receive any Satisfaction from the Applauses which she gives her self, but from the Admiration which she raises in others. She flourishes in Courts and Palaces, Theatres and Assemblies, and has no Existence but when she is looked upon.

Aurelia, though a Woman of Great Quality, delights in the Privacy of a Country Life, and passes away a great part of her Time in her own Walks and Gardens. Her Husband, who is her Bosom Friend, and Companion in her Solitudes, has been in Love with her ever since he knew her. They both abound with good Sense, consummate Virtue, and a mutual Esteem; and are a perpetual Entertainment to one another. Their Family is under so regular an Oeconomy, in its Hours of Devotion and Repast, Employment and Diversion, that it looks like a little Common-wealth within it self. They often go into Company, that they may return with the greater Delight to one another; and sometimes live in Town, not to enjoy it so properly as to grow weary of it, that they may renew in themselves the Relish of a Country Life. By this means they are happy in each other, beloved by their Children, adored by their Servants, and are become the Envy, or rather the Delight, of all that know them.

How different to this is the Life of *Fulvia!* she considers her Husband as her Steward, and looks upon Discretion and good Housewifry, as little domestick Virtues, unbecoming a Woman of Quality. She thinks Life lost in her own Family, and fancies her self out of the World when she is not in the Ring, the Play-house, or the Drawing-Room: She lives in a perpetual Motion of Body, and Restlesness of Thought, and is never easie in any one Place when she thinks, there is more Company in another. The missing of an Opera the first Night, would be more afflicting to her than the Death of a Child. She pities all the valuable Part of her own Sex, and calls every Woman of a prudent modest retired Life, a poor-spirited unpolished Creature. What a Mortification would it be to *Fulvia,* if she knew that her setting her self to View is but exposing her self, and that she grows Contemptible by being Conspicuous.

I cannot conclude my Paper, without observing that *Virgil* has very finely touched upon this Female Passion for Dress and Show, in the Character of *Camilla;* who, though she seems to have shaken off all the other Weaknesses of her Sex, is still described as a Woman in this Particular. The Poet tells us, that after having made a great Slaughter of the Enemy, she unfortunately cast her Eye on a *Trojan* who wore an embroidered Tunick, a beautiful Coat of Mail, with a Mantle of the finest Purple. *A Golden Bow,* says he, *hung upon his Shoulder; his Garment was buckled with a Golden Clasp, and his Head covered with an Helmet of the same shining Metal.* The *Amazon* immediately singled out this well-dressed Warrior, being seized with a Woman's Longing for the pretty Trappings that he was adorned with:

> _____ *Totumque incauta per agmen*
> *Fœmineo prædæ & spoliorum ardebat amore.* [4]

This heedless Pursuit after these glittering Trifles, the Poet (by a nice concealed Moral) represents to have been the Destruction of his Female Hero.

---

[4] "Heedless in her headlong pursuit, she burns with eagerness for the finery and for the spoils of battle." *Aeneid,* XI, 781-2.

. . . Locus est & pluribus Umbris.[1]—Hor.

I am sometimes very much troubled, when I reflect upon the three great Professions of Divinity, Law and Physick; how they are each of them over-burdened with Practitioners, and filled with Multitudes of Ingenious Gentlemen that starve one another.

We may divide the Clergy into Generals, Field-Officers, and Subalterns. Among the first we may reckon Bishops, Deans and Arch-Deacons. Among the second are Doctors of Divinity, Prebendaries, and all that wear Scarfs.[2] The rest are comprehended under the Subalterns. As for the first Class, our Constitution preserves it from any Redundancy of Incumbents, notwithstanding Competitors are numberless. Upon a strict Calculation, it is found that there has been a great Exceeding of late Years in the second Division, several Brevets having been granted for the converting of Subalterns into Scarf-Officers; insomuch that within my Memory the price of Lutestring is raised above two Pence in a Yard. As for the Subalterns, they are not to be numbred. Should our Clergy once enter into the corrupt Practice of the Laity, by the splitting of their Freeholds, they would be able to carry most of the Elections in *England*.

The Body of the Law is no less encumbered with superfluous Members, that are like *Virgil's* Army,[3] which he tells

---

[1] "There is room, too, for some uninvited guests."
[2] Bands of silk worn around the neck as a part of clerical costume.
[3] *Aeneid*, X, 432-433.

us was so crouded many of them had not Room to use their Weapons. This prodigious Society of Men may be divided into the Litigious and Peaceable. Under the first are comprehended all those who are carried down in Coachfulls to *Westminster-Hall,* every Morning in Term-time. *Martial's* Description of this Species of Lawyers is full of Humour:

Iras & Verba locant.

Men that hire out their Words and Anger; that are more or less passionate according as they are paid for it, and allow their Client a quantity of Wrath proportionable to the Fee which they receive from him. I must however observe to the Reader, that above three Parts of those whom I reckon among the Litigious, are such as are only quarrelsome in their Hearts, and have no Opportunity of showing their Passion at the Bar. Nevertheless, as they do not know what Strifes may arise, they appear at the Mall every Day, that they may show themselves in a Readiness to enter the Lists, whenever there shall be Occasion for them.

The Peaceable Lawyers are, in the first place, many of the Benchers of the several Inns of Court, who seem to be the Dignitaries of the Law, and are endowed with those Qualifications of Mind that accomplish a Man rather for a Ruler, than a Pleader. These Men live peaceably in their Habitations, Eating once a Day, and Dancing once a Year, for the Honour of their respective Societies.

Another numberless Branch of Peaceable Lawyers, are those young Men who being placed at the Inns of Court in order to study the Laws of their Country, frequent the Play-house more than *Westminster-Hall,* and are seen in all publick Assemblies, except in a Court of Justice. I shall say nothing of those Silent and Busie Multitudes that are employed within Doors, in the drawing up of Writings and Conveyances; nor of those greater Numbers that palliate their want of Business with a Pretense to such Chamber-practice.

If, in the third place, we look into the Profession of Physick, we shall find a most formidable Body of Men: The Sight of
them is enough to make a Man serious, for we may lay it down
as a Maxim, that When a Nation abounds in Physicians it grows
thin of People. Sir *William Temple* is very much puzzled to
find out a Reason why the Northern Hive, as he calls it, does
not send out such prodigious Swarms, and over-run the World
with *Goths* and *Vandals,* as it did formerly; but had that Excellent Author observed that there were no Students in Physick among the Subjects of *Thor* and *Woden,* and that this Science very much flourishes in the North at present, he might
have found a better Solution for this Difficulty, than any of
those he has made use of. This Body of Men, in our own Country, may be described like the *British* Army in *Cæsar's* time:
Some of them slay in Chariots, and some on Foot. If the Infantry
do less Execution than the Charioteers, it is because they cannot be carried so soon into all Quarters of the Town, and dispatch so much Business in so short a Time. Besides this Body
of Regular Troops, there are Stragglers, who without being
duly listed and enrolled, do infinite Mischief to those who are
so unlucky as to fall into their Hands.

There are, besides the above-mentioned, innumerable
Retainers to Physick, who, for want of other Patients, amuse
themselves with the stifling of Cats in an Air Pump, cutting
up Dogs alive, or impaling of Insects upon the point of a Needle
for Microscopical Observations; besides those that are employed in the gathering of Weeds, and the Chace of Butter-
flies: Not to mention the Cockleshell-Merchants and Spider-
catchers.

When I consider how each of these Professions are crouded
with Multitudes that seek their Livelihood in them, and how
many Men of Merit there are in each of them, who may be
rather said to be of the Science, than the Profession; I very
much wonder at the Humour of Parents, who will not rather
chuse to place their Sons in a way of Life where an honest Industry cannot but thrive, than in Stations where the greatest

Probity Learning and Good Sense may miscarry. How many Men are Country-Curates, that might have made themselves Aldermen of *London,* by a right Improvement of a smaller Sum of Mony than what is usually laid out upon a learned Education? A sober, frugal Person, of slender Parts and a slow Apprehension, might have thrived in Trade, though he starves upon Physick; as a Man would be well enough pleased to buy Silks of one, whom he would not venture to feel his Pulse. *Vagellius* is careful, studious and obliging, but withal a little thick-skull'd; he has not a single Client, but might have had abundance of Customers. The Misfortune is, that Parents take a Liking to a particular Profession, and therefore desire their Sons may be of it. Whereas, in so great an Affair of Life, they should consider the Genius and Abilities of their Children, more than their own Inclinations.

It is the great Advantage of a trading Nation, that there are very few in it so dull and heavy, who may not be placed in Stations of Life which may give them an Opportunity of making their Fortunes. A well-regulated Commerce is not, like Law, Physick, or Divinity, to be over-stocked with Hands; but, on the contrary, flourishes by Multitudes, and gives Employment to all its Professors. Fleets of Merchantmen are so many Squadrons of floating Shops, that vend our Wares and Manufactures in all the Markets of the World, and find out Chapmen under both the Tropicks.

No. 26   Friday, March 30, 1711.   [Addison]

Pallida mors aequo pulsat pede pauperum tabernas
  Regumque turres, o beate Sexti.
Vitae summa brevis spem nos vetat inchoare longam.
  Jam te premet nox, fabulæque manes,
Et domus exilis Plutonia . . .[1]—Hor.

When I am in a serious Humour I very often walk by my self
in *Westminster* Abby; where the Gloominess of the Place,
and the Use to which it is applied, with the Solemnity of the
Building, and the Condition of the People who lye in it, are apt
to fill the Mind with a kind of Melancholy, or rather Thought-
fulness, that is not disagreeable. I Yesterday pass'd a whole
Afternoon in the Churchyard, the Cloysters, and the Church,
amusing my self with the Tomb-stones and Inscriptions that
I met with in those several Regions of the Dead. Most of them
recorded nothing else of the buried Person, but that he was
born upon one Day and died upon another: The whole History of his Life being comprehended in those two Circumstances, that are common to all Mankind. I could not but look
upon these Registers of Existence, whether of Brass or Marble,
as a kind of Satyr upon the departed Persons; who had left no
other Memorial of them, but that they were born and that they
died. They put me in mind of several Persons mentioned in
the Battels of Heroic Poems, who have sounding Names given
them, for no other Reason but that they may be killed, and
are celebrated for nothing but being knocked on the Head.

[1] "Pale death with foot impartial knocks at the poor man's cottage and at the
palaces of kings. Despite thy fortune, the brevity of life's span forbids thy entering on far-reaching hopes. Soon the night of death shall enshroud thee, and
phantom shades, and Pluto's cheerless hall."

Γλαῦχον τε Μεδόνπα Θεζσιλοχόν τε. Hom.

Glaucumque, Medontaque, Thersilochumque. Vir.

The Life of these Men is finely described in Holy Writ by *the Path of an Arrow,* which is immediately closed up and lost.

Upon my going into the Church, I entertained my self with the digging of a Grave; and saw in every Shovel-full of it that was thrown up, the Fragment of a Bone or Skull intermixt with a kind of fresh mouldering Earth that some time or other had a Place in the Composition of an human Body. Upon this, I began to consider with my self what innumerable Multitudes of People lay confused together under the Pavement of that ancient Cathedral; how Men and Women, Friends and Enemies, Priests and Soldiers, Monks and Prebendaries, were crumbled amongst one another, and blended together in the same common Mass; how Beauty, Strength, and Youth, with Old-age, Weakness, and Deformity, lay undistinguished in the same promiscuous Heap of Matter.

After having thus surveyed this great Magazine of Mortality, as it were, in the Lump; I examined it more particularly by the Accounts which I found on several of the Monuments which are raised in every Quarter of that ancient Fabrick. Some of them were covered with such extravagant Epitaphs, that, if it were possible for the dead Person to be acquainted with them, he would blush at the Praises which his Friends have bestowed upon him. There are others so excessively modest, that they deliver the Character of the Person departed in *Greek* or *Hebrew,* and by that means are not understood once in a Twelve-month. In the Poetical Quarter, I found there were Poets who had no Monuments, and Monuments which had no Poets. I observed indeed that the present War had filled the Church with many of these uninhabited Monuments, which had been erected to the Memory of Persons whose Bodies were perhaps buried in the Plains of *Blenheim,* or in the Bosom of the Ocean.

I could not but be very much delighted with several modern Epitaphs, which are written with great Elegance of Expression and Justness of Thought, and therefore do Honour to the Living as well as to the Dead. As a Foreigner is very apt to conceive an Idea of the Ignorance or Politeness of a Nation from the Turn of their publick Monuments and Inscriptions, they should be submitted to the Perusal of Men of Learning and Genius before they are put in Execution. Sir *Cloudesly Shovel's*[2] Monument has very often given me great Offence: Instead of the brave rough *English* Admiral, which was the distinguishing Character of that plain gallant Man, he is represented on his Tomb by the Figure of a Beau, dress'd in a long Perriwig, and reposing himself upon Velvet Cushions under a Canopy of State. The Inscription is answerable to the Monument; for instead of celebrating the many remarkable Actions he had performed in the Service of his Country, it acquaints us only with the Manner of his Death, in which it was impossile for him to reap any Honour. The *Dutch,* whom we are apt to despise for want of Genius, shew an infinitely greater Taste of Antiquity and Politeness in their Buildings and Works of this nature, than what we meet with in those of our own Country. The Monuments of their Admirals, which have been erected at the publick Expence, represent them like themselves; and are adorned with rostral Crowns and naval Ornaments, with beautiful Festoons of Sea-weed, Shells, and Coral.

But to return to our Subject. I have left the Repository of our *English* Kings for the Contemplation of another Day, when I shall find my Mind disposed for so serious an Amusement. I know that Entertainments of this nature are apt to raise dark and dismal Thoughts in timorous Minds, and gloomy Imaginations; but for my own part, though I am always serious, I do not know what it is to be melancholy; and can therefore take a View of Nature in her deep and solemn Scenes, with the same Pleasure as in her most gay and delightful ones. By this means I can improve my self with those Objects, which

[2] Sir Cloudesley Shovell was a contemporary naval hero who took part in the siege of Gibralter in 1704.

others consider with Terror. When I look upon the Tombs
of the Great, every Emotion of Envy dies in me; when I read
the Epitaphs of the Beautiful, every inordinate Desire goes
out; when I meet with the Grief of Parents upon a Tomb-stone,
my Heart melts with Compassion; when I see the Tomb of
the Parents themselves, I consider the Vanity of grieving for
those whom we must quickly follow: When I see Kings lying
by those who depossed them, when I consider rival Wits placed
Side by Side, or the holy Men that divided the World with their
Contests and Disputes, I reflect with Sorrow and Astonishment on the little Competitions, Factions, and Debates of Mankind. When I read the several Dates of the Tombs, of some
that died Yesterday, and some six hundred Years ago, I consider that great Day when we shall all of us be Contemporaries;
and make our Appearance together.

Parcit
Cognatis maculis similis fera . . . [1] —Juv.

The Club of which I am a Member, is very luckily composed of such Persons as are engaged in different Ways of Life and deputed as it were out of the most conspicuous Classes of Mankind: By this Means I am furnished with the greatest Variety of Hints and Materials, and know every thing that passes in the different Quarters and Divisions, not only of this great City, but of the whole Kingdom. My Readers too have the Satisfaction to find, that there is no Rank or Degree among them who have not their Representative in this Club, and that there is always some Body present who will take Care of their respective Interests, that nothing may be written or published to the Prejudice or Infringement of their just Rights and Privileges.

I last Night sat very late in Company with this select Body of Friends, who entertained me with several Remarks which they and others had made upon these my Speculations, as also with the various Success which they had met with among their several Ranks and Degrees of Readers. WILL. HONEYCOMB told me, in the softest manner he could, that there were some Ladies (but for your Comfort, says WILL. they are not those of the most Wit) that were offended at the Liberties I had taken with the Opera and the Puppet-Show: That some of them were likewise very much surprised, that I should think such serious Points as the Dress and Equipage of Persons of Quality, proper Subjects for Raillery.

---

[1] "Wild beasts are merciful to beasts spotted like themselves."

He was going on, when Sir ANDREW FREEPORT took him up short, and told him, that the Papers he hinted at had done great Good in the City, and that all their Wives and Daughters were the better for them: And further added, that the whole City thought themselves very much obliged to me for declaring my generous Intentions to scourge Vice and Folly as they appear in a Multitude, without condescending to be a Publisher of particular Intrigues and Cuckoldoms. In short, says Sir ANDREW, if you avoid that foolish beaten Road of falling upon Aldermen and Citizens, and employ your Pen upon the Vanity and Luxury of Courts, your Paper must needs be of general Use.

Upon this my Friend the TEMPLER told Sir ANDREW, That he wondered to hear a Man of his Sense talk after that manner; that the City had always been the Province for Satyr; and that the Wits of King *Charles's* Time jested upon nothing else during his whole Reign. He then shewed, by the Examples of *Horace, Juvenal, Boileau,* and the best Writers of every Age, that the Follies of the Stage and Court had never been accounted too sacred for Ridicule, how great soever the Persons might be that patroniz'd them. But after all, says he, I think your Raillery has made too great an Excursion in attacking several Persons of the Inns of Court; and I do not believe you can shew me any Precedent for your Behaviour in that Particular.

My good Friend Sir ROGER DE COVERLEY, who had said nothing all this while, began his Speech with a Pish! and told us, That he wondered to see so many Men of Sense so very serious upon Fooleries. Let our good Friend, says he, attack every one that deserves it: I would only advise you, Mr. SPECTATOR, applying himself to me, to take Care how you meddle with Country Squires: they are the Ornaments of the *English* Nation; Men of Good Heads and sound Bodies! and let me tell you, some of them take it ill of you, that you mention Foxhunters with so little Respect.

Captain SENTRY spoke very sparingly on this Occasion. What he said was only to commend my Prudence in not touching upon the Army, and advised me to continue to act discreetly in that Point.

By this time I found every Subject of my Speculations was taken away from me, by one or other of the Club; and began to think myself in the Condition of the good Man that had one Wife who took a Dislike to his grey Hairs, and another to his black, till by their picking out what each of them had an Aversion to, they left his Head altogether bald and naked.

While I was thus musing with my self, my worthy Friend the Clergyman, who, very luckily for me, was at the Club that Night, undertook my Cause. He told us, that he wondered any Order of Persons should think themselves too considerable to be advis'd: That it was not Quality, but Innocence, which exempted Men from Reproof: That Vice and Folly ought to be attacked where-ever they could be met with, and especially when they were placed in high and conspicuous Stations of Life. He further added, That my Paper would only serve to aggravate the Pains of Poverty, if it chiefly exposed those who are already depress'd, and in some measure turned into Ridicule, by the Meanness of their Conditions and Circumstances. He afterwards proceeded to take Notice of the great Use this Paper might be of to the Publick, by reprehending those Vices which are too trivial for the Chastisement of the Law, and too fantastical for the Cognizance of the Pulpit. He then advised me to prosecute my Undertaking with Chearfulness; and assured me, that whoever might be displeased with me, I should be approved by all those whose Praises do Honour to the Persons on whom they are bestowed.

The whole Club pays a particular Deference to the Discourse of this Gentleman, and are drawn into what he says, as much by the candid ingenuous Manner with which he delivers himself, as by the Strength of Argument and Force of Reason which he makes use of. WILL. HONEYCOMB immediately agreed, that what he had said was right; and that for his Part, he would not insist upon the Quarter which he had demanded for the Ladies. Sir ANDREW gave up the City with the same Frankness. The

TEMPLER would not stand out; and was followed by Sir ROGER and the CAPTAIN: Who all agreed that I should be at Liberty to carry the War into what Quarter I pleased; provided I continued to combat with Criminals in a Body, and to assault the Vice without hurting the Person.

This Debate, which was held for the Good of Mankind, put me in mind of that which the *Roman* Triumvirate[2] were formerly engaged in, for their Destruction. Every Man at first stood hard for his Friend, till they found that by this Means they should spoil their Proscription: And at length, making a Sacrifice of all their Acquaintance and Relations, furnished out a very decent Execution.

Having thus taken my Resolutions to march on boldly in the Cause of Virtue and good Sense, and to annoy their Adversaries in whatever Degree or Rank of Men they may be found: I shall be deaf for the future to all the Remonstrances that shall be made to me on this Account. If *Punch* grows extravagant, I shall reprimand him very freely: If the Stage becomes a Nursery of Folly and Impertinence, I shall not be afraid to animadvert upon it. In short, If I meet with any thing in City, Court, or Country, that shocks Modesty or good Manners, I shall use my utmost Endeavours to make an Example of it. I must however intreat every particular Person, who does me the Honour to be a Reader of this Paper, never to think himself, or any one of his Friends or Enemies, aimed at in what is said: For I promise him, never to draw a faulty Character which does not fit at least a Thousand People; or to publish a single Paper, that is not written in the Spirit of Benevolence, and with a Love to Mankind.

[2] See *Julius Caesar*, IV, i.

No. 35   Tuesday, April 10, 1711.   [Addison]

Risu inepto res ineptior nulla est.[1] —Mart.

Among all kinds of Writing, there is none in which Authors
are more apy to miscarry than in Works of Humour, as there
is none in which they are more ambitious to excel. It is not
an Imagination that teems with Monsters, an Head that is filled
with extravagant Conceptions, which is capable of furnishing the World with Diversions of this nature; and yet if we look
into the Productions of several Writers, who set up for Men
of Humour, what wild irregular Fancies, what unnatural Dis-
tortions of Thought, do we meet with? If they speak Nonsense,
they believe they are talking Humour; and when they have
drawn together a Scheme of absurd inconsistent Ideas, they
are not able to read it over to themselves without laughing.
These poor Gentlemen endeavour to gain themselves the Reputation of Wits and Humourists, by such monstrous Conceits
as almost qualifie them for *Bedlam;* not considering that Humour should always lye under the Check of Reason, and that
it requires the Direction of the nicest Judgment, by so much
the more as it indulges it self in the most boundless Freedoms.
There is a kind of Nature that is to be observed in this sort of
Compositions, as well as in all other; and a certain Regularity of Thought which must discover the Writer to be a Man
of Sense, at the same time that he appears altogether given
up to Caprice: For my part, when I read the delirious Mirth
of an unskilful Author, I cannot be so barbarous as to divert

[1] "Nothing is more silly than a silly laugh." This motto, as Professor Bond points
out, is from Catullus, *Carmina,* 39, 16.

my self with it, but am rather apt to pity the Man, than to laugh at any thing he writes.

The Deceased Mr. *Shadwell*,[2] who had himself a great deal of the Talent which I am treating of, represents an empty Rake, in one of his Plays, as very much surprized to hear one say that breaking of Windows was not Humour; and I question not but several *English* Readers will be as much startled to hear me affirm, that many of those raving incoherent Pieces, which are often spread among us, under odd Chymerical Titles, are rather the Offsprings of a distempered Brain, than Works of Humour.

It is indeed much easier to describe what is not Humour, than what is; and very difficult to define it otherwise than as *Cowley* has done Wit, by Negatives. Were I to give my own Notions of it, I would deliver them after *Plato's* manner, in a kind of Allegory, and by supposing Humour to be a Person, deduce to him all his Qualifications, according to the following Genealogy. TRUTH was the Founder of the Family, and the Father of GOOD SENSE. GOOD SENSE was the Father of WIT, who married a Lady of a Collateral Line called MIRTH, by whom he had issue HUMOUR. HUMOUR therefore being the youngest of this Illustrious Family, and descended from Parents of such different Dispositions, is very various and unequal in his Temper; sometimes you see him putting on grave Looks and a solemn Habit, sometimes airy in his Behaviour and fantastick in his Dress: Insomuch that at different times he appears as serious as a Judge, and as jocular as a *Merry-Andrew*. But as he has a great deal of the Mother in his Constitution, whatever Mood he is in, he never fails to make his Company laugh.

But since there is an Impostor abroad, who takes upon him the Name of this young Gentleman, and would willingly pass for him in the World; to the end that well-meaning Persons may not be imposed upon by Cheats, I would desire my Readers, when they meet with this Pretender, to look into his

---

[2] Thomas Shadwell (1642-1692), one of the more successful writers of comedy in Dryden's time.

Parentage, and to examine him strictly, whether or no he be remotely allied to TRUTH, and lineally descended from GOOD SENSE? if not, they may conclude him a Counterfeit. They may likewise distinguish him by a loud and excessive Laughter, in which he seldom gets his Company to join with him. For as TRUE HUMUOR generally looks serious, whilst every Body laughs about him; FALSE HUMOUR is always laughing, whilst every Body about him looks serious. I shall only add, if he has not in him a Mixture of both Parents, that is, if he would pass for the Offspring of WIT without MIRTH, or MIRTH without WIT, you may conclude him to be altogether Spurious, and a Cheat.

The Impostor of whom I am speaking, descends Originally from FALSEHOOD, who was the Mother of NONSENSE, who was brought to Bed of a Son called FRENZY, who Married one of the Daughters of FOLLY, commonly known by the Name of LAUGHTER, on whom he begot that Monstrous Infant of which I have been here speaking. I shall set down at length the Genealogical Table of FALSE HUMOR, and, at the same time, place under it the Genealogy of TRUE HUMOUR, that the Reader may at one View behold their different Pedigrees and Relations.

FALSEHOOD.
NONSENSE.
FRENZY.____LAUGHTER.
FALSE HUMOUR.
TRUTH.
GOOD SENSE.
WIT.____MIRTH.
HUMOUR.

I might extend the Allegory, by mentioning several of the Children of FALSE HUMOUR, who are more in Number than the Sands of the Sea, and might in particular enumerate the many Sons and Daughters which he has begot in this Island. But as this would be a very invidious Task, I shall only observe in general, that FALSE HUMOUR differs from the TRUE, as a Monkey does from a Man.

First of all, He is exceedingly given to little Apish Tricks and Buffooneries.

Secondly, He so much delights in Mimickry, that it is all one to him whether he exposes by it Vice and Folly, Luxury and Avarice; or, on the contrary, Virtue and Wisdom, Pain and Poverty.

Thirdly, He is wonderfully unlucky, insomuch that he will bite the Hand that feeds him, and endeavour to ridicule both Friends and Foes indifferently. For having but small Talents, he must be merry where he *can,* not where he *should.*

Fourthly, Being entirely void of Reason, he pursues no Point either of Morality or Instruction, but is Ludicrous only for the sake of being so.

Fifthly, Being incapable of any thing but Mock-Representations; his Ridicule is always Personal, and aimed at the Vicious Man, or the Writer; not at the Vice, or at the Writing.

I have here only pointed at the whole Species of False Humourists, but as one of my principal Designs in this Paper is to beat down that malignant Spirit, which discovers it self in the Writings of the present Age, I shall not scruple, for the future, to single out any of the small Wits, that infest the World with such Compositions as are ill-natured, immoral and absurd. This is the only Exception which I shall make to the General Rule I have perscribed my self, of *attacking Multitudes:* Since every honest Man ought to look upon himself as in a Natural State of War with the Libeller and Lampooner, and to annoy them whereever they fall in his way. This is but retaliating upon them, and treating them as they treat others.

. . . Non illa colo calathisve Minervæ
Fœmineas assueta manus . . .[1]—Virg.

Some Months ago, my Friend Sir ROGER being in the Country, enclosed a Letter to me, directed to a certain Lady whom I shall here call by the Name of *Leonora,* and as it contained Matters of Consequence, desired me to deliver it to her with my own Hand. Accordingly I waited upon her Ladyship pretty early in the Morning, and was desired by her Woman to walk into her Lady's Library, till such time as she was in a Readiness to receive me. The very sound of a *Lady's Library* gave me a great Curiosity to see it; and, as it was some time before the Lady came to me, I had an Opportunity of turning over a great many of her Books, which were ranged together in a very beautiful Order. At the End of the *Folios* (which were finely bound and guilt) were great Jars of *China* placed one above another in a very noble piece of Architecture. The *Quarto's* were separated from the *Octavo's* by a pile of smaller Vessels, which rose in a delightful Pyramid. The *Octavo's* were bounded by Tea Dishes of all Shapes, Colours, and Sizes, which were so disposed on a wooden Frame, that they looked like one continued Pillar indented with the finest Strokes of Sculpture, and stained with the greatest Variety of Dyes. That Part of the Library which was designed for the Reception of Plays and Pamphlets, and other loose Papers, was inclosed in a kind of Square, consisting of one of the prettiest Gro-

[1] "Never having trained her woman's hands to Minerva's distaff or basket of wool."

tesque Works that ever I saw, and made up of Scaramouches, Lions, Monkies, Mandarines, Trees, Shells, and a thousand other odd Figures in *China* Ware. In the midst of the Room was a little Japan Table, with a Quire of gilt Paper upon it, and on the Paper a Silver Snuff-Box made in the Shape of a little Book. I found there were several other Counterfeit Books upon the upper Shelves, which were carved in Wood, and served only to fill up the Number, like Faggots in the Muster of a Regiment. I was wonderfully pleased with such a mixt kind of Furniture, as seemed very suitable both to the Lady and the Scholar, and did not know at first whether I should fancy my self in a Grotto, or in a Library.

Upon my looking into the Books, I found there were some few which the Lady had bought for her own use, but that most of them had been got together, either because she had heard them praised, or because she had seen the Authors of them. Among several that I examined, I very well remember these that follow.[2]

Ogleby's Virgil.

Dryden's Juvenal.

Cassandra.

Cleopatra.

---

[2] Leonora's amusingly helter-skelter taste is reflected in the catalogue of her books, a number of which she had obviously acquired to impress her friends as well as to improve her mind. Of this sort were probably the Latin classics—Virgil, Juvenal, and Seneca—and certainly the classic authors in wood and the "Set of *Elzivers* by the same Hand." Primarily for edification were, of course, the works of Newton, Locke, Malebranche, and Sir William Temple, as well as such moral and religious works as *Sherlock upon Death, The Ladies' Calling,* Halifax's *Advice to a Daughter,* Taylor's *Holy Living and Dying,* and Steele's *Christian Hero.* The books that she read for pleasure were the fashionable romances—*Cassandra, Cleopatra, Astræa, The Grand Cyrus,* and Sidney's *Arcadia*—and the works of a more sensational nature like Durfey's *Tales in Verse,* the *Book of Novels, The New Atalantis,* Fielding's *Tryall,* and *The Fifteen Comforts of Matrimony.* Mixed with these on her shelves were such practical stand-by's as the *Spelling Book,* the *Dictionary for the Explanation of hard Words,* Culpepper's *Midwifery,* and La Ferte's *Instructions for Country Dances.*

Astræa.

Sir *Isaac Newton's* Works.

The *Grand Cyrus:* with a Pin stuck in one of the middle Leaves.

Pembroke's Arcadia.

Lock of Human Understanding: with a Paper of Patches in it.

A Spelling Book.

A Dictionary for the Explanation of hard Words.

Sherlock upon Death.

The Fifteen Comforts of Matrimony.

Sir *William Temple's* Essays.

Father *Malbranche's* Search after Truth, translated into *English.*

A Book of Novels.

The Academy of Compliments.

Culpepper's Midwifery.

The Ladies Calling.

Tales in Verse by Mr. *Durfey:* Bound in Red Leather, gilt on the Back, and doubled down in several Places.

All the Classick Authors in Wood.

A Set of *Elzivers* by the same Hand.

Clelia: Which opened of it self in the Place that describes two Lovers in a Bower.

Baker's Chronicle.

Advice to a Daughter.

The New *Atalantis,* with a Key to it.

Mr. *Steele's* Christian Heroe.

A Prayer Book: With a Bottle of *Hungary* Water by the side of it.

Dr. *Sacheverell's* Speech.

Fielding's Tryal.

Seneca's Morals.

Taylor's Holy Living and Dying.

La Ferte's Instructions for Country Dances.

I was taking a Catalogue in my Pocket-Book of these, and several other Authors, when *Leonora* entred, and upon my presenting her with the Letter from the Knight, told me, with an unspeakable Grace, that she hoped Sir ROGER was in good Health: I answered *Yes,* for I hate long Speeches, and after a Bow or two retired.

Leonora was formerly a celebrated Beauty, and is still a very lovely Woman. She has been a Widow for two or three Years, and being unfortunate in her first Marriage, has taken a Resolution never to venture upon a second. She has no Children to take care of, and leaves the Management of her Estate to my good Friend Sir ROGER. But as the Mind naturally sinks into a kind of Lethargy, and falls asleep, that is not agitated by some Favourite Pleasures and Pursuits, *Leonora* has turned all the Passions of her Sex into a love of Books and Retirement. She converses chiefly with Men, (as she has often said her self) but it is only in their Writings; and admits of very few Male-Visitants, except my Friend Sir ROGER, whom she hears with great Pleasure, and without Scandal. As her Reading has lain very much among Romances, it has given her a very particular Turn of Thinking, and discovers it self even in her House, her Gardens, and her Furniture. Sir ROGER has entertained me an Hour together with a Description of her Country-Seat. which is situated in a kind of Wilderness, about an Hundred Miles distant from *London*, and looks like a little enchanted Palace.The Rocks about her are shaped into Artificial Grottoes, covered with Woodbines and Jessamines.[3] The Woods are cut into shady Walks, twisted into Bowers, and filled with Cages of Turtles. The Springs are made to run among Pebbles, and by that means taught to murmur very agreeably. They are likewise collected into a beautiful Lake, that is inhabited by a Couple of Swans, and empties it self by a little Rivulet which runs through a green Meadow, and is known in the Family by

[3] Addison's disapproval of the current taste for the artificial in gardening is reflected in his remarks on landscape in *The Spectator,* No. 412.

the Name of *The Purling Stream*. The Knight likewise tells me, that this Lady preserves her Game better than any of the Gentlemen in the Country; not (says Sir ROGER) that she sets so great a Value upon her Partridges and Pheasants, as upon her Larks and Nightingales. For she says that every Bird which is killed in her Ground will spoil a Consort, and that she shall certainly miss him the next Year.

When I think how odly this Lady is improved by Learning, I look upon her with a mixture of Admiration and Pity. Amidst these innocent Entertainments which she has formed to her self, how much more Valuable does she appear than those of her Sex, who employ themselves in Diversions that are less Reasonable, though more in Fashion? What Improvements would a Woman have made, who is so susceptible of Impressions from what she reads, had she been guided to such Books as have a tendency to enlighten the Understanding and rectify the Passions, as well as to those which are of little more use than to divert the Imagination?

But the manner of a Lady's employing her self usefully in Reading shall be the Subject of another Paper, in which I design to recommend such particular Books as may be proper for the Improvement of the Sex. And as this is a Subject of a very nice Nature, I shall desire my Correspondents to give me their Thoughts upon it.

No. 39   Saturday, April 14, 1711.   [Addison]

Multa fero, ut placem genus irritabile vatum,
Cum scribo . . . [1]—Hor.

As a perfect Tragedy is the noblest Production of human Nature, so it is capable of giving the Mind one of the most delightful and most improving Entertainments. A virtuous Man (says
Seneca) strugling with Misfortunes, is such a Spectacle as Gods
might look upon with Pleasure: And such a Pleasure it is which
one meets with in the Representation of a well-written Tragedy. Diversions of this kind wear out of our Thoughts every
thing that is mean and little. They cherish and cultivate that
Humanity which is the Ornament of our Nature. They soften
Insolence, sooth Affliction, and subdue the Mind to the Dis-
pensations of Providence.

It is no Wonder therefore that in all the Polite Nations of
the World, this Part of the *Drama* has met with Publick Encouragement.

The Modern Tragedy excels that of *Greece* and *Rome,*
in the Intricacy and Disposition of the Fable: But, what a Christian Writer would be ashamed to own, falls infinitely short
of it in the Moral Part of the Performance.

This I may shew more at large hereafter; and in the mean
time, that I may contribute something towards the Improvement of the *English* Tragedy, I shall take Notice, in this and
in other following Papers, of some particular Parts in it that
seem liable to Exception.

Aristotle observes, that the *Iambick* Verse in the *Greek*

[1] "Much do I endure, to soothe the fretful tribe of bards, so long as I am scrib-
bling."

Tongue was the most proper for Tragedy: Because at the same time that it lifted up the Discourse from Prose, it was that which approached nearer to it than any other kind of Verse. For, says he, we may observe that Men in ordinary Discourse very often speak *Iambicks,* without taking Notice of it. We may make the same Observation of our *English* Blank Verse, which often enters into our common Discourse, though we do not attend to it, and is such a due Medium between Rhyme and Prose, that it seems wonderfully adapted to Tragedy. I am therefore very much offended when I see a Play in Rhyme; which is as absurd in *English* as a Tragedy of *Hexameters* would have been in *Greek* or *Latin.* The Solæcism is, I think, still greater, in those Plays that have some Scenes in Rhyme and some in Blank Verse, which are to be looked upon as two several Languages; or where we see some particular Similies dignified with Rhyme, at the same time that every thing about them lyes in Blank Verse. I would not however debar the Poet from concluding his Tragedy, or, if he pleases, every Act of it, with two or three Couplets, which may have the same Effect as an Air in the *Italian* Opera after a long *Recitativo,* and give the Actor a graceful *Exit.* Besides, that we see a Diversity of Numbers in some Parts of the Old Tragedy, in order to hinder the Ear from being tired with the same continued Modulation of Voice. For the same Reason I do not dislike the Speeches in our *English* Tragedy that close with an *Hemistick,* or half Verse, notwithstanding the Person who speaks after it begins a new Verse, without filling up the preceding one; nor with abrupt Pauses and Breakings-off in the middle of a Verse, when they humour any Passion that is expressed by it.

Since I am upon this Subject, I must observe, that our *English* Poets have succeeded much better in the Stile, than in the Sentiments of their Tragedies. Their Language is very often noble and sonorous, but the Sense either very trifling or very common. On the contrary, in the ancient Tragedies, and indeed in those of *Corneille* and *Racine,* tho' the Expressions are very great, it is the Thought that bears them up and swells them. For my own part, I prefer a noble Sentiment that is depressed with homely Language, infinitely before a vulgar one that is blown up with all the Sound and Energy of Expression. Whether this Defect in our Tragedies may arise from Want of Genius, Knowledge, or Experience in the Writers, or from their Compliance with the vicious Taste of their Readers, who are better Judges of the Language than of the Sentiments, and consequently relish the one more than the other, I cannot determine. But I believe it might rectifie the Conduct both of the one and of the other, if the Writer laid down the whole Contexture of his Dialogue in plain *English,* before he turned it into Blank Verse; and if the Reader, after the Perusal of a Scene, would consider the naked Thought of every Speech in it, when divested of all its Tragick Ornaments: By this means, without being imposed upon by Words, we may judge impartially of the Thought, and consider whether it be natural or great enough for the Person that utters it, whether it deserves to shine in such a Blaze of Eloquence, or shew it self in such a Variety of Lights as are generally made use of by the Writers of our *English* Tragedy.

I must in the next place observe, that when our Thoughts are great and just, they are often obscured by the sounding Phrases, hard Metaphors, and forced Expressions in which they are cloathed. *Shakespear* is often very faulty in this Particular. There is a fine Observation in *Aristotle* to this purpose, which I have never seen quoted. The Expression, says he, ought to be very much laboured in the unactive Parts of the Fable, as in Descriptions, Similitudes, Narrations, and the like; in which the Opinions, Manners, and Passions of Men are not represented; for these (namely the Opinions, Manners, and Passions) are apt to be obscured by pompous Phrases and elaborate Expressions. *Horace,* who copy'd most of his Criticisms after *Aristotle,* seems to have had his Eye on the foregoing Rule, in the following Verses:

Et Tragicus plerumque dolet Sermone pedestri
Telephus & Peleus, cum pauper & exsul uterque,
Projicit ampullas & sesquipedalia verba,
Si curat cor Spectantis tetigisse querela.

Tragœdians too lay by their State, to grieve,
Peleus *and* Telephus, *exil'd and poor,*
Forget their swelling and gigantick Words.

Ld. ROSCOMMON.

Among our Modern *English* Poets, there is none who was better turned for Tragedy than *Lee;* if instead of favouring the Impetuosity of his Genius, he had restrained it, and kept it within its proper Bounds. His Thoughts are wonderfully suited to Tragedy, but frequently lost in such a Cloud of Words, that it is hard to see the Beauty of them: There is an infinite Fire in his Works, but so involved in Smoak, that it does not appear in half its Lustre. He frequently succeeds in the passionate Parts of the Tragedy, but more particularly where he slackens his Efforts, and eases the Stile of those Epithets and Metaphors, in which he so much abounds. What can be more natural, more soft, or more passionate, than that Line in *Statira's* Speech, where she describes the Charms of *Alexander's* Conversation?

Then he would talk: Good Gods! how he would talk!

That unexpected Break in the Line, and turning the Description of his manner of Talking into an Admiration of it, is inexpressibly beautiful, and wonderfully suited to the fond Character of the Person that speaks it. There is a Simplicity in the Words, that outshines the utmost Pride of Expression.

Otway has followed Nature in the Language of his Tragedy, and therefore shines in the Passionate Parts, more than any of our *English* Poets. As there is something Familiar and Domestick in the Fable of his Tragedy, more than in those of any other Poet, he has little Pomp, but great Force in his Expressions. For which Reason, tho' he has admirably succeeded in the tender and melting Part of his Tragedies, he sometimes falls into too great a Familiarity of Phrase in those Parts, which, by *Aristotle's* Rule, ought to have been raised and supported by the Dignity of Expression.

It has been observed by others, that this Poet has founded his Tragedy of *Venice Preserved* on so wrong a Plot, that the greatest Characters in it are those of Rebels and Traitors. Had the Hero of his Play discovered the same good Qualities in the Defence of his Country, that he shewed for its Ruin and Subversion, the Audience could not enough pity and admire him: But as he is now represented, we can only say of him, what the *Roman* Historian says of *Catiline,* that his Fall would have been glorious *(si pro Patria sic concidisset)* had he so fallen in the Service of his Country.

No. 40   Monday, April 16, 1711.   [Addison]

Ac ne forte putes me, quæ facere ipse recusem,
Cum recte tractent alii, laudare maligne;
Ille per extentum funem mihi posse videtur
Ire Poeta, meum qui pectus inaniter angit,
Irritat, mulcet, falsis terroribus implet,
Ut magus; & modo me Thebis, modo ponit Athenis.[1]—Hor.

The *English* Writers of Tragedy are possessed with a Notion, that when they represent a virtuous or innocent Person in Distress, they ought not to leave him till they have delivered him out of his Troubles, or made him triumph over his Enemies. This Error they have been led into by a ridiculous Doctrine in Modern Criticism, that they are obliged to an equal Distribution of Rewards and Punishments, and an impartial Execution of Poetical Justice. Who were the first that established this Rule I know not; but I am sure it has no Foundation in Nature, in Reason, or in the Practice of the Ancients. We find that Good and Evil happen alike to all Men on this Side the Grave; and as the principal Design of Tragedy is to raise Commiseration and Terror in the Minds of the Audience, we shall defeat this great End, if we always make Virtue and Innocence happy and successful. Whatever Crosses and Disappointments a good Man suffers in the Body of the Tragedy, they will make but small Impression on our Minds, when we know that in the

---

[1] "And lest, perchance, you may think that I begrudge praise when others are handling well what I decline to do myself, methinks that poet is able to walk a tight rope, who with airy nothings wrings my heart, inflames, soothes, fills it with vain charms like a magician, and sets me down now at Thebes, now at Athens."

last Act he is to arrive at the End of his Wishes and Desires.
When we see him engaged in the Depth of his Afflictions, we
are apt to comfort our selves, because we are sure he will find
his Way out of them; and that his Grief, how great soever it
may be at present, will soon terminate in Gladness. For this
Reason, the ancient Writers of Tragedy treated Men in their
Plays, as they are dealt with in the World, by making Virtue
sometimes happy and sometimes miserable, as they found it in
the Fable which they made choice of, or as it might affect their
Audience in the most agreeable Manner. *Aristotle* considers the
Tragedies that were written in either of these Kinds, and observes, That those which ended unhappily, had always pleased
the People, and carried away the Prize in the publick Disputes
of the Stage, from those that ended happily. Terror and Commiseration leave a pleasing Anguish in the Mind; and fix the
Audience in such a serious Composure of Thought, as is much
more lasting and delightful than any little transient Starts of
Joy and Satisfaction. Accordingly we find, that more of our
English Tragedies have succeeded, in which the Favourites
of the Audience sink under their Calamities, than those in which
they recover themselves out of them. The best Plays of this
Kind are the *Orphan*, [2] *Venice preserved, Alexander the Great,
Theodosius, All for Love, Oedipus, Oroonoko, Othello,* &c.
King *Lear* is an admirable Tragedy of the same Kind, as *Shakespear* wrote it; but as it is reformed according to the chymerical
Notion of Poetical Justice, in my humble Opinion it has lost
half its Beauty. At the same time I must allow, that there are
very noble Tragedies, which have been framed upon the other
Plan, and have ended happily; as indeed most of the good Tragedies, which have been written since the starting of the above-
mentioned Criticism, have taken this Turn: As the *Mourning*

[2] *The Orphan* and *Venice Preserved* were by Thomas Otway (1652-1685);
Alexander the Great and *Theodosius* by Nathaniel Lee (1653?-1692); *All for
Love* by John Dryden (1631-1700); *Oedipus* by Lee and Dryden; and *Oroonoko*
by Thomas Southerne (1659-1746).

Bride, Tamerlane, Ulysses, Phaedra and *Hyppolitus,*[3] with most of Mr. *Dryden's.* I must also allow, that many of *Shakespear's,* and several of the celebrated Tragedies of Antiquity, are cast in the same Form. I do not therefore dispute against this way of writing Tragedies, but against the Criticism that would establish this as the only Method; and by that Means would very much cramp the *English* Tragedy, and perhaps give a wrong Bent to the Genius of our Writers.

The Tragi-Comedy, which is the Product of the *English* Theatre, is one of the most monstrous Inventions that ever entered into a Poet's Thoughts. An Author might as well think of weaving the Adventures of *Aeneas* and *Hudibras*[4] into one Poem, as of writing such a motly Piece of Mirth and Sorrow. But the Absurdity of these Performances is so very visible, that I shall not insist upon it.

The same Objections which are made to Tragi-Comedy, may in some Measure be applied to all Tragedies that have a double Plot in them; which are likewise more frequent upon the *English* Stage, than upon any other: For though the Grief of the Audience, in such Performances, be not changed into another Passion, as in Tragi-Comedies; it is diverted upon another Object, which weakens their Concern for the principal Action, and breaks the Tide of Sorrow, by throwing it into different Channels. This Inconvenience, however, may in a great Measure be cured, if not wholly removed, by the skilful Choice of an Under-Plot, which may bear such a near Relation to the principal Design, as to contribute towards the Completion of it, and be concluded by the same Catastrophe.

There is also another Particular, which may be reckoned among the Blemishes, or rather the false Beauties, of our *English* Tragedy: I mean those particular Speeches which are commonly known by the Name of *Rants.* The warm and passionate

[3] Of these four plays, the first was written by William Congreve (1670 - 1729), the second and third by Nicholas Rowe (1674 - 1718), and the fourth by Edmund Smith (1672 - 1710).
[4] See *The Tatler,* No. 132, n.7.

Parts of a Tragedy, are always the most taking with the Audience; for which Reason we often see the Players pronouncing, in all the Violence of Action, several Parts of the Tragedy which the Author writ with great Temper, and designed that they should have been so acted. I have seen *Powell* very often raise himself a loud Clap by this Artifice. The Poets that were acquainted with this Secret, have given frequent Occasion for such Emotions in the Actor, by adding Vehemence to Words where there was no Passion, or inflaming a real Passion into Fustian. This hath filled the Mouths of our Heroes with Bombast; and given them such Sentiments, as proceed rather from a Swelling than a Greatness of Mind. Unnatural Exclamations, Curses, Vows, Blasphemies, a Defiance of Mankind, and an Outraging of the Gods, frequently pass upon the Audience for tow'ring Thoughts, and have accordingly met with infinite Applause.

I shall here add a Remark, which I am afraid our Tragick Writers may make an ill use of. As our Heroes are generally Lovers, their Swelling and Blustring upon the Stage very much recommends them to the fair Part of their Audience. The Ladies are wonderfully pleased to see a Man insulting Kings, or affronting the Gods, in one Scene, and throwing himself at the Feet of his Mistress in another. Let him behave himself insolently towards the Men, and abjectly towards the Fair One, and it is ten to one but he proves a Favourite of the Boxes. *Dryden* and *Lee,* in several of their Tragedies, have practised this Secret with good Success.

But to shew how a *Rant* pleases beyond the most just and natural Thought that is not pronounced with Vehemence, I would desire the Reader, when he sees the Tragedy of *Oedipus,* to observe how quietly the Hero is dismissed at the End of the third Act, after having pronounced the following Lines, in which the Thought is very natural, and apt to move Compassion:

> *To you, good Gods, I make my last Appeal,*
> *Or clear my Virtues, or my Crimes reveal.*

If in the Maze of Fate I blindly run,
And backward trod those Paths I sought to shun;
Impute my Errors to your own Decree:
My Hands are guilty, but my Heart is free.

Let us then observe with what Thunder-claps of Applause he leaves the Stage, after the Impieties and Execrations at the End of the fourth Act; and you will wonder to see an Audience so cursed and so pleased at the same time.

O *that as oft I have at* Athens *seen,*
  [Where, by the way, there was no Stage till many
    Years after *Oedipus.*]
  The Stage arise, and the big Clouds descend;
  So now, in very deed, I might behold
  This pond'rous Globe, and all yon marble Roof,
  Meet, like the Hands of Jove, *and crush Mankind.*
  For all the Elements, &c.

ADVERTISEMENT.

Having spoken of Mr. Powell,[5] *as sometimes raising himself Applause from the ill Taste of an Audience; I must do him the Justice to own, that he is excellently formed for a Tragœdian, and, when he pleases, deserves the Admiration of the best Judges; as I doubt not but he will in the* Conquest of Mexico, *which is acted for his own Benefit To-morrow Night.*

---

[5] A tragic actor of Addison's day.

. . . Tu non inventa reperta es. [1]—Ovid

Compassion for the Gentleman who writes the following Letter, should not prevail upon me to fall upon the Fair Sex, if it were not that I find they are frequently Fairer than they ought to be. Such Impostures are not to be tolerated in Civil Society; and I think his Misfortune ought to be made publick, as a Warning for other Men always to Examine into what they Admire.

SIR,
Supposing you to be a Person of general Knowledge, I make my Application to you on a very particular Occasion. I have a great Mind to be rid of my Wife, and hope, when you consider my Case, you will be of Opinion I have very just Pretensions to a Divorce. I am a mere Man of the Town, and have very little Improvement, but what I have got from Plays. I remember in *The Silent Woman,* the Learned Dr. *Cutberd,* or Dr. *Otter* (I forget which) makes one of the Causes of Separation to be *Error Personæ,* when a Man marries a Woman, and finds her not to be the same Woman whom he intended to marry, but another. If that be Law, it is, I presume, exactly my Case. For you are to know, Mr. SPECTATOR, that there are Women who do not let their Husbands see their Faces till they are married.

    Not to keep you in Suspense, I mean plainly, that part of the Sex who paint. They are some of them so exquisitely skilful this Way, that give them but a tolerable Pair of Eyes to set up with, and they will make Bosom, Lips, Cheeks, and Eyebrows,

[1] "Undiscovered you are discovered."

by their own Industry. As for my Dear, never Man was so in-amour'd as I was of her fair Forehead, Neck and Arms, as well as the bright Jett of her Hair; but to my great Astonishment, I find they were all the Effect of Art: Her Skin is so tarnished with this Practice, that when she first wakes in a Morning, she scarce seems young enough to be the Mother of her whom I carried to Bed the Night before. I shall take the Liberty to part with her by the first Opportunity, unless her Father will make her Portion suitable to her real, not her assumed, Coun-tenance. This I thought fit to let him and her know by your Means. I am,

  SIR,

         Your most Obedient Humble Servant.

  I cannot tell what the Law, or the Parents of the Lady will do for this Injured Gentleman, but must allow he has very much Justice on his side. I have indeed very long observed this Evil, and distinguished those of our Women who wear their own, from those in borrowed Complexions, by the *Picts*[2] and the *British*. There does not need any great Discernment to judge which are which. The *British* have a lively animated Aspect; the *Picts,* though never so Beautiful, have dead uniformed Countenances. The Muscles of a real Face sometimes swell with soft Passion, sudden Surprize, and are flushed with agree-able Confusions, according as the Objects before them, or the Ideas presented to them, affect their Imagination. But the *Picts* behold all things with the same Air, whether they are Joyful or Sad; The same fixed Insensibility appears upon all Occasions. A *Pict,* though she takes all that Pains to invite the Approach of Lovers, is obliged to keep them at a certain Distance; a Sigh in a Languishing Lover, if fetched too near her, would dissolve a Feature; and a Kiss snatched by a Forward one, might transfer the Complexion of the Mistress to the Ad-

[2] Ancient inhabitants of Britain, who according to Julius Caesar painted their bodies blue in order to frighten their enemies in battle.

mirer. It is hard to speak of these false Fair Ones, without saying something uncomplaisant, but I would only recommend to them to consider how they like coming into a Room new Painted; they may assure themselves, the near Approach of a Lady who uses this Practice is much more offensive.

WILL. HONEYCOMB told us, one Day, an Adventure he once had with a *Pict*. This Lady had Wit, as well as Beauty, at Will; and made it her Business to gain Hearts, for no other Reason, but to railly[3] the Torments of her Lovers. She would make great Advances to insnare Men, but without any manner of Scruple break off when there was no Provocation. Her Ill-Nature and Vanity made my Friend very easily Proof against the Charms of her Wit and Conversation; but her beauteous Form, instead of being blemished by her Falsehood and Inconstancy, every Day increased upon him, and she had new Attractions every time he saw her. When she observed WILL. irrevocably her Slave, she began to use him as such, and after many steps toward such a Cruelty, she at last utterly banished him. The unhappy Lover strove in vain, by servile Epistles, to revoke his Doom; till at length he was forced to the last Refuge, a round Sum of Mony to her Maid. This corrupt Attendant placed him early in the Morning behind the Hangings in her Mistress's Dressing-Room. He stood very conveniently to observe, without being seen. The *Pict* begins the Face she designed to wear that Day, and I have heard him protest she had worked a full half Hour before he knew her to be the same Woman. As soon as he saw the Dawn of that Complexion, for which he had so long languished, he thought fit to break from his Concealment, repeating that of *Cowley*:[4]

> Th' adorning Thee with so much Art,
>   Is but a barb'rous Skill;
> 'Tis like the Pois'ning of a Dart,
>   Too apt before to kill.

[3] Attack with raillery, make fun of.
[4] *Poems*, ed. A. R. Waller, p.138.

The *Pict* stood before him in the utmost Confusion, with the prettiest Smirk imaginable on the finish'd side of her Face, pale as Ashes on the other. HONEYCOMB seized all her Gally-pots and Washes, and carried off his Handkerchief full of Brushes, Scraps of *Spanish* Wooll, and Phials of Unguents. The Lady went into the Country; the Lover was cured.

It is certain no Faith ought to be kept with Cheats, and an Oath made to a *Pict* is of it self void. I would therefore exhort all the *British* Ladies to single them out, nor do I know any but *Lindamira* who should be Exempt from Discovery; for her own Complexion is so delicate, that she ought to be allowed the Covering it with Paint, as a Punishment for chusing to be the worst Piece of Art extant, instead of the Masterpiece of Nature. As for my part, who have no Expectations from Women, and consider them only as they are Part of the Species, I do not half so much fear offending a Beauty as a Woman of Sense; I shall therefore produce several Faces which have been in Publick this many Years, and never appeared; it will be a very pretty Entertainment in the Play-house (when I have abolished this Custom) to see so many Ladies, when they first lay it down, *incog.* in their own Faces.

In the mean time, as a Pattern for improving their Charms, let the Sex study the agreeable *Statira.* Her Features are enlivened with the Chearfulness of her Mind, and good Humour gives an Alacrity to her Eyes. She is Graceful without affecting an Air, and Unconcerned without appearing Careless. Her having no manner of Art in her Mind, makes her want none in her Person.

How like is this Lady, and how unlike is a *Pict,* to that Description Dr. *Donne*[5] gives of his Mistress?

> . . . . . *Her pure and eloquent Blood*
> *Spoke in her Cheeks, and so distinctly wrought,*
> *That one would almost say her Body thought.*

[5] *The Second Anniversary,* ll.244-246.

ADVERTISEMENT.

A young Gentlewoman of about Nineteen Years of Age (bred in the Family of a Person of Quality lately deceased) who Paints the Finest Flesh-colour, wants a Place, and is to be heard of at the House of Minheer Grotesque, *a* Dutch *Painter in* Barbican.

N.B. *She is also well skilled in the Drapery-part, and puts on Hoods and mixes Ribbons so as to suit the Colours of the Face with great Art and Success.*

No. 44   Friday, April 20, 1711.   [Addison]

Tu quid ego & populus mecum desideret audi.[1]—Hor.

Among the several Artifices which are put in Practice by the Poets to fill the Minds of an Audience with Terror, the first Place is due to Thunder and Lightning which are often made use of at the Descending of a God, or the Rising of a Ghost, at the Vanishing of a Devil, or at the Death of a Tyrant. I have known a Bell introduced into several Tragedies with good Effect; and have seen the whole Assembly in a very great Alarm all the while it has been ringing. But there is nothing which delights and terrifies our *English* Theatre so much as a Ghost, especially when he appears in a bloody Shirt. A Spectre has very often saved a Play, though he has done nothing but stalked across the Stage, or rose through a Cleft of it, and sunk again without speaking one Word. There may be a proper Season for these several Terrors; and when they only come in as Aids and Assistances to the Poet, they are not only to be excused, but to be applauded. Thus the sounding of the Clock in *Venice preserved*, makes the Hearts of the whole Audience quake; and conveys a stronger Terror to the Mind, than it is possible for Words to do. The Appearance of the Ghost in *Hamlet* is a Master-piece in its kind, and wrought up with all the Circumstances that can create either Attention or Horror. The Mind of the Reader is wonderfully prepared for his Reception, by the Discourses that precede it: His dumb behaviour at his first Entrance, strikes the Imagination very strongly; but every time he enters, he is still more terrifying. Who can read the Speech with which young *Hamlet* accosts him, without trembling?

[1] "Now hear what I, and with me the public, expect."

Hor. *Look, my Lord, it comes!*
Ham. *Angels and Ministers of Grace defend us!*
Be thou a Spirit of Health, or Goblin damn'd;
Bring with thee Airs from Heav'n, or Blasts from Hell;
Be thy Events wicked or Charitable;
Thou com'st in such a questionable Shape
That I will speak to thee. I'll call thee Hamlet,
King, Father, Royal Dane: *Oh! Oh! Answer me,*
Let me not burst in Ignorance; but tell
Why thy canoniz'd Bones, hearsed in Death,
Have burst their Cearments? Why the Sepulchre,
Wherein we saw thee quietly inurn'd,
Hath op'd his ponderous and marble Jaws
To cast thee up again? What may this mean?
That thou dead Coarse again in compleat Steel
Revisit'st thus the Glimpses of the Moon,
Making Night hideous?

I do not therefore find Fault with the Artifices above-mentioned, when they are introduced with Skill, and accompanied by proportionable Sentiments and Expressions in the Writing.

For the moving of Pity, our principal Machine is the Handkerchief; and indeed in our common Tragedies, we should not know very often that the Persons are in Distress by any thing they say, if they did not from time to time apply their Handkerchiefs to their Eyes. Far be it from me to think of banishing this Instrument of Sorrow from the Stage; I know a Tragedy could not subsist without it: All that I would contend for, is, to keep it from being misapplied. In a word, I would have the Actor's Tongue sympathize with his Eyes.

A disconsolate Mother, with a Child in her Hand, has frequently drawn Compassion from the Audience, and has therefore gained a Place in several Tragedies. A Modern Writer, that observed how this had took in other Plays, being resolved to double the Distress, and melt his Audience twice as much as those before him had done, brought a Princess upon the

Stage with a little Boy in one Hand and a Girl in the other. This too had a very good Effect. A third Poet being resolved to outwrite all his Predecessors, a few Years ago introduced three Children, with great Success: And, as I am informed, a young Gentleman, who is fully determined to break the most obdurate Hearts, has a Tragedy by him, where the first Person that appears upon the Stage is an afflicted Widow in her Mourning-Weeds, with half a Dozen fatherless Children attending her, like those that usually hang about the Figure of Charity. Thus several Incidents that are beautiful in a good Writer, become ridiculous by falling into the Hands of a bad one.

But among all our Methods of moving Pity or Terror, there is none so absurd and barbarous, and what more exposes us to the Contempt and Ridicule of our Neighbours, than that dreadful butchering of one another, which is so very frequent upon the *English* Stage. To delight in seeing Men stabbed, poisoned, racked, or impaled, is certainly the Sign of a cruel Temper: And as this is often practised before the *British* Audience, several *French* Criticks, who think these are grateful Spectacles to us, take Occasion from them to represent us as a People that delight in Blood. It is indeed very odd, to see our Stage strowed with Carcasses in the last Scene of a Tragedy; and to observe in the Ward-robe of the Playhouse several Daggers, Poniards, Wheels, Bowls for Poison, and many other Instruments of Death. Murders and Executions are always transacted behind the Scenes in the *French* Theatre; which in general is very agreeable to the Manners of a polite and civilised People: But as there are no Exceptions to this Rule on the *French* Stage, it leads them into Absurdities almost as ridiculous as that which falls under our present Censure. I remember in the famous Play of *Corneille,* written upon the Subject of the *Horatii* and *Curiatii;* the fierce young Hero who had overcome the *Curiatii* one after another (instead of being congratulated by his Sister for his Victory, being upbraided by her for having slain her Lover) in the height of his Passion and Resentment kills her. If any thing could extenuate so brutal an Action, it would be the doing of it on a sudden, before the Sentiments of Nature, Reason, or Manhood could take Place in him. However, to avoid *Publick Bloodshed*, as soon as his Passion is wrought to its Height, he follows his Sister the whole length of the Stage, and forbears killing her till they are both withdrawn behind the Scenes. I must confess, had he murder'd her before the Audience, the Indecency might have been greater; but as it is, it appears very unnatural, and looks like killing in cold Blood. To give my Opinion upon this Case; the Fact ought not to have been represented, but to have been told, if there was any Occasion for it.

It may not be unacceptable to the Reader, to see how *Sophocles* has conducted a Tragedy under the like delicate Circumstances. *Orestes* was in the same Condition with *Hamlet* in *Shakespear,* his Mother having murdered his Father, and taken Possession of his Kingdom, in Conspiracy with her Adulterer. That young Prince therefore, being determined to revenge his Father's Death upon those who filled his Throne, conveys himself by a beautiful Stratagem into his Mother's Apartment, with a Resolution to kill her. But because such a Spectacle would have been too shocking to the Audience, this dreadful Resolution is executed behind the Scenes: The Mother is heard calling out to her Son for Mercy; and the Son answering her, that she shewed no Mercy to his Father: After which she shrieks out that she is wounded, and by what follows we find that she is slain. I do not remember that in any of our Plays there are Speeches made behind the Scenes, though there are other Instances of this Nature to be met with in those of the Ancients: And I believe my Reader will agree with me, that there is something infinitely more affecting in this dreadful Dialogue between the Mother and her Son behind the Scenes, than could have been in any thing transacted before the Audience. *Orestes* immediately after meets the Usurper at the Entrance of his Palace; and by a very happy Thought of the Poet avoids killing him before the Audience, by telling him that he should live some Time in his present Bitterness of Soul before he would dispatch him, and by ordering him to retire into that Part of the Palace where he had slain his Father, whose Murther he would revenge in the very same Place where it was committed. By this Means the Poet observes that Decency, which *Horace* afterwards established by a Rule, of forbearing to commit Parricides or unnatural Murthers before the Audience.

> *Nec coram populo natos* Medea *trucidet.*
>
> *Let not* Medea *draw her murth'ring Knife,*
> *And spill her Childrens Blood upon the Stage.*

The *French* have therefore refined too much upon *Horace's* Rule, who never designed to banish all Kinds of Death from the Stage; but only such as had too much Horror in them, and which would have a better Effect upon the Audience when transacted behind the Scenes. I would therefore recommend to my Countrymen the Practice of the ancient Poets, who were very sparing of their publick Executions, and rather chose to perform them behind the Scenes, if it could be done with as great an Effect upon the Audience. At the same Time I must observe, that though the devoted Persons of the Tragedy were seldom slain before the Audience, which has generally something ridiculous in it, their Bodies were often produced after their Death, which has always in it something melancholy or terrifying; so that the killing on the Stage does not seem to have been avoided only as an Indecency, but also as an Improbability.

Nec pueros coram populo Medea *trucidet;*
Aut humana palam coquat exta nefarius Atreus;
Aut in avem Progne *vertatur,* Cadmus *in anguem,*
Quodcunque ostendis mihi sic, incredulus odi. — Hor.

Medea *must not draw her murth'ring Knife,*
Nor Atreus *there his horrid Feast prepare.*

Cadmus *and* Progne's *Metamorphosis,*
(She to a Swallow turn'd, he to a Snake)
And whatsoever contradicts my Sense,
I hate to see, and never can believe. —Ld. ROSCOMMON.

　　I have now gone through the several dramatick Inventions which are made use of by the ignorant Poets to supply the Place of Tragedy, and by the skilful to improve it; some of which I could wish entirely rejected, and the rest to be used with Caution. It would be an endless Task to consider Comedy in the same Light, and to mention the innumerable Shifts that small Wits put in practice to raise a Laugh. *Bullock* in a short Coat, and *Norris* in a long one, seldom fail of this Effect. In ordinary Comedies, a broad and a narrow brim'd Hat are different Characters. Sometimes the Wit of the Scene lies in a Shoulder-Belt, and sometimes in a Pair of Whiskers. A Lover running about the Stage, with his Head peeping out of a Barrel,[2] was thought a very good Jest in King *Charles* the Second's Time; and invented by one of the first Wits of that Age. But because Ridicule is not so delicate as Compassion, and because the Objects that make us laugh are infinitely more numerous than those that make us weep, there is a much greater Lattitude for comick than tragick Artifices, and by Consequence a much greater Indulgence to be allowed them.

[2] In *The Comical Revenge, or Love in a Tub* (1664), by Sir George Etherege.

No. 46   Monday, April 23, 1711.   [Addison]

Non bene junctarum discordia semina rerum.[1]—Ovid.

When I want Materials for this Paper, it is my Custom to go
Abroad in quest of Game; and when I meet any proper Subject, I take the first Opportunity of setting down an Hint of
it upon Paper. At the same Time I look into the Letters of my
Correspondents, and if I find any thing suggested in them that
may afford Matter of Speculation, I likewise enter a Minute
of it in my Collection of Materials. By this Means I frequently carry about me a whole Sheet-full of Hints, that would look
like a Rhapsody of Nonsense to any Body but my self: There
is nothing in them but Obscurity and Confusion, Raving and
Inconsistency. In short, they are my Speculations in the first
Principles, that (like the World in its Chaos) are void of all
Light, Distinction and Order.

About a Week since there happened to me a very odd
Accident, by Reason of one of these my Papers of Minutes
which I had accidentally dropped at *Lloyd's* Coffee-house,
where the Auctions are usually kept. Before I missed it, there
were a Cluster of People who had found it, and were diverting themselves with it at one End of the Coffee-house: It had
raised so much Laughter among them, before I had observed
what they were about, that I had not the Courage to own it.
The Boy of the Coffee-house, when they had done with it, carried it about in his Hand, asking every Body if they had dropped
a written Paper; but no Body challenging it, he was ordered
by those merry Gentlemen who had before persued it, to get
up into the Auction-Pulpit, and read it to the whole Room,

---

[1] "The discordant seeds of ill-joined things."

that if any one would own it they might. The Boy accordingly mounted the Pulpit, and with a very audible Voice read as follows.

MINUTES.

Sir ROGER DE COVERLY'S Country-Seat—Yes, for I hate long Speeches—Query, if a good Christian may be a Conjurer—*Childermas-day,* Saltseller, House-Dog, Screech-Owl, Cricket,—Mr. *Thomas Inkle* of *London,* in the good Ship called the *Achilles. Yarico—Egrescitque medendo*—Ghosts—The Lady's Library—Lion by Trade a Taylor—Dromedary called *Bucephalus*—Equipage the Lady's *summum bonum*—*Charles Lillie* to be taken Notice of—Short Face a Relief to Envy—Redundancies in the three Professions—King *Latinus* a Recruit—Jew devouring an Ham of Bacon—*Westminster-Abby*—*Grand Cairo*—Procrastination—*April* Fools—Blue Boars, Red Lyons, Hogs in Armour—Enter a King and two Fidlers *solus*—Admission into the Ugly Club—Beauty, how improveable—Families of true and false Humour—The Parrot's School-Mistress—Face half *Pict* half *British*—No Man to be an Hero of a Tragedy under six Foot—Club of Sighers—Letters from Flower-Pots, Elbow-Chairs, Tapestry-Figures, Lion, Thunder—The Bell rings to the Puppet-Show—Old Woman with a Beard Married to a Smock-faced Boy—My Next Coat to be turn'd up with Blue—Fable of Tongs and Gridiron—Flower Dyers—The Soldier's Prayer—Thank ye for nothing, says the Gally-Pot—*Pactolus* in Stockings, with golden Clocks to them—Bamboos, Cudgels, Drum-sticks—Slip of my Land-lady's eldest Daughter—The black Mare with a Star in her Forehead—The Barber's Pole—WILL. HONEYCOMB'S Coat-Pocket— *Cæsar's* Behaviour and my own in Parallel Circumstances—Poem in Patch-work—*Nulli gravis est percussus Achilles*—The Female Conventicler—The Ogle-Master.

The reading of this Paper made the whole Coffee-house

very merry; some of them concluded it was written by a Madman, and others by some Body that had been taking Notes out of the Spectator. One who had the Appearance of a very substantial Citizen, told us, with several politick Winks and Nods, that he wished there was no more in the Paper than what was expressed in it: That for his Part, he looked upon the Dromedary, the Gridiron, and the Barber's Pole, to signifie something more than what is usually meant by those Words; and that he thought the Coffee-man could not do better, than to carry the Paper to one of the Secretaries of State. He further added, that he did not like the Name of the outlandish Man with the Golden Clock in his Stockings. A young *Oxford* Scholar, who chanced to be with his Uncle at the Coffe-house, discovered to us who this *Pactolus* was; and by that Means turned the whole Scheme of this worthy Citizen into Ridicule. While they were making their several Conjectures upon this innocent Paper, I reached out my Arm to the Boy, as he was coming out of the Pulpit, to give it me; which he did accordingly. This drew the Eyes of the whole Company upon me; but after having cast a cursory Glance over it, and shook my Head twice or thrice at the reading of it, I twisted it into a kind of Match, and litt my Pipe with it. My profound Silence, together with the Steadiness of my Countenance, and the Gravity of my Behaviour during this whole Transaction, raised a very loud Laugh on all Sides of me; but as I had escaped all Suspicion of being the Author, I was very well satisfied; and applying my self to my Pipe and the *Post-Man,*[2] took no further Notice of any thing that passed about me.

My Reader will find, that I have already made use of above half the Contents of the foregoing Paper; and will easily suppose, that those Subjects which are yet untouched, were such Provisions as I had made for his future Entertainment. But as I have been unluckily prevented by this Accident, I shall

[2] A tri-weekly newspaper which was being published at the same time as *The Spectator.*

only give him the Letters which relate to the two last Hints. The first of them I should not have published, were I not informed that there is many an Husband who suffers very much in his private Affairs by the indiscreet Zeal of such a Partner as is hereafter mentioned; to whom I may apply the barbarous Inscription quoted by the Bishop of *Salisbury* in his Travels; *Dum nimia pia est, facta est impia.*[3]

SIR,

I Am one of those unhappy Men that are plagued with a Gospel-Gossip, so common among Dissenters (especially Friends.) Lectures in the Morning, Church-Meetings at Noon, and Preparation-Sermons at Night, take up so much of her Time, 'tis very rare she knows what we have for Dinner, unless when the Preacher is to be at it. With him come a Tribe, all Brothers and Sisters it seems; while others, really such, are deemed no Relations. If at any time I have her Company alone, she is a meer Sermon Popgun, repeating and discharging Texts, Proofs, and Applications so perpetually, that however weary I may go to Bed, the Noise in my Head will not let me sleep till towards Morning. The Misery of my Case, and great Numbers of such Sufferers, plead your Pity and speedy Relief; otherwise must expect, in a little Time, to be lectured, preached, and prayed into Want, unless the Happiness of being sooner talked to Death prevent it.

I am, &c.

R.   G.

The second Letter, relating to the Ogling Master, runs thus.

Mr. SPECTATOR,

I Am an *Irish* Gentleman, that have travelled many Years for

[3] The inscription, borrowed from Bishop Burnet's *Letters* (1686), has been translated as follows:
"Through too much piety, she became impious."

my Improvement; during which Time I have accomplished my self in the whole Art of Ogling, as it is at present practised in all the polite Nations of *Europe*. Being thus qualified, I intend, by the Advice of my Friends, to set up for an Ogling-Master. I teach the Church Ogle in the Morning, and the Play-house Ogle by Candle-light. I have also brought over with me a new flying Ogle fit for the Ring; which I teach in the Dusk of the Evening, or in any Hour of the Day by darkning one of my Windows. I have a Manuscript by me called *The compleat Ogler,* which I shall be ready to shew you upon any Occasion: In the mean time, I beg you will publish the Substance of this Letter in an Advertisement, and you will very much oblige,

Your, &c.

No. 50   Friday, April 27, 1711.   [Addison]

Nunquam aliud Natura, aliud Sapientia dixit. [1]—Juv.

When the four *Indian* Kings[2] were in this Country about a Twelve-month ago, I often mixed with the Rabble, and followed them a whole Day together, being wonderfully struck with the Sight of every Thing that is new or uncommon. I have, since their Departure, employed a Friend to make many Enquiries of their Landlord the Upholsterer, relating to their Manners and Conversation, as also concerning the Remarks which they made in this Country: For, next to the forming a right Notion of such Strangers, I should be desirous of learning what Ideas they have conceived of us.

The Upholsterer finding my Friend very inquisitive about these his Lodgers, brought him some time since a little Bundle of Papers, which he assured him were written by King *Sa Ga Yean Qua Rash Tow,* and, as he supposes, left behind by some mistake. These Papers are now translated, and contain abundance of very odd Observations, which I find this little Fraternity of Kings made during their Stay in the Isle of *Great-Britain.* I shall present my Reader with a short Specimen of them in this Paper, and may, perhaps, communicate more to him hereafter. In the Article of *London* are the following Words, which without doubt are meant of the Church of St. *Paul.*

[1] "Never does nature say one thing and wisdom another."
[2] Four Iroquois chiefs who visited London in April, 1710. Their value as a satiric device arises from the fact that familiarity has not closed their eyes to the absurdity of English customs. Compare Lemuel Gulliver's observations on the strange peoples whom he visits and Swift's remark to Stella in his *Journal* for April 28, 1711, that he has provided a "noble hint" for this number of *The Spectator.*

'On the most rising Part of the Town there stands a huge House, big enough to contain the whole Nation of which I am King. Our good Brother *E. Tow O Koam,* King of the *Rivers,* is of Opinion it was made by the Hands of that great God to whom it is consecrated. The Kings of *Granajah* and of the *Six Nations* believe, that it was created with the Earth, and produced on the same Day with the Sun and Moon. But for my own Part, by the best Information that I could get of this Matter, I am apt to think that this prodigious Pile was fashioned into the Shape it now bears by several Tools and Instruments, of which they have a wonderful Variety in this Country. It was probably at first an huge misshapen Rock that grew upon the Top of the Hill, which the Natives of the Country (after having cut it into a kind of regular Figure) bored and hollowed with incredible Pains and Industry, till they had wrought in it all those beautiful Vaults and Caverns into which it is divided at this Day. As soon as this Rock was thus curiously scooped to their Liking, a prodigious Number of Hands must have been employed in chipping the Outside of it, which is now as smooth as the Surface of a Pebble; and is in several Places hewn out into Pillars that stand like the Trunks of so many Trees bound about the Top with Garlands of Leaves. It is probable that when this great Work was begun, which must have been many Hundred Years ago, there was some Religion among this People; for they give it the Name of a Temple, and have a Tradition that it was designed for Men to pay their Devotions in. And indeed, there are several Reasons which make us think, that the Natives of this Country had formerly among them some sort of Worship; for they set apart every seventh Day as sacred: But upon my going into one of these Holy Houses on that Day, I could not observe any Circumstance of Devotion in their Behaviour: There was indeed a Man in Black who was mounted above the rest, and seemed to utter something with a great deal of Vehemence; but as for those underneath him, instead of paying their Worship to the Deity of the Place, they were most of them bowing and curt'sying to one another, and a considerable Number of them fast asleep.

'The Queen of the Country appointed two Men to attend us, that had enough of our Language to make themselves understood in some few Particulars. But we soon perceived these two were great Enemies to one another, and did not always agree in the same Story. We could make a Shift to gather out of one of them, that this Island was very much infested with a monstrous Kind of Animals, in the Shape of Men, called *Whigs;* and he often told us, that he hoped we should meet with none of them in our Way, for that if we did, they would be apt to knock us down for being Kings.

'Our other Interpreter used to talk very much of a kind of Animal called a *Tory,* that was as great a Monster as the *Whig,* and would treat us as ill for being Foreigners. These two Creatures, it seems, are born with a secret Antipathy to one another, and engage when they meet as naturally as the Elephant and the Rhinoceros. But as we saw none of either of these Species, we are apt to think that our Guides deceived us with Misrepresentations and Fictions, and amused us with an Account of such Monsters as are not really in their Country.

'These Particulars we made a Shift to pick out from the Discourse of our Interpreters; which we put together as well as we could, being able to understand but here and there a Word of what they said, and afterwards making up the meaning of it among our selves. The Men of the Country are very cunning and ingenious in handicraft Works; but withal so very idle, that we often saw young lusty raw-boned Fellows carried up and down the Streets in little covered Rooms by a Couple of Porters, who are hired for that Service. Their Dress is likewise very barbarous, for they almost strangle themselves about the Neck, and bind their Bodies with many Ligatures, that we are apt to think are the Occasion of several Distempers among them which our Country is entirely free from. Instead of those beautiful Feathers with which we adorn our Heads, they often buy up a monstrous Bush of Hair, which covers their Heads, and falls down in a large Fleece below the Middle of their

Backs; with which they walk up and down the Streets, and are as proud of it as if it was of their own Growth.

'We were invited to one of their publick Diversions, where we hoped to have seen the great Men of their Country running down a Stag or pitching a Bar, that we might have discovered who were the Persons of the greatest Abilities among them; but instead of that they conveyed us into a huge Room lighted up with abundance of Candles, where this lazy People sate still above three Hours to see several Feats of Ingenuity performed by others, who it seems were paid for it.

'As for the Women of the Country, not being able to talk with them, we could only make our Remarks upon them at a Distance. They let the Hair of their Heads grow to a great Length; but as the Men make a great Show with Heads of Hair that are none of their own, the Women, who they say have very fine Heads of Hair, tie it up in a Knot, and cover it from being seen. The Women look like Angels, and would be more beautiful than the Sun, were it not for little black Spots[3] that are apt to break out in their Faces, and sometimes rise in very odd Figures. I have observed that those little Blemishes wear off very soon; but when they disappear in one Part of the Face, they are very apt to break out in another, insomuch that I have seen a Spot upon the Forehead in the Afternoon, which was upon the Chin in the Morning.'

The Author then proceeds to shew the Absurdity of Breeches and Petticoats, with many other curious Observations, which I shall reserve for another Occasion. I cannot however conclude this Paper without taking Notice, That amidst these wild Remarks there now and then appears something very reasonable. I cannot likewise forbear observing, That we are all guilty in some Measure of the same narrow way of Thinking, which we meet with in this Abstract of the *Indian* Journal; when we fancy the Customs, Dresses, and Manners of other Countries are ridiculous and extravagant, if they do not resemble those of our own.

[3] See *The Spectator,* No. 81, on party patches.

Monday, May 7, 1711.   [Addison]

Ut pictura poesis erit . . .[1]—Hor.

Nothing is so much admired, and so little understood, as Wit. No Author that I know of has written professedly upon it; and as for those who make any Mention of it, they only treat on the Subject as it has accidentally fallen in their Way, and that too in little short Reflections, or in general declamatory Flourishes, without entring into the Bottom of the Matter. I hope therefore I shall perform an acceptable Work to my Countrymen, if I treat at large upon this Subject; which I shall endeavour to do in a Manner suitable to it, that I may not incur the Censure which a famous Critick bestows upon one who had written a Treatise upon *the Sublime* in a low groveling Stile. I intend to lay aside a whole Week for this Undertaking, that the Scheme of my Thoughts may not be broken and interrupted; and I dare promise my self, if my Readers will give me a Week's Attention, that this great City will be very much changed for the better by next *Saturday* Night.[2] I shall endeavour to make what I say intelligible to ordinary Capacities; but if my Readers meet with any Paper that in some Parts of it may be a little out of their Reach, I would not have them discouraged, for they may assure themselves the next shall be much clearer.

As the great and only End of these my Speculations is to banish Vice and Ignorance out of the Territories of *Great Britain,* I shall endeavour as much as possible to establish

---

[1] "A poem will be like a picture."
[2] Nos. 58-63 take up the whole week beginning with Monday, May 7, and ending with Saturday, May 12.

among us a Taste of polite Writing. It is with this View that I have endeavoured to set my Readers right in several Points relating to Operas and Tragedies; and shall from Time to Time impart my Notions of Comedy, as I think they may tend to its Refinement and Perfection. I find by my Bookseller that these Papers of Criticism, with that upon Humour, have met with a more kind Reception than indeed I could have hoped for from such Subjects; for which Reason I shall enter upon my present Undertaking with greater Chearfulness.

In this, and one or two following Papers, I shall trace out the History of false Wit, and distinguish the several Kinds of it as they have prevailed in different Ages of the World. This I think the more necessary at present, because I observed there were Attempts on foot last Winter to revive some of those antiquated Modes of Wit that have been long exploded out of the Commonwealth of Letters. There were several Satyrs and Panegyricks handed about in Acrostick, by which Means some of the most arrant undisputed Blockheads about the Town began to entertain ambitious Thoughts, and to set up for polite Authors. I shall therefore describe at length those many Arts of false Wit, in which a Writer does not shew himself a Man of a beautiful Genius, but of great Industry.

The first Species of false Wit which I have met with is very venerable for its Antiquity, and has produced several Pieces which have lived very near as long as the *Iliad* it self: I mean those short Poems printed among the minor *Greek* Poets, which resemble the Figure of an Egg, a Pair of Wings, an Ax, a Shepherd's Pipe, and an Altar.

As for the first, it is a little oval Poem, and may not improperly be called a Scholar's Egg. I would endeavour to hatch it, or, in more intelligible Language, to translate it into *English,* did not I find the Interpretation of it very difficult; for the Author seems to have been more intent upon the Figure of his Poem, than upon the Sense of it.

The Pair of Wings consist of twelve Verses, or rather Feathers, every Verse decreasing gradually in its Measure according to its Situation in the Wing. The Subject of it (as in the rest of the Poems which follow) bears some remote Affinity with the Figure, for it describes a God of Love, who is always painted with Wings.

The Ax methinks would have been a good Figure for a Lampoon, had the Edge of it consisted of the most satyrical Parts of the Work; but as it is in the Original, I take it to have been nothing else but the Posie of an Ax which was consecrated to *Minerva,* and was thought to have been the same that *Epeus* made use of in the building of the *Trojan* Horse; which is a Hint I shall leave to the Consideration of the Criticks. I am apt to think that the Posie was written originally upon the Ax, like those which our modern Cutlers inscribe upon their Knives; and that therefore the Posie still remains in its ancient Shape, though the Ax it self is lost.

The Shepherd's Pipe may be said to be full of Musick, for it is composed of nine different Kinds of Verses, which by their several Lengths resemble the nine Stops of the old musical Instrument, that is likewise the Subject of the Poem.

The Altar is inscribed with the Epitaph of *Troilus* the Son of *Hecuba;* which, by the way, makes me believe, that these false Pieces of Wit are much more ancient than the Authors to whom they are generally ascribed; at least I will never be perswaded, that so fine a Writer as *Theocritus* could have been the Author of any such simple Works.

It was impossible for a Man to succeed in these Performances who was not a kind of Painter, or at least a Designer: He was first of all to draw the Out-line of the Subject which he intended to write upon, and afterwards conform the Description to the Figure of his Subject. The Poetry was to contract or dilate it self according to the Mould in which it was cast. In a Word, the Verses were to be cramped or extended to the Dimensions of the Frame that was prepared for them; and to undergo the Fate of those Persons whom the Tyrant *Procrustes* used to lodge in his Iron Bed; if they were too short he stretched them on a Rack, and if they were too long chopped off a Part of their Legs, till they fitted the Couch which he had prepared for them.

Mr. *Dryden* hints at this obsolete kind of Wit in one of the following Verses, in his *Mac Fleckno;* which an *English* Reader cannot understand, who does not know that there are those little Poems abovementioned in the Shape of Wings and Altars.

> . . . . . *Chuse for thy Command*
> *Some peaceful Province in Acrostick Land:*
> *There may'st thou Wings display, and Altars raise,*
> *And torture one poor Word a thousand Ways.*

This Fashion of false Wit was revived by several Poets of the last Age,[3] and in particular may be met with among Mr. *Herbert's* Poems; and, if I am not mistaken, in the Translation of *Du Bartas.* I do not remember any other Kind of Work among the Moderns which more resembles the Performances I have mentioned, than that famous Picture of King *Charles* I. which has the whole Book of *Psalms* written in the Lines of the Face and the Hair of the Head. When I was last at *Oxford* I perused one of the Whiskers; and was reading the other, but could not go so far in it as I would have done, by reason of the Impatience of my Friends and Fellow-Travellers, who all of them pressed to see such a Piece of Curiosity. I have since heard, that there is now an eminent Writing-Master in Town, who has transcribed all the *Old Testament* in a full-bottomed Perriwig; and if the Fashion should introduce the thick Kind of Wigs which were in Vogue some few Years ago, he promises to add two or three supernumerary Locks that shall contain all the *Apocrypha.* He designed this Wig originally for King *William,* having disposed of the two Books of *Kings* in the two Forks of the Foretop; but that glorious Monarch

---

[3] In this paragraph Addison is citing poets of the seventeenth century who exercised their wit in making the typographical form of their poems provide a visual statement of its subject or theme.

dying before the Wig was finished, there is a Space left in it for the Face of any one that has a mind to purchase it.

But to return to our ancient Poems in Picture, I would humbly propose, for the Benefit of our modern Smatterers in Poetry, that they would imitate their Brethren among the Ancients in those ingenious Devices. I have communicated this Thought to a young Poetical Lover of my Acquaintance, who intends to present his Mistress with a Copy of Verses made in the Shape of her Fan; and, if he tells me true, has already finished the three first Sticks of it. He has likewise promised me to get the Measure of his Mistress's Marriage-Finger, with a Design to make a Posie in the Fashion of a Ring which shall exactly fit it. It is so very easie to enlarge upon a good Hint, that I do not question but my ingenious Readers will apply what I have said to many other Particulars; and that we shall see the Town filled in a very little time with Poetical Tippets, Handkerchiefs, Snuff-Boxes, and the like Female-Ornaments. I shall therefore conclude with a Word of Advice to those admirable *English* Authors who call themselves Pindarick Writers, that they would apply themselves to this Kind of Wit without Loss of Time, as being provided better than any other Poets with Verses of all Sizes and Dimensions.

No. 61   Thursday, May 10, 1711.   [Addison]

Non equidem hoc studeo, bullatis ut mihi nugis
Pagina turgescat, dare pondus idonea fumo. [1]—Pers.

There is no kind of false Wit which has been so recommended by the Practice of all Ages, as that which consists in a Jingle of Words, and is comprehended under the general Name of *Punning.* It is indeed impossible to kill a Weed, which the Soil has a natural Disposition to produce. The Seeds of Punning are in the Minds of all Men, and tho' they may be subdued by Reason, Reflection, and good Sense, they will be very apt to shoot up in the greatest Genius, that is not broken and cultivated by the Rules of Art. Imitation is natural to us, and when it does not raise the Mind to Poetry, Painting, Musick, or other more noble Arts, it often breaks out in Punns and Quibbles.

Aristotle, in the Eleventh Chapter of his Book of Rhetorick, describes two or three kinds of Punns, which he calls Paragrams, among the Beauties of good Writing, and produces Instances of them out of some of the greatest Authors in the *Greek* Tongue. *Cicero* has sprinkled several of his Works with Punns, and in his Book where he lays down the Rules of Oratory, quotes abundance of Sayings as Pieces of Wit, which also upon Examination prove arrant Punns. But the Age in which *the Punn* chiefly flourished, was the Reign of King *James* the First. That learned Monarch was himself a tolerable Punnster, and made very few Bishops or Privy-Counsellors that had not some time or other signalized themselves by a Clinch, or

[1] "Nay, indeed, it is no aim of mine that my page should swell with pretentious trifles, fit only to give solidity to smoke."

185

a *Connundrum*. It was therefore in this Age that the Punn appeared with Pomp and Dignity. It had before been admitted into merry Speeches and ludicrous Compositions, but was now delivered with great Gravity from the Pulpit, or pronounced in the most solemn manner at the Council-Table. The greatest Authors, in their most serious Works, made frequent use of Punns. The Sermons of Bishop *Andrews,*[2] and the Tragedies of *Shakespear,* are full of them. The Sinner was punned into Repentance by the former, as in the latter nothing is more usual than to see a Hero weeping and quibbling for a dozen Lines together.

I must add to these great Authorities, which seem to have given a kind of Sanction to this Piece of false Wit, that all the Writers of Rhetorick have treated of Punning with very great Respect, and divided the several kinds of it into hard Names, that are reckoned among the Figures of Speech, and recommended as Ornaments in Discourse. I remember a Country School-master of my Acquaintance told me once, that he had been in Company with a Gentleman, whom he looked upon to be the greatest *Paragrammatist* among the Moderns. Upon Enquiry, I found my learned Friend had dined that Day with Mr. *Swan,* the famous Punnster; and desiring him to give me some Account of Mr. *Swan's* Conversation, he told me that he generally talked in the *Paronomasia,*[3] that he sometimes gave into the *Plocè,* but that in his humble Opinion he shined most in the *Antanaclasis.*

I must not here omit, that a famous University of this Land was formerly very much infested with Punns; but whether or no this might not arise from the Fens and Marshes in which it was situated, and which are now drained, I must leave to the Determination of more skilful Naturalists.

[2] Lancelot Andrewes (1555-1626), one of the divines appointed by James I to make the authorized version of the *Bible*. He became bishop of Winchester in 1619.

[3] The rhetoricians' word for a pun. Paragram, plocè, and antanaclasis are varieties of puns.

After this short History of Punning, one would wonder how it should be so entirely banished out of the Learned World, as it is at present, especially since it had found a Place in the Writings of the most ancient Polite Authors. To account for this, we must consider, that the first Race of Authors, who were the great Heroes in Writing, were destitute of all Rules and Arts of Criticism; and for that Reason, though they excel later Writers in Greatness of Genius, they fall short of them in Accuracy and Correctness. The Moderns cannot reach their Beauties, but can avoid their Imperfections. When the World was furnished with these Authors of the first Eminence, there grew up another Set of Writers, who gained themselves a Reputation by the Remarks which they made on the Words of those who preceded them. It was one of the Employments of these Secondary Authors, to distinguish the several kinds of Wit by Terms of Art, and to consider them as more or less perfect, according as they were founded in Truth. It is no wonder therefore, that even such Authors as *Isocrates, Plato,* and *Cicero,* should have such little Blemishes as are not to be met with in Authors of a much inferior Character, who have written since those several Blemishes were discovered. I do not find that there was a proper Separation made between Punns and true Wit by any of the ancient Authors, except *Quintilian* and *Longinus.* But when this Distinction was once settled, it was very natural for all Men of Sense to agree in it. As for the Revival of this false Wit, it happened about the time of the Revival of Letters; but as soon as it was once detected, it immediately vanished and disappeared. At the same time there is no question; but as it has sunk in one Age and rose in another, it will again recover it self in some distant Period of Time, as Pedantry and Ignorance shall prevail upon Wit and Sense. And, to speak the Truth, I do very much apprehend, by some of the last Winter's Productions, which had their Sets of Admirers, that our Posterity will in a few Years degenerate into a Race of Punnsters: At least, a Man may be very excusable for any Apprehensions of this kind, that has seen *Acrosticks* handed about the Town with great Secrecie and Applause; to which I must also add a little *Epigram* called the *Witches Prayer,* that fell into Verse when it was read either backward or forward, excepting only that it Cursed one way and Blessed the other. When one sees there are actually such Pains-takers among our *British* Wits, who can tell what it may end in? If we must Lash one another, let it be with the manly Strokes of Wit and Satyr; for I am of the old Philosopher's Opinion, That if I must suffer from one or the other, I would rather it should be from the Paw of a Lion, than the Hoof of an Ass. I do not speak this out of any Spirit of Party. There is a most crying Dulness on both Sides. I have seen Tory *Acrosticks* and Whig *Anagrams,* and do not quarrel with either of them, because they are *Whigs* or *Tories,* but because they are *Anagrams* and *Acrosticks.*

But to return to Punning. Having pursued the History of a Punn, from its Original to its Downfal, I shall here define it to be a Conceit arising from the use of two Words that agree in the Sound, but differ in the Sense. The only way therefore to try a Piece of Wit, is to translate it into a different Language: If it bears the Test you may pronouce it true; but if it vanishes in the Experiment you may conclude it to have been a Punn. In short, one may say of a Punn as the Country-man described his Nightingale, that it is *vox & praeterea nihil,* a Sound, and nothing but a Sound. On the contrary, one may represent true Wit by the Description which *Aristinetus* makes of a fine Woman, when she is *dressed* she is Beautiful, when she is *undressed* she is Beautiful: Or, as *Mercerus* has translated it more Emphatically, *Induitur, formosa est: Exuitur, ipsa forma est.*

No. 62   Friday, May 11, 1711.   [Addison]

Scribendi recte Sapere est & principium & fons.[1] — Hor.

Mr. *Lock* has an admirable Reflection upon the Difference of Wit and Judgment, whereby he endeavours to shew the Reason why they are not always the Talents of the same Person. His Words are as follows: *And hence, perhaps, may be given some Reason of that common Observation, That Men who have a great deal of Wit and prompt Memories, have not always the clearest Judgment, or deepest Reason. For Wit lying most in the Assemblage of Ideas, and putting those together with Quickness and Variety, wherein can be found any Resemblance or Congruity, thereby to make up pleasant Pictures and agreeable Visions in the Fancy; Judgment, on the contrary, lies quite on the other Side, In separating carefully one from another, Ideas wherein can be found the least Difference, thereby to avoid being misled by Similitude, and by Affinity to take one thing for another. This is a Way of proceeding quite contrary to Metaphor and Allusion; wherein, for the most Part, lies that Entertainment and Pleasantry of Wit which strikes so lively on the Fancy, and is therefore so acceptable to all People.*

This is, I think, the best and most philosophical Account that I have ever met with of Wit, which generally, though not always, consists in such a Resemblance and Congruity of Ideas as this Author mentions. I shall only add to it, by way of Explanation, That every Resemblance of Ideas is not that which we call Wit, unless it be such an one that gives *Delight* and *Surprize* to the Reader: These two Properties seem essential

[1] "Of good writing the source and fount is wisdom."

189

to Wit, more particularly the last of them. In order therefore that the Resemblance in the Ideas be Wit, it is necessary that the Ideas should not lie too near one another in the Nature of things; for where the Likeness is obvious, it gives no Surprize. To compare one Man's Singing to that of another, or to represent the Whiteness of any Object by that of Milk and Snow, or the Variety of its Colours by those of the Rainbow, cannot be called Wit, unless, besides this obvious Resemblance, there be some further Congruity discovered in the two Ideas that is capable of giving the Reader some Surprize. Thus when a Poet tells us, the Bosom of his Mistress is as white as Snow, there is no Wit in the Comparison; but when he adds, with a Sigh, that it is as cold too, it then grows into Wit. Every Reader's Memory may supply him with innumerable Instances of the same Nature. For this Reason, the Similitudes in Heroick Poets, who endeavour rather to fill the Mind with great Conceptions, than to divert it with such as are new and surprizing, have seldom any thing in them that can be called Wit. Mr. *Lock's* Account of Wit, with this short Explanation, comprehends most of the Species of Wit, as Metaphors, Similitudes, Allegories, Ænigmas, Mottos, Parables, Fables, Dreams, Visions, dramatick Writings, Burlesque, and all the Methods of Allusion: As there are many other Pieces of Wit (how remote soever they may appear at first Sight from the foregoing Description) which upon Examination will be found to agree with it.

As *true Wit* generally consists in this Resemblance and Congruity of Ideas, *false Wit* chiefly consists in the Resemblance and Congruity sometimes of single Letters, as in Anagrams, Chronograms, Lipograms, and Acrosticks: Sometimes of Syllables, as in Ecchos and Doggerel Rhymes: Sometimes of Words, as in Punns and Quibbles; and sometimes of whole Sentences or Poems, cast into the Figures of *Eggs, Axes,* or *Altars.* Nay, some carry the Notion of Wit so far, as to ascribe it even to external Mimickry; and to look upon a Man as an ingenious Person, that can resemble the Tone, Posture, or Face of another.

As *true Wit* consists in the Resemblance of Ideas, and *false Wit* in the Resemblance of Words, according to the foregoing Instances; there is another kind of Wit which consists partly in the Resemblance of Ideas, and partly in the Resemblance of Words; which for Distinction Sake I shall call *mixt Wit.* This Kind of Wit is that which abounds in *Cowley,* more than in any Author that ever wrote. Mr. *Waller* has likewise a great deal of it. Mr. *Dryden* is very sparing in it. *Milton* had a Genius much above it. *Spencer* is in the same class with *Milton.* The *Italians,* even in their Epic Poetry, are full of it. Monsieur *Boileau,* who formed himself upon the Ancient Poets, has every where rejected it with Scorn. If we look after mixt Wit among the *Greek* Writers, we shall find it no where but in the Epigrammatists. There are indeed some Strokes of it in the little Poem ascribed to *Musæus,* which by that, as well as many other Marks, betrays it self to be a modern Composition. If we look into the *Latin* Writers, we find none of this mixt Wit in *Virgil, Lucretius,* or *Catullus;* very little in Horace, but a great deal of it in *Ovid,* and scarce any thing else in *Martial.*

Out of the innumerable Branches of *mixt Wit,* I shall chuse one Instance which may be met with in all the Writers of this Class. The Passion of Love in its Nature has been thought to resemble Fire; for which Reason the Words Fire and Flame are made use of to signifie Love. The witty Poets therefore have taken an Advantage from the doubtful Meaning of the Word Fire, to make an infinite Number of Witticisms. *Cowley* observing the cold Regard of his Mistress's Eyes, and at the same Time their Power of producing Love in him, considers them as Burning-Glasses made of Ice; and finding himself able to live in the greatest Extremities of Love, concludes the Torrid Zone to be habitable. When his Mistress has read his Letter written in Juice of Lemmon by holding it to the Fire, he desires her to read it over a second time by Love's Flames. When she weeps, he wishes it were inward Heat that distilled those Drops from the Limbeck. When she is absent he is beyond eighty, that is, thirty Degrees nearer the Pole than when she is with him. His ambitious Love is a Fire that naturally mounts upwards; his happy Love is the Beams of Heaven, and his unhappy Love Flames of Hell. When it does not let him sleep, it is a Flame thaw sends up no Smoak; when it is opposed by Counsel and Advice, it is a Fire that rages the more by the Wind's blowing upon it. Upon the dying of a Tree in which he had cut his Loves, he observes that his written Flames had burnt up and withered the Tree. When he resolves to give over his Passion, he tells us that one burnt like him for ever dreads the Fire. His Heart is an *Aetna,* that instead of *Vulcan's* Shop encloses *Cupid's* Forge in it. His endeavouring to drown his Love in Wine, is throwing Oil upon the Fire. He would insinuate to his Mistress, that the Fire of Love, like that of the Sun (which produces so many living Creatures) should not only warm but beget. Love in another Place cooks Pleasure at his Fire. Sometimes the Poet's Heart is frozen in every Breast, and sometimes scorched in every Eye. Sometimes he is drowned in Tears, and burnt in Love, like a Ship set on Fire in the Middle of the Sea.

The Reader may observe in every one of these Instances that the Poet mixes the Qualities of Fire with those of Love; and in the same Sentence speaking of it both as a Passion, and as real Fire, surprizes the Reader with those seeming Resemblances or Contradictions that make up all the Wit in this kind of Writing. Mixt Wit therefore is a Composition of Punn and true Wit, and is more or less perfect as the Resemblance lies in the Ideas or in the Words: Its Foundations are laid partly in Falsehood and partly in Truth: Reason puts in her Claim for one Half of it, and Extravagance for the other. The only Province therefore for this kind of Wit, is Epigram, or those little occasional Poems that in their own Nature are nothing else but a Tissue of Epigrams. I cannot conclude this Head of *mixt Wit,* without owning that the admirable Poet out of whom I have taken the Examples of it, had as much true Wit as any Author that ever writ; and indeed all other Talents of an extraordinary Genius.

It may be expected, since I am upon this Subject, that I should take Notice of Mr. *Dryden's* Definition of Wit; which, with all the Deference that is due to the Judgment of so great a Man, is not so properly a Definition of Wit, as of good Writing in general. Wit, as he defines it, is 'a Propriety of Words and Thoughts adapted to the Subject.' If this be a true Definition of Wit, I am apt to think that *Euclid* was the greatest Wit that ever set Pen to Paper: It is certain that never was a greater Propriety of Words and Thoughts adapted to the Subject, than what that Author has made use of in his Elements. I shall only appeal to my Reader, if this Definition agrees with any Notion he has of Wit: If it be a true one, I am sure Mr *Dryden* was not only a better Poet, but a greater Wit than Mr. *Cowley;* and *Virgil* a much more facetious Man than either *Ovid* or *Martial.*

Bouhours, whom I look upon to be the most penetrating of all the *French* Criticks, has taken Pains to shew, That it is impossible for any Thought to be beautiful which is not just, and has not its Foundation in the Nature of Things: That the Basis of all Wit is Truth; and that no Thought can be valuable, of which good Sense is not the Ground-work. *Boileau* has endeavoured to inculcate the same Notion in several Parts of his writings, both in Prose and Verse. This is that natural Way of Writing, that beautiful Simplicity, which we so much admire in the Compositions of the Ancients; and which no Body deviates from, but those who want Strength of Genius to make a Thought shine in its own natural Beauties. Poets who want this Strength of Genius to give that Majestick Simplicity to Nature, which we so much admire in the Works of the Ancients, are forced to hunt after foreign Ornaments, and not to let any Piece of Wit of what Kind soever escape them. I look upon these Writers as *Goths* in Poetry, who, like those in Architecture, not being able to come up to the beautiful Simplicity of the old *Greeks* and *Romans,* have endeavoured to supply its Place with all the Extravagances of an irregular Fancy. Mr. *Dryden* makes a very handsom Observation on *Ovid's* Writing a Letter from *Dido* to *Aeneas,* in the following Words: '*Ovid* (says he, speaking of *Virgil's* Fiction of *Dido* and *Aeneas*) takes it up after him, even in the same Age, and makes an Ancient Heroine of *Virgil's* new-created *Dido;* dictates a Letter for her just before her Death to the ungrateful Fugitive; and, very unluckily for himself, is for measuring a Sword with a Man so much superior in Force to him, on the same Subject. I think I may be Judge of this, because I have translated both. The famous Author of the Art of Love has nothing of his own; he borrows all from a greater Master in his own Profession, and, which is worse, improves nothing which he finds: Nature fails him, and being forced to his old Shift, he has Recourse to Witticism. This passes indeed with his soft Admirers, and gives him the Preference to *Virgil* in their Esteem.'

Were not I supported by so great an Authority as that of Mr. *Dryden,* I should not venture to observe, That the Taste of most of our *English* Poets, as well as Readers, is extremely *Gothick.*[2] He quotes Monsieur *Segrais* for a threefold Distinction of the Readers of Poetry: In the first of which he comprehends the Rabble of Readers, whom he does not treat as such with regard to their Quality, but to their Numbers and the Coarseness of their Taste. His Words are as follow: '*Segrais* has distinguished the Readers of Poetry, according to their Capacity of judging, into three Classes. [He might have said the same of Writers too, if he had pleased.] In the lowest Form he places those whom he calls *Les Petits Esprits,* such things as are our Upper-Gallery Audience in a Play-house; who like nothing but the Husk and Rind of Wit, prefer a Quibble, a Conceit, an Epigram, before solid Sense and elegant Expression: These are Mob-Readers. If *Virgil* and *Martial* stood for Parliament-Men, we know already who would carry it. But though they make the greatest Appearance in the Field, and cry the loudest, the best on 't is they are but a sort of *French* Huguenots, or *Dutch* Boors, brought over in Herds, but not Naturalized; who have not Lands of two Pounds *per Annum* in *Parnassus,*

[2] Compare *The Tatler,* No. 163, n.3., and *The Spectator,* No. 70.

and therefore are not privileged to Poll. Their Authors are of the same Level, fit to represent them on a Mountebank's Stage, or to be Masters of the Ceremonies in a Bear-Garden: Yet these are they who have the most Admirers. But it often happens, to their Mortification, that as their Readers improve their Stock of Sense (as they may by reading better Books, and by Conversation with Men of Judgment) they soon forsake them.'

I must not dismiss this Subject without observing, that as Mr. *Lock* in the Passage above-mentioned has discovered the most fruitful Source of Wit, so there is another of a quite contrary Nature to it, which does likewise branch it self out into several Kinds. For not only the *Resemblance* but the *Opposition* of Ideas does very often produce Wit; as I could shew in several little Points, Turns, and Antitheses, that I may possibly enlarge upon in some future Speculation.

> *Humano Capiti cervicem pictor Equinam*
> *Jungere si velit & varias inducere plumas*
> *Undique collatis membris, ut turpiter atrum*
> *Desinat in piscem mulier formosa superne;*
> *Spectatum admissi risum teneatis, amici?*
> *Credite, Pisones, isti tabulæ fore librum*
> *Persimilem, cujus, velut ægri somnia, venæ*
> *Finguntur species . . .*[1]—Hor.

It is very hard for the Mind to disengage it self from a Subject in which it has been long employed. The Thoughts will be rising of themselves from time to time, tho' we give them no Encouragement; as the Tossings and Fluctuations of the Sea continue several Hours after the Winds are laid.

It is to this that I impute my last Night's Dream or Vision, which formed into one continued Allegory the several Schemes of Wit, whether False, Mixed, or True, that have been the Subject of my late Papers.

Methought I was transported into a Country that was filled with Prodigies and Enchantments, governed by the Goddess of FALSEHOOD, and entitled the *Region of False Wit*. There was nothing in the Fields, the Woods, and the Rivers, that appeared natural. Several of the Trees blossomed in Leaf-Gold,

---

[1] "If a painter chose to join a human head to the neck of a horse, and to spread feathers of many a hue over limbs picked up now here now there, so that what at the top is a lovely woman ends below in a black and ugly fish, could you, my friend, if favored with a private view, refrain from laughing? Believe me, Pisos, quite like such pictures would be a book, whose idle fancies shall be shaped like a sick man's dreams . . ."

some of them produced Bone-Lace, and some of them precious Stones. The Fountains bubbled in an Opera Tune, and were filled with Stags, Wild-Boars, and Mermaids, that lived among the Waters; at the same time that Dolphins and several kinds of Fish played upon the Banks, or took their Pastime in the Meadows. The Birds had many of them golden Beaks, and human Voices. The Flowers perfumed the Air with Smells of Incense, Amber-greese, and Pulvillios;[2] and were so interwoven with one another, that they grew up in Pieces of Embroidery. The Winds were filled with Sighs and Messages of distant Lovers. As I was walking to and fro in this enchanted Wilderness, I could not forbear breaking out into Soliloquies upon the several Wonders which lay before me, when to my great Surprise I found there were artificial Ecchoes in every Walk, that by Repetitions of certain Words which I spoke, agreed with me, or contradicted me, in every thing I said. In the midst of my Conversation with these invisible Companions, I discovered in the Center of a very dark Grove a monstrous Fabrick built after the *Gothick* manner, and covered with innumerable Devices in that barbarous kind of Sculpture. I immediately went up to it, and found it to be a kind of Heathen Temple consecrated to the God of *Dullness.* Upon my Entrance I saw the Deity of the Place dressed in the Habit of a Monk, with a Book in one Hand and a Rattle in the other. Upon his right Hand was *Industry,* with a Lamp burning before her; and on his left *Caprice,* with a Monky sitting on her Shoulder. Before his Feet there stood an *Altar* of a very odd Make, which, as I afterwards found, was shaped in that manner, to comply with the Inscription that surrounded it. Upon the Altar there lay several Offerings of *Axes, Wings,* and *Eggs,* cut in Paper, and inscribed with Verses. The Temple was filled with Votaries, who applied themselves to different Diversions, as their Fancies directed them. In one Part of it I saw a Regiment of *Anagrams,* who were continually in motion, turning to the

---

[2] Perfumed powder, used especially on periwigs.

Right or to the Left, facing about, doubling their Ranks, shifting their Stations, and throwing themselves into all the Figures and Counter-marches of the most changeable and perplexed Exercise.

Not far from these was a Body of *Acrosticks,* made up of very disproportioned Persons. It was disposed into three Columns, the Officers planting themselves in a Line on the left Hand of each Column. The Officers were all of them at least Six Foot high, and made three Rows of very proper Men; but the Common Soldiers, who filled up the Spaces between the Officers were such Dwarfs, Cripples, and Scarecrows, that one could hardly look upon them without laughing. There were behind the *Acrosticks* two or three Files of *Chronograms,* which differed only from the former, as their Officers were equipped (like the Figure of Time) with an Hour-glass in one Hand, and a Scythe in the other, and took their Posts promiscuously among the private Men whom they commanded.

In the Body of the Temple, and before the very Face of the Deity, methoughts I saw the Phantom of *Tryphiodorus* the *Lipogrammatist,* engaged in a Ball with four and twenty Persons, who pursued him by turns thro' all the intricacies and Labyrinths of a Country Dance, without being able to overtake him.

Observing several to be very busie at the Western End of the *Temple,* I enquired into what they were doing, and found there was in that Quarter the great Magazine of *Rebus's.* These were several things of the most different Natures tied up in Bundles, and thrown upon one another in heaps like Faggots. You might behold an Anchor, a Nightrail, and an Hobby-horse bound up together. One of the Workmen seeing me very much surprised, told me, there was an infinite deal of Wit in several of those Bundles, and that he would explain them to me if I pleased: I thanked him for his Civility, but told him I was in very great haste at that time. As I was going out of the Temple, I observed in one Corner of it a Cluster of Men and Women laughing very heartily, and diverting themselves at a Game of *Crambo*. I heard several *double Rhymes* as I passed by them, which raised a great deal of Mirth.

Not far from these was another Set of merry People engaged at a Diversion, in which the whole Jest was to mistake one Person for another. To give Occasion for these ludicrous Mistakes, they were divided into Pairs, every Pair being covered from Head to Foot with the same kind of Dress, though perhaps there was not the least Resemblance in their Faces. By this means an old Man was sometimes mistaken for a Boy, a Woman for a Man, and a Black-a-moor for an *European,* which very often produced great Peals of Laughter. These I guessed to be a Party of *Punns*. But being very desirous to get out of this World of Magick, which had almost turned my Brain, I left the Temple, and crossed over the Fields that lay about it with all the Speed I could make. I was not gone far before I heard the Sound of Trumpets and Alarms, which seemed to proclaim the March of an Enemy; and, as I afterwards found, was in reality what I apprehended it. There appeared at a great Distance a very shining Light, and in the midst of it a Person of a most beautiful Aspect; her Name was TRUTH. On her Right Hand there marched a Male Deity, who bore several Quivers on his Shoulders, and grasped several Arrows in his Hand. His Name was *Wit*. The Approach of these two Enemies filled all the Territories of *False Wit* with an unspeakable Consternation, insomuch that the Goddess of those Regions appeared in Person upon her Frontiers, with the several inferior Deities, and the different Bodies of Forces which I had before seen in the Temple, who were now drawn up in Array, and prepared to give their Foes a warm Reception. As the March of the Enemy was very slow, it gave time to the several Inhabitants who bordered upon the *Regions of* FALSEHOOD to draw their Forces into a Body, with a Design to stand upon their Guard as Neuters, and attend the Issue of the Combat.

I must here inform my Reader, that the Frontiers of the Enchanted Region, which I have before described, were inhabited by the Species of MIXED WIT, who made a very odd

Appearance when they were mustered together in an Army. There were Men whose Bodies were stuck full of Darts, and Women whose Eyes were Burning-glasses: Men that had Hearts of Fire, and Women that had Breasts of Snow. It would be endless to describe several Monsters of the like Nature, that composed this great Army; which immediately fell asunder, and divided it self into two Parts; the one half throwing themselves behind the Banners of TRUTH, and the others behind those of FALSEHOOD.

The Goddess of FALSEHOOD was of a Gigantick Stature, and advanced some Paces before the Front of her Army; but as the dazling Light, which flowed from TRUTH, began to shine upon her, she faded insensibly; insomuch that in a little space she looked rather like an huge Phantom, than a real Substance. At length, as the Goddess of TRUTH approached still nearer to her, she fell away entirely, and vanished amidst the Brightness of her Presence; so that there did not remain the least Trace or Impression of her Figure in the Place where she had been seen.

As at the rising of the Sun the Constellations grow thin, and the Stars go out one after another, till the whole Hemisphere is extinguished; such was the vanishing of the Goddess; and not only of the Goddess her self, but of the whole Army that attended her, which sympathized with their Leader, and shrunk into Nothing, in proportion as the Goddess disappeared. At the same time the whole Temple sunk, the Fish betook themselves to the Streams, and the wild Beasts to the Woods; the Fountains recovered their Murmurs, the Birds their Voices, the Trees their Leaves, the Flowers their Scents, and the whole Face of Nature its true and genuine Appearance. Tho' I still continued asleep, I fancied my self as it were awakened out of a Dream, when I saw this Region of Prodigies restored to Woods and Rivers, Fields and Meadows.

Upon the Removal of that wild Scene of Wonders, which had very much disturbed my Imagination, I took a full Survey of the Persons of WIT and TRUTH, for indeed it was impossible to look upon the first, without seeing the other at the same time. There was behind them a strong and compact Body of Figures. The Genius of *Heroic Poetry* appeared with a Sword in her Hand, and a Lawrel on her Head. *Tragedy* was crowned with Cypress, and covered with Robes dipped in Blood. *Satyr* had Smiles in her Look, and a Dagger under her Garment. *Rhetorick* was known by her Thunderbolt; and *Comedy* by her Mask. After several other Figures, *Epigram* marched up in the Rear, who had been posted there at the Beginning of the Expedition, that he might not revolt to the Enemy, whom he was suspected to favour in his Heart. I was very much awed and delighted with the Appearance of the God of *Wit;* there was something so amiable and yet so piercing in his Looks, as inspired me at once with Love and Terror. As I was gazing on him to my unspeakable Joy, he took a Quiver of Arrows from his Shoulder, in order to make me a Present of it; but as I was reaching out my Hand to receive it of him, I knocked it against a Chair, and by that means awaked.

No. 65   Tuesday, May 15, 1711.   [Steele]

. . . Demetri teque Tigelli,
Discipularum inter Jubeo plorare cathedras. [1] — Hor.

After having at large explained what Wit is, and described
the false Appearances of it, all that Labour seems but an useless Enquiry, without some Time be spent in considering the
Application of it. The Seat of Wit, when one speaks as a Man
of the Town and the World, is the Play-house; I shall therefore fill this Paper with Reflections upon the Use of it in that
Place. The Application of Wit in the Theatre has as strong
an Effect upon the Manners of our Gentlemen, as the Taste
of it has upon the Writings of our Authors. It may, perhaps,
look like a very presumptuous Work, though not Foreign from
the Duty of a SPECTATOR, to tax the Writings of such as have
long had the general Applause of a Nation: But I shall always
make Reason, Truth, and Nature the Measures of Praise and
Dispraise; if those are for me, the Generality of Opinion is
of no Consequence against me; if they are against me, the general Opinion cannot long support me.

Without further Preface, I am going to look into some
of our most applauded Plays, and see whether they deserve
the Figure they at present bear in the Imaginations of Men,
or not.

In reflecting upon these Works, I shall chiefly dwell upon
that for which each respective Play is most celebrated. The

---

[1] "But you, Demetrius, and you, Tigellius, I bid you go whine amidst the easy
chairs of your pupils in petticoats."

202

present Paper shall be employed upon Sir *Foplin Flutter.* [2] The received Character of this Play is, That it is the Pattern of Gentile Comedy. *Dorimant* and *Harriot* are the Characters of greatest Consequence, and if these are Low and Mean, the Reputation of the Play is very Unjust.

I will take for granted, that a fine Gentleman should be honest in his Actions, and refined in his Language. Instead of this, our Hero, in this Piece, is a direct Knave in his Designs, and a Clown in his Language. *Bellair* is his Admirer and Friend, in return for which, because he is forsooth a greater Wit than his said Friend, he thinks it reasonable to perswade him to Marry a young Lady, whose Virtue, he thinks, will last no longer than 'till she is a Wife, and then she cannot but fall to his Share, as he is an irresistible fine Gentleman. The Falsehood to Mrs. *Loveit,* and the Barbarity of Triumphing over her Anguish for losing him, is another Instance of his Honesty, as well as his good Nature. As to his fine Language; he calls the Orange Woman, who, it seems, is inclined to grow Fat, *An Over-grown Jade, with a Flasket of Guts before her;* and salutes her with a pretty Phrase of, *How now, Double Tripe?* Upon the Mention of a Country Gentlewoman, whom he knows nothing of, (no one can imagine why) he *will lay his Life she is some awkward, ill-fashioned Country Toad, who not having above four Dozen of Hairs on her Head, has adorned her Baldness with a large white Fruz, that she may look Sparkishly in the Fore-front of the King's Box at an old Play.* Unnatural Mixture of senseless Common Place!

As to the Generosity of his Temper, he tells his poor Footman, *If he did not wait better*—he would turn him away, in the insolent Phrase of, *I'll Uncase you.*

Now for Mrs. *Harriot:* She laughs at Obedience to an absent Mother, whose Tenderness *Busie* describes to be so exquisite, *that she is so pleased with finding* Harriot *again,*

[2] *The Man of Mode, or Sir Fopling Flutter,* by Sir George Etherege (1635?-1691?).

that she cannot chide her for being out of the Way. This Witty Daughter, and Fine Lady, has so little Respect for this good Woman, that she Ridicules her Air in taking Leave, and cries, *In what Struggle is my poor Mother yonder? See, see, her Head tottering, her Eyes staring, and her under Lip trembling.* But all this is atoned for, because *she has more Wit than is usual in her Sex, and as much Malice, tho' she is as wild as you would wish her, and has a Demureness in her Looks that makes it so surprising!* Then to recommend her as a fit Spouse for his Hero, the Poet makes her speak her Sense of Marriage very ingeniously. *I think,* says she, *I might be brought to endure him, and that is all a reasonable Woman should expect in an Husband.* It is, methinks, unnatural that we are not made to understand how she that was bred under a silly pious old Mother, that would never trust her out of her Sight, came to be so Polite.

It cannot be denied, but that the Negligence of every thing, which engages the Attention of the sober and valuable Part of Mankind, appears very well drawn in this Piece: But it is denied, that is is necessary to the Character of a Fine Gentleman, that he should in that manner Trample upon all Order and Decency. As for the Character of *Dorimant,* it is more of a Coxcomb than that of *Foplin.* He says of one of his Companions, that a good Correspondence between them is their mutual Interest. Speaking of that Friend, he declares, their being much together *makes the Women think the better of his Understanding, and judge more favourably of my Reputation. It makes him pass upon some for a Man of very good Sense, and me upon others for a very civil Person.*

This whole celebrated Piece is a perfect Contradiction to good Manners, good Sense, and common Honesty; and as there is nothing in it but what is built upon the Ruin of Virtue and Innocence, according to the Notion of Merit in this Comedy, I take the Shooe-maker to be, in reality, the Fine Gentleman of the Play: For it seems he is an Atheist, if we may depend upon his Character as given by the Orange-Woman, who is her self far from being the lowest in the Play. She says of a Fine Man, who is *Dorimant's* Companion. There *is not such another Heathen in the Town, except the Shooe-maker.* His Pretention to be the Hero of the *Drama* appears still more in his own Description of his way of Living with his Lady. *There is,* says he, *never a Man in Town lives more like a Gentleman with his Wife than I do; I never mind her Motions; she never enquires into mine. We speak to one another civily, hate one another heartily; and because it is Vulgar to Lye and Soak together, we have each of us our several Settle-Bed.* That of *Soaking together* is as good as if *Dorimant* had spoken it himself; and, I think, since he puts Human Nature in as ugly a Form as the Circumstance will bear, and is a stanch Unbeliever, he is very much Wronged in having no part of the good Fortune bestowed in the last Act.

To speak plainly of this whole Work, I think nothing but being lost to a Sense of Innocence and Virtue can make any one see this Comedy, without observing more frequent Occasion to move Sorrow and Indignation, than Mirth and Laughter. At the same time I allow it to be Nature, but it is Nature in its utmost Corruption and Degeneracy.

No. 66   Wednesday, May 16, 1711.   [Steele]

Motus Doceri gaudet Ionicos
Matura Virgo, & fingitur Artibus
Jam nunc, & incestos amores
De Tenero meditatur Ungui.[1] — Hor.

The two following Letters are upon a Subject of very great
Importance, tho' expressed without any Air of Gravity.

'To the SPECTATOR

Sir,
I take the Freedom of asking your Advice in Behalf of
a Young Country Kinswoman of mine who is lately come
to Town, and under my Care for her Education. She is very
pretty, but you can't imagine how unformed a Creature it is.
She comes to my Hands just as Nature left her, half finished,
and without any acquired Improvements. When I look on her
I often think of the *Bell Sauvage* mentioned in one of your
Papers. Dear *Mr.* SPECTATOR, help me to make her comprehend
the visible Graces of Speech, and the dumb Eloquence of Motion; for she is at present a perfect Stranger to both. She knows
no Way to express her self but by her Tongue, and that always
to signify her Meaning. Her Eyes serve her yet only to see with,
and she is utterly a Foreigner to the Language of Looks and
Glances. In this I fancy you could help her better than any
Body. I have bestowed two Months in teaching her to Sigh
when she is not concerned, and to Smile when she is not

[1] "The maiden early takes delight in learning Grecian dances, and trains herself in coquetry even now, and plans unholy amours with passion unrestrained."
206

pleased; and am ashamed to own she makes little or no Improvement. Then she is no more able now to walk, than she was to go at a Year old. By Walking you will easily know I mean that regular but easy Motion, which gives our Person so irresistible a Grace as if we moved to Musick,[2] and is a kind of disengaged Figure, or, if I may so speak, recitative Dancing. But the want of this I cannot blame in her, for I find she has no Ear, and means nothing by Walking but to change her Place. I could pardon too her Blushing, if she knew how to carry her self in it, and if it did not manifestly injure her Complexion.

They tell me you are a Person who have seen the World, and are a Judge of fine Breeding; which makes me ambitious of some Instructions from you for her Improvement: Which when you have favoured me with, I shall further advise with you about the Disposal of this fair Forrester in Marriage; for I will make it no Secret to you, that her Person and Education are to be her Fortune.

I am, Sir,
Your very Humble Servant,
CELIMENE.'

'Sir,
Being employed by *Celimene* to make up and send to you her Letter, I make bold to recommend the Case therein mentioned to your Consideration, because she and I happen to differ a little in our Notions. I, who am a rough Man, am afraid the young Girl is in a fair Way to be spoiled: Therefore pray, Mr. SPECTATOR, let us have your Opinion of this fine thing called *Fine Breeding;* for I am afraid it differs too much from that plain thing called *Good Breeding.*

Your most humble Servant.'

The general Mistake among us in the Educating our Children, is, That in our Daughters we take Care of their Persons

---

[2] Compare Pope's couplet (*An Essay on Criticism,* II, 362-363):
       True ease in writing comes from art, not chance,
       As those move easiest who have learned to dance.

and neglect their Minds; in our Sons, we are so intent upon adorning their Minds, that we wholly neglect their Bodies. It is from this that you shall see a young Lady celebrated and admired in all the Assemblies about Town; when her elder Brother is afraid to come into a Room. From this ill Management it arises, That we frequently observe a Man's Life is half spent before he is taken Notice of; and a Woman in the Prime of her Years is out of Fashion and neglected. The Boy I shall consider upon some other Occasion, and at present stick to the Girl: And I am the more inclined to this, because I have several Letters which complain to me that my Female Readers have not understood me for some Days last past, and take themselves to be unconcerned in the present Turn of my Writings. When a Girl is safely brought from her Nurse, before she is capable of forming one simple Notion of any thing in Life, she is delivered to the Hands of her Dancing-Master; and with a Collar round her Neck, the pretty wild Thing is taught a fantastical Gravity of Behaviour, and forced to a particular Way of holding her Head, heaving her Breast, and moving with her whole Body; and all this under Pain of never having an Husband, if she steps, looks, or moves awry. This gives the young Lady wonderful Workings of Imagination, what is to pass between her and this Husband, that she is every Moment told of, and for whom she seems to be educated. Thus her Fancy is engaged to turn all her Endeavours to the Ornament of her Person, as what must determine her Good anf Ill in this Life; and she naturally thinks, if she is tall enough, she is wise enough for any thing for which her Education makes her think she is designed. To make her an agreeable Person is the main Purpose of her Parents; to that is all their Cost, to that all their Care directed; and from this general Folly of Parents we owe our present numerous Race of Coquets. These Reflections puzzle me, when I think of giving my Advice on the Subject of managing the wild Thing mentioned in the Letter of my Correspondent. But sure there is a middle Way to be followed; the Management of a young Lady's Person is not to be overlooked, but the Erudition of her Mind is much more to be regarded. According as this is managed, you will see the Mind follow the Appetites of the Body, or the Body express the Virtues of the Mind.

Cleomira dances with all the Elegance of Motion imaginable; but her Eyes are so chastised with the Simplicity and Innocence of her Thoughts, that she raises in her Beholders Admiration and good Will, but no loose Hope or wild Imagination. The true Art in this Case is, To make the Mind and Body improve together; and if possible, to make Gesture follow Thought, and not let Thought be employed upon Gesture.

Hic segetes, illic veniunt felicius uvæ;
Arborei fœtus alibi, atque injussa virescunt
Gramina. Nonne vides, croceos ut Tmolus odores,
India mittit ebur, molles sua thura Sabæi?
At Chalybes nudi ferrum, virosaque Pontus
Castorea, Eliadum palmas Epirus equarum?
Continuo has leges æternaque fœdera certis
Imposuit Natura locis . . .[1] — Virg.

There is no Place in the Town which I so much love to frequent as the *Royal Exchange.* It gives me a secret Satisfaction, and, in some measure, gratifies my Vanity, as I am an *Englishman,* to see so rich an Assembly of Country-men and Foreigners consulting together upon the private Business of Mankind, and making this Metropolis a kind of *Emporium* for the whole Earth. I must confess I look upon High-Change to be a great Council, in which all considerable Nations have their Representatives. Factors in the Trading World are what Ambassadors are in the Pollitick World; they negotiate Affairs, conclude Treaties, and maintain a good Correspondence between those wealthy Societies of Men that are divided from one another by Seas and Oceans, or live on the different Extremities of a Continent. I have often been pleased to hear Disputes ad-

[1] "Here corn, there grapes spring more luxuriantly; elsewhere young trees shoot up, and grasses unbidden. See you not, how Tmolus sends us saffron fragrance, India her ivory, the soft Sabaeans their frankincense; but the naked Chalybes give us iron, Pontus the strong-smelling beaver's oil, and Epirus the Olympian victories of her mares? From the first, Nature laid these laws and eternal covenants on certain lands."

justed between an Inhabitant of *Japan* and an Alderman of *London,* or to see a Subject of the *Great Mogul* entering into a League with one of the *Czar* of *Muscovy.* I am infinitely delighted in mixing with these several Ministers of Commerce, as they are distinguished by their different Walks and different Languages: Sometimes I am justled among a Body of *Armenians:* Sometimes I am lost in a Crowd of *Jews;* and sometimes make one in a Groupe of *Dutch-men.* I am a *Dane, Swede,* or *Frenchman* at different times, or rather fancy my self like the old Philosopher,[2] who upon being asked what Countryman he was, replied, That he was a Citizen of the World.

Though I very frequently visit this busie Multitude of People, I am known to no Body there but my Friend Sir ANDREW who often smiles upon me as he sees me bustling in the Croud, but at the same time connives at my Presence without taking any further Notice of me. There is indeed a Merchant of *Egypt,* who just knows me by sight, having formerly remitted me some Mony to *Grand Cairo;* but as I am not versed in the Modern *Coptick,* our Conferences go no further than a Bow and a Grimace.

This grand Scene of Business gives me an infinite Variety of solid and substantial Entertainments. As I am a great Lover of Mankind, my Heart naturally overflows with Pleasure at the Sight of a prosperous and happy Multitude, insomuch that at many publick Solemnities I cannot forbear expressing my Joy with Tears that have stolen down my Cheeks. For this Reason I am wonderfully delighted to see such a Body of Men thriving in their own private Fortunes, and at the same time promoting the Publick Stock; or in other Words, raising Estates for their own Families, by bringing into their Country whatever is wanting, and carrying out of it whatever is superfluous.

Nature seems to have taken a particular Care to dissemi-

[2] Diogenes.

nate her Blessings among the different Regions of the World, with an Eye to this mutual Intercourse and Traffick among Mankind, that the Natives of the several Parts of the Globe might have a kind of Dependance upon one another, and be united together by their common Interest.[3] Almost every *Degree* produces something peculiar to it. The Food often grows in one Country, and the Sauce in another. The Fruits of *Portugal* are corrected by the Products of *Barbadoes:* The Infusion of a *China* Plant sweetnd with the Pith of an *Indian* Cane: The *Philippick* Islands give a Flavour to our *European* Bowls. The single Dress of a Woman of Quality is often the Product of an Hundred Climates.[4] The Muff and the Fan come together from the different Ends of the Earth. The Scarf is sent from the Torrid Zone, and the Tippet from beneath the Pole. The Brocade Petticoat rises out of the Mines of *Peru,* and the Diamond Necklace out of the Bowels of *Indostan.*

If we consider our own Country in its natural Prospect, without any of the Benefits and Advantages of Commerce, what a barren uncomfortable Spot of Earth falls to our Share! Natural Historians tell us, that no Fruit grows originally among us, besides Hips and Haws, Acorns and Pig Nutts, with other Delicacies of the like Nature; That our climate of it self, and without the Assistances of Art, can make no further Advances towards a Plumb than to a Sloe, and carries an Apple to no greater a Perfection than a Crab: That or Melons, our Peaches, our Figs, our Apricots, and Cherries, are Strangers among us, imported in different Ages, and naturalized in our *English* Gardens; and that they would all degenerate and fall away into the Trash of our own Country, if they were wholly neglected by the Planter, and left to the Mercy of our Sun and Soil. Nor has Traffick more enriched our Vegetable World, than it has improved the whole Face of Nature among us. Our Ships are

[3] Compare Pope's *Windsor Forest,* ll. 385-400.
[4] Compare Pope's *The Rape of the Lock,* I, 129-136.

laden with the Harvest of every Climate: Our Tables are stored with Spices, and Oils, and Wines: Our Rooms are filled with Pyramids of *China,* and adorned with the Workmanship of *Japan:* Our Morning's-Draught comes to us from the remotest Corners of the Earth: We repair our Bodies by the Drugs of *America,* and repose our selves under *Indian* Canopies. My Friend Sir ANDREW calls the Vineyards of *France* our Gardens: the Spice-Islands our Hot-Beds; the *Persians* our Silk-Weavers, and the *Chinese* our Potters. Nature indeed furnishes us with bare Necessaries of Life, but Traffick gives us a great Variety of what is Useful, and at the same time supplies us with every thing that is Convenient and Ornamental. Nor is it the least Part of this our Happiness that whilst we enjoy the remotest Products of the North and Soth, we are free from those Extremities of Weather which give them Birth; That our Eyes are refreshed with the green Fields of *Britain,* at the same time that our Palates are feasted with Fruits that rise between the Tropicks.

For these Reasons there are not more useful Members in a Commonwealth than Merchants. They knit Mankind together in a mutual Intercourse of good Offices, distribute the Gifts of Nature, find Work for the Poor, add Wealth to the Rich, and Magnificence to the Great. Our *English* Merchant converts the Tin of his own Country into Gold, and exchanges his Wool for Rubies. The *Mahometans* are cloathed in our *British* Manufacture, and the Inhabitants of the Frozen Zone warmed with the Fleeces of our Sheep.

When I have been upon the *'Change,* I have often fancied one of our old Kings standing in Person, where he is represented in Effigy, and looking down upon the wealthy Concourse of People with which that Place is every Day filled. In this Case, how would he be surprized to hear all the Languages of *Europe* spoken in this little Spot of his former Dominions, and to see so many private Men, who in his Time would have been the Vassals of some powerful Baron, Negotiating like

Princes for greater Sums of Mony than were formerly to be met with in the Royal Treasury! Trade, without enlarging the *British* Territories, has given us a kind of additional Empire: It has multiplied the Number of the Rich, made our Landed Estates infinitely more Valuable than they were formerly, and added to them an Accession of other Estates as valuable as the Lands themselves.

Interdum vulgus rectum videt. [1]—Hor.

When I travelled, I took a particular Delight in hearing the Songs and Fables that are come from Father to Son, and are most in vogue among the common People of the Countries through which I passed; for it is impossible that any thing should be universally tasted and approved by a Multitude, tho' they are only the Rabble of a Nation, which hath not in it some peculiar Aptness to please and gratify the Mind of Man. Human Nature is the same in all reasonable Creatures; and whatever falls in with it, will meet with Admirers amongst Readers of all Qualities and Conditions. *Moliere,* as we are told by Monsieur *Boileau,* used to read all his Comedies to an old Woman who was his House-keeper, [2] as she sat with him at her Work by the Chimney-Corner; and could fortel the Success of his Play in the Theatre, from the Reception it met at his Fire-Side: For he tells us the Audience always followed the old Woman, and never failed to laugh in the same Place.

I know nothing which more shews the essential and inherent Perfection of Simplicity of Thought, above that which I call the Gothick Manner in Writing, than this, that the first pleases all Kinds of Palates, and the latter only such as have formed to themselves a wrong artificial Taste upon little fanciful Authors and Writers of Epigram. *Homer, Virgil,* or *Milton,* so far as the Language of their Poems is understood, will

[1] "At times the public sees aright."
[2] A parallel anecdote is told by Swift of Lord Falkland in *A Letter to a Young Gentleman Lately Entered into Holy Orders.*

please a Reader of plain common Sense, who would neither relish nor comprehend an Epigram of *Martial,* or a Poem of *Cowley:* So, on the contrary, an ordinary Song or Ballad that is the Delight of the common People, cannot fail to please all such Readers as are not unqualified for the Entertainment by their Affectation or Ignorance; and the Reason is plain, because the same Paintings of Nature which recommend it to the most ordinary Readers, will appear Beautiful to the most refined.

The old Song of *Chevy-Chase* is the favourite Ballad of the common People of *England;* and *Ben. Johnson* used to say he had rather have been the Author of it than of all his Works. Sir *Philip Sidney* in his Discourse of Poetry speaks of it in the following Words; *I never heard the old Song of* Piercy *and* Douglas, *that I found not my Heart more moved than with a Trumpet; and yet it is sung by some blind Crowder with no rougher Voice than rude Stile; which being so evil apparelled in the Dust and Cobweb of that uncivil Age, what would it work trimmed in the gorgeous Eloquence of* Pindar? For my own Part, I am so professed an Admirer of this antiquated Song, that I shall give my Reader a Critick upon it, without any further Apology for so doing.

The greatest Modern Criticks have laid it down as a Rule, That an Heroick Poem should be founded upon some important Precept of Morality, adapted to the Constitution of the Country in which the Poet writes. *Homer* and *Virgil* have formed their Plans in this View. As *Greece* was a Collection of many Governments, who suffered very much among themselves, and gave the *Persian* Emperor, who was their common Enemy, many Advantages over them by their mutual Jealousies and Animosities, *Homer,* in order to establish among them an Union, which was so necessary for their Safety, grounds his Poem upon the Discords of the several *Grecian* Princes who were engaged in a Confederacy against an *Asiatick* Prince, and the several Advantages which the Enemy gained by such their

Discords. At the Time the Poem we are now treating of was written, the Dissentions of the Barons, who were then so many petty Princes, ran very high, whether they quarrelled among themselves, or with their Neighbours, and produced unspeakable Calamities to the Country: The Poet, to deter Men from such unnatural Contentions, describes a bloody Battel and dreadful Scene of Death, occasioned by the mutual Feuds which reigned in the Families of an *English* and *Scotch* Nobleman. That he designed this for the Instruction of his Poem, we may learn from his four last Lines, in which, after the Example of the modern Tragedians, he draws from it a Precept for the Benefit of his Readers.

> *God save the King, and bless the Land*
> *In Plenty, Joy, and Peace;*
> *And grant henceforth that foul Debate*
> *'Twixt Noblemen may cease.*

The next Point observed by the greatest Heroic Poets, hath been to celebrate Persons and Actions which do Honour to their Country: Thus *Virgil's* Hero was the Founder of *Rome,* *Homer's* a Prince of *Greece;* and for this Reason *Valerius Flaccus* and *Statius,* who were both *Romans,* might be justly derided for having chosen the Expedition of the *Golden Fleece* and the *Wars of Thebes,* for the Subjects of their Epic Writings.

The Poet before us, has not only found out an Hero in his own Country, but raises the Reputation of it by several beautiful Incidents. The *English* are the first who take the Field, and the last who quit it. The *English* bring only Fifteen hundred to the Battel, the *Scotch* Two thousand. The *English* keep the Field with Fifty three: The *Scotch* retire with Fifty five: All the rest on each Side being slain in Battel. But the most remarkable Circumstance of this Kind is the different Manner in which the *Scotch* and *English* Kings receive the News

of this Fight, and of the great Mens Deaths who commanded
in it.

> *This News was brought to* Edinburgh,
>   *Where* Scotland's *King did reign,*
> *That brave Earl* Douglas *suddenly*
>   *Was with an Arrow slain.*
>
> *O heavy News, King* James *did say,*
>   Scotland *can Witness be,*
> *I have not any Captain more*
>   *Of such Account as he.*
>
> *Like Tydings to King* Henry *came*
>   *Within as short a Space,*
> *That* Piercy *of* Northumberland
>   *Was slain in* Chevy-Chace.
>
> *Now God be with him, said our King,*
>   *Sith 'twill no better be,*
> *I trust I have within my Realm*
>   *Five hundred as good as he.*
>
> *Yet shall not* Scot *nor* Scotland *say*
>   *But I will Vengeance take,*
> *And be revenged on them all*
>   *For brave Lord* Piercy's *sake.*
>
> *This Vow full well the King perform'd*
>   *After on* Humble-down,
> *In one Day Fifty Knights were slain*
>   *With Lords of great Renown.*
>
> *And of the rest of small Account*
>   *Did many Thousands dye,* &c.

At the same Time that our Poet shews a laudable Partiality

to his Country-men, he represents the *Scots* after a Manner not unbecoming so bold and brave a People.

> *Earl* Douglas *on a milk-white Steed,*
> *Most like a Baron bold,*
> *Rode foremost of the Company*
> *Whose Armour shone like Gold.*

His Sentiments and Actions are every Way suitable to an Hero. One of us two, says he, must dye: I am an Earl as well as your self, so that you can have no Pretence for refusing the Combat: However, says he, 'tis Pity, and indeed would be a Sin, that so many innocent Men should perish for our Sakes, rather let you and I end our Quarrel in single Fight.

> *E'er thus I will out-braved be,*
> *One of us two shall dye:*
> *I know thee well, an Earl thou art,*
> *Lord* Piercy, *so am I.*

> *But trust me,* Piercy, *Pity it were,*
> *And great Offence, to kill*

> *Any of these our harmless Men,*
> *For they have done no Ill.*

> *Let thou and I the Battel try,*
> *And set our Men aside;*
> *Accurst be he, Lord* Piercy *said,*
> *By whom this is deny'd.*

When these brave Men had distinguished themselves in the Battel and in single Combat with each other, in the Midst of a generous Parly, full of heroic Sentiments, the *Scotch* Earl falls; and with his Dying Words encourages his Men to revenge his Death, representing to them, as the most bitter Circumstance of it, that his Rival saw him fall.

> With that there came an Arrow keen
>   Out of an English bow,
> Which struck Earl Douglas to the Heart
>   A deep and deadly Blow.
>
> Who never spoke more Words than these,
>   Fight on my merry Men all;
> For why, my Life is at an End,
>   Lord Piercy sees my fall.

Merry Men, in the Language of those Times, is no more than a chearful Word for Companions and Fellow-Soldiers. A passage in the Eleventh Book of *Virgil's Aeneids* is very much to be admired, where *Camilla* in her last agonies, instead of weeping over the Wound she had received, as one might have expected from a Warrior of her Sex, considers only (like the Hero of whom we are now speaking) how the Battel should be continued after her Death.

> *Tum sic expirans,* &c.
> A gathering Mist o'erclouds her chearful Eyes;
> And from her Cheeks the rosy colour flies.
> Then, turns to her, whom, of her Female Train,
> She trusted most, and thus she speaks with Pain.
> Acca, 'tis past! He swims before my Sight,
> Inexorable Death; and claims his Right.
> Bear my last Words to Turnus, fly with speed,
> And bid him timely to my Charge succeed:
> Repel the Trojans, and the Town relieve:
> Farewell. . . .

Turnus did not die in so Heroic a Manner; tho' our Poet seems to have had his eye upon *Turnus's* Speech in the last Verse.

Lord Piercy *sees my Fall.*

...Vicisti, & victum tendere palmas
Ausonii videre...

Earl *Piercy's* Lamentation over his Enemy is generous, beautiful, and passionate; I must only caution the Reader not to let the Simplicity of the Stile, which one may well pardon in so old a Poet, prejudice him against the Greatness of the Thought.

> *Then leaving Life Earl* Piercy *took*
> *   The dead Man by the Hand,*
> *And said, Earl* Douglas *for thy Life*
> *   Would I had lost my Land.*
>
> *O Christ! My very Heart doth bleed*
> *   With Sorrow for thy Sake;*
> *For sure a more renowned Knight*
> *   Mischance did never take.*

That beautiful Line *Taking the dead Man by the Hand,* will put the Reader in Mind of *Æneas's* Behaviour towards *Lausus,* whom he himself had Slain as he came to the Rescue of his aged Father.

> *At vero ut vultum vidit morientis, & ora,*
> *Ora modis Anchisiades pallentia miris:*
> *Ingemuit, miserans graviter, dextramque tetendit, &c.*
>
> *The pious Prince beheld young* Lausus *dead;*
> *He griev'd, he wept; then grasp'd his Hand, and said,*
> *Poor hapless Youth! What Praises can be paid*
> *To Worth so great!...*

I shall take another Opportunity to consider the other Parts of this old Song.

No. 75   Saturday, May 26, 1711.   [Steele]

Omnis Aristippum decuit color & status & res.[1]—Hor.

It was with some Mortification that I suffered the Raillery of
a Fine Lady of my Acquaintance, for Calling, in one of my
Papers,[2] *Dorimant* a Clown. She was so unmerciful as to take
Advantage of my invincible Taciturnity, and on that occasion,
with great Freedom to consider the Air, the Height, the Face,
the Gesture of him who could pretend to Judge so arrogantly
of Gallantry. She is full of Motion, Janty and lively in her Impertinence, and one of those that commonly pass, among the
Ignorant, for Persons who have a great deal of Humour. She
had the Play of Sir *Fopling* in her Hand, and after she had said
it was happy for her there was not so charming a Creature as
Dorimant now living, she began with a Theatrical Tone of
Voice to read, by way of Triumph over me, some of his Speeches. *'Tis she, that lovely Hair, that easie Shape, those wanton
Eyes, and all those melting Charms about her Mouth, which*
Medley *spoke of; I'll follow the Lottery, and put in for a Prize
with my Friend* Bell-air.

> *In Love the Victors from the Vanquish'd fly;*
> *They fly that wound, and they pursue that dye.*[3]

Then turning over the Leaves, she reads alternately, and speaks.

> *And you and* Loveit *to her Cost shall find,*
> *I fathom all the Depths of Womankind.*

[1] "To Aristippus every form of life was fitting, every condition and circumstance."
[2] No. 65, which Steele had devoted to *The Man of Mode* on May 15.
[3] *The Man of Mode,* III iii.

222

Oh the Fine Gentleman! But here, continues she, is the Passage I admire most, where he begins to Teize *Loveit,* and Mimick Sir *Fopling.* Oh the pretty Satyr, in his resolving to be a Coxcomb to please, since Noise and Nonsense have such powerful Charms!

> *I, that I may Successful prove,*
> *Transform my self to what you love.* [4]

Then how like a Man of the Town, so Wild and Gay is that!

> *The Wise will find a Difference in our Fate,*
> *You Wed a Woman, I a good Estate.* [5]

It would have been a very wild Endeavour for a Man of my Temper to offer any Opposition to so nimble a Speaker as my Fair Enemy is, but her Discourse gave me very many Reflections, when I had left her Company. Among others, I could not but consider, with some Attention, the false Impressions the generality (the Fair Sex more especially) have of what should be intended, when they say a *Fine Gentleman;* and could not help revolving that Subject in my Thoughts, and settling, as it were, an Idea of that Character in my own Imagination.

No Man ought to have the Esteem of the rest of the World, for any Actions which are disagreeable to those Maxims which prevail, as the Standards of Behaviour, in the Country wherein he lives. What is opposite to the eternal Rules of Reason and good Sense, must be excluded from any Place in the Carriage of a Well-bred Man. I did not, I confess, explain my self enough on this Subject, when I called *Dorimant* a Clown, and made it an Instance of it, that he called the *Orange Wench, Double-Tripe:* I should have shewed, that Humanity obliges a Gentleman to give no Part of Humankind Reproach, for what

---

[4] *The Man of Mode,* V, i.
[5] *The Man of Mode,* IV, ii.

they, whom they Reproach, may possibly have in Common with the most Virtuous and Worthy amongst us. When a Gentleman speaks Coarsly, he has dressed himself Clean to no purpose: The Cloathing of our Minds certainly ought to be regarded before that of our Bodies. To betray in a Man's Talk a corrupted Imagination, is a much greater Offence against the Conversation of Gentlemen, than any Negligence of Dress imaginable. But this Sense of the Matter is so far from being received among People even of Condition, that *Vocifer* passes for a Fine Gentleman. He is Loud, Haughty, Gentle, Soft, Lewd, and Obsequious by turns, just as a little Understanding and great Impudence prompt him at the present Moment. He passes among the Silly Part of our Women for a Man of Wit, because he is generally in Doubt. He Contradicts with a Shrug, and confutes with a certain Sufficiency, in professing such or such a Thing is above his Capacity. What makes his Character the pleasanter is, that he is a professed Deluder of Women; and because the empty Coxcomb has no Regard to any thing that is of it self Sacred and Inviolable, I have heard an unmarried Lady of Fortune say, it is a Pity so fine a Gentleman as *Vocifer* is so great an Atheist. The Crowds of such inconsiderable Creatures that infest all Places of Assembling, every Reader will have in his Eye from his own Observation; but would it not be worth considering what Sort of Figure a Man who formed himself upon those Principles among us, which are agreeable to the Dictates of Honour and Religion, would make in the familiar and ordinary Occurrences of Life?

I hardly have observed any one fill his several Duties of Life better than *Ignotus.* All the Under-parts of his Behaviour, and such as are exposed to common Observation, have their rise in him from great and noble Motives. A firm and unshaken Expectation of another Life, makes him become this; Humanity and good Nature, fortified by the Sense of Virtue, has the same Effect upon him, as the Neglect of all Goodness has upon many others. Being firmly Established in all Matters of Importance, that certain Inattention which makes Men's Actions look easie, appears in him with greater Beauty: By a thorough Contempt of little Excellencies, he is perfectly Master of them. This Temper of Mind leaves him under no necessity of Studying his Air, and he has this peculiar Distinction, that his Negligence is unaffected.

He that can work himself into a Pleasure in considering this Being as an uncertain one, and think to reap an Advantage by its Discontinuance, is in a fair way of doing all Things with a graceful Unconcern, and Gentlemanlike Ease. Such a one does not behold his Life as a short, transient, perplexing State, made up of trifling Pleasures and great Anxieties; but sees it in quite another Light; his Griefs are Momentary, and his Joys Immortal. Reflection upon Death is not a gloomy and sad Thought of Resigning every Thing that he Delights in, but it is a short Night followed by an endless Day. What I would here contend for is, that the more Virtuous the Man is, the nearer he will naturally be to the Character of Genteel and Agreeable. A Man whose Fortune is Plentiful, shews an Ease in his Countenance, and Confidence in his Behaviour, which he that is under Wants and Difficulties cannot assume. It is thus with the State of the Mind; he that governs his Thoughts with the everlasting Rules of Reason and Sense, must have something so inexpressibly Graceful in his Words and Actions, that every Circumstance must become him. The Change of Persons or Things around him do not at all alter his Situation, but he looks disinterested in the Occurrences with which others are distracted, because the greatest purpose of his Life is to maintain an Indifference both to it and all its Enjoyments. In a word, to be a Fine Gentleman, is to be a Generous and a Brave Man. What can make a Man so much in constant good Humour and Shine, as we call it, than to be supported by what can never fail him, and to believe that whatever happens to him was the best thing that could possibly befal him, or else he on whom it depends would not have permitted it to have befallen him at all?

No. 80   Friday, June 1, 1711.   [Steele]

Cœlum non animum mutant qui trans mare current. [1]—Hor.

In the Year 1688, and on the same Day of that Year, were
born in *Cheapside,* [2] *London,* two Females of exquisite Feature and Shape; the one we shall call *Brunetta,* the other *Phillis.* [3]
A close Intimacy between their Parents made each of them the
first Acquaintance the other knew in the World: They played,
dressed Babies, [4] acted Visitings, learned to Dance and make
Curtsies, together. They were inseparable Companions in all
the little Entertainments their tender Years were capable of:
Which innocent Happiness continued till the Beginning of
their fifteenth Year, when it happened that Mrs. *Phillis* had
an Head-dress on which became her so very well, that instead
of being beheld any more with Pleasure for their Amity to each
other, the Eyes of the Neighbourhood were turned to remark
them with Comparison of their Beauty. They now no longer
enjoyed the Ease of Mind and pleasing Indolence in which
they were formerly happy, but all their Words and Actions
were misinterpreted by each other, and every Excellence in
their Speech and Behaviour was looked upon as an Act of Emu-
lation to surpass the other. These Beginnings of Dis-inclination
soon improved into a Formality of Behaviour, a general Coldness, and by natural Steps into an irreconcileable Hatred.

[1] "Those who hurry across the sea change their climate but not their mind."
[2] A street in the heart of London's business district, where many successful
bankers and merchants lived and conducted their businesses.
[3] Evidence that there is an actual incident behind this story is given by Professor
Bond in his edition of *The Spectator,* I, 342.
[4] Dolls.

These two Rivals for the Reputation of Beauty, were in their Stature, Countenance and Mein so very much alike, that if you were speaking of them in their Absence, the Words in which you described the one must give you an Idea of the other. They were hardly distinguishable, you would think, when they were apart, tho' extreamly different when together. What made their Enmity the more entertaining to all the rest of their Sex was, that in Detraction from each other neither could fall upon Terms which did not hit her self as much as her Adversary. Their Nights grew restless with Meditation of new Dresses to out-vie each other, and inventing new Devices to recall Admirers, who observed the Charms of the one rather than those of the other on the last Meeting. Their Colours failed at each other's Appearance, flushed with Pleasure at the Report of a Disadvantage, and their Countenances withered upon Instances of Applause. The Decencies to which Women are obliged, made these Virgins stifle their Resentment so far as not to break into open Violences, while they equally suffered the Torments of a regulated Anger. Their Mothers, as it is usual, engaged in the Quarrel, and supported the several Pretensions of the Daughters with all that ill-chosen sort of Expence which is common with People of plentiful Fortunes and mean Taste. The Girls preceded their Parents like Queens of *May,* in all the gaudy Colours imaginable, on every *Sunday* to Church, and were exposed to the Examination of the Audience for Superiority of Beauty.

During this constant Struggle it happened, that *Phillis* one Day at publick Prayers smote the Heart of a gay *West-Indian,* who appeared in all the Colours which can affect an Eye that could not distinguish between being fine and tawdry. This *American* in a Summer-Island Suit was too shining and too gay to be resisted by *Phillis,* and too intent upon her Charms to be diverted by any of the laboured Attractions of *Brunetta.* Soon after, *Brunetta* had the Mortification to see her Rival disposed of in a wealthy Marriage, while she was only addressed to in a Manner that shewed she was the Admiration of all Men, but the Choice of none. *Phillis* was carried to the Habitation of her Spouse in *Barbadoes: Brunetta* had the ill Nature to enquire for her by every Opportunity, and had the Misfortune to hear of her being attended by numerous Slaves, fanned into Slumbers by successive Hands of them, and carried from Place to Place in all the Pomp of barbarous Magnificence. *Brunetta* could not endure these repeated Advices, but employed all her Arts and Charms in laying Baits for any of Condition of the same Island, out of a meer Ambition to confront her once more before she died. She at last succeeded in her Design, and was taken to Wife by a Gentleman whose Estate was contiguous to that of her Enemy's Husband. It would be endless to ennumerate the many Occasions on which these irreconcileable Beauties laboured to excel each other; but in Process of Time it happened, that a Ship put into the Island consigned to a Friend of *Phillis,* who had Directions to give her the Refusal of all Goods for Apparel, before *Brunetta* could be alarmed of their Arrival. He did so, and *Phillis* was dressed in a few Days in a Brocade more gorgeous and costly than had ever before appeared in that Latitude. *Brunetta* languished at the Sight, and could by no Means come up to the Bravery of her Antagonist. She communicated her Anguish of Mind to a faithful Friend, who by an Interest in the Wife of *Phillis's* Merchant, procured a Remnant of the same Silk for *Brunetta. Phillis* took Pains to appear in all publick Places where she was sure to meet *Brunetta; Brunetta* was now prepared for the Insult, and came to a publick Ball in a plain black Silk Mantua, attended by a beautiful Negro Girl in a Petticoat of the same Brocade with which *Phillis* was attired. This drew the Attention of the whole Company; upon which the unhappy *Phillis* swooned away, and was immediately conveyed to her House. As soon as she came to her self she fled from her Husband's House, went on board a Ship in the Road, and is now landed in inconsolable Despair at *Plymouth.*

POSTSCRIPT.

After the above melancholy Narration, it may perhaps be a Relief to the Reader to peruse the following Expostulation.

To Mr. SPECTATOR.

The just Remonstrance of affronted That.[5]

Tho' I deny not the Petition of Mr. *Who* and *Which,* yet You should not suffer them to be rude, and to call honest People Names: For that bears very hard on some of those Rules of Decency, which You are justly famous for establishing. They may find Fault, and correct Speeches in the Senate and at the Bar: But let them try to get *themselves* so *often* and with so much *Eloquence* repeated in a Sentence, as a great Orator doth frequently introduce me.

My Lords! (says he) with humble Submission, *That* that I say is this: that, *That* that, that Gentleman has advanced, is not *That,* that he should have proved to your Lordships. Let these two questionary Petitioners try to do thus with their *Whos* and their *Whiches.*

What great Advantage was I of to Mr. *Dryden* in his *Indian Emperor,*

You force me still to answer You in *That,*

to furnish out a Rhime to *Morat?* And what a poor Figure would Mr. *Bayes* have made without his *Egad and all That?* How can a judicious Man distinguish one thing from another, without saying *This here,* or *That there?* And how can a sober Man, without using the *Expletives* of Oaths (in which indeed the Rakes and Bullies have a great Advantage over others)

[5] *The Spectator's* concern about the use of "that" as a pronoun appears in numerous changes from "that" to "which" or "who" in preparing the octavo edition of the essays.

make a Discourse of any tolerable Length, without *That is;* and if he be a very grave Man indeed, without *That is to say?* And how instructive as well as entertaining are those usual Expressions in the Mouths of great Men, *Such things as That,* and *The like of That.*

I am not against reforming the Corruptions of Speech You mention, and own there are proper Seasons for the Introduction of other Words besides *That;* but I scorn as much to supply the Place of a *Who* or a *Which* at every Turn, as they are *unequal* always to fill mine; and I expect good Language and civil Treatment, and hope to receive it for the future: *That,* that I shall only add is, that I am,

Yours,

THAT.

No. 81   Saturday, June 2, 1711.   [Addison]

Qualis ubi audito venantum murmure Tigris
Horruit in maculas . . .[1]—Statius.

About the middle of last Winter I went to see an *Opera* at the
Theatre in the *Hay-Market,* where I could not but take notice
of two Parties of very Fine Women, that had placed themselves
in the opposite Side-Boxes, and seemed drawn up in a kind
of Battle-Array one against another. After a short Survey of
them, I found they were *Patched* differently; the Faces, on
one Hand, being Spotted on the Right Side of the Forehead,
and those upon the other on the Left. I quickly perceived that
they cast Hostile Glances upon one another; and that their
Patches were placed in those different Situations, as Party-
Signals to distinguish Friends from Foes. In the Middle-Boxes,
between these two opposite Bodies, were several Ladies who
Patched indifferently on both sides of their Faces, and seemed
to sit there with no other Intention but to see the *Opera.* Upon
Enquiry I found, that the Body of *Amazons* on my Right Hand,
were Whigs;[2] and those on my Left, Tories; and that those
who had placed themselves in the Middle-Boxes were a Neutral Party, whose Faces had not yet declared themselves. These
last, however, as I afterwards found, diminished daily, and
took their Party with one Side or the other; insomuch that
I observed in several of them, the Patches which were before
dispersed equally, are now all gone over to the Whig or Tory

[1] "Just as when a tigress hearing the noise of hunters breaks out in angry
spots . . ."
[2] In the summer of 1711 party animosities were running particularly high over
the terms of the peace, the succession, and constitutional issues.

231

Side of the Face. The Censorious say, That the Men whose
Hearts are aimed at are very often the Occasions that one part
of the Face is thus Dishonoured, and lyes under a kind of Disgrace, while the other is so much Set off and Adorned by the
Owner; and that the Patches turn to the Right or to the Left,
according to the Principles of the Man who is most in Favour.
But whatever may be the Motives of a few Fantastical Coquets,
who do not Patch for the Publick Good, so much as for their
own Private Advantage; it is certain, that there are several
Women of Honour who Patch out of Principle, and with an
Eye to the Interest of their Country. Nay, I am informed, that
some of them adhere so steadfastly to their Party, and are so
far from Sacrificing their Zeal for the Publick to their Passion
for any particular Person, that in a late Draught of Marriage-
Articles a Lady has stipulated with her Husband, That, whatever
his Opinions are, she shall be at Liberty to Patch on which side
she pleases.

I must here take notice, that *Rosalinda*, a Famous Whig
Partizan, has most unfortunately a very beautiful Mole on the
Tory part of her Forehead; which, being very conspicuous,
has occasioned many Mistakes, and given an Handle to her
Enemies to misrepresent her Face, as though it had Revolted
from the Whig Interest. But whatever this natural Patch may
seem to intimate, it is well known that her Notions of Government are still the same. This unlucky Mole however has misled several Coxcombs; and, like the hanging out of false Colours, made some of them converse with *Rosalinda* in what
they thought the Spirit of her Party, when on a sudden she
has given them an unexpected Fire, that has sunk them all at
once. If *Rosalinda* is unfortunate in her Mole, *Nigranilla* is
as unhappy in a Pimple, which forces her, against her Inclinations, to Patch on the Whig side.

I am told that many Virtuous Matrons, who formerly
have been taught to believe that this Artificial Spotting of
the Face was unlawful, are now reconciled by a Zeal for their

Cause, to what they could not be prompted by a Concern for their Beauty. This way of declaring War upon one another, puts me in mind of what is reported of the Tigress, that several Spots rise in her Skin when she is angry; or as Mr. *Cowley* has imitated the Verses that stand as the Motto of this Paper,

> . . . *She Swells with angry Pride,*
> *And calls forth all her Spots on ev'ry side.*

When I was in the Theatre the time above-mentioned, I had the Curiosity to count the Patches on both Sides, and found the Tory patches to be about twenty Stronger than the Whig; but to make amends for this small Inequality, I the next Morning found the whole Puppet-show filled with Faces spotted after the Whiggish manner. Whether or no the Ladies had re-treated hither in order to rally their Forces I cannot tell; but the next Night they came in so great a Body to the Opera, that they outnumbered the Enemy.

This Account of Party-Patches will, I am afraid, appear improbable to those who live at a distance from the fashionable World; but as it is a Distinction of a very singular Nature, and what perhaps may never meet with a Parallel, I think I should not have discharged the Office of a faithful Spectator had I not recorded it.

I have, in former Papers, endeavoured to expose this Party-Rage in Women, as it only serves to aggravate the Hatreds and Animosities that reign among Men, and in a great mea-sure deprives the Fair Sex of those peculiar Charms with which Nature has endowed them.

When the *Romans* and *Sabines* were at War, and just upon the point of giving Battle, the Women, who were allied to both of them, interposed with so many Tears and Intreaties, that they prevented the mutual Slaughter which threatned both Parties, and united them together in a firm and lasting Peace.

I would recommend this noble Example to our *British*

Ladies, at a time when their Country is torn with so many unnatural Divisions, that if they continue, it will be a Misfortune to
be born in it. The *Greeks* thought it so improper for Women
to interest themselves in Competitions and Contentions, that
for this Reason, among others, they forbad them, under Pain
of Death, to be present at the *Olympick* Games, notwithstanding these were the Publick Diversions of all *Greece.*

As our *English* Women excel those of all Nations in Beauty,
they should endeavour to outshine them in all other Accomplishments proper to the Sex, and to distinguish themselves as
tender Mothers and faithful Wives, rather than as furious Par-
tizans. Female Virtues are of a Domestick turn. The Family
is the proper Province for Private Women to Shine in. If they
must be showing their Zeal for the Publick, let it not be against
those who are perhaps of the same Family, or at least of the
same Religion or Nation, but against those who are the open,
professed, undoubted Enemies of their Faith, Liberty, and
Country. When the *Romans* were pressed with a Foreign Enemy, the Ladies voluntarily contributed all their Rings and Jewels
to assist the Government under a publick Exigence; which
appeared so laudable an Action in the Eyes of their Countrymen, that from thenceforth it was permitted by a Law to pronounce publick Orations at the Funeral of a Woman in Praise
of the deceased Person, which till that time was peculiar to
Men. Would our *English* Ladies, instead of sticking on a Patch
against those of their own Country, shew themselves so truly
Publick-spirited as to Sacrifice every one her Necklace against
the Common Enemy, what Decrees ought not to be made in
favour of them?

Since I am recollecting upon this Subject such Passages
as occur to my Memory out of ancient Authors, I cannot omit
a Sentence in the Celebrated Funeral Oration of *Pericles,* which
he made in Honour of those Brave *Athenians* that were Slain
in a Fight with the *Lacedemonians.* After having addressed
himself to the several Ranks and Orders of his Countrymen,

and shewn them how they should behave themselves in the Publick Cause, he turns to the Female part of his Audience; 'And as for you (says he) I shall advise you in very few Words: Aspire only to those Virtues that are peculiar to your Sex; follow your natural Modesty, and think it your greatest Commendation not to be talked of one way or other.'

No. 82   Monday, June 4, 1711.   [Steele]

... *Caput domina venale sub hasta.* [1]—Juv.

Passing under *Ludgate* the other Day I heard a Voice bawling
for Charity, which I thought I had somewhere heard before.
Coming near to the Grate, the Prisoner called me by my Name,
and desired I would throw something into the Box: I was out
of Countenance for him, and did as he bid me, by putting in
half a Crown. I went away reflecting upon the strange Constitution of some Men, and how meanly they behave themselves
in all Sorts of Conditions. The Person who begged of me is
now, as I take it, Fifty: I was well acquainted with him till about
the Age of Twenty five; at which Time a good Estate fell to
him, by the Death of a Relation. Upon coming to this unexpected good Fortune, he ran into all the Extravagancies imaginable;
was frequently in drunken Disputes, broke Drawers Heads,
talked and swore loud; was unmannerly to those above him,
and insolent to those below him. I could not but remark, that
it was the same Baseness of Spirit which worked in his Behaviour in both Fortunes: The same little Mind was insolent in
Riches, and shameless in Poverty. This Accident made me
muse upon the Circumstance of being in Debt in general, and
solve in my Mind what Tempers were most apt to fall into this
Errour of Life, as well as the Misfortune it must needs be to
languish under such Pressures. As for my self, my natural Aversion to that Sort of Conversation which makes a Figure with
the Generality of Mankind, exempts me from any Tempta-
tions to Expence; and all my Business lies within a very nar-

[1] "Or put up slaves for sale under the authority of the spear."

row Compass, which is, only to give an honest Man who takes care of my Estate proper Vouchers for his quarterly Payments to me, and observe what Linnen my Laundress brings and takes away with her once a Week: My Steward brings his Receipt ready for my signing, and I have a pretty Implement with the respective Names of Shirts, Cravats, Handkerchiefs and Stockings, with proper Numbers to know how to reckon with my Laundress. This being almost all the Business I have in the World for the Care of my own Affairs, I am at full Leisure to observe upon what others do, with Relation to their Equipage and Oeconomy.

When I walk the Street, and observe the Hurry about me in this Town,

> *Where with like Haste, tho' different Ways, they run;*
> *Some to undo, and some to be undone.*[2]

I say, when I behold this vast Variety of Persons and Humours, with the Pains they both take for the Accomplishment of the Ends mentioned in the above Verses of *Denham,* I cannot much wonder at the Endeavour after Gain; but am extreamly astonished that Men can be so insensible of the Danger of running into Debt. One would think it impossible a Man who is given to contract Debts should know, that his Creditor has from that Moment in which he transgresses Payment, so much as that Demand comes to in his Debtor's Honour, Liberty and Fortune. One would think he did not know, that his Creditor can say the worst thing imaginable of him, to wit, *That he is unjust,* without Defamation; and can sieze his Person, without being guilty of an Assault. Yet such is the loose and abandoned Turn of some Mens Minds, that they can live under these constant Apprehensions, and still go on to encrease the Cause of them. Can there be a more low and servile Condition, than to be ashamed, or afraid, to see any one Man breath-

[2] Sir John Denham, *Cooper's Hill* (1642), ll. 31-32.

ing? Yet he that is much in debt, is in that Condition with relation to twenty different People. There are indeed Circumstances wherein Men of honest Natures may become liable to Debts, by some unadvised Behaviour in any great Point of their Life, or mortgaging a Man's Honesty as a Security for that of another, and the like; but these Instances are so particular and circumstantiated, that they cannot come within general Considerations: For one such Case as one of these, there are ten, where a Man, to keep up a Farce of Retinue and Grandeur within his own House, shall shrink at the Expectation of surly Demands at his Doors. The Debtor is the Creditor's Criminal, and all the Officers of Power and State whom we behold make so great a Figure, are no other than so many Persons in Authority to make good his Charge against him. Humane Society depends upon his having the Vengeance Law allots him; and the Debtor owes his Liberty to his Neighbour, as much as the Murderer does his Life to his Prince.

Our Gentry are, generally speaking, in debt; and many Families have put it into a kind of Method of being so from Generation to Generation. The Father mortgages when his Son is very young; and the Boy is to marry as soon as he is at Age, to redeem it, and find Portions for his Sisters. This, forsooth, is no great Inconvenience to him; for he may wench, keep a publick Table, or feed Dogs, like a worthy *English* Gentleman, till he has outrun half his Estate, and leave the same Incumbrance upon his First-born; and so on, till one Man of more Vigour than ordinary goes quite thorough the Estate, or some Man of Sense comes into it, and scorns to have an Estate in Partnership, that is to say, liable to the Demand or Insult of any Man living. There is my Friend Sir ANDREW, tho' for many Years a great and general Trader, was never the Defendant in a Law Suit, in all the Perplexity of Business, and the Iniquity of Mankind at present: No one had any Colour for the least Complaint against his Dealings with him. This is certainly as uncommon, and in its Proportion as laudable in a Citizen, as it is in a General never to have suffered a Disadvantage in Fight.

How different from this Gentleman is *Jack Truepenny,* who has been an old Acquaintance of Sir ANDREW and my self from Boys, but could never learn our Caution. *Jack* has a whorish unresisting good Nature, which makes him incapable of having a Property in any thing. His Fortune, his Reputation, his Time and his Capacity, are at any Man's Service that comes first. When he was at School, he was whipp'd thrice a Week for Faults he took upon him to excuse others; since he came into the Business of the World, he has been arrested twice or thrice a Year for Debts he had nothing to do with but as Surety for others; and I remember when a Friend of his had suffered in the Vice of the Town, all the Physick his Friend took was conveyed to him by *Jack,* and inscribed, 'A Bolus or an Electuary for Mr. *Truepenny.*' *Jack* had a good Estate left him, which came to nothing; because he believed all who pretended to Demands upon it. This Easiness and Credulity destroy all the other Merit he has; and he has all his Life been a Sacrifice to others, without ever receiving Thanks or doing one good Action.

I will end this Discourse with a Speech which I heard *Jack* make to one of his Creditors (of whom he deserved gentler Usage) after lying a whole Night in Custody at his Suit.

SIR,
Your Ingratitude for the many Kindnesses I have done you, shall not make me unthankful for the Good you have done me, in letting me see there is such a Man as you in the World. I am obliged to you for the Diffidence I shall have all the rest of my Life: *I shall hereafter trust no Man so far as to be in his Debt.*

Quid Domini facient, audent cum talia Fures?[1]—Virg.

May 30, 1711

Mr. SPECTATOR,

I have no small Value for your Endeavours to lay before the World what may escape their Observation, and yet highly conduces to their Service. You have, I think, succeeded very well on many Subjects; and seem to have been conversant in very different Scenes of Life. But in the Considerations of Mankind, as a SPECTATOR, you should not omit Circumstances which relate to the inferiour Part of the World, any more than those which concern the greater. There is one thing in particular which I wonder you have not touched upon, and that is, the general Corruption of Manners in the Servants of *Great Britain*. I am a Man that have travelled and seen many Nations, but have for seven Years last past resided constantly in *London* or within twenty Miles of it: In this Time I have contracted a numerous Acquaintance among the best Sort of People, and have hardly found one of them happy in their Servants. This is Matter of great Astonishment to Foreigners, and all such as have visited foreign Countries; especially since we cannot but observe, That there is no Part of the World where Servants have those Privileges and Advantages as in *England:* They have no where else such plentiful Diet, large Wages, or indulgent Liberty:

---

[1] "What nonsense would the fool thy master prate,
 When thou, his knave, canst talk at such a rate!"

—Dryden's translation.

There is no Place wherein they labour less, and yet where they are so little respectful, more wasteful, more negligent, or where they so frequently change their Masters. To this I attribute, in a great Measure, the frequent Robberies and Losses which we suffer on the high Road and in our own Houses. That indeed which gives me the present Thought of this Kind, is, that a careless Groom of mine has spoiled me the prettiest Pad in the World, with only riding him ten Miles; and I assure you, if I were to make a Register of all the Horses I have known thus abused by Negligence of Servants, the Number would mount a Regiment. I wish you would give us your Observations, that we may know how to treat these Rogues, or that we Masters may enter into Measures to reform them. Pray give us a Speculation in general about Servants, and you make me

                                              Yours,
Pray do not omit   Philo-Britannicus.
the Mention of Grooms
in particular.'

This honest Gentleman, who is so desirous that I should write a Satyr upon Grooms, has a great deal of Reason for his Resentment; and I know no Evil which touches all Mankind so much, as this of the Misbehaviour of Servants.

The Complaint of this Letter runs wholly upon Men-Servants; and I can attribute the Licentiousness which has at present prevailed among them, to nothing but what an hundred before me have ascribed it to, The Custom of giving Board-Wages:[2] This one Instance of false Oeconomy, is sufficient to debauch the whole Nation of Servants, and makes them as it were but for some Part of their Time in that Quality. They are either attending in Places where they meet and run into Clubs, or else, if they wait at Taverns, they eat after their Masters, and reserve their Wages for other Occasions. From hence it arises, That they are but in a lower Degree what their Mas-

---

[2] An allowance made to servants who were expected to provide their own food.

ters themselves are; and usually affect an Imitation of their Manners: And you have in Liveries Beaux, Fops, and Coxcombs, in as high Perfection, as among People that keep Equipages. It is a common Humour among the Retinue of People of Quality, when they are in their Revels, that is when they are out of their Masters Sight, to assume in an humourous Way the Names and Titles of those whose Liveries they wear. By which Means Characters and Distinctions become so familiar to them, that it is to this, among other Causes, one may impute a certain Insolence among our Servants, that they take no Notice of any Gentleman though they know him ever so well, except he is an Acquaintance of their Masters.

My Obscurity and Taciturnity leave me at Liberty, without Scandal, to dine, if I think fit, at a common Ordinary, in the meanest as well as the most sumptuous House of Entertainment. Falling in the other Day at a Victualling-house near the House of Peers, I heard the Maid come down and tell the Landlady at the Bar, That my Lord Bishop swore he would throw her out at Window if she did not bring up more Mildbeer, and that my Lord Duke would have a double Mug of Purle. My Surprise was encreased, in hearing loud and rustick Voices speak and answer to each other upon the publick Affairs, by the Names of the most Illustrious of our Nobility; till of a sudden one came running in, and cryed the House was rising. Down came all the Company together, and away: The Ale-house was immediately filled with Clamour, and scoring one Mug to the Marquis of such a Place, Oyl and Vinegar to such an Earl, three Quarts to my new Lord for wetting his Title, and so forth. It is a thing too notorious to mention the Crowds of Servants, and their Insolence, near the Courts of Justice, and the Stairs towards the supreme Assembly; where there is an universal Mockery of all Order, such riotous Clamour and licentious Confusion, that one would think the whole Nation lived in Jest, and there were no such thing as Rule and Distinction among us.

The next Place of Resort, wherein the servile World are

let loose, is at the Entrance of *Hide-Park,* while the Gentry are at the Ring. Hither People bring their Lacqueys out of State, and here it is that all they say at their Tables and act in their Houses is communicated to the whole Town. There are Men of Wit in all Conditions of Life; and mixing with these People at their Diversions, I have heard Coquets and Prudes as well rallied, and Insolence and Pride exposed, (allowing for their want of Education,) with as much Humour and good Sense, as in the politest Companies. It is a general Observation, That all Dependants run in some Measure into the Manners and Behaviour of those whom they serve: You shall frequently meet with Lovers and Men of Intrigue among the Lacqueys, as well as *White's*[3] or in the Side-Boxes. I remember some Years ago an Instance of this Kind. A Footman to a Captain of the Guard used frequently, when his Master was out of the Way, to carry on Amours and make Assignations in his Master's Cloaths. The Fellow had a very good Person, and there are very many Women that think no farther than the Outside of a Gentleman; besides which, he was almost as learned a Man as the Collonel himself. I say, thus qualified, the Fellow could scrawl *Billets doux* so well, and furnish a Conversation on the common Topicks, that he had, as they call it, a great deal of good Business on his Hands. It happened one Day, that coming down a Tavern-stairs in his Master's fine Guard-Coat, with a well-dressed Woman masked, he met the Collonel coming up with other Company; but with a ready Assurance he quitted his Lady, came up to him, and said, *Sir, I know you have too much Respect for your self to cane me in this honourable Habit: But you see there is a Lady in the Case, and I hope on that Score also you will put off your Anger till I have told you all another Time.* After a little Pause the Collonel cleared up his Countenance, and with an Air of Familiarity whispered his Man apart, *Sirrah, bring the Lady with you to ask Pardon for you;* then aloud, *Look to it* Will. I'll never forgive you else. The Fel-

---

[3] The smartest of the chocolate-houses of the day.

low went back to his Mistress, and telling her with a loud Voice and an Oath, That was the honestest Fellow in the World, conveyed her to an Hackney-Coach.

But the many Irregularities committed by Servants in the Places above-mentioned, as well as in the Theatres, of which Masters are generally the Occasions, are too various not to need being resumed on another Occasion.

No. 94   Monday, June 18, 1711.   [Addison]

. . . Hoc est
Vivere bis, vita posse priore frui. [1]—Mart.

The last Method which I proposed in my *Saturday's* Paper, for filling up those empty Spaces of Life which are so tedious and burthensome to idle People, is the employing our selves in the Pursuit of Knowledge. I remember Mr. *Boyle,* [2] speaking of a certain Mineral, tells us, That a Man may consume his whole Life in the Study of it, without arriving at the Knowledge of all its Qualities. The Truth of it is, there is not a single Science, or any Branch of it, that might not furnish a Man with Business for Life, though it were much longer than it is.

I shall not here engage on those beaten Subjects of the Usefulness of Knowledge, nor of the Pleasure and Perfection it gives the Mind, nor on the Methods of attaining it, nor recommend any particular Branch of it, all which have been the Topicks of many other Writers; but shall indulge my self in a Speculation that is more uncommon, and may therefore perhaps be more entertaining.

I have before shewn how the unemployed Parts of Life appear long and tedious, and shall here endeavour to shew how those Parts of Life which are exercised in Study, Reading, and the Pursuits of Knowledge, are long but not tedious; and by that Means discover a Method of lengthening our Lives, and at the same Time of turning all the Parts of them to our Advantage.

[1] "This is to live twice, to be able to enjoy the life already lived."
[2] In *The Usefulness of Natural Philosophy* (*Works,* ed. 1772), II, 11.

Mr. *Lock* observes, "That we get the Idea of Time, or Duration, by reflecting on that Train of Ideas which succeed one another in our Minds: That for this Reason, when we sleep soundly without dreaming, we have no Perception of Time, or the Length of it, whilst we sleep; and that the Moment wherein we leave off to think, till the Moment we begin to think again, seem to have no Distance." To which the Author adds; "And so, I doubt not, but it would be to a waking Man, if it were possible for him to keep only one *Idea* in his Mind, without Variation, and the Succession of others: And we see, that one who fixes his Thoughts very intently on one thing, so as to take but little Notice of the Succession of *Ideas* that pass in his Mind whilst he is taken up with that earnest Contemplation, lets slip out of his Account a good Part of that Duration, and thinks that Time shorter than it is.[3]

We might carry this Thought further, and consider a Man as, on one Side, shortening his Time by thinking on nothing, or but a few things; so, on the other, as lengthening it, by employing his Thoughts on many Subjects, or by entertaining a quick and constant Succession of Ideas. Accordingly Monsieur *Mallebranche,* in his *Enquiry after Truth,*[4] (which was published several Years before Mr. *Lock's Essay on Humane Understanding*) tells us, That it is possible some Creatures may think Half an Hour as long as we do a thousand Years; or look upon that Space of Duration which we call a Minute, as an Hour, a Week, a Month, or an whole Age.

This Notion of Monsieur *Mallebranche,* is capable of some little Explanation from what I have quoted out of Mr. *Lock;* for if our Notion of Time is produced by our reflecting on the Succession of Ideas in our Mind, and this Succession may be infinitely accelerated or retarded, it will follow, that different Beings may have different Notions of the same Parts of Duration, according as their Ideas, which we suppose are equally

[3] In *An Essay Concerning Human Understanding,* Book II, Chapter 14.
[4] Book I, Chapter viii.

distinct in each of them, follow one another in a greater or less Degree of Rapidity.

There is a famous Passage in the *Alcoran*,[5] which looks as if *Mahomet* had been possessed of the Notion we are now speaking of. It is there said, That the Angel *Gabriel* took *Mahomet* out of his Bed one Morning to give him a Sight of all things in the seven Heavens, in Paradise, and in Hell, which the Prophet took a distinct View of; and after having held ninety thousand Conferences with God, was brought back again to his Bed. All this, says the *Alcoran*, was transacted in so small a Space of Time, that *Mahomet*, at his Return, found his Bed still warm, and took up an Earthen Pitcher (which was thrown down at the very Instant that the Angel *Gabriel* carried him away) before the Water was all spilt.

There is a very pretty Story in the *Turkish* Tales which relates to this Passage of that famous Impostor, and bears some Affinity to the Subject we are now upon. A Sultan of Ægypt, who was an Infidel, used to laugh at this Circumstance in *Mahomet's* Life, as what was altogether impossible and absurd: But conversing one Day with a great Doctor in the Law, who had the Gift of working Miracles, the Doctor told him, he would quickly convince him of the Truth of this Passage in the History of *Mahomet*, if he would consent to do what he should desire of him. Upon this the Sultan was directed to place himself by an huge Tub of Water, which he did accordingly; and as he stood by the Tub amidst a Circle of his great Men, the holy Man bid him plunge his Head into the Water, and draw it up again: The King accordingly thrust his Head into the Water, and at the same time found himself at the Foot of a Mountain on a Sea-shore. The King immediately began to rage against his Doctor for this Piece of Treachery and Witchcraft; but at length, knowing it was in vain to be angry, he set himself to think on proper Methods for getting a Livelihood in this

---

[5] This passage and the story in the following paragraph are from *Turkish Tales* (1708), pp. 18-19, 25-41.

strange Country: Accordingly he applied himself to some People whom he saw at work in a neighbouring Wood; these People conducted him to a Town that stood at a little Distance from the Wood, where after some Adventures he married a Woman of great Beauty and Fortune. He lived with this Woman so long till he had by her seven Sons and seven Daughters: He was afterwards reduced to great Want, and forced to think of plying in the Streets as a Porter for his Livelyhood. One Day as he was walking alone by the Sea-Side, being seized with many melancholy Reflections upon his former and his present State of Life, which had raised a Fit of Devotion in him, he threw off his Cloaths with a Design to wash himself, according to the Custom of the *Mahometans,* before he said his Prayers.

After his first Plunge into the Sea, he no sooner raised his Head above the Water, but he found himself standing by the Side of the Tub, with the great Men of his Court about him, and the holy Man at his Side: He immediately upbraided his Teacher for having sent him on such a Course of Adventures, and betray'd him into so long a State of Misery and Servitude; but was wonderfully surprized when he heard that the State he talked of was only a Dream and Delusion; that he had not stirred from the Place where he then stood; and that he had only dipped his Head into the Water, and immediately taken it out again.

The *Mahometan* Doctor took this Occasion of instructing the Sultan, that nothing was impossible with God; and that *He,* with whom a Thousand Years are but as one Day, can if he pleases make a single Day, nay a single Moment, appear to any of his Creatures as a thousand Years.

I shall leave my Reader to compare these Eastern Fables with the Notions of those two great Philosophers whom I have quoted in this Paper; and shall only, by way of Application, desire him to consider how we may extend Life beyond its natural Dimensions, by applying ourselves diligently to the Pursuits of Knowledge.

The Hours of a wise Man are lengthened by his Ideas, as those of a Fool are by his Passions: The Time of the one is long, because he does not know what to do with it; so is that of the other, because he distinguishes every Moment of it with useful or amusing Thought; or in other Words, because the one is always wishing it away, and the other always enjoying it.

How different is the View of past Life, in the Man who is grown old in Knowledge and Wisdom, from that of him who is grown old in Ignorance and Folly? The latter is like the Owner of a barren Country, that fills his Eye with the Prospect of naked Hills and Plains which produce nothing either profitable or ornamental; the other beholds a beautiful and spacious Landskip, divided into delightful Gardens, green Meadows, fruitful Fields, and can scarce cast his Eye on a single Spot of his Possesions, that is not covered with some beautiful Plant or Flower.

No. 96   Wednesday, June 20, 1711.   [Steele]

. . . *amicum*
Mancipium domino, & frugi . . .[1] Hor.

Mr. SPECTATOR,

I have frequently read your Discourse upon Servants, and, as I am one my self, have been much offended, that in that Variety of Forms wherein you considered the Bad, you found no Place to mention the Good. There is however one Observation of yours I approve, which is, That there are Men of Wit and good Sense among all Orders of Men; and that Servants report most of the Good or Ill which is spoken of their Masters. That there are Men of Sense who live in Servitude, I have the Vanity to say I have felt to my woful Experience. You attribute very justly the Source of our general Iniquity to Board-Wages, and the Manner of living out of a domestick Way: But I cannot give you my Thoughts on this Subject any Way so well, as by a short Account of my own Life to this the Forty fifth Year of my Age; that is to say, from my being first a Foot-boy at Fourteen, to my present Station of a Nobleman's Porter in the Year of my Age above-mentioned.

Know then, that my Father was a poor Tenant to the Family of Sir *Stephen Rackrent:* Sir *Stephen* put me to School, or rather made me follow his Son *Harry* to School, from my Ninth Year; and there, though Sir *Stephen* paid something for my Learning, I was used like a Servant, and was forc'd to get what Scraps of Learning I could by my own Industry, for the Schoolmaster took very little Notice of me. My young Mas-

[1] " . . . a slave loyal to his master and honest. . . ."
250

ter was a Lad of very sprightly Parts; and my being constantly about him and loving him, was no small Advantage to me. My Master loved me extremely, and has often been whipped for not keeping me at a Distance. He used always to say, That when he came to his Estate I should have a Lease of my Father's Tenement for nothing. I came up to Town with him to *Westminster* School; at which Time he taught me, at Night, all he learnt, and put me to find out Words in the Dictionary when he was about his Exercise. It was the Will of Providence that Master *Harry* was taken very ill of a Fever, of which he died within ten Days after his first falling sick. Here was the first Sorrow I ever knew; and I assure you, Mr. SPECTATOR, I remember the beautiful Action of the sweet Youth in his Fever, as fresh as if it were Yesterday. If he wanted any thing, it must be given him by *Tom:* When I let any thing fall through the Grief I was under, he would cry, Do not beat the poor Boy: Give him some more Julep for me, no Body else shall give it me. He wold strive to hide his being so bad, when he saw I could not bear his being in so much Danger, and comforted me, saying, *"Tom, Tom,* have a good Heart." When I was holding a Cup at his Mouth he fell into Convulsions; and at this very Time I hear my dear Master's last Groan. I was quickly turned out of the Room, and left to sob and beat my Head against the Wall at my Leisure. The Grief I was in was inexpressible; and every Body thought it would have cost me my Life. In a few Days my old Lady, who was one of the Housewives of the World, thought of turning me out of Doors, because I put her in Mind of her Son. Sir *Stephen* proposed putting me to Prentice, but my Lady being an excellent Manager, would not let her Husband throw away his Money in Acts of Charity. I had Sense enough to be under the utmost Indignation, to see her discard with so little Concern one her Son had loved so much; and went out of the House to ramble whereever my Feet would carry me.

The third Day after I left Sir *Stephen's* Family, I was strolling up and down the Walks in the *Temple.* A young Gentleman of the House, who (as I heard him say afterwards) seeing me half starved and well dressed, thought me an Equipage ready to his Hand, after very little Enquiry more than *did I want a Master?* bid me follow him: I did so, and in a very little while thought my self the happiest Creature in this World. My Time was taken up in carrying Letters to Wenches, or Messages to young Ladies of my Master's Acquaintance. We rambled from Tavern to Tavern, to the Play-house, the Mulberry-garden, and all Places of Resort; where my Master engaged every Night in some new Amour, in which and drinking he spent all his Time when he had Money. During these Extravagancies I had the Pleasure of lying on the Stairs of a Tavern half a Night, playing at Dice with other Servants, and the like Idlenesses. When my Master was moneyless, I was generally employed in transcribing amorous Pieces of Poetry, old Songs, and new Lampoons. This Life held till my Master married, and he had then the Prudence to turn me off because I was in the Secret of his Intreagues.

I was utterly at a Loss what Course to take next; when at last I applied my self to a Fellow-sufferer, one of his Mistresses, a Woman of the Town. She happening at that Time to be pretty full of Money, cloathed me from Head to Foot; and knowing me to be a sharp Fellow, employed me accordingly. Sometimes I was to go abroad with her, and when she had pitched upon a young Fellow she thought for her Turn, I was to be dropped as one she could not trust. She would often cheapen Goods at the *New Exchange;*[2] and when she had a Mind to be attacked, she would send me away on an Errand. When an humble Servant and she were beginning a Parley, I came immediately, and told her Sir *John* was come home; then she would order another Coach to prevent being dogged. The Lover makes Signs to me as I get behind the Coach, I shake

---

[2] A fashionable shopping district south of the Strand. A scene from the third act of Wycherley's *The Country Wife* takes place at the New Exchange.

my Head it was impossible: I leave my Lady at the next Turning, and follow the Cully to know how to fall in his Way on another Occasion. Besides good Offices of this Nature, I writ all my Mistress's Love-letters; some from a Lady that saw such a Gentleman at such a Place in such a coloured Coat, some shewing the Terrour she was in of a jealous old Husband, others explaining that the Severity of her Parents was such (tho' her Fortune was settled) that she was willing to run away with such a one tho' she knew he was but a younger Brother. In a Word, my Half-Education and Love of idle Books, made me outwrite all that made Love to her by way of Epistle; and as she was extreamly cunning, she did well enough in Company by a Skilful Affectation of the greatest Modesty. In the Midst of all this, I was surprized with a Letter from her and a Ten Pound Note.

Honest Tom,
You will never see me more. I am married to a very cunning Country-Gentleman, who might possibly guess something if I kept you still; therefore farewell.

When this Place was lost also in Marriage, I was resolved to go among quite another People for the Future; and got in Butler to one of those Families where there is a Coach kept, three or four Servants, a clean House, and a good general Outside upon a small Estate. Here I lived very comfortably for some Time, till I unfortunately found my Master, the very gravest Man alive, in the Garret with the Chambermaid. I knew the World too well to think of staying there; and the next Day pretended to have received a Letter out of the Country that my Father was dying, and got my Discharge with a Bounty for my Discretion.

The next I lived with was a peevish single Man, whom I stay'd with for a Year and a Half. Most Part of the Time I passed very easily; for when I began to know him, I minded no more than he meant what he said; so that one Day in good Humour he said, *I was the best Man he ever had, by my want of Respect to him.*

These, Sir, are the chief Occurrences of my other Places I have been in, where I have been the strangest Fellow in the World, where no Body in the World had such Servants as they, where sure they were the unluckiest People in the World in Servants, and so forth. All I mean by this Representation, is, To shew you that we poor Servants are not (what you called us too generally) all Rogues; but that we are what we are, according to the Example of our Superiors. In the Family I am now in, I am guilty of no one Sin but Lying; which I do with a grave Face in my Gown and Staff every Day I live, and almost all Day long, in denying my Lord to impertinent Suitors, and my Lady to unwelcome Visitants. But, Sir, I am to let you know, that I am, when I can get abroad, a Leader of the Servants: I am he that keep Time with beating my Cudgel against the Boards in the Gallery at an Opera; I am he that am touched so properly at a Tragedy, when the People of Quality are staring at one another during the most important Incidents: When you hear in a Crowd a Cry in the right Place, an Humm where the Point is touched in a Speech, or an Hussa set up where it is the Voice of the People; you may conclude it is begun, or joined by,

SIR,

Your more than humble Servant,
Thomas Trusty.

No. 105   Saturday, June 30, 1711.   [Addison]

. . . *Id arbitror*
Adprime in vita esse utile, ne quid nimis. [1] —Ter. Andr.

My Friend WILL. HONEYCOMB, values himself very much upon
what he calls the Knowledge of Mankind, which has cost him
many Disasters in his Youth; for WILL. reckons every Misfortune that he has met with among the Women, and every Ren-
counter among the Men, as Parts of his Education; and fancies he should never have been the Man he is, had not he broke
Windows, knocked down Constables, disturbed honest People with his Midnight Serenades, and beat up a lewd Woman's
Quarters, when he was a young Fellow. The engaging in Adventures of this nature, WILL. calls the studying of Mankind; and
terms this Knowledge of the Town, the Knowledge of the
World. WILL. ingenuously confesses, that for half his Life his
Head ached every Morning with reading of Men over-night; and
at present comforts himself under certain Pains which he endures from time to time, that without them he could not have
been acquainted with the Gallantries of the Age. This WILL.
looks upon as the Learning of a Gentleman, and regards all
other kinds of Science as the Accomplishments of one whom he
calls a Scholar, a Bookish Man, or a Philosopher.

  For these Reasons WILL. shines in mixed Company, where
he has the Discretion not to go out of his Depth, and has often
a certain way of making his real Ignorance appear a seeming
one. Our Club however has frequently caught him tripping,
at which times they never spare him. For as WILL. often insults

[1] "'Nothing to excess' is in my opinion an excellent motto."

us with the Knowledge of the Town, we sometimes take our Revenge upon him by our Knowledge of Books.

He was last Week producing two or three Letters which he writ in his Youth to a Coquet Lady. The Raillery of them was natural, and well enough for a meer Man of the Town; but, very unluckily, several of the Words were wrong spelt. WILL. laught this off at first as well as he could, but finding himself pushed on all sides, and especially by the *Templer,* he told us, with a little Passion, that he never liked Pedantry in Spelling, and that he spelt like a Gentleman, and not like a Scholar: Upon this WILL. had Recourse to his old Topick of shewing the narrow Spiritedness, the Pride, and Ignorance of Pedants; which he carried so far, that upon my retiring to my Lodgings, I could not forbear throwing together such Reflections as occurred to me upon that Subject.

A Man who has been brought up among Books, and is able to talk of nothing else, is a very indifferent Companion, and what we call a Pedant. But, methinks, we should enlarge the Title, and give it every one that does not know how to think out of his Profession, and particular way of Life.

What is a greater Pedant than a meer Man of the Town? Barr him the Play-houses, a Catalogue of the reigning Beauties, and an Account of a few fashionable Distempers that have befallen him, and you strike him Dumb. How many a pretty Gentleman's Knowledge lies all within the Verge of the Court? He will tell you the Names of the Principal Favourites, repeat the shrewd Sayings of a Man of Quality, whisper an Intreague that is not yet blown upon by common Fame; or, if the Sphere of his Observations is a little larger than ordinary, will perhaps enter into all the Incidents, Turns, and Revolutions in a Game of Ombre.[2] When he has gone thus far he has shown you the whole Circle of his Accomplishments, his Parts are drained, and he is disabled from any further Conversation. What are

[2] Note the prominence of the game of ombre in the third canto of Pope's *Rape of the Lock.*

these but rank Pedants? and yet these are the Men who value themselves most on their Exemption from the Pedantry of Colleges.

I might here mention the Military Pedant, who always talks in a Camp, and is storming Towns, making Lodgments, and fighting Battels from one end of the Year to the other. Every thing he speaks smells of Gunpowder; if you take away his Artillery from him, he has not a Word to say for himself. I might likewise mention the Law Pedant, that is perpetually putting Cases, repeating the Transactions of *Westminster-Hall,* wrangling with you upon the most indifferent Circumstances of Life, and not to be convinced of the Distance of a Place, or of the most trivial Point in Conversation, but by dint of Argument. The State-Pedant is wrapt up in News, and lost in Politicks. If you mention either of the Kings of *Spain* or *Poland,* he talks very notably; but if you go out of the *Gazette,* you drop him. In short, a meer Courtier, a meer Soldier, a meer Scholar, a meer any thing, is an insipid Pedantick Character, and equally ridiculous.

Of all the Species of Pedants, which I have mentioned, the Book-Pedant is much the most supportable; he has at least an exercised Understanding, and a Head which is full though confused, so that a Man who converses with him may often receive from him hints of things that are worth knowing, and what he may possibly turn to his own Advantage, tho' they are of little use to the Owner. The worst kind of Pedants among Learned Men, are such as are naturally endued with a very small Share of common Sense, and have read a great number of Books without Taste or Distinction.

The Truth of it is, Learning, like Travelling, and all other Methods of Improvement, as it finishes good Sense, so it makes a silly Man ten thousand times more insufferable, by supplying variety of Matter to his Impertinence, and giving him an Opportunity of abounding in Absurdities.

Shallow Pedants cry up one another much more than Men of solid and useful Learning. To read the Titles they give an

Editor, or Collator of a Manuscript, you would take him for the Glory of the Common-Wealth of Letters, and the Wonder of his Age; when perhaps upon Examination you find that he has only Rectify'd a *Greek* Particle, or laid out a whole Sentence in proper Commas.[3]

They are obliged indeed to be thus lavish of their Praises, that they may keep one another in Countenance; and it is no wonder if a great deal of Knowledge, which is not capable of making a Man Wise, has a natural Tendency to make him Vain and Arrogant.

[3] Compare the satiric portrait of Tom Folio in *The Tatler,* No. 158.

No. 106   Monday, July 2, 1711.   [Addison]

. . . Hinc tibi copia
Manabit ad plenum, benigno
Ruris honorum opulenta cornu.[1] —Hor.

Having often received an Invitation from my Friend Sir ROGER DE COVERLY to pass away a Month with him in the Country, I last Week accompanied him thither, and am settled with him for some Time at his Country-house, where I intend to form several of my ensuing Speculations.[2] Sir ROGER, who is very well acquainted with my Humour, lets me rise and go to Bed when I please, dine at his own Table or in my Chamber as I think fit, sit still and say nothing without bidding me be merry. When the Gentlemen of the Country come to see him, he only shews me at a Distance: As I have been walking in his Fields I have observed them stealing a Sight of me over an Hedge, and have heard the Knight desiring them not to let me see them, for that I hated to be stared at.

    I am the more at Ease in Sir ROGER's Family, because it consists of sober and staid Persons; for as the Knight is the best Master in the World, he seldom changes his Servants; and as he is beloved by all about him, his Servants never care for leaving him: By this Means his Domesticks are all in Years, and grown old with their Master. You would take his Valet de Chambre for his Brother, his Butler is gray-headed, his Groom

---

[1] "In this spot shall rich abundance of the glories of the field flow to the full for thee from bounteous horn."

[2] The Spectator's visit with Sir Roger in the country occupied the whole month of July (compare No. 131), when many of Addison's readers were themselves leaving London for the country.

is one of the gravest Men that I have ever seen, and his Coachman has the Looks of a Privy-Counsellor. You see the Goodness of the Master even in the old House-dog, and in a gray Pad that is kept in the Stable with great Care and Tenderness out of Regard to his past Services, tho' he has been useless for several Years.

I could not but observe with a great deal of Pleasure the Joy that appeared in the Countenances of these ancient Domesticks upon my Friend's Arrival at his Country-Seat. Some of them could not refrain from Tears at the Sight of their old Master; every one of them press'd forward to do something for him, and seemed discouraged if they were not employed. At the same Time the good old Knight, with a Mixture of the Father and the Master of the Family, tempered the Enquiries after his own Affairs with several kind Questions relating to themselves. This Humanity and Good-nature engages every Body to him, so that when he is pleasant upon any of them, all his Family are in good Humour, and none so much as the Person whom he diverts himself with: On the Contrary, if he coughs, or betrays any Infirmity of old Age, it is easy for a Stander-by to observe a secret Concern in the Looks of all his Servants.

My worthy Friend has put me under the particular Care of his Butler, who is a very prudent Man, and, as well as the rest of his Fellow-Servants, wonderfully desirous of pleasing me, because they have often heard their Master talk of me as of his particular Friend.

My chief Companion, when Sir ROGER is diverting himself in the Woods or the Fields, is a very venerable Man who is ever with Sir ROGER, and has lived at his House in the Nature of a Chaplain above thirty Years. This Gentleman is a Person of good Sense and some Learning, of a very regular Life and obliging Conversation: He heartily loves Sir ROGER, and knows that he is very much in the old Knight's Esteem; so that he lives in the Family rather as a Relation than a Dependant.

I have observed in several of my Papers, that my Friend Sir ROGER, amidst all his good Qualities, is something of an

Humourist; and that his Virtues, as well as Imperfections, are as it were tinged by a certain Extravagance, which makes them particularly *his,* and distinguishes them from those of other Men. This Cast of Mind, as it is generally very innocent in it self, so it renders his Conversation highly agreeable, and more delightful than the same Degree of Sense and Virtue would appear in their common and ordinary Colours. As I was walking with him last Night, he ask'd me how I liked the good Man whom I have just now mentioned? and without staying for my Answer, told me, That he was afraid of being insulted with Latin and Greek at his own Table; for which Reason, he desired a particular Friend of his at the University to find him out a Clergyman rather of plain Sense than much Learning, of a good Aspect, a clear Voice, a sociable Temper, and, if possible, a Man that understood a little of Back-Gammon. My Friend, says Sir ROGER, found me out this Gentleman, who, besides the Endowments required of him, is, they tell me, a good Scholar though he does not shew it. I have given him the Parsonage of the Parish; and because I know his Value, have settled upon him a good Annuity for Life. If he outlives me, he shall find that he was higher in my Esteem than perhaps he thinks he is. He has now been with me thirty Years; and though he does not know I have taken Notice of it, has never in all that Time asked any thing of me for himself, tho' he is every Day solliciting me for something in Behalf of one or other of my Tenants his Parishioners. There has not been a Law-Suit in the Parish since he has lived among them: If any Dispute arises, they apply themselves to him for the Decision; if they do not acquiesce in his Judgment, which I think never happened above once, or twice at most, they appeal to me. At his first settling with me, I made him a Present of all the good Sermons which have been printed in *English,* and only begged of him that every *Sunday* he wold pronounce one of them in the Pulpit. Accordingly, he has digested them into such a Series, that they follow one another naturally, and make a continued System of practical Divinity.

As Sir ROGER was going on in his Story, the Gentleman

we were talking of came up to us; and upon the Knight's asking him who preached to Morrow (for it was *Saturday* Night) told us, the Bishop of St. *Asaph* in the Morning, and Doctor *South* in the Afternoon. He then shewed us his List of Preachers for the whole Year, where I saw with a great deal of Pleasure Archbishop *Tillotson,* Bishop *Saunderson,* Doctor *Barrow,* Doctor *Calamy,* with several living Authors who have published Discourses of Practical Divinity. I no sooner saw this venerable Man in the Pulpit, but I very much approved of my Friend's insisting upon the Qualifications of a good Aspect and a clear Voice; for I was so charmed with the Gracefulness of his Figure and Delivery, as well as with the Discourses he pronounced, that I think I never passed any Time more to my Satisfaction. A Sermon repeated after this Manner, is like the Composition of a Poet in the Mouth of a graceful Actor.

I could heartily wish that more of our Country-Clergy would follow this Example; and instead of wasting their Spirits in laborious Compositions of their own, would endeavour after a handsome Elocution, and all those other Talents that are proper to enforce what has been penned by greater Masters. This would not only be more easy to themselves, but more edifying to the People.

No. 108   Wednesday, July 4, 1711.   [Addison]

Gratis anhelans, multa agendo nihil agens. [1] —Phaed.

As I was Yesterday Morning walking with Sir ROGER before his House, a Country-Fellow brought him a huge Fish, which, he told him, Mr. *William Wimble* had caught that very Morning; and that he presented it, with his Service, to him, and intended to come and dine with him. At the same Time he delivered a Letter, which my Friend read to me as soon as the Messenger left him.

'*Sir* ROGER,

I Desire you to accept of a Jack, which is the best I have caught this Season. I intend to come and stay with you a Week, and see how the Perch bite in the *Black River*. I observed, with some Concern, the last Time I saw you upon the Bowling-Green, that your Whip wanted a Lash to it: I will bring half a Dozen with me that I twisted last Week, which I hope will serve you all the Time you are in the Country. I have not been out of the Saddle for six Days last past, having been at *Eaton* with Sir *John's* eldest Son. He takes to his Learning hugely.
I am,
       SIR,
              Your humble Servant,
                   Will. Wimble.'

This extraordinary Letter, and Message that accompanied it, made me very curious to know the Character and Quality

[1] "Out of breath to no purpose, and very busy about nothing."

263

of the Gentleman who sent them; which I found to be as follows; *Will. Wimble* is younger Brother to a Baronet, and descended of the ancient Family of the *Wimbles.* He is now between Forty and Fifty; but being bred to no Business and born to no Estate, he generally lives with his elder Brother as Superintendant of his Game. He hunts a Pack of Dogs better than any Man in the Country, and is very famous for finding out a Hare. He is extremely well versed in all the little Handicrafts of an idle Man: He makes a *May*-fly to a Miracle; and furnishes the whole Country with Angle-Rods. As he is a good-natur'd officious Fellow, and very much esteemed upon Account of his Family, he is a welcome Guest at every House, and keeps up a good Correspondence among all the Gentlemen about him. He carries a Tulip-Root in his Pocket from one to another, or exchanges a Puppy between a couple of Friends that live perhaps in the opposite Sides of the County. *Will.* is a particular Favourite of all the young Heirs, whom he frequently obliges with a Net that he has weaved, or a Setting-dog that he has *made* himself: He now and then presents a Pair of Garters of his own knitting to their Mothers or Sisters; and raises a great deal of Mirth among them, by enquiring as often as he meets them *how they wear?* These Gentleman-like Manufactures and obliging little Humours, make *Will.* the Darling of the Country.

Sir ROGER was proceeding in the Character of him, when we saw him make up to us, with two or three Hazle-twigs in his Hand that he had cut in Sir ROGER's Woods, as he came through them, in his Way to the House. I was very much pleased to observe on one Side the hearty and sincere Welcome with which Sir ROGER received him, and on the other the secret Joy which his Guest discovered at Sight of the good old Knight. After the first Salutes were over, *Will.* desired Sir ROGER to lend him one of his Servants to carry a Set of Shuttle-cocks he had with him in a little Box to a Lady that liv'd about a Mile off, to whom it seems he had promised such a Present for above this half Year. Sir ROGER's Back was no sooner turn'd, but honest *Will.* began to tell me of a large Cock-Pheasant that he had sprung in one of the neighbouring Woods, with two or three other Adventures of the same Nature. Odd and uncommon Characters are the Game that I look for, and most delight in; for which Reason I was as much pleased with the Novelty of the Person that talked to me, as he could be for his Life with the springing of a Pheasant, and therefore listned to him with more than ordinary Attention.

In the Midst of his Discourse the Bell rung to Dinner, where the Gentleman I have been speaking of had the Pleasure of seeing the huge Jack, he had caught, served up for the first Dish in a most sumptuous Manner. Upon our sitting down to it he gave us a long Account how he had hooked it, played with it, foiled it, and at length drew it out upon the Bank, with several other Particulars that lasted all the first Course. A Dish of Wild-fowl that came afterwards furnished Conversation for the rest of the Dinner, which concluded with a late Invention of *Will's* for improving the Quail Pipe.

Upon withdrawing into my Room after Dinner, I was secretly touched with Compassion towards the honest Gentleman that had dined with us; and could not but consider with a great deal of Concern, how so good an Heart and such busy Hands were wholly employed in Trifles; that so much Humanity should be so little beneficial to others, and so much Industry so little advantageous to himself. The same Temper of Mind and Application to Affairs might have recommended him to the publick Esteem, and have raised his Fortune in another Station of Life. What Good to his Country or himself might not a Trader or Merchant have done with such useful tho' ordinary Qualifications?

Will. Wimble's is the Case of many a younger Brother of a great Family, who had rather see their Children starve like Gentlemen, than thrive in a Trade or Profession that is beneath their Quality. This Humour fills several Parts of *Europe* with Pride and Beggary. It is the Happiness of a trading Nation, like ours, that the younger Sons, tho' uncapable of any liberal Art or Profession, may be placed in such a Way of Life, as may perhaps enable them to vie with the best of their Family: Accordingly we find several Citizens that were launched into the World with narrow Fortunes, rising by an honest Industry to greater Estates than those of their elder Brothers. It is not improbable but *Will.* was formerly tried at Divinity, Law, or Physick; and that finding his Genius did not lie that Way, his Parents gave him up at length to his own Inventions: But certainly, however improper he might have been for Studies of a higher Nature, he was perfectly well turned for the Occupations of Trade and Commerce. As I think this is a Point which cannot be too much inculcated, I shall desire my Reader to compare what I have here written with what I have said in my Twenty first Speculation.

No. 109   Thursday, July 5, 1711.   [Steele]

Abnormis sapiens [1]—Hor.

I was this Morning walking in the Gallery, when Sir ROGER
enter'd at the end opposite to me, and advancing towards me,
said, he was glad to meet me among his Relations the DE
COVERLEYS, and hoped I liked the Conversation of so much
good Company, who were as silent as my self. I knew he alluded
to the Pictures, and as he is a Gentleman who does not a little
value himself upon his ancient Descent, I expected he would
give me some Account of them. We were now arrived at the upper End of the Gallery, when the Knight faced towards one of
the Pictures, and as we stood before it, he entered into the Matter, after his blunt way of saying things, as they occur to his
Imagination, without regular Introduction, or Care to preserve
the appearance of Chain of Thought.

It is, said he, worth while to consider the Force of Dress;
and how the Persons of one Age differ from those of another,
merely by that only. One may observe also that the General
Fashion of one Age has been follow'd by one particular Set
of People in another, and by them preserved from one Generation to another. Thus the vast Jetting Coat and small Bonnet,
which was the Habit in *Harry* the Seventh's time, is kept on
in the Yeomen of the Guard; not without a good and Politick
View, because they look a Foot taller, and a Foot and an half
broader: Besides, that the Cap leaves the Face expanded,
and consequently more Terrible, and fitter to stand at the Entrance of Palaces.

[1] "Unschooled in formal learning."

This Predecessor of ours, you see, is dressed after this manner, and his Cheeks would be no larger than mine were he in a Hat as I am. He was the last Man that won a Prize in the Tilt-Yard (which is now a Common Street before *Whitehall*). You see the broken Lance that lyes there by his right Foot; He shivered that Lance of his Adversary all to pieces; and bearing himself, look you Sir, in this manner, at the same time he came within the Target of the Gentleman who rode again him, and taking him with incredible Force before him on the Pummel of his Saddle, he in that manner rid the Turnament over, with an Air that shewed he did it rather to perform the Rule of the Lists, than Expose his Enemy; however, it appeared he knew how to make use of a Victory, and with a gentle Trot he marched up to a Gallery where their Mistress sat (for they were Rivals) and let him down with laudable Courtesy and pardonable Insolence. I don't know but it might be exactly where the Coffee-house is now.

You are to know this my Ancestor was not only of a military Genius but fit also for the Arts of Peace, for he play'd on the Base-viol as well as any Gentleman at Court; you see where his Viol hangs by his Basket-hilt Sword. The Action at the Tilt-yard you may be sure won the Fair Lady, who was a Maid of Honour, and the greatest Beauty of her time; here she stands, the next Picture. You see, Sir, my Great Great Great Grand-Mother has on the new-fashioned Petticoat, except that the Modern is gathered at the Waste; my Grandmother appears as is she stood in a large Drum, wheras the Ladies now walk as if they were in a Go-Cart. For all this Lady was bred at Court, she became an Excellent Country-Wife, she brought ten Children, and when I shew you the Library, you shall see in her own hand (allowing for the Difference of the Language,) the best Receipt now in *England* both for an Hasty-Pudding and a Whitepot.

If you please to fall back a little, because it is necessary to look at the three next Pictures at one View; these are three Sisters. She on the right Hand, who is so very beautiful, dyed a Maid; the next to her, still handsomer, had the same Fate, against her Will; this homely thing in the middle had both their Portions added to her own, and was Stolen by a neighbouring Gentleman, a Man of Stratagem and Resolution, for he poisoned three Mastiffs to come at her, and knocked down two Dear-stealers in carrying her off. Misfortunes happen in all Families: The Theft of this Romp and so much Money, was no great matter to our Estate. But the next Heir that possessed it was this soft Gentleman, whom you see there: Observe the small Buttons, the little Boots, the Laces, the Slashes about his Cloaths, and above all the Posture he is drawn in, (which to be sure was his own chusing;) you see he sits with one Hand on a Desk writing, and looking as it were another way, like an easie Writer,[2] or a Sonneteer: He was one of those that had too much Wit to know how to live in the World; he was a Man of no Justice, but great good Manners; he ruined every body that had any thing to do with him, but never said a rude thing in his Life; the most indolent Person in the World, he would sign a Deed that passed away half his Estate with his Gloves on, but would not put on his Hat before a Lady if it were to save his Country. He is said to be the first that made Love by squeezing the Hand. He left the Estate with ten thousand Pounds Debt upon it, but however by all Hands I have been informed that he was every way the finest Gentleman in the World. That Debt lay heavy on our House for one Generation, but it was retrieved by a Gift from that Honest Man you see there, a Citizen of our Name, but nothing at all a-kin to us. I know Sir ANDREW FREEPORT has said behind my Back, that this Man was descended from one of the ten Children of the Maid of Honour I shewed you above. But it was never made out; we winked at the thing indeed, because Mony was wanting at that time.

---

[2] Compare Steele's comment on "Insects called easie Writers" in *The Tatler*, No. 9, and Pope's reference to "the Mob of Gentlemen who wrote with Ease" in *To Augustus*, 1. 108.

Here I saw my Friend a little embarrassed, and turned my Face to the next Portraiture.

Sir ROGER went on with his Account of the Gallery in the following manner. This Man (pointing to him I look'd at) I take to be the Honour of our House. Sir HUMPHREY DE COVERLEY; he was in his Dealings as punctual as a Tradesman, and as generous as a Gentleman. He would have thought himself as much undone by breaking his Word, as if it were to be followed by Bankrupcy. He served his Country as Knight of this Shire to his dying Day: He found it no easie matter to maintain an Integrity in his Words and Actions, even in things that regarded the Offices which were incumbent upon him, in the care of his own Affairs and Relations of Life, and therefore dreaded (tho' he had great Talents) to go into Employments of State, where he must be exposed to the Snares of Ambition. Innocence of Life and great Ability were the distinguishing Parts of his Character; the latter, he had often observed, had led to the Destruction of the former, and used frequently to lament that Great and Good had not the same Signification. He was an Excellent Husbandman, but had resolved not to exceed such a degree of Wealth; all above it he bestowed in secret Bounties many Years after the Sum he aimed at for his own use was attained. Yet he did not slacken his Industry, but to a decent old Age spent the Life and Fortune which was superfluous to himself, in the Service of his Friends and Neighbours.

Here we were called to Dinner, and Sir ROGER ended the Discourse of this Gentleman, by telling me, as we followed the Servant, that this his Ancestor was a Brave Man, and narrowly escaped being killed in the Civil Wars; for, said he, he was sent out of the Field upon a private Message the Day before the Battle of *Worcester*. The Whim of narrowly escaping, by having been within a Day of Danger; with other Matters abovementioned, mixed with good Sense, left me at a Loss whether I was more delighted with my Friend's Wisdom or Simplicity.

No. 110   Friday, July 6, 1711.   [Addison]

Horror ubique animos, simul ipsa silentia terrent.[1] —Virg.

At a little Distance from Sir ROGER'S House, among the Ruins of an old Abby, there is a long Walk of aged Elms; which are shot up so very high, that when one passes under them, the Rooks and Crows that rest up on the Tops of them seem to be Cawing in another Region. I am very much delighted with this Sort of Noise, which I consider as a kind of natural Prayer to that Being who supplies the Wants of his whole Creation, and, who in the beautiful Language of the *Psalms,* feedeth the young Ravens that call upon him. I like this Retirement the better, because of an ill Report it lies under of being *haunted;* for which Reason (as I have been told in the Family) no living Creature ever walks in it besides the Chaplain. My good Friend the Butler desired me with a very grave Face not to venture myself in it after Sun-set, for that one of the Footmen had been almost frighted out of his Wits by a Spirit that appeared to him in the Shape of a black Horse without an Head; to which he added, that about a Month ago one of the Maids coming home late that Way with a Pail of Milk upon her Head, heard such a Rustling among the Bushes that she let it fall.

I was taking a Walk in this Place last Night between the Hours of Nine and Ten, and could not but fancy it one of the most proper Scenes in the World for a Ghost to appear in. The Ruins of the Abby are scattered up and down on every Side, and half covered with Ivy and Elder-Bushes, the Harbours

[1] "All things were full of Horrour and Affright,
    And dreadful ev'n the silence of the Night."

—Dryden's *Virgil.*

271

of several solitary Birds which seldom make their Appearance till the Dusk of the Evening. The Place was formerly a Church-yard, and has still several Marks in it of Graves and Burying-Places. There is such an Eccho among the old Ruins and Vaults, that if you stamp but a little louder than ordinary you hear the Sound repeated. At the same Time the Walk of Elms, with the Croaking of the Ravens which from time to time are heard from the Tops of them, looks exceeding solemn and vener-able. These Objects naturally raise Seriousness and Attention; and when Night heightens the Awfulness of the Place, and pours out her supernumerary Horrours upon every thing in it, I do not at all wonder that weak Minds fill it with Spectres and Apparitions.

Mr. LOCKE,[2] in his Chapter of the Association of Ideas, has very curious Remarks to shew how by the Prejudice of Education one Idea often introduces into the Mind a whole Set that bear no Resemblance to one another in the Nature of things. Among several Examples of this Kind, he produces the following Instance. *The Ideas of Goblins and Sprights have really no more to do with Darkness than Light: Yet let but a foolish Maid inculcate these often on the Mind of a Child, and raise them there together, possibly he shall never be able to separate them again so long as he lives; but Darkness shall ever afterwards bring with it those frightful Ideas, and they shall be so joyned, that he can no more bear the one than the other.*

As I was walking in this Solitude, where the Dusk of the Evening conspired with so many other Occasions of Terrour, I observed a Cow grazing not far from me, which an Imagina-tion that is apt to *startle* might easily have construed into a black Horse without an Head; and I dare say the poor Foot-man lost his Wits upon some such trivial Occasion.

My Friend Sir ROGER has often told me with a great deal of Mirth, that at his first coming to his Estate he found three Parts of his House altogether useless; that the best Room in

---

[2] *An Essay Concerning Human Understanding,* III, xxxiii.

it had the Reputation of being haunted, and by that Means was locked up; that Noises had been heard in his long Gallery, so that he could not get a Servant to enter it after eight a Clock at Night; that the Door of one of his Chambers was nailed up, because there went a Story in the Family that a Butler had formerly hanged himself in it; and that his Mother, who lived to a great Age, had shut up half the Rooms in the House, in which either her Husband, a Son, or Daughter had died. The Knight seeing his Habitation reduced to so small a Compass, and himself in a Manner shut out of his own House, upon the Death of his Mother ordered all the Apartments to be flung open, and *exorcised* by his Chaplain, who lay in every Room one after another, and by that Means dissipated the Fears which had so long reigned in the Family.

I should not have been thus particular upon these ridiculous Horrours, did not I find them so very much prevail in all Parts of the Country. At the same Time I think a Person who is thus terrify'd with the Imagination of Ghosts and Spectres much more reasonable, than one who contrary to the Reports of all Historians sacred and prophane, ancient and modern, and to the Traditions of all Nations, thinks the Appearance of Spirits fabulous and groundless: Could not I give my self up to this general Testimony of Mankind, I should to the Relations of particular Persons who are now living, and whom I cannot distrust in other Matters of Fact. I might here add, that not only the Historians, to whom we may joyn the Poets, but likewise the Philosophers of Antiquity have favoured this Opinion. *Lucretius* himself, though by the Course of his Philosophy he was obliged to maintain that the Soul did not exist separate from the Body, makes no Doubt of the Reality of Apparitions, and that Men have often appeared after their Death. This I think very remarkable; he was so pressed with the Matter of Fact which he could not have the Confidence to deny, that he was forced to account for it by one of the most absurd unphilosophical Notions that was ever started. He tells us, That the Surfaces of all Bodies are perpetually flying off from their respective Bodies, one after another; and that these Surfaces or thin Cases that included each other whilst they were joined in the Body like the Coats of an Onion, are sometimes seen entire when they are separated from it; by which Means we often behold the Shapes and Shadows of Persons who are either dead or absent.

I shall dismiss this Paper with a Story out of *Josephus,* not so much for the Sake of the Story itself, as for the moral Reflections with which the Author concludes it, and which I shall here set down in his own Words. *Glaphyra* the Daughter of King *Archilaus,* after the Death of her two first Husbands (being married to a third, who was Brother to her first Husband, and so passionately in Love with her that he turn'd off his former Wife to make Room for this Marriage) had a very odd kind of Dream. She fancied that she saw her first Husband coming towards her, and that she embraced him with great Tenderness; when in the Midst of the Pleasure which she expressed at the Sight of him, he reproached her after the following Manner: *Glaphyra,* says he, thou hast made good the old Saying, That Women are not to be trusted. Was not I the Husband of thy Virginity? have I not Children by thee? How couldst thou forget our loves so far as to enter into a second Marriage, and after that into a third, nay to take for thy Husband a Man who has so shamelessly crept into the Bed of his Brother? However, for the Sake of our passed Loves, I shall free thee from thy present Reproach, and make thee mine for ever. *Glaphyra* told this Dream to several Women of her Acquaintance, and died soon after. I thought this Story might not be impertinent in this Place, wherein I speak of those Kings: Besides that, the Example deserves to be taken Notice of, as it contains a most certain Proof of the Immortality of the Soul, and of Divine Providence. If any Man thinks these Facts incredible, let him enjoy his Opinion to himself; but let him not endeavour to disturb the Belief of others, who by Instances of this Nature are excited to the Study of Virtue.

Ἀθανάτους μὲν πρῶτα θεοὺς, νόμῳ ὡς διάκειται,
τιμα.[1]—Pyth.

I am always very well pleased with a Country *Sunday;* and think, if keeping holy the Seventh Day were only a human Institution, it would be the best Method that could have been thought of for the polishing and civilizing of Mankind. It is certain the Country-People would soon degenerate into a kind of Savages and Barbarians, were there not such frequent Returns of a stated Time, in which the whole Village meet together with their best Faces, and in their cleanliest Habits, to converse with one another upon indifferent Subjects, hear their Duties explained to them, and join together in Adoration of the supreme Being. *Sunday* clears away the Rust of the whole Week, not only as it refreshes in their Minds the Notions of Religion, but as it puts both the Sexes upon appearing in their most agreeable Forms, and exerting all such Qualities as are apt to give them a Figure in the Eye of the Village. A Country-Fellow distinguishes himself as much in the *Church-yard,* as a Citizen does upon the *Change;* the whole Parish-Politicks being generally discuss'd in that Place either after Sermon or before the Bell rings.

My Friend Sir ROGER being a good Churchman, has beautified the Inside of his Church with several Texts of his own chusing: He has likewise given a handsome Pulpit-Cloth, and railed in the Communion-Table at his own Expence. He has

---

[1] "First to the Gods thy humble Homage pay;
The greatest this, and first of Laws, obey."

—Rowe's   translation.

often told me, that at his coming to his Estate he found his Parishioners very irregular; and that in order to make them kneel and join in the Responses, he gave every one of them a Hassock and a Common-prayer Book; and at the same Time employed an itinerant Singing-Master, who goes about the Country for that Purpose, to instruct them rightly in the Tunes of the Psalms; upon which they now very much value themselves, and indeed out-do most of the Country Churches that I have ever heard.

As Sir ROGER is Landlord to the whole Congregation, he keeps them in very good Order, and will suffer no Body to sleep in it besides himself; for if by Chance he has been surprized into a short Nap at Sermon, upon recovering out of it he stands up and looks about him, and if he sees any Body else nodding, either wakes them himself, or sends his Servant to them. Several other of the old Knight's Particularities break out upon these Occasions: Sometimes he will be lengthening out a Verse in the Singing-Psalms, half a Minute after the rest of the Congregation have done with it; sometimes, when he is pleased with the Matter of his Devotion, he pronounces *Amen* three or four times to the same Prayer; and sometimes stands up when every Body else is upon their Knees, to count the Congregation, or see if any of his Tenants are missing.

I was Yesterday very much surprized to hear my old Friend, in the Midst of the Service, calling out to one *John Matthews* to mind what he was about, and not disturb the Congregation. This *John Matthews* it seems is remarkable for being an idle Fellow, and at that Time was kicking his Heels for his Diversion. This Authority of the Knight, though exerted in that odd Manner which accompanies him in all Circumstances of Life, has a very good Effect upon the Parish, who are not polite enough to see any thing ridiculous in his Behaviour; besides that, the general good Sense and Worthiness of his Character, make his Friends observe these little Singularities as Foils that rather set off than blemish his good Qualities.

As soon as the Sermon is finished, no Body presumes to stir till Sir ROGER is gone out of the Church. The Knight walks down from his Seat in the Chancel between a double Row of his Tenants, that stand bowing to him on each Side; and every now and then enquires how such an one's Wife, or Mother, or Son, or Father do whom he does not see at Church; which is understood as a secret Reprimand to the Person that is absent.

The Chaplain has often told me, that upon a Catechizing-day, when Sir ROGER has been pleased with a Boy that answers well, he has ordered a Bible to be given him next Day for his Encouragement; and sometimes accompanies it with a Flitch of Bacon to his Mother. Sir ROGER has likewise added five Pounds a Year to the Clerk's Place; and that he may encourage the young Fellows to make themselves perfect in the Church-Service, has promised upon the Death of the present Incumbent, who is very old, to bestow it according to Merit.

The fair Understanding between Sir ROGER and his Chaplain, and their mutual Concurrence in doing Good, is the more remarkable, because the very next Village is famous for the Differences and Contentions that rise between the Parson and the 'Squire, who live in a perpetual State of War. The Parson is always preaching at the 'Squire, and the 'Squire to be revenged on the Parson never comes to Church. The 'Squire has made all his Tenants Atheists and Tithe-Stealers; while the Parson instructs them every *Sunday* in the Dignity of his Order, and insinuates to them in almost every Sermon, that he is a better Man than his Patron. In short, Matters are come to such an Extremity, that the 'Squire has not said his Prayers either in publick or private this half Year; and that the Parson threatens him, if he does not mend his Manners, to pray for him in the Face of the whole Congregation.

Feuds of this Nature, though too frequent in the Country, are very fatal to the ordinary People; who are so used to be dazled with Riches, that they pay as much Deference to the Understanding of a Man of an Estate, as of a Man of Learning; and are very hardly brought to regard any Truth, how important soever it may be, that is preached to them, when they know there are several Men of five hundred a Year who do not believe it.

. . . Hærent infixi Pectore vultus. [1] — Virg.

In my first Description of the Company in which I pass most of my Time, it may be remembered that I mentioned a great Affliction which my Friend Sir ROGER had met with in his Youth, which was no less than a Disappointment in Love. It happened this Evening, that we fell into a very pleasing Walk at a Distance from his House: As soon as we came into it, 'It is,' quoth the good old Man, looking round him with a Smile, 'very hard, that any Part of my Land should be settled upon one who has used me so ill as the perverse Widow [2] did; and yet I am sure I could not see a Sprig of any Bough of this whole Walk of Trees, but I should reflect upon her and her Severity. She has certainly the finest Hand of any Woman in the World. You are to know this was the Place wherein I used to muse upon her; and by that Custom I can never come into it, but the same tender Sentiments revive in my Mind, as if I had actually walked with that beautiful Creature under these Shades. I have been Fool enough to carve her Name on the Bark of several of these Trees; so unhappy is the Condition of Men in Love, to attempt the removing of their Passion by the Methods which serve only to imprint it deeper. She has certainly the finest Hand of any Woman in the World.'

Here followed a profound Silence; and I was not displeased to observe my Friend falling so naturally into a Discourse, which I had ever before taken Notice he industriously avoided. After

---

[1] "His looks cling fast within her bosom," or, as Steele applies the quotation, "Her [the widow's] looks cling fast within his [Sir Roger's] bosom."
[2] See *The Spectator,* No. 2, n.2.

a very long Pause, he entered upon an Account of this great Circumstance in his Life, with an Air which I thought raised my *Idea* of him above what I had ever had before; and gave me the Picture of that chearful Mind of his, before it received that Stroke which has ever since affected his Words and Actions. But he went on as follows.

'I came to my Estate in my Twenty second Year, and resolved to follow the Steps of the most worthy of my Ancestors, who have inhabited this spot of Earth before me, in all the Methods of Hospitality and good Neighbourhood, for the Sake of my Fame; and in Country Sports and Recreations, for the Sake of my Health. In my Twenty third Year I was obliged to serve as Sheriff of the County; and in my Servants, Officers, and whole Equipage, indulged the Pleasure of a young Man (who did not think ill of his own Person) in taking that publick Occasion of shewing my Figure and Behaviour to Advantage. You may easily imagine to your self what Appearance I made, who am pretty tall, rid well, and was very well dressed, at the Head of a whole County, with Musick before me, a Feather in my Hat, and my Horse well bitted. I can assure you I was not a little pleased with the kind Looks and Glances I had from all the Balconies and Windows, as I rode to the Hall where the Assizes were held. But when I came there, a beautiful Creature in a Widow's Habit sat in Court, to hear the Event of a Cause concerning her Dower. This commanding Creature (who was born for Destruction of all who behold her) put on such a Resignation in her Countenance, and bore the Whispers of all around the Court with such a pretty Uneasiness, I warrant you, and then recovered her self from one Eye to another, till she was perfectly confused by meeting something so wistful in all she encountered, that at last, with a Murrain to her, she cast her bewitching Eye upon me. I no sooner met it, but I bowed like a great surprized Booby; and knowing her Cause to be the first which came on, I cried, like a captivated Calf as I was, Make Way for the Defendant's Witnesses. This sudden Partiality made all the County immediately see the Sheriff also was become a Slave to the fine Widow. During the Time her Cause was upon Trial, she behaved her self, I warrant you, with such a deep Attention to her Business, took Opportunities to have little Billets handed to her Counsel, then would be in such a pretty Confusion, occasioned, you must know, by acting before so much Company, that not only I but the whole Cort was prejudiced in her Favour; and all that the next Heir to her Husband had to urge, was thought so groundless and frivolous, that when it came to her Counsel to reply, there was not half so much said as every one besides in the Court thought he could have urged to her Advantage. You must understand, Sir, this perverse Woman is one of those unaccountable Creatures that secretly rejoyce in the Admiration of Men, but indulge themselves in no further Consequences. Hence it is that she has ever had a Train of Admirers, and she removes from her Slaves in Town to those in the Country, according to the Seasons of the Year. She is a reading Lady, and far gone in the Pleasures of Friendship: She is always accompanied by a Confident, who is Witness to her daily Protestations against our Sex, and consequently a Bar to her first Steps towards Love, upon the Strength of her own Maxims and Declarations.

However, I must needs say this accomplished Mistress of mine has distinguished me above the rest, and has been known to declare Sir ROGER DE COVERLY was the tamest and most human of all the Brutes in the Country. I was told she said so by one who thought he rallied me; but upon the Strength of this slender Encouragement of being thought least detestable, I made new Liveries, new paired my Coach-Horses, sent them all to Town to be bitted, and taught to throw their Legs well, and move altogether, before I pretended to cross the Country and wait upon her. As soon as I thought my Retinue suitable to the Character of my Fortune and Youth, I set out from hence to make my Addresses. The particular Skill of this Lady has ever been to inflame your Wishes, and yet command Respect. To make her Mistress of this Art, she has a greater Share of Knowledge, Wit, and good Sense, than is usual even among

Men of Merit. The she is beautiful beyond the Race of Women. If you won't let her go on with a certain Artifice with her Eyes, and the Skill of Beauty, she will arm her self with her real Charms, and strike you with Admiration instead of Desire. It is certain that if you were to behold the whole Woman, there is that Dignity in her Aspect, that Composure in her Motion, that Complacency in her Manner, that if her Form makes you hope, her Merit makes you fear. But then again, she is such a desperate Scholar, that no Country-Gentleman can approach her without being a Jest. As I was going to tell you, when I came to her House I was admitted to her Presence with great Civility; at the same Time she placed her self to be first seen by me in such an Attitude, as I think you call the Posture of a Picture, that she discovered new Charms, and I at last came towards her with such an Awe as made me speechless. This she no sooner observed but she made her Advantage of it, and began a Discourse to me concerning Love and Honour, as they both are followed by Pretenders, and the real Votaries to them. When she discussed these Points in a Discourse, which I verily believe was as learned as the best Philosopher in *Europe* could possibly make, she asked me whether she was so happy as to fall in with my Sentiments on these important Particulars. Her Confident sat by her, and upon my being in the last Confusion and Silence, this malicious Aide of hers turning to her says, I am very glad to observe Sir ROGER pauses upon this Subject, and seems resolved to deliver all his Sentiments upon the Matter when he pleases to speak. They both kept their Countenances, and after I had sat half an Hour meditating how to behave before such profound Casuists, I rose up and took my Leave. Chance has since that Time thrown me very often in her Way, and she as often has directed a Discourse to me which I do not understand. This Barbarity has kept me ever at a Distance from the most beautiful Object my Eyes ever beheld. It is thus also she deals with all Mankind, and you must make Love to her, as you would conquer the Sphinx, by posing her. But were she like other Women, and that there were any talking to her, how constant must the Pleasure of that Man be, who could converse with a Creature—But, after all, you may be sure her Heart is fixed on some one or other; and yet I have been credibly informed; but who can believe half that is said! After she had done speaking to me, she put her Hand to her Bosom and adjusted her Tucker. Then she cast her Eyes a little down, upon my beholding her too earnestly. They say she sings excellently: Her Voice in her ordinary Speech has something in it inexpressibly sweet. You must know I dined with her at a publick Table the Day after I first saw her, and she helped me to some Tansy in the Eye of all the Gentlemen in the Country: She has certainly the finest Hand of any Woman in the World. I can assure you, Sir, were you to behold her, you would be in the same Condition; for as her Speech is Musick, her Form is Angelick. But I find I grow irregular while I am talking of her; but indeed it would be Stupidity to be unconcerned at such Perfection. Oh the excellent Creature, she is as inimitable to all Women, as she is inaccessible to all Men!'

I found my Friend begin to rave, and insensibly led him towards the House, that we might be joined by some other Company; and am convinced that the Widow is the secret Cause of all that Inconsistency which appears in some Parts of my Friend's Discourse; tho' he has so much Command of himself as not directly to mention her, yet according to that of *Martial,* which one knows not how to render into *English, Dum tacet hanc loquitur.* I shall end this Paper with that whole Epigram, which represents with much Humour my honest Friend's Condition.

> *Quicquid agit Rufus, nihil est nisi Nævia Rufo:*
> *Si guadet, si flet, si tacet, hanc loquitur:*
> *Cænat, propinat, poscit, negat, annuit, una est*
> *Nævia; si non sit Nævia, mutus erit.*
> *Scriberet hesterna Patri cum Luce salutem,*
> *Nævia lux, inquit, Nævia numen, ave.*

Let Rufus *weep, rejoice, stand, sit, or walk,*
Still he can nothing but of Nævia *talk;*
Let him eat, drink, ask Questions, or dispute,
Still he must speak of Nævia, *or be mute.*
He writ to his Father, ending with this Line,
I am, my Lovely Nævia, *ever thine.*

No. 117   Saturday, July 14, 1711.   [Addison]

... *Ipsi sibi somnia fingunt.* [1]—Virg.

There are some Opinions in which a Man should stand Neuter, without engaging his Assent to one side or the other. Such a hovering Faith as this, which refuses to settle upon any Determination, is absolutely necessary in a Mind that is careful to avoid Errors and Prepossessions. When the Arguments press equally on both sides in Matters that are indifferent to us, the safest method is to give up our selves to neither.

It is with this Temper of Mind that I consider the Subject of Witchcraft. When I hear the Relations that are made from all Parts of the World, not only from *Norway* and *Lapland,* from the *East* and *West Indies,* but from every particular Nation in *Europe,* I cannot forbear thinking that there is such an Intercourse and Commerce with Evil Spirits, as that which we express by the Name of Witchcraft. [2] But when I consider that the ignorant and credulous Parts of the World abound most in these Relations, and that the Persons among us who are supposed to engage in such an Infernal Commerce are People of a weak Understanding and crazed Imagination, and at the same time reflect upon the many Impostures and Delusions of this Nature that have been detected in all Ages, I endeavour to suspend my Belief till I hear more certain Accounts than any which have yet come to my Knowledge. In short, when I consider the Question, Whether there are such Persons in the World as those we call Witches? my Mind is divided between the two oppo-

---

[1] "They fashion their own dreams."
[2] This sentence and the next illustrate one of the intellectual dilemmas in which the neoclassic "rationalist" found himself.

site Opinions; or rather (to speak my Thoughts freely) I believe in general that there is, and has been such a thing as Witchcraft; but at the same time can give no Credit to any Particular Instance of it.

I am engaged in this Speculation, by some Occurrences that I met with Yesterday, which I shall give my Reader an Account of at large. As I was walking with my Friend Sir ROGER by the side of one of his Woods, an old Woman applied her self to me for my Charity. Her Dress and Figure put me in mind of the following Description in *Otway*. [3]

> *In a close Lane as I pursu'd my Journey,*
> *I spy'd a wrinkled Hag, with Age grown double,*
> *Picking dry Sticks, and mumbling to her self.*
> *Her Eyes with scalding Rheum were gall'd and red;*
> *Cold Palsy shook her Head; her Hands seem'd wither'd;*
> *And on her Crooked Shoulders had she wrapp'd*
> *The tatter'd Remnants of an old striped Hanging,*
> *Which serv'd to keep her Carcass from the Cold:*
> *So there was nothing of a-piece about her.*
> *Her lower Weeds were all o'er coarsly patch'd*
> *With diff'rent-colour'd Rags, black, red, white, yellow,*
> *And seem'd to speak Variety of Wretchedness.*

As I was musing on this Description, and comparing it with the Object before me, the Knight told me, that this very old Woman had the Reputation of a Witch all over the Country, that her Lips were observed to be always in Motion, and that there was not a Switch about her House which her Neighbours did not believe had carried her several hundreds of Miles. If she chanced to stumble, they always found Sticks or Straws that lay in the Figure of a Cross before her. If she made any Mistake at Church, and cryed *Amen* in a wrong Place, they never failed to conclude that she was saying her Prayers backwards. There was not a Maid in the Parish that would take

[3] *The Orphan,* Act II.

a Pin of her, though she should offer a Bag of Money with it. She goes by the Name of *Moll White,* and has made the Country ring with several imaginary Exploits which are palmed upon her. If the Dairy Maid does not make her Butter come so soon as she would have it, *Moll White* is at the bottom of the Churn. If a Horse sweats in the Stable, *Moll White* has been upon his Back. If a Hare makes an unexpected Escape from the Hounds, the Huntsman curses *Moll White.* Nay, (says Sir ROGER) I have known the Master of the Pack, upon such an Occasion, send one of his Servants to see if *Moll White* had been out that Morning.

This Account raised my Curiosity so far, that I begged my Friend Sir ROGER to go with me into her Hovel, which stood in a solitary Corner under the side of the Wood. Upon our first entring Sir ROGER winked to me, and pointed at something that stood behind the Door, which upon looking that way I found to be an old Broomstaff. At the same time he whispered me in the Ear to take notice of a Tabby Cat that sat in the Chimney-Corner, which, as the Knight told me, lay under as bad a Report as *Moll White* her self; for besides that *Moll* is said often to accompany her in the same Shape, the Cat is reported to have spoken twice or thrice in her Life, and to have played several Pranks above the Capacity of an ordinary Cat.

I was secretly concerned to see Human Nature in so much Wretchedness and Disgrace, but at the same time could not forbear smiling to hear Sir ROGER, who is a little puzzled about the old Woman, advising her as a Justice of Peace to avoid all Communication with the Devil, and never to hurt any of her Neighbours' Cattle. We concluded our Visit with a Bounty, which was very acceptable.

In our Return home Sir ROGER told me, that old *Moll* had been often brought before him for making Children spit Pins, and giving Maids the Night-Mare; and that the Country People would be tossing her into a Pond and trying Experiments with her every Day, if it was not for him and his Chaplin.

I have since found, upon Enquiry, that Sir ROGER was

several times staggered with the Reports that had been brought him concerning this old Woman, and would frequently have bound her over to the County Sessions, had not his Chaplin with much ado perswaded him to the contrary.

I have been the more particular in this Account, because I hear there is scarce a Village in *England* that has not a *Moll White* in it. When an old Woman begins to doat, and grow chargeable to a Parish, she is generally turned into a Witch, and fills the whole Country with extravagant Fancies, imaginary Distempers, and terrifying Dreams. In the mean time, the poor Wretch that is the innocent Occasion of so many Evils begins to be frighted at her self, and sometimes confesses secret Commerces and Familiarities that her Imagination forms in a delirious old Age. This frequently cuts off Charity from the greatest Objects of Compassion, and inspires People with a Malevolence towards those poor decrepid Parts of our Species, in whom Human Nature is defaced by Infirmity and Dotage.

No. 120   Wednesday, July 18, 1711.   [Addison]

. . . Equidem credo, quia sit Divinitus illis
Ingenium . . .[1]—Virg.

My Friend Sir ROGER is very often merry with me, upon my passing so much of my Time among his Poultry: He has caught me twice or thrice looking after a Bird's Nest, and several Times sitting an Hour or two together near an Hen and Chickens. He tells me he believes I am personally acquainted with every Fowl about his House; calls such a particular Cock my Favourite; and frequently complains that his Ducks and Geese have more of my Company than himself.

I must confess I am infinitely delighted with those Speculations of Nature which are to be made in a Country-Life; and as my Reading has very much lain among Books of natural History, I cannot forbear recollecting upon this Occasion the several Remarks which I have met with in Authors, and comparing them with what falls under my own Observation: The Arguments for Providence drawn from the natural History of Animals, being in my Opinion demonstrative.

The Make of every Kind of Animal is different from that of every other Kind; and yet there is not the least Turn in the Muscles or Twist in the Fibres of any one, which does not render them more proper for that particular Animal's Way of Life than any other Cast or Texture of them would have been.

The most violent Appetites in all Creatures are *Lust* and *Hunger:* The first, is a perpetual Call upon them to propagate their Kind; the latter, to preserve themselves.

---

[1] "Methinks they have wisdom from on high."

It is astonishing to consider the different Degrees of Care that descend from the Parent to the Young, so far as is absolutely necessary for the leaving a Posterity. Some Creatures cast their Eggs as Chance directs them, and think of them no farther, as Insects and several Kinds of Fish: Others of a nicer Frame, find out proper Beds to deposite them in, and there leave them; as the Serpent, the Crocodile and Ostrich: Others hatch their Eggs and tend the Birth, till it is able to shift for its self.

What can we call the Principle which directs every different Kind of Bird to observe a particular Plan in the Structure of its Nest, and directs all the same Species to work after the same Model? It cannot be *Imitation;* for though you hatch a Crow under a Hen, and never let it see any of the Works of its own Kind, the Nest it makes shall be the same, to the laying of a Stick, with all the other Nests of the same Species. It cannot be *Reason;* for were Animals indued with it to as great a Degree as Man, their Buildings would be as different as ours, according to the different Conveniencies that they would propose to themselves.

Is it not remarkable, that the same Temper of Weather which raises this genial Warmth in Animals, should cover the Trees with Leaves and the Fields with Grass for their Security and Concealment, and produce such infinite Swarms of Insects for the Support and Sustenance of their respective Broods?

Is it not wonderful, that the Love of the Parent should be so violent while it lasts; and that it should last no longer than is necessary for the Preservation of the Young?

The Violence of this natural Love is exemplified by a very barbarous Experiment; which I shall quote at Length as I find it in an excellent Author, and hope my Readers will pardon the mentioning such an Instance of Cruelty, because there is nothing can so effectually shew the Strength of that Principle in Animals of which I am here speaking. 'A Person who was well skilled in Dissections opened a Bitch, and as she lay in the most exquisite Tortures offered her one of her young Puppies, which she immediately fell a licking; and for the Time seemed insensible of her own Pain: On the Removal, she kept her Eye fixt on it, and began a wailing sort of Cry, which seemed rather to proceed from the Loss of her young one, than the Sense of her own Torments.'

But notwithstanding this natural Love in Brutes is much more violent and intense than in rational Creatures, Providence has taken Care that it should be no longer troublesome to the Parent than it is useful to the Young; for so soon as the Wants of the latter cease, the Mother withdraws her Fondness and leaves them to provide for themselves: And what is a very remarkable Circumstance in this Part of Instinct, we find that the Love of the Parent may be lengthened out beyond its usual Time if the Preservation of the Species requires it; as we may see in Birds that drive away their Young as soon as they are able to get their Livelihood, but continue to feed them if they are tied to the Nest or confined within a Cage, or by any other Means appear to be out of a Condition of supplying their own Necessities.

This natural Love is not observed in Animals to ascend from the Young to the Parent, which is not at all necessary for the Continuance of the Species: Nor indeed in reasonable Creatures does it rise in any Proportion, as it spreads it self downwards; for in all Family-Affection, we find Protection granted and Favours bestowed, are greater Motives to Love and Tenderness; than Safety, Benefits, or Life received.

One would wonder to hear Sceptical Men disputing for the Reason of Animals, and telling us it is only our Pride and Prejudices that will not allow them the Use of that Faculty.

Reason shews it self in all Occurrences of Life; whereas the Brute makes no Discovery of such a Talent, but in what immediately regards his own Preservation, or the Continuance of his Species. Animals in their Generation are wiser than the Sons of Men; but their Wisdom is confined to a few Particulars, and lies in a very narrow Compass. Take a Brute out of his Instinct, and you find him wholly deprived of Understanding. To use an Instance that comes often under Observation.

With what Caution does the Hen provide her self a Nest in Places unfrequented, and free from Noise and Disturbance? When she has laid her Eggs in such a Manner that she can cover them, what Care does she take in turning them frequently, that all Parts may partake of the vital Warmth? When she leaves them to provide for her necessary Sustenance, how punctually does she return before they have Time to cool, and become incapable of producing an Animal? In the Summer you see her giving her self greater Freedoms, and quitting her Care for above two Hours together; but in Winter, when the Rigour of the Season would chill the Principles of Life, and destroy the young one, she grows more assiduous in her Attendance, and stays away but half the Time. When the Birth approaches, with how much Nicety and Attention does she help the Chick to break its Prison? Not to take Notice of her covering it from the Injuries of the Weather, providing it proper Nourishment, and teaching it to help it self; nor to mention her forsaking the Nest, if after the usual Time of reckoning the young one does not make its Appearance. A Chymical Operation could not be followed with greater Art or Diligence, than is seen in the hatching of a Chick; tho' there are many other Birds that shew an infinitely greater Sagacity in all the forementioned Particulars.

But at the same Time the Hen, that has all this seeming Ingenuity, (which is indeed absolutely necessary for the Propagation of the Species) considered in other Respects, is without the least Glimmerings of Thought or Common Sense. She mistakes a Piece of Chalk for an Egg, and sits upon it in the same Manner: She is insensible of any Increase or Diminution in the Number of those she lays: She does not distinguish between her own and those of another Species; and when the Birth appears of never so different a Bird, will cherish it for her own. In all these Circumstances, which do not carry an immediate Regard to the Subsistence of her self or her Species, she is a very Ideot.

There is not in my Opinion any thing more mysterious in Nature than this Instinct in Animals, which thus rises above Reason, and falls infinitely short of it. It cannot be accounted for by any Properties in Matter, and at the same Time works after so odd a Manner, that one cannot think it the Faculty of an intellectual Being. For my own Part, I look upon it as upon the Principle of Gravitation in Bodies, which is not to be explained by any known Qualities inherent in the Bodies themselves, nor from any Laws of Mechanism, but, according to the best Notions of the greatest Philosophers, is an immediate Impression from the first Mover, and the Divine Energy acting in the Creatures.[2]

[2] Compare *The Spectator*, No. 465.

Comes jucundus in via pro vehiculo est. [1]—Publ. Syr., *Frag.*

A Man's first Care should be to avoid the Reproaches of his own Heart; his next, to escape the Censures of the World: If the last interferes with the former, it ought to be entirely neglected; but otherwise, there cannot be a greater Satisfaction to an honest Mind, than to see those Approbations which it gives itself seconded by the Applauses of the Publick: A Man is more sure of his Conduct, when the Verdict which he passes upon his own Behaviour is thus warranted, and confirmed by the Opinion of all that know him.

My worthy Friend Sir ROGER is one of those who is not only at Peace within himself, but beloved and esteemed by all about him. He receives a suitable Tribute for his universal Benevolence to Mankind, in the Returns of Affection and Good-will, which are paid him by every one that lives within his Neighbourhood. I lately met with two or three odd Instances of that general Respect which is shewn to the good old Knight. He would needs carry *Will. Wimble* and myself with him to the County-Assizes: As we were upon the Road *Will. Wimble* joyned a couple of plain Men who rid before us, and conversed with them for some Time; during which my Friend Sir ROGER acquainted me with their Characters.

The first of them, says he, that has a Spaniel by his Side, is a Yeoman of about an hundred Pounds a Year, an honest Man: He is just within the Game-Act, and qualified to kill an Hare or a Pheasant: He knocks down a Dinner with his Gun

[1] "An agreeable companion on the road is as good as a coach."

294

twice or thrice a Week; and by that Means lives much cheaper than those who have not so good an Estate as himself. He would be a good Neighbour if he did not destroy so many Partridges: In short, he is a very sensible Man; shoots flying; and has been several Times Foreman of the Petty-Jury.

The other that rides along with him is *Tom Touchy,* a Fellow famous for *taking the Law* of every Body. There is not one in the Town where he lives that he has not sued at a Quarter-Sessions. The Rogue had once the Impudence to go to Law with the *Widow.* His Head is full of Costs, Damages, and Ejectments: He plagued a couple of honest Gentlemen so long for a Trespass in breaking one of his Hedges, till he was forced to sell the Ground it enclosed to defray the Charges of the Prosecution: His Father left him fourscore Pounds a Year; but he has *cast* and been cast so often, that he is not now worth thirty. I suppose he is going upon the old Business of the Willow-Tree.

As Sir ROGER was giving me this Account of *Tom Touchy,* *Will. Wimble* and his two Companions stopped short till we came up to them. After having paid their Respects to Sir ROGER, *Will.* told him that Mr. *Touchy* and he must appeal to him upon a Dispute that arose between them. *Will.* it seems had been giving his Fellow Traveller an Account of his angling one Day in such a Hole; when *Tom Tochy,* instead of hearing out his Story, told him, that Mr. such an One, if he pleased, might *take the Law of him* for fishing in that Part of the River. My Friend Sir ROGER heared them both, upon a round Trot; and after having paused some Time told them, with the Air of a Man who would not give his Judgment rashly, that *much might be said on both Sides.* They were neither of them dissatisfied with the Knight's Determination, because neither of them found himself in the Wrong by it: Upon which we made the best of our Way to the Assizes.

The Court was sat before Sir ROGER came, but notwithstanding all the Justices had taken their Places upon the Bench, they made Room for the old Knight at the Head of them; who for his Reputation in the Country took Occasion to whisper in the Judge's Ear, That *he was glad his Lordship had met with so much good Weather in his Circuit.* I was listening to the Proceedings of the Court with much Attention, and infinitely pleased with that great Appearance and Solemnity which so properly accompanies such a publick Administration of our Laws; when, after about an Hour's Sitting, I observed to my great Surprize, in the Midst of a Trial, that my Friend Sir ROGER was getting up to speak. I was in some Pain for him, till I found he had acquitted himself of two or three Sentences, with a Look of much Business and great Intrepidity.

Upon his first Rising the Court was hushed, and a general Whisper ran among the Country-People that Sir ROGER *was up.* The Speech he made was so little to the Purpose, that I shall not trouble my Readers with an Account of it; and I believe was not so much designed by the Knight himself to inform the Court, as to give him a Figure in my Eye, and keep up his Credit in the Country.

I was highly delighted, when the Court rose, to see the Gentlemen of the Country gathering about my old Friend, and striving who should compliment him most; at the same Time that the ordinary People gazed upon him at a Distance, not a little admiring his Courage, that was not afraid to speak to the Judge.

In our Return home we met with a very odd Accident; which I cannot forbear relating, because it shews how desirous all who know Sir ROGER are of giving him Marks of their Esteem. When we were arrived upon the Verge of his Estate, we stopped at a little Inn to rest our selves and our Horses. The Man of the House had it seems been formerly a Servant in the Knight's Family; and to do Honour to his old Master, had some Time since, unknown to Sir ROGER, put him up in a Sign-post before the Door; so that *the Knight's Head* had hung out upon the Road about a Week before he himself knew any thing of the Matter. As soon as Sir ROGER was acquainted with it, finding that his Servant's Indiscretion proceeded wholly from Affection and Good-will, he only told him that he had made him too high a Compliment; and when the Fellow seemed to think that could hardly be, added with a more decisive Look, That it was too great an Honour for any Man under a Duke; but told him at the same time that it might be altered with a very few Touches, and that he himself would be at the Charge of it. Accordingly they got a Painter by the Knight's Directions to add a pair of Whiskers to the Face, and by a litte Aggravation of the Features to change it into the *Saracen's Head.* I should not have known this Story, had not the Inn-keeper upon Sir ROGER's alighting told him in my Hearing, That his Honour's Head was brought back last Night with the Alterations that he had ordered to be made in it. Upon this my Friend with his usual Chearfulness related the Particulars above-mentioned, and ordered the Head to be brought into the Room. I could not forbear discovering greater Expressions of Mirth than ordinary upon the Appearance of this monstrous Face, under which, notwithstanding it was made to frown and stare in a most extraordinary Manner, I could still discover a distant Resemblance of my old Friend. Sir ROGER, upon seeing me laugh, desired me to tell him truly if I thought it possible for People to know him in that Disguise. I at first kept my usual Silence; but upon the Knight's conjuring me to tell him whether it was not still more like himself than a *Saracen,* I composed my Countenance in the best Manner I could, and replied, *That much might be said on both Sides.*

These several Adventures, with the Knight's Behaviour in them, gave me as pleasant a Day as ever I met with in any of my Travels.

No. 124   Monday, July 23, 1711.   [Addison]

Μέγα βιβγίον, μέγα κακόν.[1]

A man who publishes his Works in a Volume, has an infinite Advantage over one who communicates his Writings to the World in loose Tracts and single Pieces. We do not expect to meet with any thing in a bulky Volume, till after some heavy Preamble, and several Words of Course, to prepare the Reader for what follows: Nay, Authors have established it as a Kind of Rule, That a Man ought to be dull sometimes; as the most severe Reader makes Allowances for many Rests and Nodding-places in a Voluminous Writer. This gave Occasion to the famous *Greek* Proverb which I have chosen for my Motto, *That a great Book is a great Evil.*

On the contrary, those who publish their Thoughts in distinct Sheets, and as it were by Piece-meal, have none of these Advantages. We must immediately fall into our Subject, and treat every part of it in a lively Manner, or our Papers are thrown by as dull and insipid: Our Matter must lie close together, and either be wholly new in itself, or in the Turn it receives from our Expressions. Were the Books of our best Authors thus to be retailed to the Publick, and every Page submitted to the Taste of forty or fifty thousand Readers, I am afraid we should complain of many flat Expressions, trivial Observations, beaten Topicks, and common Thoughts, which go off very well in the Lump. At the same Time, notwithstanding some Papers may be made up of broken Hints and irreg-

[1]Addison's own version of the Greek proverb is given at the end of the first paragraph.

ular Sketches, it is often expected that every Sheet should be a kind of Treatise, and make out in Thought what it wants in Bulk: That a Point of Humour should be worked up in all its Parts; and a Subject touched upon in its most essential Articles, without the Repetitions, Tautologies, and Enlargements that are indulged to longer Labours. The ordinary Writers of Morality prescribe to their Readers after the Galenick Way; their Medicines are made up in large Quantities. An Essay Writer must practise in the Chymical Method, and give the Virtue of a full Draught in a few Drops. Were all Books reduced thus to their Quintessence, many a bulky Author would make his Appearance in a Penny Paper: There would be scarce such a thing in Nature as a Folio: The Works of an Age would be contained on a few Shelves; not to mention Millions of Volumes that would be utterly annihilated.

I cannot think that the Difficulty of furnishing out separate Papers of this Nature has hindered Authors from communicating their Thoughts to the World after such a Manner: Though I must confess I am amazed that the Press should be only made use of in this Way by News-Writers, and the Zealots of Parties; as if it were not more advantageous to Mankind to be instructed in Wisdom and Virtue, than in Politicks; and to be made good Fathers, Husbands, and Sons, than Counsellors and Statesmen. Had the Philosophers and great Men of Antiquity, who took so much Pains in order to instruct Mankind, and leave the World wiser and better than they found it; had they, I say, been possessed of the Art of Printing, there is no Question but they would have made such an Advantage of it, in dealing out their Lectures to the Publick. Our common Prints would be of great Use were they thus calculated to diffuse good Sense through the Bulk of a People, to clear up their Understandings, animate their Minds with Virtue, dissipate the Sorrows of a heavy Heart, or unbend the Mind from its more severe Employments with innocent Amusements.[2]

[2] Compare *The Spectator,* No. 10.

When Knowledge, instead of being bound up in Books, and kept in Libraries and Retirements, is thus obtruded upon the Publick; when it is canvassed in every Assembly, and exposed upon every Table; I cannot forbear reflecting upon that Passage in the *Proverbs, Wisdom cryeth without, she uttereth her Voice in the Streets: She cryeth in the chief Place of Concourse, in the Openings of the Gates. In the City she uttereth her Words, saying, How long, ye simple ones, will ye love Simplicity? and the Scorners delight in their Scorning? and Fools hate Knowledge?*

The many Letters which come to me from Persons of the best Sense in both Sexes, (for I may pronounce their Characters from their Way of Writing) do not a little encourage me in the Prosecution of this my Undertaking: Besides that, my Bookseller tells me, the Demand for these my Papers increases daily. It is at his Instance that I shall continue my *rural Speculations* to the End of this Month; several having made up separate Sets of them, as they have done before of those relating to Wit, to Operas, to Points of Morality, or Subjects of Humour.

I am not at all mortified, when sometimes I see my Works thrown aside by Men of no Taste nor Learning. There is a kind of Heaviness and Ignorance that hangs upon the Minds of ordinary Men, which is too thick for Knowledge to break through: Their Souls are not to be enlightened.

———— *Nox atra cava circumvolat umbra.*

To these I must apply the Fable of the Mole, That after having consulted many Oculists for the bettering of his Sight, was at last provided with a good Pair of Spectacles; but upon his endeavouring to make use of them, his Mother told him very prudently, "That Spectacles, though they might help the Eye of a Man, could be of no use to a Mole." It is not therefore for the Benefit of Moles that I publish these my daily Essays.

But besides such as are Moles through Ignorance, there are others who are Moles through Envy. As it is said in the Latin Proverb, "That one Man is a Woolf to another;" so, generally speaking, one Author is a Mole to another Author. It is impossible for them to discover Beauties in one another's Works; they have Eyes only for Spots and Blemishes: They can indeed see the Light, as it is said of the Animals which are their Namesakes, but the Idea of it is painful to them; they immediately shut their Eyes upon it, and withdraw themselves into a wilful Obscurity. I have already caught two or three of these dark undermining Vermin, and intend to make a String of them, in order to hang them up in one of my Papers, as an Example to all such voluntary Moles.

No. 125   Tuesday, July 24, 1711.   [Addison]

Ne pueri, ne tanta animis assuescite bella:
Neu patriæ validas in viscera vertite vires.[1]—Vir.

My worthy Friend Sir ROGER, when we are talking of the Malice
of Parties, very frequently tells us an Accident that happened
to him when he was a School-Boy, which was at the Time when
the Feuds ran high between the Round-heads and Cavaliers.
This worthy Knight being then but a Strippling, had Occasion
to enquire which was the Way to St. *Anne's* Lane, upon which
the Person whom he spoke to, instead of answering his Question, called him a young Popish Cur, and asked him who had
made *Anne* a Saint? The Boy being in some Confusion, enquired of the next he met, which was the Way to *Anne's* Lane;
but was called a Prick-eared Cur for his Pains, and instead
of being shewn the Way, was told, that she had been a Saint
before he was born, and would be one after he was hanged.
Upon this, says Sir ROGER, I did not think fit to repeat the former Question, but going into every Lane of the Neighbourhood, asked what they called the Name of that Lane. By which
ingenious Artifice he found out the Place he enquired after,
without giving Offence to any Party. Sir ROGER, generally closes
this Narrative with Reflections on the Mischief that Parties
do in the Country; how they spoil good Neighbourhood, and
make honest Gentlemen hate one another; besides that they
manifestly tend to the Prejudice of the Land-Tax, and the Destruction of the Game.

[1] "Embrace again, my sons, be foes no more;
  Nor stain your country with her children's gore!"
                       —Dryden's translation.

There cannot a greater Judgment befall a Country than such a dreadful Spirit of Division as rends a Government into two distinct People, and makes them greater Strangers and more averse to one another, than if they were actually two different Nations. The Effects of such a Division are pernicious to the last degree, not only with Regard to those Advantages which they give the Common Enemy, but to those private Evils which they produce in the Heart of almost every particular Person. This influence is very fatal both to Men's Morals and their Understandings; It sinks the Virtue of a Nation, and not only so, but destroys even Common Sense.

A furious Party-Spirit, when it rages in its full Violence, exerts itself in Civil War and Bloodshed: and when it is under its greatest Restraints naturally breaks out in Falshood, Detraction, Calumny, and a partial Administration of Justice. In a Word, it fills a Nation with Spleen and Rancour, and extinguishes all the Seeds of Good-Nature, Compassion and Humanity.

Plutarch says very finely, That a Man should not allow himself to hate even his Enemies, because, says he, if you indulge this Passion in some Occasions, it will rise of it-self in others; if you hate your Enemies, you will contract such a vicious Habit of Mind, as by Degrees will break out upon those who are your Friends, or those who are indifferent to you. I might here observe how admirably this Precept of Morality (which derives the Malignity of Hatred from the Passion itself, and not from its Object) answers to that great Rule[2] which was dictated to the World about an Hundred Years before this Philosopher wrote; but instead of that, I shall only take notice, with a real Grief of Heart, that the Minds of many good Men among us appear sowered with Party-Principles, and alienated from one another in such a manner, as seems to me altogether inconsistent with the Dictates either of Reason or Religion. Zeal for a Publick Cause is apt to breed Passions in the Hearts

[2] "Love your enemies, do good to them that hate you."—*Luke,* vi, 27.

of virtuous Persons, to which the Regard of their own private Interest would never have betrayed them.

If this Party-Spirit has so ill an Effect on our Morals, it has likewise a very great one upon our Judgments. We often hear a poor insipid Paper or Pamphlet cryed up, and sometimes a noble Piece depreciated, by those who are of a different Principle from the Author. One who is actuated by this Spirit is almost under an Incapacity of discerning either real Blemishes or Beauties. A Man of Merit in a different Principle, is like an Object seen in two different Mediums, that appears crooked or broken, however streight and entire it may be in itself. For this Reason there is scarce a Person of any Figure in *England* who does not go by two contrary Characters, as opposite to one another as Light and Darkness. Knowledge and Learning suffer in a particular manner from this strange Prejudice, which at present prevails amongst all Ranks and Degrees in the *British* Nation. As Men formerly became eminent in learned Societies by their Parts and Acquisitions, they now distinguish themselves by the Warmth and Violence with which they espouse their respective Parties. Books are valued upon the like Considerations: An Abusive Scurrilous Style passes for Satyr, and a dull Scheme of Party-Notions is called fine Writing.

There is one Piece of Sophistry practised by both Sides, and that is the taking any scandalous Story that has been ever whispered or invented of a private Man, for a known undoubted Truth, and raising suitable Speculations upon it. Calumnies that have been never proved, or have been often refuted, are the ordinary Postulatums of these infamous Scribblers, upon which they proceed as upon first Principles granted by all Men, though in their Hearts they know they are false, or at best very doubtful. When they have laid these Foundations of Scurrility, it is no wonder that their Superstructure is every way answerable to them. If this shameless Practice of the present Age endures much longer, Praise and Reproach will cease to be Motives of Action in good Men.

There are certain Periods of Time in all Governments when this inhuman Spirit prevails. *Italy* was long torn in pieces by the *Guelfes* and *Gibellines,* and *France* by those who were for and against the League: But it is very unhappy for a Man to be born in such a stormy and tempestuous Season. It is the restless Ambition of Artful Men that thus breaks a People into Factions, and draws several well-meaning Persons to their Interest by a Specious Concern for their Country. How many honest Minds are filled with uncharitable and barbarous Notions, out of their Zeal for the Publick Good? What Cruelties and Outrages would they not commit against Men of an adverse Party, whom they would honour and esteem, if instead of considering them as they are represented, they knew them as they are? Thus are Persons of the greatest Probity seduced into shameful Errors and Prejudices, and made bad Men even by that noblest of Principles, the Love of their Country. I cannot here forbear mentioning the Famous *Spanish* Proverb, *If there were neither Fools nor Knaves in the World, all People would be of one Mind.*

For my own part, I could heartily wish that all Honest Men would enter into an Association, for the Support of one another against the Endeavours of those whom they ought to look upon as their Common Enemies, whatsoever side they may belong to. Were there such an honest Body of Neutral Forces, we should never see the worst of Men in great Figures of Life, because they are useful to a Party; nor the best unregarded, because they are above practising those Methods which would be grateful to their Faction. We should then single every Criminal out of the Herd, and hunt him down, however formidable and overgrown he might appear: On the contrary, we should shelter distressed Innocence, and defend Virtue, however beset with Contempt or Ridicule, Envy or Defamation. In short, we should not any longer regard our Fellow-Subjects as Whigs or Tories, but should make the Man of Merit our Friend, and the Villain our Enemy.

No. 130   Monday, July 30, 1711.   [Addison]

. . . *Semperque recentes*
Convectare juvat præedas, & vivere rapto.[1] — Virg.

As I was Yesterday riding out in the Fields with my Friend Sir
ROGER, we saw at a little Distance from us a Troop of Gypsies.
Upon the first Discovery of them, my Friend was in some
Doubt whether he should not exert the *Justice of the Peace*
upon such a Band of lawless Vagrants; but not having his Clerk
with him, who is a necessary Counsellour on these Occasions,
and fearing that his Poultry might fare the worse for it, he let
the Thought drop: But at the same Time gave me a particular Account of the Mischiefs they do in the Country, in stealing Peoples Goods and spoiling their Servants. If a stray Piece
of Linnen hangs upon an Hedge, says Sir ROGER, they are sure
to have it; if a Hog loses his Way in the Fields, it is ten to one
but he becomes their Prey; our Geese cannot live in Peace
for them; if a Man prosecutes them with Severity, his Hen-roost
is sure to pay for it: They generally straggle into these Parts
about this Time of the Year; and set the Heads of our Servant-
Maids so agog for Husbands, that we do not expect to have
any Business done, as it should be, whilst they are in the Country. I have an honest Dairy-Maid who crosses their Hands with
a Piece of Silver every Summer; and never fails being promised the handsomest young Fellow in the Parish for her Pains.
Your Friend the Butler has been Fool enough to be seduced
by them; and though he is sure to lose a Knife, a Fork, or a

[1] "The rude Equicolae his rule obey'd;
  Hunting their sport, and plund'ring was their trade."
                                    —Dryden's translation.

Spoon every Time his Fortune is told him, generally shuts himself up in the Pantry with an old Gypsie for above half an Hour once in a Twelve-month. Sweet-hearts are the things they live upon, which they bestow very plentifully upon all those that apply themselves to them. You see now and then some handsome young Jades among them: The Sluts have often very white Teeth and black Eyes.

Sir ROGER observing that I listned with great Attention to his Account of a People who were so entirely new to me, told me, That if I would they should tell us our Fortunes. As I was very well pleased with the Knight's Proposal, we rid up and communicated our Hands to them. A *Cassandra* of the Crew, after having examined my Lines very diligently, told me, That I loved a pretty Maid in a Corner, that I was a good Woman's Man, with some other Particulars which I do not think proper to relate. My Friend Sir ROGER alighted from his Horse, and exposing his Palm to two or three that stood by him, they crumpled it into all Shapes, and diligently scanned every Wrinkle that could be made in it; when one of them who was older and more Sun-burnt than the rest, told him, That he had a Widow in his Line of Life: Upon which the Knight cryed, Go, go, you are an idle Baggage; and at the same time smiled upon me. The Gypsie finding he was not displeased in his Heart, told him, after a further Enquiry into his Hand, that his True-love was constant, and that she should dream of him to Night. My old Friend cryed pish, and bid her go on. The Gypsie told him that he was a Batchelour, but would not be so long; and that he was dearer to some Body than he thought: The Knight still repeated, She was an idle Baggage, and bid her go on. Ah Master says the Gypsie, that roguish Leer of yours makes a pretty Woman's Heart ake; you ha'n't that Simper about the Mouth for Nothing——The uncouth Gibberish with which all this was uttered, like the Darkness of an Oracle, made us the more attentive to it. To be short, the Knight left the Money with her that he had crossed her Hand with, and got up again on his Horse.

As we were riding away, Sir ROGER told me, that he knew several sensible People who believed these Gypsies now and then foretold very strange things; and for Half an Hour together appeared more jocund than ordinary. In the Height of his good Humour, meeting a common Beggar upon the Road who was no Conjuror, as he went to relieve him he found his Pocket was pickt: That being a Kind of Palmistry at which this Race of Vermin are very dexterous.

I might here entertain my Reader with Historical Remarks on this idle profligate People, who infest all the Countries of *Europe*, and live in the Midst of Governments in a kind of Commonwealth by themselves. But instead of entering into Observations of this Nature, I shall fill the remaining part of my Paper with a Story which is still fresh in *Holland*, and was printed in one of our Monthly Accounts about twenty Years ago. As the *Trekschuyt*, or Hackney-boat, which carries Passengers from *Leiden* to *Amsterdam*, was putting off, a Boy running along the Side of the Canal, desir'd to be taken in; which the Master of the Boat refused, because the Lad had not quite Money enough to pay the usual Fare. An eminent Merchant being pleased with the Looks of the Boy, and secretly touched with Compassion towards him, paid the Money for him, and ordered him to be taken on board. Upon talking with him afterwards, he found that he could speak readily in three or four Languages, and learned upon further Examination that he had been stolen away when he was a Child by a Gypsy, and had rambled ever since with a Gang of those Strolers up and down several Parts of *Europe*. It happened that the Merchant, whose Heart seems to have inclined towards the Boy by a secret kind of Instinct, had himself lost a Child some Years before. The Parents, after a long Search for him, gave him for drowned in one of the Canals with which that Country abounds; and the Mother was so afflicted at the Loss of a fine Boy, who was her only Son, that she died for Grief of it. Upon laying together all Particulars, and examining the several Moles and Marks by which the Mother used to describe the Child when he was first missing, the Boy proved to be the Son of the Merchant, whose Heart had so unaccountably melted at the Sight of him. The Lad was very well pleased to find a Father, who was so rich, and likely to leave him a good Estate; the Father, on the other Hand, was not a little delighted to see a Son return to him, whom he had given for lost, with such a Strength of Constitution, Sharpness of Understanding, and Skill in Languages. Here the printed Story leaves off; but if I may give Credit to Reports, our Linguist having received such extraordinary Rudiments towards a good Education, was afterwards trained up in every thing that becomes a Gentleman; wearing off by little and little all the vicious Habits and Practices that he had been used to in the Course of his Peregrinations: Nay, it is said, that he has since been employed in foreign Courts upon National Business, with great Reputation to himself and Honour to those who sent him, and that he has visited several Countries as a publick Minister, in which he formerly wandered as a Gypsy.

No. 131   Tuesday, July 31, 1711.   [Addison]

. . . Ipsæ rursum concedite Silvæ. [1] — Virg.

It is usual for a Man who loves Country Sports to preserve
the Game in his own Grounds, and divert himself upon those
that belong to his Neighbour. My Friend Sir ROGER generally
goes two or three Miles from his House, and gets into the Frontiers of his Estate, before he beats about in search of an Hare
or Partridge, on purpose to spare his own Fields, where he
is always sure of finding Diversion when the worst comes to
the worst. By this means the Breed about his House has time
to encrease and multiply, besides that the Sport is the more
agreeable where the Game is the harder to come at, and does
not lie so thick as to produce any Perplexity or Confusion in
the Pursuit. For these Reasons the Country Gentleman, like
the Fox, seldom preys near his own Home.

   In the same manner I have made a Month's Excursion
out of the Town, which is the great Field of Game for Sports-
men of my Species, to try my Fortune in the Country, where
I have started several Subjects, and hunted them down,[2] with
some Pleasure to my self, and I hope to others. I am here forced
to use a great deal of Diligence before I can spring any thing
to my Mind, whereas in Town, whilst I am following one Character, it is ten to one but I am crossed in my Way by another,
and put up such a Variety of odd Creatures in both Sexes, that
they foil the Scent of one another, and puzzle the Chace. My
greatest Difficulty in the Country is to find Sport, and in Town

---

[1] "Once more farewell, ye woods!"
[2] A particularly effective use of a metaphor common in Addison's day. Compare
Dryden, Preface to *Annus Mirabilis,* and Pope, *An Essay on Man,* I, 9-14.

to chuse it. In the mean time, as I have given a whole Month's Rest to the Cities of *London* and *Westminster,* I promise my self abundance of new Game upon my return thither.

It is indeed high time for me to leave the Country, since I find the whole Neighbourhood begin to grow very inquisitive after my Name and Character. My love of Solitude, Taciturnity, and particular way of Life, having raised a great Curiosity in all these Parts.

The Notions which have been framed of me are various; some look upon me as very proud, and some as very melancholy. *Will. Wimble,* as my Friend the Butler tells me, observing me very much alone, and extreamly silent when I am in Company, is afraid I have killed a Man. The Country People seem to suspect me for a Conjurer; and some of them hearing of the Visit that I made to *Moll. White,* will needs have it that Sir ROGER has brought down a Cunning Man with him, to cure the old Woman, and free the Country from her Charms. So that the Character which I go under in part of the Neighbourhood, is what they here call a *White*[3] *Witch.*

A Justice of Peace, who lives about five Miles off, and is not of Sir ROGER'S Party, has it seems said twice or thrice at his Table, that he wishes Sir ROGER does not harbour a Jesuit in his House, and that he thinks the Gentlemen of the Country would do very well to make me give some Account of my self.

On the other side, some of Sir ROGER'S Friends are afraid the old Knight is imposed upon by a designing Fellow; and as they have heard that he converses very promiscuously when he is in Town, do not know but he has brought down with him some discarded Whig, that is sullen, and says nothing, because he is out of Place.

Such is the Variety of Opinions that are here entertained of me, so that I pass among some for a disaffected Person, and among others for a Popish Priest; among some for a Wizard,

[3] Free of harmful intent. See *The Spectator,* No. 117.

and among others for a Murderer; and all this for no other Reason, that I can imagine, but because I do not hoot and hollow and make a Noise. It is true my Friend Sir ROGER, tells them *that it is my way,* and that I am only a Philosopher, but that will not satisfy them. They think there is more in me than he discovers, and that I do not hold my Tongue for nothing.

For these and other Reasons I shall set out for *London* to Morrow, having found by Experience that the Country is not a Place for a Person of my Temper, who does not love Jollity, and what they call Good-Neighbourhood. A Man that is out of Humour when an unexpected Guest breaks in upon him, and does not care for sacrificing an Afternoon to every Chance-comer; that will be the Master of his own Time, and the Pursuer of his own Inclinations, makes but a very unsociable Figure in this kind of Life. I shall therefore retire into the Town, if I may make use of that Phrase, and get into the Crowd again as fast as I can, in order to be alone. I can there raise what Speculations I please upon others without being observed my self, and at the same time enjoy all the Advantages of Company with all the Privileges of Solitude. In the mean while, to finish the Month, and conclude these my Rural Speculations, I shall here insert a Letter from my Friend WILL. HONEYCOMB, who has not lived a Month for these forty Years out of the Smoke of *London,* and rallies me after his way upon my Country Life.

'*Dear* SPEC.

I suppose this Letter will find thee picking of Daisies, or smelling to a Lock of Hay, or passing away thy time in some innocent Country Diversion of the like nature. I have however Orders from the Club to summon thee up to Town, being all of us cursedly afraid thou wilt not be able to relish our Company, after thy Conversations with *Moll. White* and *Will. Wimble.* Prithee don't send us up any more Stories of a Cock and a Bull, nor frighten the Town with Spirits and Witches. Thy Speculations begin to smell confoundly of Woods and Meadows. If thou dost not come up quickly, we shall conclude that thou art in Love with one of Sir ROGER's Dairy Maids. Service to the Knight. Sir ANDREW is grown the Cock of the Club since he left us, and if he does not return quickly will make every Mother's Son of us Common-wealths Men.

Dear SPEC,
Thine Eternally,
WILL. HONEYCOMB.'

No. 157   Thursday, August 30, 1711.   [Steele]

. . . *Genius natale comes qui Temperat astrum*
Naturæ deus humanæ, Mortalis in unum
Quodque caput . . . [1] — Hor.

I am very much at a Loss to express by any Word that occurs
to me in our Language that which is understood by *Indoles*
in Latin. The natural Disposition to any particular Art, Science,
Profession, or Trade, is very much to be consulted in the Care
of Youth, and studied by Men for their own Conduct when
they form to themselves any Scheme of Life. It is wonderfully
hard indeed for a Man to judge of his own Capacity impartially;
that may look great to me which may appear little to another,
and I may be carried by Fondness towards my self so far, as
to attempt things too high for my Talents and Accomplishments: But it is not methinks so very difficult a Matter to make
a Judgment of the Abilities of others, especially of those who
are in their Infancy. My common-place Book directs me on this
Occasion to mention the Dawning of Greatness in *Alexander,*
who being asked in his Youth to contend for a Prize in the
Olympick Games, answered he would if he had Kings to run
against him. *Cassius,* who was one of the Conspirators against
Caesar, gave as great a Proof of his Temper, when in his Childhood he struck a Play-fellow, the Son of *Sylla,* for saying his
Father was Master of the *Roman* People. *Scipio* is reported
to have answered (when some Flatterers at Supper were asking him what the *Romans* should do for a General after his

[1] "Genius, that companion who rules our star of birth, the god of human nature,
though mortal for each single life."

314

Death), Take *Marius*. *Marius* was then a very Boy, and had given no Instances of his Valour; but it was visible to *Scipio* from the Manners of the Youth, that he had a Soul formed for the Attempt and Execution of great Undertakings. I must confess I have very often with much Sorrow bewailed the Misfortune of the Children of *Great Britain,* when I consider the Ignorance and Undiscerning of the Generality of School-masters. The boasted Liberty we talk of is but a mean Reward for the long Servitude, the many Heart Aches and Terrours, to which our Childhood is exposed in going through a Grammar-School: Many of these stupid Tyrants exercise their Cruelty without any Manner of Distinction of the Capacities of Children, or the Intention of Parents in their Behalf. There are many excellent Tempers which are worthy to be nourished and cultivated with all possible Diligence and Care, that were never designed to be acquainted with *Aristotle, Tully,* or *Virgil;* and there are as many who have Capacities for understanding every Word those great Persons have writ, and yet were not born to have any Relish of their Writings. For want of this common and obvious discerning in those who have the Care of Youth, we have so many Hundred unaccountable Creatures every Age whipped up into great Scholars, that are for ever near a right Understanding, and will never arrive at it. These are the Scandal of Letters, and these are generally the Men who are to teach others. The Sense of Shame and Honour is enough to keep the World it self in Order without Corporal Punishment, much more to train the Minds of uncorrupted and innocent Children. It happens, I doubt not, more than once in a Year, that a Lad is chastised for a Blockhead, when it is good Apprehension that makes him incapable of knowing what his Teacher means: A brisk Imagination very often may suggest an Errour, which a Lad could not have fallen into if he had been as heavy in conjecturing as his Master in explaining: But there is no Mercy even towards a wrong Interpretation of his Meaning, the Sufferings of the Scholar's Body are to rectify the Mistakes of his Mind.

I am confident that no Boy who will not be allured to Letters without Blows, will ever be brought to any thing with them. A great or good Mind must necessarily be the worse for such Indignities: and it is a sad Change to lose of its Virtue for the Improvement of its Knowledge. No one who has gone through what they call a great School, but must remember to have seen Children of excellent and ingenuous Natures, (as has afterwards appeared in their Manhood;) I say no Man has passed through this Way of Education, but must have seen an ingenuous Creature expiring with Shame, with pale Looks, beseeching Sorrow, and silent Tears, throw up its honest Eyes, and kneel on its tender Knees to an inexorable Blockhead, to be forgiven the false Quantity of a Word in making a Latin Verse: The Child is punished, and the next Day he commits a like Crime, and so a third with the same Consequence. I would fain ask any reasonable Man whether this Lad, in the Simplicity of his native Innocence, full of Shame, and capable of any Impression from that Grace of Soul, was not fitter for any Purpose in this Life, than after that Spark of Virtue is extinguished in him, tho' he is able to write twenty Verses in an Evening?

Seneca says, after his exalted Way of talking, *As the immortal Gods never learnt any Virtue, tho' they are endued with all that is good; so there are some Men who have so natural a Propensity to what they should follow, that they learn it almost as soon au they hear it.* Plants and Vegetables are cultivated into the Production of finer Fruit than they would yield without that Care; and yet we cannot entertain Hopes of producing a tender conscious Spirit into Acts of Virtue, without the same Methods as is used to cut Timber, or give new Shape to a Piece of Stone.

It is wholly to this dreadful Practice that we may attribute a certain Hardness and Ferocity which some Men, tho' liberally educated, carry about them in all their Behaviour. To be bred like a Gentleman, and punished like a Malefactor, must, as we see it does, produce that illiberal Sauciness which we see sometimes in Men of Letters.

The *Spartan* Boy who suffered the Fox (which he had stolen and hid under his Coat) to eat into his Bowels, I dare say had not half the Wit or Petulance which we learn at great Schools among us: But the glorious Sense of Honour, or rather Fear of Shame, which he demonstrated in that Action, was worth all the Learning in the World without it.

It is methinks a very melancholy Consideration, that a little Negligence can spoil us, but great Industry is necessary to improve us; the most excellent Natures are soon depreciated, but evil Tempers are long before they are exalted into good Habits. To help this by Punishments, is the same thing as killing a Man to cure him of a Distemper; when he comes to suffer Punishment in that one Circumstance, he is brought below the Existence of a rational Creature, and is in the State of a Brute that moves only by the Admonition of Stripes. But since this Custom of educating by the Lash is suffered by the Gentry of *Great Britain,* I would prevail only that honest heavy Lads may be dismissed from Slavery sooner than they are at present, and not whipped on to their fourteenth or fifteenth Year, whether they expect any Progress from them or not. Let the Child's Capacity be forthwith examined, and he sent to some Mechanick Way of Life, without Respect to his Birth, if Nature design'd him for nothing higher; let him go before he has innocently suffered, and is debased into a Dereliction of Mind for being what it is no Guilt to be, a plain Man. I would not here be supposed to have said, that our learned Men of either Robe who have been whipped at School, are not still Men of noble and liberal Minds; but I am sure they had been much more so than they are, had they never suffered that Infamy.

But tho' there is so little Care, as I have observed, taken, or Observation made of the natural Strain of Men, it is no small Comfort to me, as a SPECTATOR, that there is any right Value set upon the *bona Indoles*[2] of other Animals; as appears by

[2] Inborn soundness.

the following Advertisement handed about the County of *Lincoln,* and subscribed by *Enos Thomas,* a Person whom I have not the Honour to know, but suppose to be profoundly learned in Horse-Flesh.

A Chesnut Horse called Caesar, *bred by* James Darcey, *Esq; at* Sedbury *near* Richmond *in the County of* York; *his Grandam was his old royal Mare, and got by* Blunderbuss, *which was got by* Hemsly Turk, *and he got Mr.* Courant*'s* Arabian, *which got Mr.* Minshul*'s* Jewstrump. *Mr.* Caesar *sold him to a Nobleman (coming five Years old, when he had but one Sweat) for three hundred Guineas. A Guinea a Leap and Trial, and a Shilling the Man.*

Enos   Thomas.

No. 159   Saturday, September 1, 1711. [Addison]

. . . Omnem, quæ nunc obducta tuenti
Mortales hebetat visus tibi, & humida circum
Caligat, nubem eripiam . . .[1] — Virg.

When I was at *Grand Cairo* I picked up several Oriental Manuscripts, which I have still by me. Among others I met with one
entitled, *The Visions of Mirzah,* which I have read over with
great Pleasure. I intend to give it to the Publick when I have
no other Entertainment for them; and shall begin with the first
Vision, which I have translated Word for Word as follows.

'On the fifth Day of the Moon, which according to the
Custom of my Forefathers I always keep holy, after having
washed my self and offered up my Morning Devotions, I as-
cended the high Hills of *Bagdat,* in order to pass the rest of
the Day in Meditation and Prayer. As I was here airing my
self on the Tops of the Mountains, I fell into a profound Contemplation on the Vanity of humane Life; and passing from
one Thought to another, Surely, said I, Man is but a Shadow
and Life a Dream. Whilst I was thus musing, I cast my Eyes
towards the Summit of a Rock that was not far from me, where
I discovered one in the Habit of a Shepherd, with a little Musical Instrument in his Hand. As I looked upon him he applied
it to his Lips, and began to play upon it. The Sound of it was
exceeding sweet, and wrought into a Variety of Tunes that
were inexpressibly melodious, and altogether different from
any thing I had ever heard. They put me in mind of those heav-

[1] "All the cloud, which now, drawn over thy sight, dulls thy mortal vision and
with dark pall enshrouds thee, I will tear away."

319

enly Airs that are played to the departed Souls of good Men upon their first Arrival in Paradise, to wear out the Impressions of their last Agonies, and qualify them for the Pleasures of that happy Place. My Heart melted away in secret Raptures.

I had been often told that the Rock before me was the Haunt of a Genius; and that several had been entertained with Musick who had passed by it, but never heard that the Musician had before made himself visible. When he had raised my Thoughts, by those transporting Airs which he played, to taste the Pleasures of his Conversation, as I looked upon him like one astonished, he beckoned to me, and by the waving of his Hand directed me to approach the Place where he sat. I drew near with that Reverence which is due to a superior Nature; and as my Heart was entirely subdued by the captivating Strains I had heard, I fell down at his Feet and wept. The Genius smiled upon me with a Look of Compassion and Affability that familiarized him to my Imagination, and at once dispelled all the Fears and Apprehensions with which I approached him. He lifted me from the Ground, and taking me by the Hand, *Mirzah,* said he, I have heard thee in thy Soliloquies, follow me.

He then led me to the highest Pinnacle of the Rock, and placing me on the Top of it, Cast thy Eyes Eastward, said he, and tell me what thou seest. I see, said I, a huge Valley and a prodigious Tide of Water rolling through it. The Valley that thou seest, said he, is the Vale of Misery, and the Tide of Water that thou seest is Part of the great Tide of Eternity. What is the Reason, said I, that the Tide I see rises out of a thick Mist at one End, and again loses it self in a thick Mist at the other? What thou seest, said he, is that Portion of Eternity which is called Time, measured out by the Sun, and reaching from the Beginning of the World to its Consummation. Examine now, said he, this Sea that is thus bounded with Darkness at both Ends, and tell me what thou discoverest in it. I see a Bridge, said I, standing in the Midst of the Tide. The Bridge thou seest, said he, is humane Life; consider it attentively. Upon a more leisurely Survey of it, I found that it consisted of threescore and ten entire Arches, with several broken Arches, which added to those that were entire made up the Number about an hundred. As I was counting the Arches, the Genius told me that this Bridge consisted at first of a thousand Arches; but that a great Flood swept away the rest, and left the Bridge in the ruinous Condition I now beheld it.[2] But tell me further, said he, what thou discoverest on it. I see Multitudes of People passing over it, said I, and a black Cloud hanging on each End of it. As I looked more attentively, I saw several of the Passengers dropping thro' the Bridge, into the great Tide that flowed underneath it; and upon further Examination, perceived there were innumerable Trap-doors that lay concealed in the Bridge, which the Passengers no sooner trod upon, but they fell through them into the Tide and immediately disappeared. These hidden Pit-falls were set very thick at the Entrance of the Bridge, so that Throngs of People no sooner broke through the Cloud, but many of them fell into them. They grew thinner towards the Middle, but multiplied and lay closer together towards the End of the Arches that were entire.

There were indeed some Persons, but their Number was very small, that continued a kind of hobbling March on the broken Arches, but fell through one after another, being quite tired and spent with so long a Walk.

I passed some Time in the Contemplation of this wonderful Structure, and the great Variety of Objects which it presented. My Heart was filled with a deep Melancholy to see several dropping unexpectedly in the Midst of Mirth and Jollity, and catching at every thing that stood by them to save themselves. Some were looking up towards the Heavens in a thoughtful Posture, and in the Midst of a Speculation stumbled and fell out of Sight. Multitudes were very busy in the Pursuit of

[2] A reference, apparently, to the shortening of human life as part of the decay of nature following the Flood. Compare Donne's *An Anatomy of the World*, II. 111-134.

Bubbles that glittered in their Eyes and danced before them, but often when they thought themselves within the Reach of them their Footing failed and down they sunk. In this Confusion of Objects, I observed some with Scymetars in their Hands, and others with Urinals, who ran to and fro upon the Bridge, thrusting several Persons on Trap-doors which did not seem to lie in their Way, and which they might have escaped had they not been thus forced upon them.

The Genius seeing me indulge my self in this melancholy Prospect, told me I had dwelt long enough upon it: Take thine Eyes off the Bridge, said he, and tell me if thou yet seest any thing thou dost not comprehend. Upon looking up, What mean said I, those great Flights of Birds that are perpetually hovering about the Bridge, and settling upon it from Time to Time? I see Vultures, Harpyes, Ravens, Cormorants; and among many other feathered Creatures several little winged Boys, that perch in great Numbers upon the middle Arches. These said the Genius, are Envy, Avarice, Superstition, Despair, Love, with the like Cares and Passions that infest humane Life.

I here fetched a deep Sigh. Alas, said I, Man was made in vain! How is he given away to Misery and Mortality! tortured in Life, and swallowed up in Death! The Genius being moved with Compassion towards me, bid me quit so uncomfortable a Prospect: Look no more, said he, on Man in the first Stage of his Existence, in his setting out for Eternity; but cast thine Eye on that thick Mist into which the Tide bears the several Generations of Mortals that fall into it. I directed my Sight as I was ordered, and (whether or no the good Genius strengthened it with any supernatural Force, or dissipated Part of the Mist that was before too thick for the Eye to penetrate) I saw the Valley opening at the further End, and spreading forth into an immense Ocean, that had a huge Rock of Adamant running through the Midst of it, and dividing it into two equal Parts. The Clouds still rested on one Half of it, insomuch that I could discover nothing in it, but the other appeared to me a vast Ocean planted with innumerable Islands, that were covered with Fruits and Flowers, and interwoven with a thousand little shining Seas that ran among them. I could see Persons dressed in glorious Habits, with Garlands upon their Heads, passing among the Trees, lying down by the Sides of Fountains, or resting on Beds of Flowers; and could hear a confused Harmony of singing Birds, falling Waters, humane Voices, and musical Instruments. Gladness grew in me upon the Discovery of so delightful a Scene. I wished for the Wings of an Eagle, that I might fly away to those happy Seats; but the Genius told me there was no Passage to them, except through the Gates of Death that I saw opening every Moment upon the Bridge. The Islands, said he, that lie so fresh and green before thee, and with which the whole Face of the Ocean appears spotted as far as thou canst see, are more in Number than the Sands on the Sea-shore; there are Myriads of Islands behind those which thou here discoverest, reaching further than thine Eye or even thine Imagination can extend it self. These are the Mansions of good Men after Death, who according to the Degree and Kinds of Virtue in which they excelled, are distributed among these several Islands, which abound with Pleasures of different Kinds and Degrees, suitable to the Relishes and Perfections of those who are settled in them; every Island is a Paradise accommodated to its respective Inhabitants. Are not these, O *Mirzah,* Habitations worth contending for? Does Life appear miserable, that gives thee Opportunities of earning such a Reward? Is Death to be feared, that will convey thee to so happy an Existence? Think not Man was made in vain, who has such an Eternity reserved for him. I gazed with inexpressible Pleasure on these happy Islands. At length, said I, shew me now, I beseech thee, the Secrets that lie hid under those dark Clouds which cover the Ocean on the other Side of the Rock of Adamant. The Genius making me no Answer, I turned about to address my self to him a second time, but I found that he had left me; I then turned again to the Vision which I had been so long contemplating, but instead of the rolling Tide, the arched Bridge, and the happy Islands, I saw nothing but the long hollow Valley of *Bagdat,* with Oxen, Sheep, and Camels grazing upon the Sides of it.'

The End of the first Vision of Mirzah.

No. 160   Monday, September 3, 1711.   [Addison]

. . . *Cui mens divinior, atque os*
Magna sonaturum, des nominis hujus honorem. [1] —Hor.

There is no Character more frequently given to a Writer, than
that of being a Genius. I have heard many a little Sonneteer
called a *fine Genius.* There is not an Heroick Scribler in the
Nation, that has not his Admirers who think him a *great Genius;*
and as for your Smatterers in Tragedy, there is scarce a Man
among them who is not cried up by one or other for a *prodi-*
gious Genius.

My Design in this Paper is to consider what is properly
a great Genius, and to throw some Thoughts together on so
uncommon a Subject.

Among great Genius's, those few draw the Admiration
of all the World upon them, and stand up as the Prodigies of
Mankind, who by the meer Strength of natural Parts, and without any Assistance of Art or Learning, have produced Works
that were the Delight of their own Times and the Wonder of
Posterity. [2] There appears something nobly wild and extravagant in these great natural Genius's, that is infinitely more
beautiful than all the Turn and Polishing of what the *French*
call a *Bel Esprit,* by which they would express a Genius refined
by Conversation, Reflection, and the Reading of the most polite
Authors. The greatest Genius which runs through the Arts

[1] "If one has a soul divine and a tongue of noble utterance, to such give the
honor of that name."
[2] Addison is here reflecting on the "grace beyond the reach of art" which Pope
treats in *An Essay on Criticism,* I, 140 - 160.

and Sciences, takes a kind of Tincture from them, and falls unavoidably into Imitation.

Many of these great natural Genius's that were never disciplined and broken by Rules of Art, are to be found among the Ancients, and in particular among those of the more Eastern Parts of the World. *Homer* has innumerable Flights that *Virgil* was not able to reach, and in the Old Testament we find several Passages more elevated and sublime than any in *Homer*. At the same Time that we allow a greater and more daring Genius to the Ancients, we must own that the greatest of them very much failed in, or, if you will, that they were much above the Nicety and Correctness of the Moderns. In their Similitudes and Allusions, provided there was a Likeness, they did not much trouble themselves about the Decency of the Comparison: Thus *Solomon* resembles the Nose of his Beloved to the Tower of *Libanon* which looketh toward *Damascus;* as the Coming of a Thief in the Night, is a Similitude of the same Kind in the New Testament. It would be endless to make Collections of this Nature: *Homer* illustrates one of his Heroes encompassed with the Enemy, by an Ass in a Field of Corn that has his Sides belaboured by all the Boys of the Village without stirring a Foot for it; and another of them tossing to and fro in his Bed and burning with Resentment, to a Piece of Flesh broiled on the Coals. This particular Failure in the Ancients, opens a large Field of Raillerie to the little Wits, who can laugh at an Indecency but not relish the Sublime in these Sorts of Writings. The present Emperor of *Persia,* conformable to this Eastern way of Thinking, amidst a great many pompous Titles, denominates himself the Sun of Glory, and the *Nutmeg of Delight.* In short, to cut off all Cavelling against the Ancients, and particularly those of the warmer Climates, who had most Heat and Life in their Imaginations, we are to consider that the Rule of observing what the *French* call the *Bienseance* in an Allusion, has been found out of latter Years and in the colder Regions of the World; where we would make some Amends for our want of Force and Spirit, by a scrupulous Nicety and Exactness in our Compositions. Our Countryman *Shakespear* was a remarkable Instance of this first kind of great Genius's.

I cannot quit this Head without observing that *Pindar* was a great Genius of the first Class, who was hurried on by a Natural Fire and Impetuosity to vast Conceptions of things, and noble Sallies of Imagination. At the same time, can any thing be more ridiculous than for Men of a sober and moderate Fancy to imitate this Poet's Way of Writing in those monstrous Compositions which go among us under the Name of Pindaricks? When I see People copying Works, which, as *Horace* has represented them, are singular in their Kind and inimitable; when I see Men following Irregularities by Rule, and by the little Tricks of Art straining after the most unbounded Flights of Nature, I cannot but apply to them that Passage in *Terence*.

> . . . *incerta hæc si tu postules*
> *Ratione certa facere, nihilo plus agas,*
> *Quam si des operam, ut cum ratione insanias.* [3]

In short a modern pindarick Writer compared with *Pindar*, is like a Sister among the *Camisars*[4] compared with *Virgil's* Sybil: There is the Distortion, Grimace, and outward Figure, but nothing of that divine Impulse which raises the Mind above it self, and makes the Sounds more than humane.

There is another kind of Great Genius's which I shall place in a second Class, not as I think them inferior to the first, but only for distinction's sake as they are of a different kind. This second Class of great Genius's are those that have formed them-

[3] "If you tried to turn these uncertainties into certainties by a system of reasoning, you would accomplish no more than if you systematically set about being mad."

[4] A lay sister in a community of fanatical French protestants, some of whom had come to England a few years earlier and were known as "the French Prophets."

selves by Rules, and submitted the Greatness of their natural Talents to the Corrections and Restraints of Art. Such among the *Greeks* were *Plato* and *Aristotle,* among the *Romans Virgil* and *Tully,* among the *English Milton* and Sir *Francis Bacon.*

The Genius in both these Classes of Authors may be equally great, but shews it self after a different Manner. In the first it is like a rich Soil in a happy Climate, that produces a whole Wilderness of noble Plants rising in a thousand beautiful Landskips without any certain Order or Regularity. In the other it is the same rich Soil under the same happy Climate, that has been laid out in Walks and Parterres, and cut into Shape and Beauty by the Skill of the Gardener.

The great Danger in these latter kind of Genius's, is, least they cramp their own Abilities too much by Imitation, and form themselves altogether upon Models, without giving the full Play to their own natural Parts. An Imitation of the best Authors is not to compare with a good Original; and I believe we may observe that very few Writers make an extraordinary Figure in the World, who have not something in their Way of thinking or expressing themselves that is peculiar to them and entirely their own.

It is odd to consider what great Genius's are sometimes thrown away upon Trifles.

I once saw a Shepherd, says a famous *Italian* Author, who used to divert himself in his Solitudes with tossing up Eggs and catching them again without breaking them: In which he had arrived to so great a Degree of Perfection, that he would keep up four at a Time for several Minutes together playing in the Air, and falling into his Hand by Turns. I think, says the Author, I never saw a greater Severity than in this Man's Face; for by his wonderful Perseverance and Application, he had contracted the Seriousness and Gravity of a Privy-Councellour; and I could not but reflect with my self, that the same Assiduity and Attention, had they been rightly applied, might have made him a greater Mathematician than *Archimedes.*

No. 181   Thursday, September 27, 1711. [Addison]

His lachrymis vitam damus, & miserescimus ultro. [1] — Virg.

I am more pleased with a Letter that is filled with Touches of Nature than of Wit. The following one is of this kind.

'SIR,
  Among all the Distresses which happen in Families, I do not remember that you have touched upon the Marriage of Children without the Consent of their Parents. I am one of these unfortunate Persons. I was about Fifteen when I took the Liberty to chuse for my self, and have ever since languished under the Displeasure of an inexorable Father, who, though he sees me happy in the best of Husbands, and blessed with very fine Children, can never be prevailed upon to forgive me. He was so kind to me before this unhappy Accident, that indeed it makes my Breach of Duty, in some measure, inexcusable; and at the same time creates in me such a Tenderness towards him, that I love him above all things, and would die to be reconciled to him. I have thrown my self at his Feet, and besought him with Tears to pardon me, but he always pushes me away, and spurns me from him; I have written several Letters to him, but he will neither open nor receive them. About two Years ago I sent my little Boy to him, dressed in new Apparel, but the Child returned to me crying, because he said his Grand-father would not see him, and had ordered him to be put out of his House. My Mother is won over to my side, but dares not mention me to my Father for fear of provoking him.

[1] "Moved by these tears we pity him and grant him life."

About a Month ago he lay sick upon his Bed, and in great Danger of his Life; I was pierced to the Heart at the News, and could not forbear going to enquire after his Health. My Mother took this Opportunity of speaking in my behalf: She told him with abundance of Tears that I was come to see him, that I could not speak to her for weeping, and that I should certainly break my Heart if he refused at that time to give me his Blessing, and be reconciled to me. He was so far from relenting towards me, that he bid her speak no more of me, unless she had a Mind to disturb him in his last Moments; for, Sir, you must know that he has the Reputation of an honest and religious Man, which makes my Misfortune so much the greater. God be thanked he is since recovered, but his severe Usage has given me such a Blow that I shall soon sink under it, unless I may be relieved by any Impressions which the reading of this in your Paper may make upon him.

I am, &c.'

Of all Hardnesses of Heart, there is none so inexcusable as that of Parents towards their Children. An obstinate, inflexible, unforgiving Temper, is odious upon all Occasions, but here it is unnatural. The Love, Tenderness and Compassion, which are apt to arise in us towards those who depend upon us, is that by which the whole World of Life is upheld. The Supreme Being, by the transcendent Excellency and Goodness of his Nature, extends his Mercy towards all his Works; and because his Creatures have not such a spontaneous Benevolence and Compassion towards those who are under their Care and Protection, he has implanted in them an Instinct, that supplies the Place of this inherent Goodness. I have illustrated this kind of Instinct in former Papers, and have shewn how it runs thro' all the Species of Brute Creatures, as indeed the whole Animal Creation subsists by it.

This Instinct in Man is more general and uncircumscribed than in Brutes, as being enlarged by the Dictates of Reason and Duty. For if we consider our selves attentively, we shall find that we are not only enclined to Love those who descend from us, but that we bear a kind of στοργή or natural Affection to every thing which relies upon us for its Good and Preservation. Dependance is a perpetual Call upon Humanity, and a greater Incitement to Tenderness and Pity than any other Motive whatsoever.

The Man therefore who, notwithstanding any Passion or Resentment, can overcome this powerful Instinct, and extinguish natural Affection, debases his Mind even below Brutality, frustrates, as much as in him lies, the great Design of Providence, and strikes out of his Nature one of the most Divine Principles that is planted in it.

Among innumerable Arguments which might be brought against such an unreasonable Proceeding, I shall only insist on one. We make it the Condition of our Forgiveness that we forgive others. In our very Prayers we desire no more than to be treated by this kind of Retaliation. The Case therefore before us seems to be what they call *a Case in point;* the relation between the Child and Father, being what comes nearest to that between a Creature and its Creator. If the Father is inexorable to the Child who has offended, let the Offence be of never so high a Nature, how will he address him self to the Supreme Being, under the tender Appellation of a Father, and desire of him such a Forgiveness as he himself refuses to grant?

To this I might add many other Religious, as well as many Prudential Considerations; but if the last mentioned Motive does not prevail, I despair of succeeding by any other, and shall therefore conclude my Paper with a very remarkable Story, which is recorded in an old Chronicle published by *Freher* among the Writers of the *German* History.

Eginhart, who was Secretary to *Charles* the Great, became exceeding Popular by his Behaviour in that Post. His great Abilities gained him the Favour of his Master, and the Esteem of the whole Court. *Imma,* the Daughter of the Emperor, was so pleased with his Person and Conversation, that she fell in

Love with him. As she was one of the greatest Beauties of the Age, *Eginhart* answered her with a more than equal Return of Passion. They stifled their Flames for some time, under Apprehension of the fatal Consequences that might ensue. *Eginhart* at length resolving to hazard all, rather than live deprived of one whom his Heart was so much set upon, conveyed himself one Night into the Princess's Apartment, and knocking gently at the Door, was admitted as a Person who had something to communicate to her from the Emperor. He was with her in private most part of the Night; but upon his preparing to go away about Break of Day, he observed that there had fallen a great snow during his Stay with the Princess: This very much perplexed him, least the Prints of his Feet in the Snow might make Discoveries to the King, who often used to visit his Daughter in the Morning. He acquainted the Princess *Imma* with his Fears, who after some Consultations upon the Matter, prevailed upon him to let her carry him through the Snow upon her own Shoulders. It happened, that the Emperor not being able to sleep, was at that time up and walking in his Chamber, when upon looking through the Window he perceived his Daughter tottering under her Burden, and carrying his first Minister across the Snow; which she had no sooner done, but she returned again with the utmost speed to her own Apartment. The Emperor was extremely troubled and astonished at this Accident; but resolved to speak nothing of it 'till a proper Opportunity. In the mean time *Eginhart* knowing that what he had done could not be long a Secret; determined to retire from Court, and in order to it begged the Emperor that he would be pleased to dismiss him, pretending a kind of Discontent at his not having been rewarded for his long Services. The Emperor would not give a direct Answer to his Petition, but told him he would think of it, and appointed a certain Day when he would let him know his Pleasure. He then called together the most faithful of his Counsellors, and acquainting them with his Secretary's Crime, asked them their Advice in so delicate an Affair. They most of them gave their Opinion, that the Person could not be too severely punished, who had thus dishonoured his Master. Upon the whole Debate, the Emperor declared it was his Opinion, that *Eginhart's* Punishment would rather encrease than diminish the Shame of his Family; and that therefore he thought it the most adviseable to wear out the Memory of the Fact, by Marrying him to his Daughter. Accordingly *Eginhart* was called in, and acquainted by the Emperor, that he should no longer have any Pretence of complaining his Services were not rewarded, for that the Princess *Imma* should be given him in Marriage, with a Dower suitable to her Quality; which was soon after performed accordingly.

No. 226   Monday, November 19, 1711.   [Steele]

Mutum est pictura poema.[1]—Hor.

I have very often lamented and hinted my Sorrow in several Speculations, that the Art of Painting is made so little Use of the Improvement of our Manners. When we consider that it places the Action of the Person represented in the most agreeable Aspect imaginable, that it does not only express the Passion or Concern as it sits upon him who is drawn, but has under those Features the Height of the Painter's Imagination, What strong Images of Virtue and Humanity might we not expect would be instilled into the Mind from the Labours of the Pencil? This is a Poetry which would be understood with much less Capacity, and less Expence of Time, than what is taught by Writings; but the Use of it is generally perverted, and that admirable Skill prostituted to the basest and most unworthy Ends. Who is the better Man for beholding the most beautiful *Venus,* the best wrought *Bacchanal,* the Images of sleeping *Cupids,* languishing Nymphs, or any of the Representations of Gods, Goddesses, Demygods, Satyrs, *Polyphemes,* Sphinxes or Fauns? But if the Virtues and Vices which are sometimes pretended to be represented under such Draughts, were given us by the Painter in the Characters of real Life, and the Persons of Men and Women whose Actions have rendered them laudable or infamous; we should not see a good History-Piece without receiving an instructive Lecture. There needs no other Proof of this Truth, than the Testimony of every reasonable Crea-

[1] "A picture is a silent poem." This statement is not from Horace but is attributed by Plutarch to Simonides.

ture who has seen the Cartons[2] in Her Majesty's Gallery at *Hampton-Court:* These are Representations of no less Actions than those of our Blessed Saviour and his Apostles. As I now sit and recollect the warm Images which the admirable *Raphael* has raised, it is impossible, even from the faint Traces in ones's Memory of what one has not seen these two Years, to be unmoved at the Horrour and Reverence which appears in the whole Assembly when the mercenary Man fell down dead; at the Amazement of the Man born blind, when he first receives Sight; or at the graceless Indignation of the Sorcerer, when he is struck blind. The Lame, when they first find Strength in their Feet, stand Doubtful of their new Vigour. The heavenly Apostles appear acting these great things, with a deep Sense of the Infirmities which they relieve, but no Value of themselves who administer to their Weakness. They know themselves to be but Instruments; and the generous Distress they are painted in when divine Honours are offered to them, is a Representation in the most exquisite Degree of the Beauty of Holiness. When St. *Paul* is preaching to the *Athenians,* with what wonderful Art are almost all the different Tempers of Mankind represented in that elegant Audience? You see one credulous of all that is said, another wrapt up in deep Suspence, another saying there is some Reason in what he says, another angry that the Apostle destroys a favourite Opinion which he is unwilling to give up, another wholly convinced and holding out his Hands in Rapture; while the Generality attend, and wait for the Opinion of those who are of leading Characters in the Assembly. I will not pretend so much as to mention that Chart on which is drawn the Appearance of our Blessed Lord after his Resurrection. Present Authority, late Suffering, Humility and Majesty, Despotick Command and Divine Love, are at once seated in his Celestial Aspect. The Figures of the Eleven Apostles are all in the same Passion of Admiration, but dis-

---

[2] The famous Raphael cartoons, acquired by Charles I and now in the Victoria and Albert Museum in London.

cover it differently according to their Characters. *Peter* receives his Master's Orders on his Knees with an Admiration mixed with a more particular Attention: The two next with a more open Extasie, though still constrained by the Awe of the Divine Presence: The beloved Disciple, whom I take to be the Right of the two first Figures, has in his Countenance Wonder drowned in Love; and the last Personage, whose Back is towards the Spectator and his Side towards the Presence, one would fancy to be St. *Thomas,* as abashed by the Conscience of his former Diffidence; which perplexed Concern it is possible *Raphael* thought too hard a Task to draw but by this Acknowledgment of the Difficulty to describe it.

The whole Work is an Exercise of the highest Piety in the Painter; and all the Touches of a religious Mind are expressed in a manner much more forcible than can possibly be performed by the most moving Eloquence. These invaluable Pieces are very justly in the Hands of the greatest and most pious Soveraign in the World; and cannot be the frequent Object of every one at their own Leisure: But as an Engraver is to the Painter, what a Painter is to an Author, it is worthy Her Majesty's Name, that she has encouraged that noble Artist, Monsieur *Dorigny,* to publish these Works of *Raphael.* We have of this Gentleman a Piece of the Transfiguration, which is held a Work second to none in the World.

Methinks it would be ridiculous in our People of Condition, after their large Bounties to Foreigners of no Name or Merit, should they overlook this Occasion of having, for a trifling Subscription, a Work which it is impossible for a Man of Sense to behold, without being warmed with the noblest Sentiments that can be inspired by Love, Admiration, Compassion, Contempt of this World, and Expectation of a Better.

It is certainly the greatest Honour we can do our Country, to distinguish Strangers of Merit who apply to us with Modesty and Diffidence, which generally accompanies Merit. No Opportunity of this Kind ought to be neglected; and a modest Behaviour should alarm us to examine whether we do not lose something excellent under that Disadvantage in the Possessor of that Quality. My Skill in Paintings, where one is not directed by the Passion of the Pictures, is so inconsiderable, that I am in very great Perplexity when I offer to speak of any Performances of Painters of Landskips, Buildings, or single Figures. This makes me at a Loss how to mention the Pieces which Mr. *Boul* exposes to Sale by Auction on *Wednesday* next in *Shandois-street:* But having heard him commended by those who have bought of him heretofore for great Integrity in his Dealing, and overheard him himself (tho' a laudable Painter) say nothing of his own was fit to come into the Room with those he had to sell, I feared I should lose an Occasion of serving a Man of Worth in omitting to speak of his Auction.

ADVERTISEMENT

There is arrived from Italy *a Painter who acknowledges himself the greatest Person of the Age in that Art, and is willing to be as renowned in this Island as he declares he is in foreign Parts.*

The Doctor paints the Poor for nothing.

No. 235   Thursday, November 29, 1711. [Addison]

. . . *Populares*
Vincentum strepitus . . . [1] — Hor.

There is nothing which lies more within the Province of a Spectator than Publick Shows and Diversions; and as among these there are none which can pretend to vie with those Elegant Entertainments that are exhibited in our Theatres, I think it particularly Incumbent on me to take Notice of every thing that is remarkable in such numerous and refined Assemblies.

It is observed, that of late Years, there has been a certain Person in the Upper Gallery of the Play-house, who when he is pleased with any thing that is acted upon the Stage, expresses his Approbation by a loud Knock upon the Benches, or the Wainscot, which may be heard over the whole Theatre. This Person is commonly known by the Name of the *Trunk-maker in the Upper Gallery.* Whether it be, that the Blow he gives on these Occasions resembles that which is often heard in the Shops of such Artizans, or that he was supposed to have been a real Trunk-maker, who after the finishing of his Day's Work, used to unbend his Mind at these Publick Diversions with his Hammer in his Hand, I cannot certainly tell. There are some, I know, who have been foolish enough to imagine it is a Spirit which haunts the Upper-Gallery, and from time to time makes those strange Noises; and the rather, because he is observed to be louder than ordinary every time the Ghost of *Hamlet* appears. Others have reported, that it is a Dumb Man, who

[1] "Able to drown the clamors of the pit."

has chosen this way of uttering himself, when he is transported with any thing he sees or hears. Others will have it to be the Play-house Thunderer, that exerts himself after this manner in the Upper-Gallery, when he has nothing to do upon the Roof.

But having made it my business to get the best Information I cou'd in a matter of this Moment, I find that the Trunk-maker, as he is commonly called, is a large black Man, whom no body knows. He generally leans forward on a huge Oaken Plant with great Attention to every thing that passes upon the Stage. He is never seen to Smile; but upon hearing any thing that pleases him, he takes up his Staff with both Hands, and lays it upon the next piece of Timber that stands in his way with exceeding Vehemence: After which he composes himself in his former Posture, 'till such time as something new sets him again at Work.

It has been observed his Blow is so well timed, that the most judicious Critick could never except against it. As soon as any shining Thought is expressed in the Poet, or any uncommon Grace appears in the Actor, he smites the Bench or Wainscot. If the Audience does not concur with him, he smites a second time; and if the Audience is not yet awaked, looks round him with great Wrath, and repeats the Blow a third time, which never fails to produce the Clap. He sometimes lets the Audience begin the Clap of themselves, and at the Conclusion of their Applause ratifies it with a single Thwack.

He is of so great use to the Play-house, that it is said a former Director of it, upon his not being able to pay his Attendance by reason of Sickness, kept one in Pay to officiate for him 'till such time as he recovered; but the Person so employed, tho' he laid about him with incredible Violence, did it in such wrong Places, that the Audience soon found out it was not their old Friend the Trunk-maker.

It has been remarked, that he has not yet exerted himself with Vigour this Season. He sometimes plies at the Opera; and upon *Nicolini's* first Appearance, was said to have demolished three Benches in the Fury of his Applause. He has broken half a dozen Oaken Plants upon *Dogget*,[2] and seldom goes away from a Tragedy of *Shakespear*, without leaving the Wainscot extreamly shattered.

The Players do not only connive at this his obstreperous Approbation, but very chearfully repair at their own Cost whatever Damages he makes. They had once a Thought of erecting a kind of Wooden Anvil for his use, that should be made of a very sounding Plank, in order to render his Stroaks more deep and mellow; but as this might not have been distinguished from the Musick of a Kettle Drum, the Project was laid aside.

In the mean while I cannot but take notice of the great use it is to an Audience, that a Person should thus preside over their Heads, like the Director of a Consort, in order to awaken their Attention, and beat Time to their Applauses. Or to raise my Simile, I have sometimes fancied the Trunk-maker in the Upper Gallery to be like *Virgil*'s Ruler of the Winds, seated upon the Top of a Mountain, who, when he struck his Sceptre upon the side of it, roused an Hurricane, and set the whole Cavern in an Uproar.

It is certain the Trunk-maker has saved many a good Play, and brought many a graceful Actor into Reputation, who would not otherwise have been taken notice of. It is very visible, as the Audience is not a little abashed, if they find themselves betrayed into a Clap, when their Friend in the Upper-Gallery does not come into it; so the Actors do not value themselves upon the Clap, but regard it as a meer *Brutum fulmen,* or empty Noise, when it has not the Sound of the Oaken Plant in it. I know it has been given out by those who are Enemies to the Trunk-maker, that he has sometimes been bribed to be in the Interest of a bad Poet, or a vicious Player; but this is a Surmise, which has no Foundation; his Stroaks are always just, and his Admonitions seasonable; he does not deal about his Blows at Random, but always hits the right Nail upon the Head. The

[2] Thomas Doggett (1670?-1721), a popular comedian.

inexpressible Force wherewith he lays them on, sufficiently shews the Evidence and Strength of his Conviction. His Zeal for a good Author is indeed outragious, and breaks down every force and Partition, every Board and Plank, that stands within the Expression of his Applause.

As I do not care for terminating my Thoughts in Barren Speculations, or in Reports of pure Matter of Fact, without drawing something from them for the Advantage of my Countrymen, I shall take the Liberty to make an humble Proposal, that whenever the Trunkmaker shall depart this Life, or whenever he shall have lost the Spring of his Arm by Sickness, Old Age, Infirmity, or the like, some able-bodied Critick should be advanced to this Post, and have a competent Salary settled on him for Life, to be furnished with Bamboos for Opera's, Crabtree-Cudgels for Comedies, and Oaken Plants for Tragedy, at the publick Expence. And to the End that this Place should always be disposed of, according to Merit, I would have none preferred to it, who has not given convincing Proofs, both of a sound Judgment and a strong Arm, and who could not, upon Occasion, either knock down an Ox or write a Comment upon *Horace*'s Art of Poetry. In short, I would have him a due Composition of *Hercules* and *Apollo,* and so rightly qualify'd for this important Office, that the *Trunk-maker* may not be missed by our Posterity.

No. 239   Tuesday, December 4, 1711.   [Addison]

. . . Bella, horrida Bella ![1]—Virg.

I have sometimes amused my self with considering the several Methods of managing a Debate, which have obtained in the World.

The first Races of Mankind used to dispute, as our ordinary People do now-a-days, in a kind of wild Logick, uncultivated by Rules of Art.

Socrates introduced a Catachetical Method of Arguing. He would ask his Adversary Question upon Question, till he had convinced him out of his own Mouth that his Opinions were wrong. This way of debating drives an Enemy up into a Corner, seizes all the Passes through which he can make an Escape, and forces him to surrender at Discretion.

Aristotle changed this Method of Attack, and invented a great variety of little Weapons, called Syllogisms. As in the *Socratic* way of Dispute you agree to every thing which your Opponent advances, in the *Aristotelic* you are still denying and contradicting some part or other of what he says. *Socrates* conquers you by Stratagem, *Aristotle* by Force: The one takes the Town by Sapp, the other Sword in Hand.

The Universities of *Europe,* for many Years, carried on their Debates by Syllogism, insomuch that we see the Knowledge of several Centuries laid out into Objections and Answers, and all the good Sense of the Age cut and minced into almost an Infinitude of Distinctions.

When our Universities found that there was no End

[1] "Wars, grim wars!"

of wrangling this way, they invented a kind of Argument, which is not reducible to any Mood or Figure in *Aristotle*. It was called the *Argumentum Basilinum* (others write it *Bacilinum* and *Baculinum*) which is pretty well expressed in our *English* Word Club-Law. When they were not able to confute their Antagonist, they knock'd him down. It was their Method in these Polemical Debates first to discharge their Syllogisms, and afterwards to betake themselves to their Clubs, till such time as they had one way or other confounded their Gainsayers. There is in *Oxford* a narrow Defilé, (to make use of a Military Term) where the Partisians used to Encounter, for which Reason it still retains the Name of *Logic Lane*. I have heard an old Gentleman, a Physician, make his Boasts, that when he was a young Fellow he marched several times at the Head of a Troop of *Scotists,* and Cudgell'd a Body of *Smiglesians* half the length of *High-street;* till they had dispersed themselves for Shelter into their respective Garrisons.

This Humour, I find, went very far in *Erasmus's* Time. For that Author tells us, That upon the Revival of *Greek* Letters most of the Universities in *Europe* were divided into *Greeks* and *Trojans.* The latter were those who bore a mortal Enmity to the Language of the *Grecians,* insomuch that if they met with any who understood it, they did not fail to treat him as a Foe. *Erasmus* himself had, it seems, the Misfortune to fall into the Hands of a Party of *Trojans,* who laid him on with so many Blows and Buffets, that he never forgot their Hostilities to his dying Day.

There is a way of managing an Argument not much unlike the former, which is made use of by States and Communities, when they draw up a hundred thousand Disputants on each side, and convince one another by dint of Sword. A certain grand Monarch[2] was so sensible of his Strength in this way of Reasoning, that he writ upon his great Guns ____ *Ratio ultima Regum.* The Logick of Kings. But God be thanked he is now

[2] Louis XIV.

pretty well baffled at his own Weapons. When one has to do with a Philosopher of this kind, one should remember the old Gentleman's Saying who had been engaged in an Argument with one of the *Roman* Emperors. Upon his Friend's telling him, That he wonder'd he would give up the Question, when he had visibly the better of the Dispute, *I am never ashamed,* says he, *to be Confuted by one who is Master of Fifty Legions.*

I shall but just mention another kind of Reasoning, which may be called Arguing by Poll; and another which is of equal force, in which Wagers are made use of as Arguments, according to the celebrated Line in *Hudibras.* [3]

But the most notable way of managing a Controversie is that which we may call *Arguing by Torture.* This is a Method of Reasoning which has been made use of with the poor Refugees, and which was so fashionable in our Country during the Reign of Queen *Mary,* that in a Passage of an Author quoted by Monsieur *Bayle,* it is said, the Price of Wood was raised in *England,* by reason of the Executions that were made in *Smithfield.* These Disputants convince their Adversaries with a *Sorites* commonly called a Pile of Faggots. The Rack is also a kind of Syllogism which has been used with good Effect, and has made multitudes of Converts. Men were formerly disputed out of their Doubts, reconciled to Truth by force of Reason, and won over to Opinions by the Candour, Sense and Ingenuity of those who had the Right of their Side; but this method of Conviction operated too slowly. Pain was found to be much more Enlightning than Reason. Every Scruple was looked upon as Obstinacy, and not to be removed but by several Engines invented for that purpose. In a Word, the Application of Whips, Racks, Gibbets, Gallies, Dungeons, Fire and Faggot, in a Dis-

---

[3] A satiric poem by Samuel Butler (1612-80). The couplet to which Addison alludes runs as follows:
> Quoth she, I've heard old cunning *Stagers*
> Say, Fools for *Arguments* use wagers.

pute, may be looked upon as Popish Refinements upon the old Heathen Logick.

There is another way of Reasoning which seldom fails, tho' it be of a quite different Nature to that I have last mentioned. I mean convincing a Man by ready Mony, or, as it is ordinarily called, Bribing a Man to an Opinion. This Method has often proved successful, when all the others have been made use of to no purpose. A Man who is furnished with Arguments from the Mint, will convince his Antagonist much sooner than one who draws them from Reason and Philosophy. Gold is a wonderful Clearer of the Understanding: It dissipates every Doubt and Scruple in an Instant: Accommodates it self to the meanest Capacities; Silences the Loud and Clamorous, and brings over the most Obstinate and Inflexible. *Philip* of *Macedon* was a Man of most Invincible Reason this way. He refuted by it all the Wisdom of *Athens,* confounded their Statesmen, struck their Orators Dumb, and at length argued them out of all their Liberties.

Having here touched upon the several Methods of Disputing, as they have prevailed in different Ages of the World, I shall very suddenly give my Reader an Account of the whole Art of Cavilling; which shall be a full and satisfactory Answer to all such Papers and Pamphlets as have yet appeared against the *Spectator.*

No. 253   Thursday, December 20, 1711. [Addison]

Indignor quicquam reprehendi, non quia crasse
Compositum, illepideve putetur, sed quia nuper.[1]—Hor.

There is nothing which more denotes a great Mind, than the Abhorrence of Envy and Detraction. This Passion reigns more among bad Poets, than among any other Set of Men.

As there are none more ambitious of Fame, than those who are conversant in Poetry, it is very natural for such as have not succeeded in it to depreciate the Works of those who have. For since they cannot raise themselves to the Reputation of their Fellow-Writers, they must endeavour to sink it to their own Pitch, if they would still keep themselves upon a Level with them.

The greatest Wits that ever were produced in one Age, lived together in so good an Understanding, and celebrated one another with so much Generosity, that each of them receives an additional Lustre from his Contemporaries, and is more famous for having lived with Men of so extraordinary a Genius, than if he had himself been the sole Wonder of the Age. I need not tell my Reader, that I here point at the Reign of *Augustus,* and I believe he will be of my Opinion, that neither *Virgil* nor *Horace* would have gained so great a Reputation in the World, had they not been the Friends and Admirers of each other. Indeed all the great Writers of that Age, for whom singly we have so great an Esteem, stand up together as Vouchers for one another's Reputation. But at the same

---

[1] "I am vexed that any work is censured, not because it is coarse or crude in style, but because it is recent."

346

time that *Virgil* was celebrated by *Gallus, Propertius, Horace, Varius, Tucca* and *Ovid,* we know that *Bavius* and *Mævius* were his declared Foes and Calumniators.

In our own Country a Man seldom sets up for a Poet, without attacking the Reputation of all his Brothers in the Art. The Ignorance of the Moderns, the Scribblers of the Age, the Decay of Poetry, are the Topicks of Detraction, with which he makes his Entrance into the World: But how much more noble is the Fame that is built on Candour and Ingenuity, according to those beautiful Lines of Sir *John Denham,* in his Poem on *Fletcher's* Works!

> *But whither am I straid? I need not raise*
> *Trophies to thee from other Men's Dispraise;*
> *Nor is thy Fame on lesser Ruins built,*
> *Nor needs thy juster Title the foul Guilt*
> *Of Eastern Kings, who to secure their Reign*
> *Must have their Brothers, Sons, and Kindred slain.*

I am sorry to find that an Author, who is very justly esteemed among the best Judges, has admitted some Stroaks of this Nature into a very fine Poem, I mean *The Art of Criticism,*[2] which was published some Months since, and is a Masterpiece in its Kind. The Observations follow one another like those in *Horace's Art of Poetry,* without that methodical Regularity which would have been requisite in a Prose Author. They are some of them uncommon, but such as the Reader must assent to, when he sees them explained with that Elegance and Perspicuity in which they are delivered. As for those which are the most known, and the most received, they are placed in so beautiful a Light, and illustrated with such apt Allusions, that they have in them all the Graces of Novelty, and make

---

[2] Addison is here referring to Pope's *Essay on Criticism,* which had appeared the previous May. See Professor Bond's comprehensive note on the literary relationship at this time between Addison and Pope. (*The Spectator,* ed. Donald F. Bond, II, 483).

the Reader, who was before acquainted with them, still more convinced of their Truth and Solidity. And here give me Leave to mention what Monsieur *Boileau* has so very well enlarged upon in the Preface to his Works, that Wit and fine Writing doth not consist so much in advancing Things that are new, as in giving things that are known an agreeble Turn. It is impossible, for us who live in the later Ages of the World, to make Observations in Criticism, Morality, or in any Art or Science, which have not been touched upon by others. We have little else left us, but to represent the common Sense of Mankind in more strong, more beautiful, or more uncommon Lights. If a Reader examines *Horace's* Art of Poetry, he will find but very few Precepts in it, which he may not meet with in *Aristotle,* and which were not commonly known by all the Poets of the *Augustan* Age. His Way of Expressing and Applying them, not his Invention of them, is what we are chiefly to admire.

For this Reason I think there is nothing in the World so tiresome as the Works of those Criticks, who write in a positive dogmatick Way, without either Language, Genius or Imagination. If the Reader would see how the best of the *Latin* Criticks writ, he may find their Manner very beautifully described in the Characters of *Horace, Petronius, Quintilian* and *Longinus,* as they are drawn in the Essay of which I am now speaking.

Since I have mentioned *Longinus,* who in his Reflections has given us the same Kind of Sublime, which he observes in the several Passages that occasioned them; I cannot but take notice, that our *English* Author has after the same manner exemplified several of his Precepts in the very Precepts themselves. I shall produce two or three Instances of this Kind. Speaking of the insipid Smoothness which some Readers are so much in Love with, he has the following Verses.

> *These* Equal Syllables *alone require,*
> *Tho' oft the Ear the* open Vowels *tire,*

> *While* Expletives *their feeble Aid* do *join,*
> *And ten low Words oft creep in one dull Line.*

The gaping of the Vowels in the second Line, the Expletive *do* in the third, and the ten Monosyllables in the fourth, give such a Beauty to this Passage, as would have been very much admired in an Ancient Poet. The Reader may observe the following Lines in the same View:

> *A* needless Alexandrine *ends the Song,*
> *That like a wounded Snake, drags its slow Length along.*

And afterwards,

> *'Tis not enough no Harshness gives Offence,*
> *The* Sound *must seem an* Eccho *to the* Sense.
> Soft *is the Strain when* Zephir *gently blows,*
> *And the* smooth Stream *in* smoother Numbers *flows;*
> *But when loud Surges lash the sounding Shore,*
> *The* hoarse, rough Verse *shou'd like the* Torrent *roar.*
> *When* Ajax *strives, some Rock's vast Weight to throw,*
> *The* Line *too* labours, *and the* Words *move* slow;
> *Not so, when swift* Camilla *scours the Plain,*
> *Flies o'er th' unbending Corn, and skims along the Main.*

The beautiful Distich upon *Ajax* in the foregoing Lines, puts me in mind of a Description in *Homer*'s Odyssey, which none of the Criticks have taken notice of. It is where *Sisyphus* is represented lifting his Stone up the Hill, which is no sooner carried to the Top of it, but it immediately tumbles to the Bottom. This double Motion of the Stone is admirably described in the Numbers of these Verses. As in the four first it is heaved up by several *Spondees,* intermixed with proper Breathing-places, and at last trundles down in a continued Line of *Dactyls.*

> Καὶ μιῶ Σίουφον εἰσεῖδον, χορατέρ' ἄλγ εχοντυ,
> Λᾶαν βαδάζονζα πελώριον ἀμφοτέρῃοιν.

Ἤτοι ὁ μῒ, οχηειη Γόεζι Ο χεροίν το ποσίν τε,
Λᾶδι ἄνω ὤζεόχε ποτὶ λόφον. ᾽δι᾽ ὅτε μέλλοι
Ἄαπον ὑπερδαλέεν τότ᾽ λποζρέψοοχε Κραμαρὶς,
Αμτις ἔπεζα πέδονδε ηλίνδιζ λᾶας ἀνρδής.[3]

It would be endless to quote Verses out of *Virgil* which
have this particular Kind of Beauty in the Numbers; but I may
take an Occasion in a future Paper to shew several of them
which have escaped the Observation of others.

I cannot conclude this Paper without taking notice that
we have three Poems in our Tongue, which are of the same
Nature, and each of them a Master-piece in its Kind; the Essay
on Translated Verse, the Essay on the Art of Poetry, and the
Essay upon Criticism.

[3] "I turn'd my eye, and as I turn'd survey'd
     A mournful vision! the *Sisyphyan* shade;
   With many a weary step, and many a groan,
   Up the high hill he heaves a huge round stone;
   The huge round stone, resulting with a bound,
     Thunders impetuous down, and smoaks along the ground.
                                        The Odyssey, XI, 733-8.
                                     Trans. Pope, III (1725), 109.

No. 267   Saturday, January 5, 1711 - 12.   [Addison]

Cedite Romani Scriptores, cedite Graii.[1] — Propert.

There is Nothing in Nature so irksome as general Discourses, especially when they turn chiefly upon Words. For this Reason I shall wave the Discussion of that Point which was started some Years since, Whether *Milton's Paradise Lost* may be called an Heroick Poem? Those who will not give it that Title may call it (if they please) a *Divine Poem.* It will be sufficient to its Perfection, if it has in it all the Beauties of the highest Kind of Poetry; and as for those who alledge it is not an Heroick Poem, they advance no more to the Diminution of it, than if they should say *Adam* is not *Æneas,* nor *Eve Helen.*

I shall therefore examine it by the Rules of Epic Poetry, and see whether it falls short of the *Iliad* or *Æneid,* in the Beauties which are essential to that Kind of Writing. The first Thing to be consider'd in an Epic Poem, is the Fable, which is perfect or imperfect, according as the Action which it relates is more or less so. This Action should have three Quailfications in it. First, It should be but one Action. Secondly, It should be an entire Action; and Thirdly, it should be a great Action. To consider the Action of the *Iliad, Æneid,* and *Paradise Lost,* in these three several Lights. *Homer* to preserve the Unity of his Action hastens into the Midst of Things, as *Horace* has observed: Had he gone up to *Leda's* Egg, or begun much later, even at the Rape of *Helen,* or the Investing of *Troy,* it is manifest that the Story of the Poem would have been a Series of several Actions. He therefore opens his Poem with the Dis-

[1] "Yield ye, bards of Rome, yield ye, singers of Greece."

cord of his Princes, and with great Art interweaves in the several succeeding Parts of it, an Account of every Thing material which relates to them, and had passed before that fatal Dissension. After the same Manner *Æneas* makes his first Appearance in the *Tyrrhene* Seas, and within Sight of *Italy,* because the Action proposed to be celebrated was that of his settling himself in *Latium.* But because it was necessary for the Reader to know what had happened to him in the taking of *Troy,* and in the preceding Parts of his Voyage, *Virgil* makes his Heroe relate it by Way of Episode in the second and third Books of the *Æneid.* The Contents of both which Books come before those of the first Book in the Thread of the Story, tho' for preserving of this Unity of Action, they follow them in the Disposition of the Poem. *Milton,* in Imitation of these two great Poets, opens his *Paradise Lost,* with an infernal Council plotting the Fall of Man, which is the Action he proposed to celebrate; and as for those great Actions which preceded, in Point of Time, the Battle of the Angels, and the Creation of the World, (which would have entirely destroyed the Unity of his principal Action, had he related them in the same Order that they happened) he cast them into the fifth, sixth, and seventh Books, by way of Episode to this noble Poem.

Aristotle himself allows, that *Homer* has nothing to boast of as to the Unity of his Fable, tho' at the same Time that great Critick and Philosopher endeavours to palliate this Imperfection in the *Greek* Poet, by imputing it in some Measure to the very Nature of an Epic Poem. Some have been of Opinion, that the *Æneid* labours also in this Particular, and has Episodes which may be looked upon as Excrescencies rather than as Parts of the Action. On the contrary, the Poem which we have now under our Consideration, hath no other Episodes than such as naturally arise from the Subject, and yet is filled with such a Multitude of astonishing Incidents, that it gives us at the same Time a Pleasure of the greatest Variety, and of the greatest Simplicity.

I must observe also, that as *Virgil* in the Poem which was

designed to celebrate the Original of the *Roman* Empire, has described the Birth of its great Rival, the *Carthaginian* Commonwealth: *Milton* with the like Art in his Poem on the Fall of Man, has related the Fall of those Angels who are his professed Enemies. Besides the many other Beauties in such an Episode, it's running parallel with the great Action of the Poem, hinders it from breaking the Unity so much as another Episode would have done, that had not so great an Affinity with the principal Subject. In short, this is the same Kind of Beauty which the Criticks admire in the *Spanish Fryar,* or the *Double Discovery,*[2] where the two different Plots look like Counterparts and Copies of one another.

The second Qualification required in the Action of an Epic Poem is, that it should be an *entire* Action: An Action is entire when it is compleat in all its Parts; or as *Aristotle* describes it, when it consists of a Beginning, a Middle, and an End. Nothing should go before it, be intermix'd with it, or follow after it, that is not related to it. As on the contrary, no single Step should be omitted in that just and regular Process which it must be supposed to take from its Original to its Consummation. Thus we see the Anger of *Achilles* in its Birth, its Continuance and Effects; and *Æneas*'s Settlement in *Italy,* carried on through all the Oppositions in his Way to it both by Sea and Land. The Action in *Milton* excels (I think) both the former in this Particular; we see it contrived in Hell, executed upon Earth, and punished by Heaven. The Parts of it are told in the most distinct Manner, and grow out of one another in the most natural Method.

The third Qualification of an Epic Poem is its *Greatness.* The Anger of *Achilles* was of such Consequence, that it embroiled the Kings of *Greece,* destroy'd the Heroes of *Troy,* and engaged all the Gods in Factions. *Æneas*'s Settlement in *Italy* produced the *Caesars,* and gave Birth to the *Roman* Empire. *Milton*'s Subject was still greater than either of the

[2] By John Dryden.

former; it does not determine the Fate of single Persons or Nations, but of a whole Species. The united Powers of Hell are joined together for the Destruction of Mankind, which they effected in Part, and would have completed, had not Omnipotence it self interposed. The principal Actors are Man in his greatest Perfection, and Woman in her highest Beauty. Their Enemies are the fallen Angels: The Messiah their Friend, and the Almighty their Protector. In short, every Thing that is great in the whole Circle of Being, whether within the Verge of Nature, or out of it, has a proper Part assigned it in this noble Poem.

In Poetry, as in Architecture, not only the Whole, but the principal Members, and every Part of them, should be Great. I will not presume to say, that the Book of Games in the *Æneid,* or that in the *Iliad,* are not of this Nature, nor to reprehend *Virgil's* Simile of a Top, and many other of the same Nature in the *Iliad,* as liable to any Censure in this Particular; but I think we may say, without derogating from those wonderful Performances, that there is an unquestionable Magnificence in every Part of *Paradise Lost,* and indeed a much greater than could have been formed upon any Pagan System.

But *Aristotle,* by the Greatness of the Action, does not only mean that it should be great in its Nature, but also in its Duration, or in other Words, that it should have a due Length in it, as well as what we properly call Greatness. The just Measure of this Kind of Magnitude, he explains by the following Similitude. An Animal, no bigger than a Mite, cannot appear perfect to the Eye, because the Sight takes it in at once, and has only a confused Idea of the Whole, and not a distinct Idea of all its Parts; If on the contrary you should suppose an Animal of ten thousand Furlongs in Length, the Eye would be so filled with a single Part of it, that it could not give the Mind an Idea of the Whole. What these Animals are to the Eye, a very short or a very long Action would be to the Memory. The first would be, as it were, lost and swallowed up by it, and the other difficult to be contained in it. *Homer* and *Virgil* have shewn their principal Art in this Particular; the Action of the *Iliad,* and that of the *Æneid,* were in themselves exceeding short, but are so beautifully extended and diversified by the Invention of *Episodes,* and the Machinery of Gods, with the like poetical Ornaments, that they make up an agreeable Story sufficient to employ the Memory without overcharging it. *Milton's* Action is enriched with such a Variety of Circumstances, that I have taken as much Pleasure in reading the Contents of his Books, as in the best invented Story I ever met with. It is possible, that the Traditions on which the *Iliad* and *Æneid* were built, had more Circumstances in them than the History of *the Fall of Man,* as it is related in Scripture. Besides it was easier for *Homer* and *Virgil* to dash the Truth with Fiction, as they were in no danger of offending the Religion of their Country by it. But as for *Milton,* he had not only a very few Circumstances upon which to raise his Poem, but was also obliged to proceed with the greatest Caution in every Thing that he added out of his own Invention. And, indeed, notwithstanding all the Restraints he was under, he has filled his Story with so many surprising Incidents, which bear so close an Analogy with what is delivered in Holy Writ, that it is capable of pleasing the most delicate Reader, without giving Offence to the most scrupulous.

The modern Criticks have collected from several Hints in the *Iliad* and *Æneid* the Space of Time, which is taken up by the Action of each of those Poems; but as a great Part of *Milton's* Story was transacted in Regions that lie out of the Reach of the Sun and the Sphere of Day, it is impossible to gratifie the Reader with such a Calculation, which indeed would be more curious than instructive; None of the Criticks, either Antient or Modern, having laid down Rules to circumscribe the Action of an Epic Poem with any determined Number of Years, Days or Hours.

This Piece of Criticism on Milton's *Paradise Lost shall be carried on in the following* Saturdays *Papers.*

No. 285   Saturday, January 26, 1711-12.   [Addison]

Ne, quicunque Deus, quicunque adhibebitur heros,
Regali conspectus in auro nuper & ostro,
Migret in Obscuras humili sermone tabernas:
Aut, dum vitat humum, nubes & inania captet.[1]—Hor.

Having already treated of the Fable, the Characters, and Sentiments in the *Paradise Lost,* we are in the last Place to consider the *Language;* and as the learned World is very much divided upon *Milton,* as to this Point, I hope they will excuse me if I appear particular in any of my Opinions, and encline to those who judge the most advantagiously of the Author.

It is requisite that the Language of an heroick Poem should be both perspicuous and sublime. In proportion as either of these two Qualities are wanting, the Language is imperfect. Perspicuity is the first and most necessary Qualification; insomuch, that a good-natured Reader sometimes overlooks a little Slip even in the Grammar or Syntax, where it is impossible for him to mistake the Poet's Sense. Of this Kind is that Passage in *Milton,* wherein he speaks of *Satan.*

> . . . *God and his Son except,*
> *Created Thing Nought valu'd he nor shunn'd.*

And that in which he describes *Adam* and *Eve.*

---

[1] "No god, no hero, who shall be brought upon the stage, and whom we have just beheld in royal gold and purple, shall shift with the vulgar speech into dingy hovels, or, while shunning the ground, catch at clouds and emptiness."

Adam *the goodliest Man of Men since born*
His Sons, the fairest of her Daughters Eve.

It is plain, that in the former of these Passages, according to the natural Syntax, the Divine Persons mentioned in the first Line are represented as created Beings; and that in the other, *Adam* and *Eve* are confounded with their Sons and Daughters. Such little Blemishes as these, when the Thought is great and natural, we should, with *Horace,* impute to a pardonable Inadvertency, or to the Weakness of humane Nature, which cannot attend to each minute Particular, and give the last finishing to every Circumstance in so long a Work. The ancient Criticks therefore, who were acted by a Spirit of Candour, rather than that of Cavilling, invented certain Figures of Speech, on purpose to palliate little Errors of this Nature in the Writings of those Authors, who had so many greater Beauties to atone for them.

If Clearness and Perspicuity were only to be consulted, the Poet would have Nothing else to do but to cloath his Thoughts in the most plain and natural Expressions. But, since it often happens that the most obvious Phrases, and those which are used in ordinary Conversation, become too familiar to the Ear, and contract a Kind of Meanness by passing through the Mouths of the Vulgar, a Poet should take particular Care to guard himself against idiomatick Ways of Speaking. *Ovid* and *Lucan* have many Poornesses of Expression upon this Account, as taking up with the first Phrases that offered, without putting themselves to the Trouble of looking after such as would not only have been natural, but also elevated and sublime. *Milton* has but few Faillings in this Kind, of which, however, you may meet with some Instances, as in the following Passages.

Embrio's and Idiots, Eremites and Fryars
White, Black, and Grey, *with all their* Trumpery,
Here Pilgrims roam . . .

> *. . . A while Discourse they hold,*
> No fear lest Dinner cool; *when thus began*
> *Our Author . . .*
> *Who of all Ages to succeed, but feeling*
> *The Evil on him brought by me, will curse*
> *My Head, ill fare our Ancestor impure,*
> For this we may thank *Adam . . .*

The great Masters in Composition know very well that many an elegant Phrase becomes improper for a Poet or an Orator, when it has been debased by common Use. For this Reason the Works of ancient Authors, which are written in dead Languages, have a great Advantage over those which are written in Languages that are now spoken. Were there any mean Phrases or Idioms in *Virgil* and *Homer,* they would not shock the Ear of the most delicate modern Reader, so much as they would have done that of an old *Greek* or *Roman,* because we never hear them pronounced in our Streets, or in ordinary Conversation.

It is not therefore sufficient, that the Language of an Epic Poem be perspicuous, unless it be also sublime. To this End it ought to deviate from the common Forms and ordinary Phrases of Speech. The Judgment of a Poet very much discovers it self in shunning the common Roads of Expression, without falling into such Ways of Speech as may seem stiff and unnatural; he must not swell into a false Sublime, by endeavouring to avoid the other Extream. Among the *Greeks, Eschylus,* and sometimes *Sophocles,* were guilty of this Fault; among the *Latins, Claudian* and *Statius;* and among our own Countrymen, *Shakespear* and *Lee.* In these Authors the Affectation of Greatness often hurts the Perspicuity of the Stile, as in many others the Endeavour after Perspicuity prejudices its Greatness.

Aristotle has observed, that the Idiomatick Stile may be avoided, and the Sublime formed, by the following Methods. First, by the Use of Metaphors, like those in *Milton.*

> Imparadised *in one another's Arms,*
> . . . *And in his Hand a Reed*
> *Stood waving* tipt *with Fire;* . . .
> *The grassie Clods now* calv'd. . . .

In these and innumerable other Instances, the Metaphors are very bold, but beautiful: I must however observe, that the Metaphors are not thick sown in *Milton,* which always savours too much of Wit, that they never clash with one another, which as *Aristotle* observes, turns a Sentence into a Kind of an Enigma or Riddle; and that he seldom makes Use of them where the proper and natural Words will do as well.

Another Way of raising the Language, and giving it a poetical Turn, is to make Use of the Idioms of other Tongues. *Virgil* is full of the *Greek* Forms of Speech, which the Criticks call *Hellenisms,* as *Horace* in his Odes abounds with them much more than *Virgil.* I need not mention the several Dialects which *Homer* has made Use of for this End. *Milton* in conformity with the Practice of the ancient Poets, and with *Aristotle's* Rule, has infused a great many *Latinisms,* as well as *Graecisms,* and sometimes *Hebraisms,* into the Language of his Poem, as towards the Beginning of it.

> Nor *did they* not *perceive the evil Plight*
> *In which they were, or the fierce Pains* not *feel.*
> *Yet to their Gen'ral's Voice they soon obey'd.*
> . . . *Who shall tempt with wandring Feet*
> *The dark unbottom'd infinite Abyss,*
> *And through the* palpable Obscure *find out his Way,*
> *His uncouth Way, or spread his airy Flight*
> *Upborn with indefatigable Wings*
> *Over the* vast Abrupt! . . .
> . . . *So both ascend*
> *In the Visions of God.* . . .   B. 2.

Under this Head may be reckoned the placing the Adjective after the Substantive, the Transposition of Words, the turning the Adjective into a Substantive, with several other foreign Modes of Speech, which this Poet has naturalized to give his Verse the greater Sound, and throw it out of Prose.

The third Method mentioned by *Aristotle,* is what agrees with the Genius of the *Greek* Language more than with that of any other Tongue, and is therefore more used by *Homer* than by any other Poet. I mean the length'ning of a Phrase by the Addition of Words, which may either be inserted or omitted, as also by the extending or contracting of particular Words by the Insertion or Omission of certain Syllables. *Milton* has put in Practice this Method of raising his Language, as far as the Nature of our Tongue will permit, as in the Passage abovementioned, *Eremite,* for what is Hermite in common Discourse. If you observe the Measure of his Verse, he has with great Judgment suppressed a Syllable in several Words, and shortned those of two Syllables into one, by which Method, besides the abovementioned Advantage, he has given a greater Variety to his Numbers. But this Practice is more particularly remarkable in the Names of Persons and of Countries, as *Beelzebub, Hessebon,* and in many other Particulars, wherein he has either changed the Name, or made Use of that which is not the most commonly known, that he might the better deviate from the Language of the Vulgar.

The same Reason recommended to him several old Words, which also makes his Poem appear the more venerable, and gives it a greater Air of Antiquity.

I must likewise take Notice, that there are in *Milton* several Words of his own Coining, as *Cerberean, miscreated, Hell-doom'd, Embryon* Atoms, and many Others. If the Reader is offended at this Liberty in our *English* Poet, I would recommend him to a Discourse in *Plutarch,* which shews us how frequently *Homer* has made Use of the same Liberty.

Milton, by the abovementioned Helps, and by the Choice of the noblest Words and Phrases which our Tongue would afford him, has carried our Language to a greater Height than any of the *English* Poets have ever done before or after him, and made the Sublimity of his Stile equal to that of his Sentiments.

I have been the more particular in these Observations of *Milton*'s Stile, because it is that Part of him in which he appears the most singular. The Remarks I have here made upon the Practice of other Poets, with my Observations out of *Aristotle,* will perhaps alleviate the Prejudice which some have taken to his Poem upon this Account; tho' after all, I must confess, that I think his Stile, tho' admirable in general, is in some Places too much stiffened and obscured by the frequent Use of those Methods, which *Aristotle* has prescribed for the raising of it.

This Redundancy of those several Ways of Speech which *Aristotle* calls *foreign Language,* and with which *Milton* has so very much enriched, and in some Places darkned the Language of his Poem, was the more proper for his Use, because his Poem is written in blank Verse; Rhyme, without any other Assistance, throws the Language off from Prose, and very often makes an indifferent Phrase pass unregarded; but where the Verse is not built upon Rhymes, there Pomp of Sound, and Energy of Expression, are indispensably necessary to support the Stile, and keep it from falling into the Flatness of Prose.

Those who have not a Taste for this Elevation of Stile, and are apt to ridicule a Poet when he departs from the common Forms of Expression, would do well to see how *Aristotle* has treated an ancient Author, called *Euclid,* for his insipid Mirth upon this Occasion. Mr. *Dryden* used to call this Sort of Men his Prose-Criticks.

I should, under this Head of the Language, consider *Milton's* Numbers, in which he has made Use of several Elisions, that are not customary among other *English* Poets, as may be particularly observed in his cutting off the letter *Y,* when it precedes a Vowel. This, and some other Innovations in the Measure of his Verse, has varied his Numbers in such a Manner, as makes them incapable of satiating the Ear, and cloying the Reader, which the same uniform Measure would certainly have done, and which the perpetual Returns of Rhime never fail to do in long narrative Poems. I shall close these Reflections upon the Language of *Paradise Lost,* with observing that *Milton* has copied after *Homer,* rather than *Virgil,* in the Length of his Periods, the Copiousness of his Phrases, and the running of his Verses into one another.

No. 290   Friday, February 1, 1711-12.   [Steele]

Projicit ampullas & sesquipedalia verba. [1] —Hor.

The Players, who know I am very much their Friend, take all Opportunities to express a Gratitude to me for being so. They could not have a better Occasion of obliging me, than one which they lately took Hold of. They desired my Friend WILL HONEYCOMB to bring me to the Reading of a new Tragedy, it is called *The Distressed Mother.* [2] I must confess, tho' some Days are passed since I enjoyed that Entertainment, the Passions of the several Characters dwell strongly upon my Imagination; and I congratulate to the Age, that they are at last to see Truth and humane Life represented in the Incidents which concern Heroes and Heroines. The Stile of the Play is such as becomes those of the first Education, and the Sentiments worthy those of the highest Figure. It was a most exquisite Pleasure to me, to observe real Tears drop from the Eyes of those who had long made it their Profession to dissemble Affliction; and the Player who read, frequently throw down the Book, till he had given Vent to the Humanity which rose in him at some irresistible Touches of the imagined Sorrow. We have seldom had any Female Distress on the Stage, which did not, upon cool Imagination, appear to flow from the Weakness rather than the Misfortune of the Person represented: But in this Tragedy you are not entertained with the ungoverned Passions of such as are enamoured of each other meerly as they are Men and Women, but their Regards are founded upon

[1] "He throws aside his bombast and polysyllabic words."
[2] By Ambrose Philips (1674-1749), who belonged to Addison's circle of wits at Button's Coffee-house. *The Distressed Mother,* adapted from Racine's *Andromaque,* was first acted March 17, 1712.

high Conceptions of each other's Virtue and Merit; and the Character which gives Name to the Play, is one who has behaved her self with heroick Virtue in the most important Circumstances of a female Life, those of a Wife, a Widow, and a Mother. If there be those whose Minds have been too attentive upon the Affairs of Life, to have any Notion of the Passion of Love in such Extremes as are known only to particular Tempers, yet in the above-mentioned Considerations, the Sorrow of the Heroine will move even the Generality of Mankind. Domestick Virtues concern all the World, and there is no one living who is not interested that *Andromache* should be an imitable Character. The generous Affection to the Memory of her deceased Husband, that tender Care for her Son, which is ever heightned with the Consideration of his Father, and these Regards preserved in spite of being tempted with the Possession of the highest Greatness, are what cannot but be venerable even to such an Audience as at present frequents the *English* Theatre. My Friend WILL HONEYCOMB commended several tender Things that were said, and told me they were very genteel; but whispered me, that he feared the Piece was not busy enough for the present Taste. To supply this, he recommended to the Players to be very careful in their Scenes, and above all Things, that every Part should be perfectly new dress'd. I was very glad to find that they did not neglect my Friend's Admonition, because there are a great many in his Class of Criticism who may be gained by it; but indeed the Truth is, that as to the Work it self, it is every where Nature. The Persons are of the highest Quality in Life, even that of Princes; but their Quality is not represented by the Poet with Direction that Guards and Waiters should follow them in every Scene, but their Grandure appears in greatness of Sentiments, flowing from Minds worthy their Condition. To make a Character truly Great, this Author understands that it should have its Foundation in superior Thoughts and Maxims of Conduct. It is very certain, that many an honest Woman would make no Difficulty, tho' she had been the Wife of *Hector,* for the Sake of a Kingdom, to marry the Enemy of her Husband's Family and Country; and indeed who can deny but she might be still an honest Woman, but no Heroine? That may be defensible, nay laudable in one Character, which would be in the highest Degree exceptionable in another. When *Cato Uticensis* killed himself, *Cottius,* a *Roman* of ordinary Quality and Character, did the same Thing; upon which one said, smiling, '*Cottius* might have lived tho' *Caesar* has seized the *Roman* Liberty.' *Cottius's* Condition might have been the same, let Things at the Upper-End of the World pass as they would. What is further very extraordinary in this Work, is, that the Persons are all of them laudable, and their Misfortunes arise rather from unguarded Virtue than Propensity to Vice. The Town has an Opportunity of doing it self Justice in supporting the Representations of Passion, Sorrow, Indignation, even Despair it self, within the Rules of Decency, Honour, and good Breeding; and since there is no one can flatter himself his Life will be always fortunate, they may here see Sorrow as they would wish to bear it whenever it arrives.

'*Mr.* SPECTATOR,

I am appointed to act a Part in the new Tragedy, called *The Distressed Mother:* It is the celebrated Grief of *Orestes* which I am to personate; but I shall not act as I ought, for I shall feel it too intimately to be able to utter it. I was last Night repeating a Paragraph to my self, which I took to be an Expression of Rage, and in the Middle of the Sentence there was a Stroke of Self-pity, which quite unmanned me. Be pleased, Sir, to print this Letter, that when I am oppressed in this Manner at such an Interval, a certain Part of the Audience may not think I am out; and I hope with this Allowance to do it to Satisfaction.

I am,

Sir,

Your most humble Servant,
George   Powell.'[3]

---

[3] Compare *The Spectator,* No. 40.

'*Mr.* SPECTATOR,

As I was walking t' other Day in the *Park,* I saw a Gentleman with a very short Face;⁴ I desire to know whether it was you. Pray inform me as soon as you can, lest I become the most heroick *Hecatissa*'s Rival.

Your humble Servant to Command,

Sophia.'

'*Dear Madam,*

It is not me you are in love with, for I was very ill, and kept my Chamber all that Day.

Your most humble Servant,

The SPECTATOR.'

⁴In No. 17, Steele had equipped Mr. Spectator with a physical characteristic of Steele's own, a face "which is not quite so long as it is broad."

No. 294 Wednesday, February 6, 1711-12. [Steele]

Difficile est plurimum virtutem revereri qui semper secunda fortuna sit usus.[1] —Tull. *ad Herennium.*

Insolence is the Crime of all others which every Man is most apt to rail at; and yet is there one Respect in which almost all Men living are guilty of it, and that is in the Case of laying a greater Value upon the Gifts of Fortune than we ought. It is here in *England* come into our very Language, as a Propriety of Distinction, to say, when we would speak of Persons to their Advantage, they are People of Condition. There is no Doubt but the proper Use of Riches implies that a Man should exert all the good Qualities imaginable; and if we mean by a Man of Condition or Quality one, who, according to the Wealth he is Master of, shews himself just, beneficent, and charitable, that Term ought very deservedly to be had in the highest Veneration; but when Wealth is used only as it is the Support of Pomp and Luxury, to be rich is very far from being a Recommendation to Honour and Respect. It is indeed the greatest Insolence imaginable, in a Creature who would feel the Extremes of Thirst and Hunger if he did not prevent his Appetites before they call upon him, to be so forgetful of the common Necessity of humane Nature as never to cast an Eye upon the Poor and Needy. The Fellow who escaped from a Ship which struck upon a Rock in the West, and joined with the Country-People to destroy his Brother Sailors and make her a Wreck, was Thought a most execrable Creature; but does not every Man who enjoys the Possession of what he nat-

[1] "It is difficult for a man always accustomed to good fortune to have a very great reverence for virtue."

urally wants, and is unmindful of the unsupplied Distress of other Men, betray the same Temper of Mind? When a Man looks about him, and with Regard to Riches and Poverty beholds some drawn in Pomp and Equipage, and they and their very Servants with an Air of Scorn and Triumph overlooking the Multitude that pass by them: And in the same Street a Creature of the same Make crying out in the Name of all that is good and sacred to behold his Misery, and give him some Supply against Hunger and Nakedness; who would believe these two Beings were of the same Species? But so it is, that the Consideration of Fortune has taken up all our Minds, and, as I have often complained, Poverty and Riches stand in our Imaginations in the Places of Guilt and Innocence. But in all Seasons there will be some Instances of Persons who have Souls too large to be taken with popular Prejudices, and while the rest of Mankind are contending for Superiority in Power and Wealth, have their Thoughts bent upon the Necessities of those below them. The Charity-Schools which have been erected of late Years, are the greatest Instances of publick Spirit the Age has produced: But indeed when we consider how long this Sort of Beneficence has been on Foot, it is rather from the good Management of those Institutions, than from the Number or Value of the Benefactions to them, that they make so great a Figure. One would think it impossible, that in the Space of fourteen Years there should not have been five thousand Pounds bestowed in Gifts this Way, nor sixteen hundred Children, including Males and Females, put out into Methods of Industry. It is not allowed me to speak of Luxury and Folly with the severe Spirit they deserve; I shall only therefore say, I shall very readily compound with any Lady in a Hoop-Petticoat, if she gives the Price of one half Yard of the Silk towards cloathing, feeding, and instructing an innocent helpless Creature of her own Sex in one of these Schools. The Consciousness of such an Action will give her Features a nobler Life on this illustrious Day, than all the Jewels that can hang in her Hair, or can be clustred in her Bosom. It would be uncourtly to speak in harsher Words to the Fair, but to Men one may take a little more Freedom. It is monstrous how a Man can live with so little Reflection, as to fancy he is not in a Condition very · unjust, and disproportioned to the rest of Mankind, while he enjoys Wealth, and exerts no Benevolence or Bounty to others. As for this particular Occasion of these Schools, there cannot any offer more worthy a generous Mind. Would you do an handsome Thing without Return? do it for an Infant that is not sensible of the Obligation: Would you do it for publick Good? do it for one who would be an honest Artificer: Would you do it for the Sake of Heaven? give it to one who shall be instructed in the Worship of him for whose Sake you gave it. It is methinks a most laudable Institution, this, if it were of no other Expectation than that of producing a Race of good and useful Servants, who will have more than a liberal, a religious Education. What would not a Man do, in common Prudence, to lay out in Purchase of one about him, who would add to all his Orders he gave the Weight of the Commandments to inforce an Obedience to them? for one who would consider his Master as his Father, his Friend, and Benefactor upon the easy Terms, and in Expectation of no other Return but moderate Wages and gentle Usage? It is the common Vice of Children to run too much among the Servants; from such as are educated in these Places they would see Nothing but Lowliness in the Servant, which would not be disingenuous in the Child. All the ill Offices and defamatory Whispers, which take their Birth from Domesticks, would be prevented if this Charity could be made universal; and a good Man might have a Knowledge of the whole Life of the Persons he designs to take into his House for his own Service, or that of his Family or Children, long before they were admitted. This would create endearing Dependencies; and the Obligation would have a paternal Air in the Master, who would be relieved from much Care and Anxiety from the Gratitude and Diligence of an humble Friend attending him as his Servant. I fall into this Discourse from a Letter sent to me, to give me Notice that Fifty Boys would be clothed and take their Seats (at the Charge of some generous Benefactors) in St. *Bride's* Church on *Sunday* next. I wish I could promise to my self any Thing which my Correspondent seems to expect from a Publication of it in this Paper; for there can be Nothing added to what so many excellent and learned Men have said on this Occasion: But that there may be something here which would move a generous Mind, like that of him who writ to me, I shall transcribe an handsome Paragraph of Dr. *Snape's* Sermon on these Charities, which my Correspondent enclosed with this Letter.

The wise Providence has amply compensated the Disadvantages of the Poor and Indigent, in wanting many of the Conveniencies of this Life, by a more abundant Provision for their Happiness in the next. Had they been higher born, or more richly endowed, they would have wanted this Manner of Education, of which those only enjoy the Benefit, who are low enough to submit to it; where they have such Advantages without Money, and without Price, as the Rich cannot purchase with it. The Learning which is giv'n, is generally more edifying to them, than that which is sold to others: Thus do they become more exalted in Goodness, by being depressed in Fortune, and their Poverty is, in reality, their Preferment.

. . . volet hæc sub luce videri,
Judicis argutum quæ non formidat acumen. [1]—Hor.

I have seen in the Works of a modern Philosopher, a Map of the Spots in the Sun. My last Paper of the Faults and Blemishes in *Milton's Paradise Lost,* may be considered as a Piece of the same Nature. To pursue the Allusion: As it is observed, that among the bright Parts of the luminous Body above-mentioned, there are some which glow more intensely, and dart a stronger Light than others; so, notwithstanding I have already shewn *Milton's* Poem to be very beautiful in general, I shall now proceed to take notice of such Beauties as appear to me more exquisite than the rest. *Milton* has proposed the Subject of his Poem in the following Verses.

> *Of Mans first disobedience, and the fruit*
> *Of that forbidden tree, whose mortal taste*
> *Brought Death into the World and all our woe,*
> *With loss of* Eden, *'till one greater Man*
> *Restore us, and regain the blissful Seat,*
> *Sing Heav'nly Muse . . . . .*

These Lines are perhaps as plain, simple and unadorned as any of the whole Poem, in which Particular the Author has

---

[1] "[A poem is like a picture: one strikes your fancy more the nearer you stand; another the farther away. This courts the shade], that will wish to be seen in the light, and dreads not the critical insight of the judge."

conform'd himself to the Example of *Homer,* and the Precept of *Horace.*

His Invocation to a Work which turns in a great Measure upon the Creation of the World, is very properly made to the Muse who inspired *Moses* in those Books from whence our Author drew his Subject, and to the Holy Spirit who is therein represented as operating after a particular Manner in the first Production of Nature. This whole Exordium rises very happily into noble Language and Sentiment, as I think the Transition to the Fable is exquisitely beautiful and natural.

The Nine-days Astonishment,[2] in which the Angels lay entranced after their dreadful Overthrow and Fall from Heaven, before they could recover either the Use of Thought or Speech, is a noble *Circumstance,* and very finely imagined. The Division of Hell[3] into Seas of Fire, and into firm Ground impregnated with the same furious Element, with that particular Circumstance of the Exclusion of *Hope* from those Infernal Regions, are Instances of the same great and fruitful Invention.

The Thoughts in the first Speech and Description of *Satan,*[4] who is one of the principal Actors, in this Poem, are wonderfully proper to give us a full Idea of him. His Pride, Envy and Revenge, Obstinacy, Despair and Impenitence, are all of them very artfully interwoven. In short, his first Speech is a Complication of all those Passions which discover themselves separately in several other of his Speeches in the Poem. The whole Part of this great Enemy of Mankind is filled with such Incidents as are very apt to raise and terrify the Reader's Imagination. Of this Nature, in the Book now before us, is his being the first that awakens out of the general Trance, with his Posture on the burning Lake, his rising from it, and the Description of his Shield and Spear.

[2] *Paradise Lost,* I, 50-53.
[3] I, 59-69.
[4] I, 84-124.

Thus Satan *talking to his nearest mate,*
With head up-lift above the wave, and eyes
That sparkling blazed, his other parts beside
Prone on the Flood, extended long and large,
Lay floating many a rood . . . . .
Forthwith upright he rears from off the pool
His mighty Stature; on each hand the flames
Driv'n backward slope their pointing Spires, and
In Billows, leave i' th' midst a horrid vale. (rowl'd
Then with expanded wings he steers his flight
Aloft, incumbent on the dusky Air
That felt unusual weight . . . . .
. . . . . His pondrous Shield
Ethereal temper, massie, large and round
Behind him cast; the broad circumference
Hung on his Shoulders like the Moon, whose orb
Thro' Optick Glass the Tuscan *Artists view*
At Ev'ning from the top of Fesole,
Or in Valdarno *to descry new Lands,*
Rivers or Mountains on her spotty Globe.
His Spear to equal which the tallest pine
Hewn on Norwegian *Hills to be the Mast*
Of some great Ammiral, were but a wand
He walk'd with to support uneasy Steps
Over the burning Marl . . . . .

To which we may add his Call to the fallen Angels that
lay plunged and stupified in the Sea of Fire.

He call'd so loud, that all the hollow deep
Of Hell resounded . . . . .

But there is no single Passage in the whole Poem worked
up to a greater Sublimity, than that wherein his Person is described in those celebrated Lines:

> . . . . . *He, above the rest*
> *In shape and gesture proudly eminent*
> *Stood like a Tower,* &c.

His Sentiments are every way answerable to his Character, and suitable to a created Being of the most exalted and
most depraved Nature. Such is that in which he takes Possession of his Place of Torments.

> . . . . . *Hail Horrors, hail*
> *Infernal World, and thou profoundest Hell*
> *Receive thy new Possessor, one who brings*
> *A mind not to be changed by place or time.*

And afterwards,

> . . . . . *Here at least*
> *We shall be free; th' Almighty hath not built*
> *Here for his envy, wil not drive us hence:*
> *Here we may reign secure, and in my choice*
> *To reign is worth aambiition, tho' in Hell:*
> *Better to reign in Hell, than serve in Heaven.*

Amidst those Impieties which this Enraged Spirit utters
in other Places of the Poem, the Author has taken care to introduce none that is not big with Absurdity, and incapable
of shocking a Religious Reader; his Words, as the Poet himself describes them, bearing only a *Semblance of Worth, not
Substance*. He is likewise with great Art described as owning
his Adversary to be Almighty. Whatever perverse Interpretation he puts on the Justice, Mercy, and other Attributes of
the Supreme Being, he frequently confesses his Omnipotence,
that being the Perfection he was forced to allow him, and the

only Consideration which could support his Pride under the Shame of his Defeat.

Nor must I here omit that beautiful Circumstance of his bursting out in Tears, upon his Survey of those innumerable Spirits whom he had involved in the same Guilt and Ruin with himself.

> . . . . . *He now prepared*
> *To speak; whereat their doubled ranks they bend*
> *From wing to wing, and half enclose him round*
> *With all his Peers: Attention held them mute.*
> *Thrice he assay'd, and thrice in spite of Scorn*
> *Tears such as Angels weep, burst forth* . . . . .

The catalogue of Evil Spirits has Abundance of Learning in it, and a very agreeable Turn of Poetry, which rises in a great measure from his describing the Places where they were worshipped, by those beautiful Marks of Rivers, so frequent among the Antient Poets. The Author had doubtless in this Place[5] *Homer's* Catalogue of Ships, and *Virgil's* List of Warriors in his view. The Character of *Moloch* and *Belial* prepare the Reader's Mind for their respective Speeches and Behaviour in the second and sixth Book. The Account of *Thammuz* is finely Romantick, and suitable to what we read among the Antients of the Worship which was paid to that Idol.

The Passage in the Catalogue, explaining the manner how Spirits transform themselves by Contraction, or Enlargement of their Dimensions, is introduced with great Judgment, to make way for several supprising Accidents in the Sequel of the Poem. There follows one, at the very End of the First Book, which is what the *French* Criticks call *Marvellous,* but at the same Time *probable* by reason of the Passage last mentioned.

[5] I, 376-521. Addison cites for comparison Homer's catalogue of ships (*Iliad*, II, 494ff.) and Virgil's catalogue of warriors (*Aeneid*, VII, 647ff.).

As soon as the Infernal Palace is finished, we are told the Multitude and Rabble of Spirits immediately shrunk themselves into a small Compass, that there might be Room for such a numberless Assembly in this capacious Hall. But it is the Poet's Refinement upon this Thought, which I most admire, and which is indeed very noble in its self. For he tells us, that notwithstanding the vulgar, among the fallen Spirits, contracted their Forms, those of the first Rank and Dignity still preserved their natural Dimensions.[6]

> Thus incorporal Spirits to smallest Forms
> Reduc'd their Shapes immense, and were at large
> Though without Number still amidst the Hall
> Of that infernal Court. But far within,
> And in their own Dimensions like themselves,
> The Great Seraphick Lords and Cherubim,
> In close recess and Secret conclave sate,
> A thousand Demy Gods on Golden Seats,
> Frequent and full . . . . .

The Character of *Mammon,* and the Description of the *Pandemonium,* are full of Beauties.

There are several other Strokes in the First Book[7] wonderfully poetical, and Instances of that Sublime Genius so peculiar to the Author. Such is the Description of *Azazel's* Stature, and of the Infernal Standard, which he unfurls; as also of that ghastly Light, by which the Fiends appear to one another in their Place of Torments.

> The Seat of Desolation, void of Light,
> Save what the glimm'ring of those livid Flames
> Casts pale and dreadful . . . . .

The Shout of the whole Host of fallen Angels when drawn up in Battel Array:

[6] I, 423-31.
[7] I, 533-39.

. . . . . *The Universal Host up sent*
A Shout that tore Hell's Concave, and beyond
Frighted the Reign of Chaos *and old Night.*

The Review, which the Leader makes of his Infernal Army:

. . . . . *He thro' the armed files*
Darts his experienc'd eye, and soon traverse
The whole Battalion views, their order due,
Their Vizages and Stature as of Gods,
Their number last he sums. And now his Heart
Distends with Pride, and hard'ning in his strength
Glories . . . . .

The Flash of Light, which appeared upon the drawing of their Swords;

He spake: and to confirm his Words out flew
Millions of flaming Swords, drawn from the Thighs
Of mighty Cherubim; *the sudden Blaze*
Far round illumin'd Hell . . . . .

The sudden Production of the *Pandæmanium;*

Anon out of the Earth a Fabrick huge
Rose like an Exhalation, with the Sound
Of dulcet Symphonies and Voices sweet.

The artificial Illuminations made in it

. . . . . *From the arched Roof*
Pendent by subtle Magick, many a Row
Of Starry Lamps and blazing Crescets, fed
With Naphtha *and* Asphaltus, *yielded Light*
As from a Sky . . . . .

There are also several noble Similes and Allusions in the

first Book of *Paradise Lost*. And here I must observe, that when *Milton* alludes either to Things or Persons, he never quits his Simile till it rises to some very great Idea, which is often foreign to the Occasion that gave Birth to it. The Resemblance does not, perhaps, last above a Line or two, but the Poet runs on with the Hint, till he has raised out of it some glorious Image or Sentiment, proper to inflame the Mind of the Reader, and to give it that sublime Kind of Entertainment, which is suitable to the Nature of an Heroick Poem. Those, who are acquainted with *Homer's* and *Virgil's* Way of Writing, cannot but be pleased with this Kind of Structure in *Milton's* Similitudes. I am the more particular on this Head, because ignorant Readers, who have formed their Taste upon the quaint Similes, and little Turns of Wit, which are so much in Vogue among modern Poets, cannot relish these Beauties which are of a much higher Nature, and are therefore apt to censure *Milton's* Comparisons, in which they do not see any surprising Points of Likeness. Monsieur *Perrault* was a Man of this vitiated Relish, and for that very Reason has endeavoured to turn into Ridicule several of *Homer's* Similitudes, which he calls *Comparaisons a longue queue, Long-tail'd Comparisons*. I shall conclude this Paper on the First Book of *Milton* with the Answer which Monsieur *Boileau* makes to *Perrault* on this Occasion; Comparisons, says he, in Odes and Epic Poems are not introduced only to illustrate and embellish the Discourse, but to amuse and relax the Mind of the Reader, by frequently disengaging him from too painful an Attention to the principal Subject, and by leading him into other agreeable Images. *Homer,* says he, excelled in this Particular, whose Comparisons abound with such Images of Nature as are proper to relieve and diversifie his Subjects. He continually instructs the Reader, and makes him take notice, even in Objects which are every Day before our Eyes, of such Circumstances as we should not otherwise have observed. *To this he adds, as a Maxim universally acknowledged,* that it is not necessary in Poetry for the Points of the Comparison to correspond with one another exactly, but that a general Resemblance is sufficient, and that too much Nicety in this Particular savours of the Rhetorician and Epigrammatist.

In short, if we look into the Conduct of *Homer, Virgil* and *Milton,* as the great Fable is the Soul of each Poem, so to give their Works an agreeable Variety, their Episodes are so many short Fables, and their Similes so many short Episodes; to which you may add, if you please, that their Metaphors are so many short Similes. If the Reader considers the Comparisons in the first Book of *Milton,*[8] of the Sun in an Eclipse, of the sleeping *Leviathan,* of the Bees swarming about their Hive, of the fairy Dance, in the View wherein I have here placed them, he will easily discover the great Beauties that are in each of those Passages.

[8] I, 594-99, 200-210, 768-75, 780-88.

No. 324   Wednesday, March 12, 1711-12.   [Steele]

O curvæ in terris animæ, & cœlestium inanes. [1]—Pers.

Mr. SPECTATOR,

The Materials you have collected together towards a general History of Clubs, make so bright a Part of your Speculations, that I think it is but a Justice we all owe the learned World to furnish you with such Assistances as may promote that useful Work. For this Reason I could not forbear communicating to you some imperfect Informations of a Set of Men (if you will allow them a Place in that Species of Being) who have lately erected themselves into a Nocturnal Fraternity, under the Title of *The Mohock Club,* a Name borrowed it seems from a Sort of *Cannibals* in *India,* who subsist by Plundering and Devouring all the Nations about them. The President is stiled *Emperor of the Mohocks;* and his Arms are a *Turkish Crescent,* which his Imperial Majesty bears at present in a very extraordinary Manner engraven upon his Forehead. Agreeable to their Name, the avowed Design of their Institution is Mischief; and upon this Foundation all their Rules and Orders are framed. An outragious Ambition of doing all possible Hurt to their Fellow-Creatures, is the great Cement of their Assembly, and the only Qualification required in the Members. In order to exert this Principle in its full Strength and Perfection, they take Care to drink themselves to a Pitch, that is, beyond the Possibility of attending to any Motions of Reason or Humanity; then make a general Sally, and attack all that are so unfortunate as to walk the Streets through which they patroll.

---

[1] "O souls bowed down to earth and void of all celestial thoughts."

Some are knock'd down, others stabb'd, others cut and carbonado'd. To put the Watch to a total Rout, and mortify some of those inoffensive Militia, is reckon'd a *Coup d'eclat.* The particular Talents by which these *Misanthropes* are distinguished from one another, consist in the various Kinds of Barbarities which they execute upon their Prisoners. Some are celebrated for a happy Dexterity in Tipping the Lion upon them; which is perform'd by squeezing the Nose flat to the Face, and boring out the Eyes with their Fingers: Others are called the Dancing-Masters, and teach their Scholars to cut Capers by running Swords thro' their Legs; a new Invention, whether originally *French* I cannot tell: A third Sort are the Tumblers, whose Office it is to set Women upon their Heads, and commit certain Indecencies, or rather Barbarities, on the Limbs which they expose. But these I forbear to mention, because they can't but be very shocking to the Reader, as well as the SPECTATOR. In this Manner they carry on a War against Mankind; and by the standing Maxims of their Policy, are to enter into no Alliances but one, and that is Offensive and Defensive with all Bawdy-Houses in general, of which they have declared themselves Protectors and Guarantees.

I must own, Sir, these are only broken incoherent Memoirs of this wonderful Society, but they are the best I have been yet able to procure; for being but of late Establishment, it is not ripe for a just History: And to be serious, the chief Design of this Trouble is to hinder it from ever being so. You have been pleas'd, out of a Concern for the Good of your Countrymen, to act under the Character of SPECTATOR not only the Part of a Looker-on, but an Overseer of their Actions; and whenever such Enormities as this infest the Town, we immediately fly to you for Redress. I have Reason to believe, that some thoughtless Youngsters, out of a false Notion of Bravery, and an immoderate Fondness to be distinguished for Fellows of Fire, are insensibly hurry'd into this senseless scandalous Project: Such will probably stand corrected by your Reproofs, especially if you inform them, that it is not Courage for half a Score Fellows, mad with Wine and Lust, to set upon two or three soberer than themselves; and that the Manners of *Indian* Savages are no becoming Accomplishments to an *English* fine Gentleman. Such of them as have been Bullies and Scowrers of a long Standing, and are grown Veterans in this Kind of Service, are I fear too hardned to receive any Impressions from your Admonitions. But I beg you would recommend to their Perusal your ninth Speculation: They may there be taught to take Warning from the Club of Duellists; and be put in Mind, that the common Fate of those Men of Honour was to be hang'd.

I am,

March the 10th,   *SIR,*

1711 - 12.   *Your most humble Servant,*

Philanthropos.

The following Letter is of a quite contrary Nature; but I add it here that the Reader may observe at the same View, how amiable Ignorance may be when it is shewn in its Simplicities, and how detestable in Barbarities. It is written by an honest Countryman to his Mistress, and came to the Hands of a Lady of good Sense wrapped about a Thread-Paper, who has long kept it by her as an Image of artless Love.

To her I very much Respect, Mrs. Margaret Clark.

Lovely, and oh that I could write loving Mrs. *Margaret Clark,* I pray you let Affection excuse Presumption. Having been so happy as to enjoy the Sight of your sweet Countenance and comely Body, sometimes when I had Occasion to buy Treacle or Liquorish Powder at the Apothecary's Shop, I am so enamour'd with you, that I can no more keep close my flaming Desire to become your Servant. And I am the more bold now to write to your sweet self, because I am now my own Man, and may match where I please; for my Father is taken away, and now I am come to my Living, which is Ten

Yard Land, and a House; and there is never a Yard of Land in our Field but it is as well worth ten Pound a Year as a Thief is worth a Halter; and all my Brothers and Sisters are provided for: Besides I have good Houshold-stuff, though I say it, both Brass and Pewter, Linnens and Woollens; and though my House be thatched, yet, if you and I match, it shall go hard but I will have one Half of it slated. If you think well of this Motion, I will wait upon you as soon as my new Cloaths is made and Hay-Harvest is in. I could, though I say it, have good—, The rest is torn off; and Posterity must be contented to know that Mrs. *Margaret Clark* was very pretty, but are left in the Dark as to the Name of her Lover.

No. 335   Tuesday, March 25, 1712.   [Addison]

Respicere exemplar vitæ morumque jubebo
Doctum imitatorem, & vivas hinc ducere voces.[1] — Hor.

My Friend Sir ROGER DE COVERLY, when we last met together
at the Club, told me, that he had a great Mind to see the new
Tragedy[2] with me, assuring me at the same Time, that he had
not been at a Play these twenty Years. The last I saw, says Sir
ROGER, was the *Committee*,[3] which I should not have gone
to neither, had not I been told before-hand that it was a good
Church of *England* Comedy. He then proceeded to enquire
of me who this Distress'd Mother was, and upon hearing that
she was *Hector*'s Widow, he told me, that her Husband was
a brave Man, and that when he was a School-boy he had read
his Life at the end of the Dictionary. My Friend asked me, in
the next Place, if there would not be some Danger in coming
home late, in case the *Mohocks*[4] should be abroad. I assure
you, says he, I thought I had fallen into their Hands last Night,
for I observ'd two or three lusty black Men that followed me
half way up *Fleet street,* and mended their Pace behind me,
in Proportion as I put on to get away from them. You must
know, continued the Knight with a Smile, I fancied they had
a mind to *hunt* me; for I remember an honest Gentleman in my

---

[1] "I would advise one who has learned the imitative art to look to manners for
a model."
[2] *The Distressed Mother.* See *The Spectator,* No. 290, n.2.
[3] A comedy by Sir Robert Howard (1626 - 1698), who appeared as Crites in Dryden's *Essay of Dramatic Poesy.*
[4] A band of young rakes and bullies who for several weeks had been terroriz-
ing the Town.

Neighbourhood, who was serv'd such a Trick in King *Charles* the Second's Time; for which Reason he has not ventured himself in Town ever since. I might have shown them very good Sport, had this been their Design, for as I am an old Fox-hunter, I should have turned and dodged, and have play'd them a thousand Tricks they had never seen in their Lives before. Sir ROGER added, that if these Gentlemen had any such Intention, they did not succeed very well in it, for I threw them out, says he, at the End of *Norfolk-street,* where I doubled the Corner, and got Shelter in my Lodgings before they could imagine what was become of me. However, says the Knight, if Captain SENTRY will make one with us to Morrow Night, and if you will both of you call upon me about Four a-Clock, that we may be at the House before it is full, I will have my own Coach in Readiness to attend you, for *John* tells me he has got the Fore-Wheels mended.

The Captain, who did not fail to meet me there at the appointed Hour, bid Sir ROGER fear nothing, for that he had put on the same Sword which he made use of at the Battel of *Steen-kirk.* Sir ROGER'S Servants, and among the rest my old Friend the Butler, had, I found, provided themselves with good Oaken Plants, to attend their Master upon this Occasion. When we had plac'd him in his Coach, with my self at his Left Hand, the Captain before him, and his Butler at the Head of his Foot-men in the Rear, we convoy'd him in Safety to the Play-house; where, after having march'd up the Entry in good Order, the Captain and I went in with him, and seated him betwixt us in the Pit. As soon as the House was full, and the Candles lighted, my old Friend stood up and looked about him with that Pleasure, which a Mind seasoned with Humanity naturally feels in it self, at the Sight of a Multitude of People who seem pleased with one another, and partake of the same common Entertainment. I could not but fancy to my self, as the old Man stood up in the Middle of the Pit, that he made a very proper Center to a Tragick Audience. Upon the Entring of *Pyrrhus,* the Knight told me, that he did not believe the King of *France* himself had a better Strut. I was indeed very attentive to my old Friend's Remarks, because I looked upon them as a Piece of Natural Criticism, and was well pleased to hear him at the Conclusion of almost every Scene, telling me that he could not imagine how the Play would end. One while he appear'd much concerned for *Andromache;* and a little while after as much for *Hermione;* and was extremely puzzled to think what would become of *Pyrrhus.*

When Sir ROGER saw *Andromache's* obstinate Refusal to her Lover's Importunities, he whispered me in the Ear, that he was sure she would never have him; to which he added, with a more than ordinary Vehemence, You can't imagine, Sir, what 'tis to have to do with a Widow. Upon *Pyrrhus* his threatning afterwards to leave her, the Knight shook his Head, and muttered to himself, Ay, do if you can. This Part dwelt so much upon my Friend's Imagination, that at the Close of the Third Act, as I was thinking of something else, he whispered in my Ear, These Widows, Sir, are the most perverse Creatures in the World.[5] But pray, says he, you that are a Critick, is this Play according to your Dramatick Rules, as you call them? Should your People in Tragedy always talk to be understood? Why, there is not a single Sentence in this Play that I do not know the Meaning of.

The Fourth Act very luckily begun before I had Time to give the old Gentleman an Answer; Well, says the Knight, sitting down with great Satisfaction, I suppose we are now to see *Hector's* Ghost. He then renewed his Attention, and, from Time to Time, fell a praising the Widow. He made, indeed, a little Mistake as to one of her Pages, whom, at his first Entring, he took for *Astyanax;* but he quickly set himself right in that Particular, though, at the same time, he owned he should have been very glad to have seen the little Boy, who, says he, must needs be a very fine Child by the Account that is given of him. Upon *Hermione's* going off with a Menace to *Pyrrhus,*

[5] See *The Spectator,* No. 113.

the Audience gave a loud Clap, to which Sir ROGER added, On my Word, a notable young Baggage.

As there was a very remarkable Silence and Stillness in the Audience during the whole Action, it was natural for them to take the Opportunity of these Intervals between the Acts, to express their Opinion of the Players, and of their respective Parts. Sir ROGER hearing a Cluster of them praise *Orestes,* struck in with them, and told them, that he thought his Friend *Pylades* was a very sensible Man; As they were afterwards applauding *Pyrrhus,* Sir ROGER put in a second time. And let me tell you, says he, though he speaks but little, I like the old Fellow in Whiskers as well as any of them. Captain SENTRY, seeing two or three Waggs who sat near us, lean with an attentive Ear towards Sir ROGER, and fearing lest they should smoak the Knight, pluck'd him by the Elbow, and whispered something in his Ear, that lasted till the Opening of the Fifth Act. The Knight was wonderfully attentive to the Account which *Orestes* gives of *Pyrrhus* his Death, and at the Conclusion of it, told me it was such a bloody Piece of Work, that he was glad it was not done upon the Stage. Seeing afterwards *Orestes* in his raving Fit, he grew more than ordinary serious, and took Occasion to moralize (in his Way) upon an evil Conscience, adding, that *Orestes, in his Madness, looked as if he saw something.*

As we were the first that came into the House, so we were the last that went out of it; being resolved to have a clear Passage for our old Friend, whom we did not care to venture among the Justling of the Crowd. Sir ROGER went out fully satisfy'd with his Entertainment, and we guarded him to his Lodgings in the same manner that we brought him to the Play-house; being highly pleased, for my own Part, not only with the Performance of the excellent Piece which had been presented, but with the Satisfaction which it had given to the good old Man.

No. 370   Monday, May 5, 1712.   [Steele]

Totus mundus agit Histrionem. [1]

Many of my fair Readers, as well as very gay and well-received
Persons of the other Sex, are extreamly perplexed at the *Latin*
Sentences at the Head of my Speculations; I do not know
whether I ought not to indulge them with Translations of each
of them: However, I have to Day taken down from the Top
of the Stage in *Drury-Lane* a Bit of *Latin* which often stands
in their View, and signifies that *the whole World acts the Player.*
It is certain that if we look all round us and behold the different Employments of Mankind, you hardly see one who is not,
as the Player is, in an assumed Character. The Lawyer, who
is vehement and loud in a Cause wherein he knows he has not
the Truth of the Question on his Side, is a Player as to the personated Part, but incomparably meaner than he as to the Pros-
titution of himself for Hire; because the Pleader's Falshood
introduces Injustice, the Player feigns for no other End but
to divert or instruct you. The Divine, whose Passions transport him to say any thing with any View but promoting the
Interests of true Piety and Religion, is a Player with a still greater Imputation of Guilt in Proportion to his depreciating a Character more sacred. Consider all the different Pursuits and Employments of Men, and you will find half their Actions tend
to nothing else but Disguise and Imposture; and all that is done
which proceeds not from a Man's very self is the Action of
a Player. For this Reason it is that I make so frequent Mention of the Stage: It is, with me, a Matter of the highest Con-

[1] "All the world plays the role of actor."

sideration what Parts are well or ill performed, what Passions or Sentiments are indulged or cultivated, and consequently what Manners and Customs are transfused from the Stage to the World, which reciprocally imitate each other. As the Writers of Epick Poems introduce shadowy Persons and represent Vices and Virtues under the Characters of Men and Women; so I, who am a SPECTATOR in the World, may perhaps sometimes make use of the Names of the Actors on the Stage, to represent or admonish those who transact Affairs in the World. When I am commending *Wilks*[2] for representing the Tenderness of a Husband and a Father in *Mackbeth,* the Contrition of a reformed Prodigal in *Harry* the Fourth, the winning Emptiness of a young Man of Good-nature and Wealth[3] in *the Trip to the Jubilee,* the Officiousness of an artful Servant[4] in *the Fox:* When thus I celebrate *Wilks,* I talk to all the World who are engaged in any of those Circumstances. If I were to speak of Merit neglected, misapplied, or misunderstood, might not I say *Eastcourt* has a great Capacity? but it is not the Interest of others who bear a Figure on the Stage that his Talents were understood; it is their Business to impose upon him what cannot become him, or keep out of his Hands any thing in which he would shine. Were one to raise a Suspicion of himself in a Man who passes upon the World for a fine Thing, in order to alarm him, one might say, if Lord *Foppington*[5] were not on the Stage, (*Cibber* acts the false Pretentions to a genteel Behaviour so very justly), he would have in the generality of Mankind more that would admire than deride him. When we come to characters directly comical, it is not to be imagined what Effect a well regulated Stage would have upon Men's Manners. The Craft of an Usurer, the Absurdity of a rich Fool,

[2] Robert Wilks (1665-1732), an able actor in tragedy as well as in comedy, though he excelled in the latter.
[3] Sir Harry Wildair in Farquhar's *The Constant Couple; or, a Trip to the Jubilee* (1699).
[4] Mosca in Jonson's *Volpone.*
[5] A character in *The Careless Husband* (1704) by Colley Cibber (1671-1757). The role was often played by Cibber himself.

the awkard Roughness of a Fellow of half Courage, the ungraceful Mirth of a Creature of half Wit, might be for ever put out of Countenance by proper parts for *Dogget*.[6] *Johnson*[7] by acting *Corbacchio* the other Night, must have given all who saw him a through Detestation of aged Avarice. The petulancy of a peevish old Fellow, who loves and hates he knows not why, is very excellently performed by the Ingenious Mr. *William Penkethman*[8] in the *Fop's Fortune;* where, in the Character of *Don Cholerick Snap Shorto de Testy,* he answers no Questions but to those whom he likes, and wants no Account of any thing from those he approves. Mr. *Penkethman* is also Master of as many Faces in the Dumb-Scene, as can be expected from a Man in the Circumstances of being ready to perish out of Fear and Hunger: He wonders throughout the whole Scene very masterly, without neglecting his Victuals. If it be, as I have heard it sometimes mentioned, a great Qualification for the World to follow Business and Pleasure too, what is it in the ingenious Mr. *Penkethman* to represent a Sense of Pleasure and Pain at the same time; as you may see him do this Evening?

As it is certain that a Stage ought to be wholly suppressed, or judiciously encouraged, while there is one in the Nation, Men turned for regular Pleasure cannot employ their Thoughts more usefully for the Diversion of Mankind, than by convincing them that it is in themselves to raise this Entertainment to the greatest Height. It would be a great Improvement, as well as Embellishment to the Theatre, if Dancing were more regarded, and taught to all the Actors. One who has the Advantage of such an agreeable girlish Person as Mrs. *Bicknell,*[9] joyned with her Capacity of Imitation, could in proper Gesture

<hr>

[6] See *The Spectator,* No. 235, n.2.
[7] Benjamin Johnson (d.1742), famous for his playing of Corbaccio in Jonson's *Volpone.*
[8] William Pinkethman (d.1725), who had a popular success in Colley Cibber's *Love Makes a Man; or, the Fop's Fortune* (1701).
[9] A skillful young actress who played hoydenish roles in comedies by Wycherley, Vanbrugh, and Congreve.

and Motion represent all the decent Characters of Female Life. An amiable Modesty in one Aspect of a Dancer, an assumed Confidence in another, a sudden Joy in another, a falling off with an Impatience of being beheld, a Return towards the Audience with an unsteady Resolution to approach them, and a well-acted Solicitude to please, would revive in the Company all the fine Touches of Mind raised in observing all the Objects of Affection or Passion they had before beheld. Such elegant Entertainments as these, would polish the Town into Judgment in their Gratifications; and Delicacy in Pleasure is the first Step People of Condition take in Reformation from Vice. Mrs. *Bicknell* has the only Capacity for this sort of Dancing of any on the Stage; and I dare say all who see her Performance to Morrow Night, when sure the Romp will do her best for her own Benefit, will be of my Mind.

No. 409   Thursday, June 19, 1712.   [Addison]

. . . Musæo contingens cuncta lepore.[1]—Lucr.

Gratian very often recommends *the fine Taste,* as the utmost Perfection of an accomplished Man. As this Word arises very often in Conversation, I shall endeavour to give some Account of it, and to lay down Rules how we may know whether we are possessed of it, and how we may acquire that fine Taste of Writing, which is so much talked of among the Polite World.

Most Languages make use of this Metaphor, to express that Faculty of the Mind, which distinguishes all the most concealed Faults and nicest Perfections in Writing. We may be sure this Metaphor would not have been so general in all Tongues, had there not been a very great Conformity between that Mental Taste, which is the Subject of this Paper, and that Sensitive Taste which gives us a Relish of every different Flavour that affects the Palate. Accordingly we find, there are as many Degrees of Refinement in the intellectual Faculty, as in the Sense, which is marked out by this common Denomination.

I knew a Person who possessed the one in so great a Perfection, that after having tasted ten different Kinds of Tea, he would distinguish, without seeing the Colour of it, the particular Sort which was offered him; and not only so, but any two Sorts of them that were mixt together in an equal Proportion; nay, he has carried the Experiment so far, as upon tasting the Composition of three different Sorts, to name the Parcels from whence the three several Ingredients were taken. A man of a fine Taste in Writing will discern after the same

[1] "Touching all with the Muse's grace."

392

manner, not only the general Beauties and Imperfections of an Author, but discover the several Ways of thinking and expressing himself, which diversify him from all other Authors, with the several Foreign Infusions of Thought and Language, and the particular Authors from whom they were borrowed.

After having thus far explained what is generally meant by a fine Taste in Writing, and shewn the Propriety of the Metaphor which is used on this Occasion, I think I may define it to be *that Faculty of the Soul, which discerns the Beauties of an Author with Pleasure, and the Imperfections with Dislike.* If a Man would know whether he is possessed of this Faculty, I would have him read over the celebrated Works of Antiquity, which have stood the Test of so many different Ages and Countries; or those Works among the Moderns, which have the Sanction of the Politer Part of our Contemporaries. If upon the Perusal of such Writings he does not find himself delighted in an extraordinary Manner, or if, upon reading the admired Passages in such Authors, he finds a Coldness and Indifference in his Thoughts, he ought to conclude, not (as is too usual among tasteless Readers) that the Author wants those Perfections which have been admired in him, but that he himself wants the Faculty of discovering them.

He should, in the second Place, be very careful to observe, whether he tastes the distinguishing Perfections, or, if I may be allowed to call them so, the Specifick Qualities of the Author whom he peruses; whethec he is particularly pleased with *Livy* for his Manner of telling a Story, with *Sallust* for his entring into those internal Principles of Action which arise from the Characters and Manners of the Persons he describes, or with *Tacitus* for his displaying those outward Motives of Safety and Interest, which give birth to the whole Series of Transactions which he relates.

He may likewise consider, how differently he is affected by the same Thought, which presents it self in a great Writer, from what he is when he finds it delivered by a Person of an ordinary Genius. For there is as much difference in apprehending a Thought cloathed in *Cicero*'s Language, and that of a common Author, as in seeing an Object by the Light of a Taper, or by the Light of the Sun.

It is very difficult to lay down Rules for the Acquirement of such a Taste as that I am here speaking of. The Faculty must in some degree be born with us, and it very often happens, that those who have other Qualities in Perfection are wholly void of this. One of the most eminent Mathematicians of the Age has assured me, that the greatest Pleasure he took in reading *Virgil,* was in examining *Æneas* his Voyage by the Map; as I question not but many a Modern Compiler of History would be delighted with little more in that Divine Author, than the bare Matters of Fact.

But notwithstanding this Faculty must in some measure be born with us, there are several Methods for Cultivating and Improving it, and without which it will be very uncertain, and of little use to the Person that possesses it. The most natural Method for this Purpose is to be conversant among the Writings of the most Polite Authors. A Man who has any Relish for fine Writing, either discovers new Beauties, or receives stronger Impressions from the Masterly Stroaks of a great Author every time he peruses him: Besides that he naturally wears himself into the same manner of Speaking and Thinking.

Conversation with Men of a Polite Genius is another Method for improving our Natural Taste. It is impossible for a Man of the greatest Parts to consider any thing in its whole Extent, and in all its variety of Lights. Every Man, besides those general Observations which are to be made upon an Author, forms several Reflections that are peculiar to his own manner of Thinking; so that Conversation will naturally furnish us with Hints which we did not attend to, and make us enjoy other Men's Parts and Reflections as well as our own. This is the best Reason I can give for the Observation which several have made, that Men of great Genius in the same way of Writing seldom rise up singly, but at certain Periods of Time appear together, and in a Body; as they did at *Rome* in the Reign of *Augustus,* and in *Greece* about the Age of *Socrates*. I cannot think that *Corneille, Racine, Moliere, Boileau, la Fontaine, Bruyere, Bossu,* or the *Daciers,* would have written so well as they have done, had they not been Friends and Contemporaries.

It is likewise necessary for a Man who would form to himself a finished Taste of good Writing, to be well versed in the Works of the best *Criticks* both Ancient and Modern. I must confess that I could wish there were Authors of this Kind, who, beside the Mechanical Rules which a Man of very little Taste may discourse upon, would enter into the very Spirit and Soul of fine Writing, and shew us the several Sources of that Pleasure which rises in the Mind upon the Perusal of a noble Work. Thus altho' in Poetry it be absolutely necessary that the Unities of Time, Place and Action, with other Points of the same Nature, should be thoroughly explained and understood; there is still something more essential to the Art, something that elevates and astonishes the Fancy, and gives a Greatness of Mind to the Reader, which few of the Criticks besides *Longinus* have considered.

Our general Taste in *England* is for Epigram, turns of Wit, and forced Conceits, which have no manner of Influence, either for the bettering or enlarging the Mind of him who reads them, and have been carefully avoided by the greatest Writers, both among the Ancients and Moderns. I have endeavoured in several of my Speculations to banish this *Gothic* Taste,[2] which has taken Possession among us. I entertained the Town for a Week together with an Essay upon Wit, in which I endeavoured to detect several of those false Kinds which have been admired in the different Ages of the World; and at the same time to shew wherein the Nature of true Wit consists. I afterwards gave an Instance of the great Force which lyes in a natural Simplicity of Thought to affect the Mind of the Reader, from such vulgar Pieces as have little else besides this single Qualification to recommend them. I have likewise examined the

[2] See *The Spectator,* Nos. 61, 62.

Works of the greatest Poet which our Nation or perhaps any other has produced, and particularized most of those rational and manly Beauties which give a Value to that Divine Work. I shall next *Saturday* enter upon an Essay *on the Pleasures of the Imagination*,[3] which, though it shall consider that Subject at large, will perhaps suggest to the Reader what it is that gives a Beauty to many Passages of the finest Writers both in Prose and Verse. As an Undertaking of this Nature is entirely new, I question not but it will be received with Candour.

[3] *The Spectator*, Nos. 411-421.

No. 411   Saturday, June 21, 1712.   [Addison]

Avia Pieridum peragro loca, nullius ante
Trita solo; juvat integros accedere fonteis;
Atque haurire: . . .[1]—Lucr.

Our Sight is the most perfect and most delightful of all our Senses. It fills the Mind with the largest Variety of Ideas, converses with its Objects at the greatest Distance, and continues the longest in Action without being tired or satiated with its proper Enjoyments. The Sense of Feeling can indeed give us a Notion of Extension, Shape, and all other Ideas that enter at the Eye, except Colours; but at the same time it is very much streightned and confined in its Operations, to the Number, Bulk, and Distance of its particular Objects. Our Sight seems designed to supply all these Defects, and may be considered as a more delicate and diffusive Kind of Touch, that spreads its self over an infinite Multitude of Bodies, comprehends the largest Figures, and brings into our reach some of the most remote Parts of the Universe.

It is this Sense which furnishes the Imagination with its Ideas; so that by the Pleasures of the Imagination or Fancy (which I shall use promiscuously) I here mean such as arise from visible Objects, either when we have them actually in our View, or when we call up their Ideas into our Minds by Paintings, Statues, Descriptions, or any the like Occasion. We cannot indeed have a single Image in the Fancy that did not make its first Entrance through the Sight; but we have the Pow-

[1] "I traverse pathless tracts of the Muses never yet trodden by any foot; I love to approach virgin springs and there to drink."

er of retaining, altering and compounding those Images, which we have once received, into all the Varieties of Picture and Vision that are most agreeable to the Imagination; for by this Faculty a Man in a Dungeon is capable of entertaining himself with Scenes and Landskips more beautiful than any that can be found in the whole Compass of Nature.

There are few Words in the *English* Language which are employed in a more loose and uncircumscribed Sense than those of the *Fancy* and the *Imagination*. I therefore thought it necessary to fix and determine the Notion of these two Words, as I intend to make use of them in the Thread of my following Speculations, that the Reader may conceive rightly what is the Subject which I proceed upon. I must therefore desire him to remember, that by the Pleasures of the Imagination, I mean only such Pleasures as arise originally from Sight, and that I divide these Pleasures into two Kinds: My Design being first of all to discourse of those Primary Pleasures of the Imagination, which entirely proceed from such Objects as are before our Eyes; and in the next place to speak of those Secondary Pleasures of the Imagination which flow from the Ideas of visible Objects, when the Objects are not actually before the Eye, but are called up into our Memories, or formed into agreeable Visions of Things that are either Absent or Fictitious.

The Pleasures of the Imagination, taken in their full Extent, are not so gross as those of Sense, nor so refined as those of the Understanding. The last are, indeed, more preferable, because they are founded on some new Knowledge or Improvement in the Mind of Man; yet it must be confest, that those of the Imagination are as great and as transporting as the other. A beautiful Prospect delights the Soul, as much as a Demonstration; and a Description in *Homer* has charm'd more Readers than a Chapter in *Aristotle*. Besides, the Pleasures of the Imagination have this Advantage, above those of the Understanding, that they are more obvious, and more easie to be acquired. It is but opening the Eye, and the Scene enters. The

Colours paint themselves on the Fancy, with very little Attention of Thought or Application of Mind in the Beholder. We are struck, we know not how, with the Symmetry of any thing we see, and immediately assent to the Beauty of an Object, without enquiring into the particular Causes and Occasions of it.

A Man of a Polite Imagination is let into a great many Pleasures, that the Vulgar are not capable of receiving. He can converse with a Picture, and find an agreeable Companion in a Statue. He meets with a secret Refreshment in a Description, and often feels a greater Satisfaction in the Prospect of Fields and Meadows, than another does in the Possession. It gives him, indeed, a kind of Property in every thing he sees, and makes the most rude uncultivated Parts of Nature administer to his Pleasures: So that he looks upon the World, as it were, in another Light, and discovers in it a Multitude of Charms, that conceal themselves from the generality of Mankind.

There are, indeed, but very few who know how to be idle and innocent, or have a Relish of any Pleasures that are not Criminal; every Diversion they take is at the Expence of some one Virtue or another, and their very first Step out of Business is into Vice or Folly. A Man should endeavour, therefore, to make the Sphere of his innocent Pleasures as wide as possible, that he may retire into them with Safety, and find in them such a Satisfaction as a wise Man would not blush to take. Of this Nature are those of the Imagination, which do not require such a Bent of Thought as is necessary to our more serious Employments, nor at the same Time, suffer the Mind to sink into that Negligence and Remissness, which are apt to accompany our more sensual Delights, but, like a gentle Exercise to the Faculties, awaken them from Sloth and Idleness, without putting them upon any Labour or Difficulty.

We might here add, that the Pleasures of the Fancy are more conducive to Health, than those of the Understanding, which are worked out by Dint of Thinking, and attended with too violent a Labour of the Brain. Delightful Scenes, whether in Nature, Painting, or Poetry, have a kindly Influence on the Body, as well as the Mind, and not only serve to clear and brighten the Imagination, but are able to disperse Grief and Melancholy, and to set the Animal Spirits in pleasing and agreeable Motions. For this Reason Sir *Francis Bacon,* in his Essay upon Health, has not thought it improper to prescribe to his Reader a Poem or a Prospect, where he particularly dissuades him from knotty and subtle Disquisitions, and advises him to pursue Studies that fill the Mind with splendid and illustrious Objects, as Histories, Fables and Contemplations of Nature.

I have in this Paper, by way of Introduction, settled the Notion of those Pleasures of the Imagination which are the Subject of my present Undertaking, and endeavoured, by several Considerations, to recommend to my Reader the Pursuit of those Pleasures. I shall, in my next Paper, examine the several Sources from whence these Pleasures are derived.

No. 412   Monday, June 23, 1712.   [Addison]

. . . Divisum sic breve fiet Opus. [1]—Mart.

I shall first consider those Pleasures of the Imagination, which
arise from the actual View and Survey of outward Objects:
And these, I think, all proceed from the Sight of what is *Great,
Uncommon,* or *Beautiful.* There may, indeed, be something
so terrible or offensive, that the Horrour or Loathsomeness
of an Object may over-bear the Pleasure which results from
its *Greatness, Novelty* or *Beauty;* but still there will be such
a Mixture of Delight in the very Disgust it gives us, as any of
these three Qualifications are most conspicuous and prevailing.

By *Greatness,* I do not only mean the Bulk of any single
Object, but the Largeness of a whole View, considered as one
entire Piece. Such are the Prospects of an open Champian
Country, a vast uncultivated Desart, of huge Heaps of Mountains, high Rocks and Precipices, or a wide Expanse of Waters,
where we are not struck with the Novelty or Beauty of the Sight,
but with that rude kind of Magnificence which appears in many
of these stupendous Works of Nature. Our Imagination loves
to be filled with an Object, or to grasp at any thing that is too
big for its Capacity. We are flung into a pleasing Astonishment
at such unbounded Views, and feel a delightful Stilness and
Amazement in the Soul at the Apprehension of them. The
Mind of Man naturally hates every thing that looks like a Re-
straint upon it, and is apt to fancy it self under a sort of Confinement, when the Sight is pent up in a narrow Compass, and

[1] "Divided the work will thus become brief."

shortned on every side by the Neighbourhood of Walls or Mountains. On the contrary, a spacious Horizon is an Image of Liberty, where the Eye has Room to range abroad, to expatiate at large on the Immensity of its Views, and to lose it self amidst the Variety of Objects that offer themselves to its Observation. Such wide and undetermined Prospects are as pleasing to the Fancy, as the Speculations of Eternity or Infinitude are to the Understanding. But if there be a Beauty or Uncommonness joined with this Grandeur, as in a troubled Ocean, a Heaven adorned with Stars and Meteors, or a spacious Landskip cut out into Rivers, Woods, Rocks, and Meadows, the Pleasure still grows upon us, as it arises from more than a single Principle.

Every thing that is *new* or *uncommon* raises a Pleasure in the Imagination, because it fills the Soul with an agreeable Surprise, gratifies its Curiosity, and gives it an Idea of which it was not before possest. We are indeed so often conversant with one Sett of Objects, and tired out with so many repeated Shows of the same Things, that whatever is *new* or *uncommon* contributes a little to vary human Life, and to divert our Minds, for a while, with the Strangeness of its Appearance: It serves us for a Kind of Refreshment, and takes off from that Satiety we are apt to complain of in our usual and ordinary Entertainments. It is this that bestows Charms on a Monster, and makes even the Imperfections of Nature please us. It is this that recommends Variety, where the Mind is every Instant called off to something new, and the Attention not suffered to dwell too long, and waste it self on any particular Object. It is this, likewise, that improves what is great or beautiful, and makes it afford the Mind a double Entertainment. Groves, Fields, and Meadows, are at any Season of the Year pleasant to look upon, but never so much as in the opening of the Spring, when they are all new and fresh, with their first Gloss upon them, and not yet too much accustomed and familiar to the Eye. For this Reason there is nothing that more enlivens a Prospect than Rivers, Jetteaus, or Falls of Water, where the Scene is perpetually shifting, and entertaining the Sight every Moment with something that is new. We are quickly tired with looking upon Hills and Vallies, where every thing continues fixt and settled in the same Place and Posture, but find our Thoughts a little agitated and relieved at the Sight of such Objects as are ever in Motion, and sliding away from beneath the Eye of the Beholder.

But there is nothing that makes its way more directly to the Soul than *Beauty,* which immediately diffuses a secret Satisfaction and Complacency through the Imagination, and gives a Finishing to any thing that is Great or Uncommon. The very first Discovery of it strikes the Mind with an inward Joy, and spreads a Chearfulness and Delight through all its Faculties. There is not perhaps any real Beauty or Deformity more in one piece of Matter than another, because we might have been so made, that whatsoever now appears loathsom to us, might have shewn it self agreeable; but we find by Experience, that there are several Modifications of Matter which the Mind, without any previous Consideration, pronounces at first sight Beautiful or Deformed. Thus we see that every different Species of sensible Creatures has its different Notions of Beauty, and that each of them is most affected with the Beauties of its own Kind. This is no where more remarkable than in Birds of the same Shape and Proportion, where we often see the Male determined in his Courtship by the single Grain or Tincture of a Feather, and never discovering any Charms but in the Colour of its Species.[2]

> *The feather'd Husband to his Partner true,*
> *Preserves connubial Rites inviolate.*
> *With cold Indifference every Charm he sees,*
> *The milky Whiteness of the stately Neck,*
> *The shining Down, proud Crest, and purple Wings;*

[2] The nineteen lines of Latin verse by Addison which appeared here in the early editions were translated as follows in a duodecimo edition of 1744. Compare *The Spectator,* No. 120.

> *But cautious with a searching Eye explores*
> *The female Tribes, his proper Mate to find,*
> *With kindred Colours mark'd: Did he not so,*
> *The Grove with painted Monsters wou'd abound,*
> *Th' ambiguous Product of unnatural Love.*
> *The Black-bird hence selects her sooty Spouse;*
> *The Nightingale her musical Compeer,*
> *Lur'd by the well-known Voice: the Bird of Night,*
> *Smit with her dusky Wings and greenish Eyes,*
> *Woos his dun Paramour. The beauteous Race*
> *Speak the chaste Loves of their Progenitors;*
> *When, by the Spring invited, they exult*
> *In Woods and Fields, and to the Sun unfold*
> *Their Plumes, that with paternal Colours glow.*

There·is a second Kind of *Beauty* that we find in the several Products of Art and Nature, which does not work in the Imagination with that Warmth and Violence as the Beauty that appears in our proper Species, but is apt however to raise in us a secret Delight, and a kind of Fondness for the Places or Objects in which we discover it. This consists either in the Gaiety or Variety of Colours, in the Symmetry and Proportion of Parts, in the Arrangement and Disposition of Bodies, or in a just Mixture and Concurrence of all together. Among these several Kinds of Beauty the Eye takes most Delight in Colours. We no where meet with a more glorious or pleasing Show in Nature, than what appears in the Heavens at the rising and setting of the Sun, which is wholly make up of those different Stains of Light that shew themselves in Clouds of a different Situation. For this Reason we find the Poets, who are always addressing themselves to the Imagination, borrowing more of their Epithets from Colours than from any other Topic.

As the Fancy delights in every thing that is Great, Strange, or Beautiful, and is still more pleased the more it finds of these Perfections in the same Object, so it is capable of receiving a new Satisfaction by the Assistance of another Sense. Thus any continued Sound, as the Musick of Birds, or a Fall of Water, awakens every moment the Mind of the Beholder, and makes him more attentive to the several Beauties of the Place that lye before him. Thus if there arises a Fragrancy of Smells or Perfumes, they heighten the Pleasures of the Imagination, and make even the Colours and Verdure of the Landskip appear more agreeable; for the Ideas of both Senses recommend each other, and are pleasanter together than when they enter the Mind separately: As the different Colours of a Picture, when they are well disposed, set off one another, and receive an additional Beauty from the Advantage of their Situation.

. . . mentis gratissimus Error. [1] —Hor.

There is a kind of Writing, wherein the Poet quite loses sight of Nature, and entertains his Reader's Imagination with the Characters and Actions of such Persons as have many of them no Existence, but what he bestows on them. Such are Fairies, Witches, Magicians, Demons, and departed Spirits. This Mr. *Dryden* calls *the Fairy Way of Writing,* which is, indeed, more difficult than any other that depends on the Poet's Fancy, because he has no Pattern to follow in it, and must work altogether out of his own Invention.

There is a very odd turn of Thought required for this sort of Writing, and it is impossible for a Poet to succeed in it, who has not a particular Cast of Fancy, and an Imagination naturally fruitful and superstitious. Besides this, he ought to be very well versed in Legends and Fables, antiquated Romances, and the Traditions of Nurses and old Women, that he may fall in with our natural Prejudices, and humour those Notions which we have imbibed in our Infancy.[2] For, otherwise, he will be apt to make his Fairies talk like People of his own Species, and not like other Setts of Beings, who converse with different Objects, and think in a different manner from that of Mankind;

Sylvis deducti caveant, me Judice, Fauni

[1] "The dearest illusion of the heart."
[2] Compare *The Rape of the Lock,* I, 29-36.

Ne velut innati triviis, ac pæne forenses,
Aut nimium teneris juvenentur versibus[3] . . .- Hor.

I do not say with Mr. *Bays* in the *Rehearsal,* that Spirits must not be confined to speak Sense, but it is certain their Sense ought to be a little discoloured, that it may seem particular, and proper to the Person and Condition of the Speaker.

These Descriptions raise a pleasing kind of Horrour in the Mind of the Reader, and amuse his Imagination with the Strangeness and Novelty of the Persons who are represented in them. They bring up into our Memory the Stories we have heard in our Childhood, and favour those secret Terrors and Apprehensions to which the Mind of Man is naturally subject. We are pleased with surveying the different Habits and Behaviours of Foreign Countries, how much more must we be delighted and surprised when we are led, as it were, into a new Creation, and see the Persons and Manners of another Species? Men of cold Fancies, and Philosophical Dispositions, object to this kind of Poetry, that it has not Probability enough to affect the Imagination. But to this it may be answered, that we are sure, in general, there are many intellectual Beings in the World besides our selves, and several Species of Spirits, who are subject to different Laws and Oeconomies from those of Mankind; when we see, therefore, any of these represented naturally, we cannot look upon the Representation as altogether impossible; nay, many are prepossest with such false Opinions, as dispose them to believe these particular Delusions; at least, we have all heard so many pleasing Relations in favour of them, that we do not care for seeing through the Falshood, and willingly give our selves up to so agreeable an Imposture.

The Ancients have not much of this Poetry among them,

---

[3] "When the fauns are brought from the forest, they should, methinks, beware of behaving as though they were born at the crossways and almost as dwelling in the Forum, playing the young bloods with their mawkish verses."

for, indeed, almost the whole Substance of it owes its Original to the Darkness and Superstition of later Ages, when pious Frauds were made use of to amuse Mankind, and frighten them into a Sense of their Duty. Our Forefathers looked upon Nature with more Reverence and Horrour, before the World was enlightened by Learning and Philosophy, and loved to astonish themselves with the Apprehensions of Witchcraft, Prodigies, Charms and Enchantments. There was not a Village in *England* that had not a Ghost in it, the Church-yards were all haunted, every large Common had a Circle of Fairies belonging to it, and there was scarce a Shepherd to be met with who had not seen a Spirit.

Among all the Poets of this Kind our *English* are much the best, by what I have yet seen, whether it be that we abound with more Stories of this Nature, or that the Genius of our Country is fitter for this sort of Poetry. For the *English* are naturally Fanciful, and very often disposed by that Gloominess and Melancholly of Temper, which is so frequent in our Nation, to many wild Notions and Visions, to which others are not so liable.

Among the *English, Shakespear* has incomparably excelled all others. That noble Extravagance of Fancy, which he had in so great Perfection, thoroughly qualified him to touch this weak superstitious Part of his Reader's Imagination; and made him capable of succeeding, where he had nothing to support him besides the Strength of his own Genius. There is something so wild and yet so solemn in the Speeches of his Ghosts, Fairies, Witches, and the like Imaginary Persons, that we cannot forbear thinking them natural, tho' we have no Rule by which to judge of them, and must confess, if there are such Beings in the World, it looks highly probable they should talk and act as he has represented them.

There is another sort of Imaginary Beings, that we sometimes meet with among the Poets, when the Author represents any Passion, Appetite, Virtue or Vice, under a visible Shape, and makes it a Person or an Actor in his Poem. Of this Nature are the Descriptions of Hunger and Envy in *Ovid,* of Fame in *Virgil,* and of Sin and Death in *Milton.* We find a whole Creation of the like shadowy Persons in *Spencer,* who had an admirable Talent in Representations of this kind. I have discoursed of these Emblematical Persons in former Papers, and shall therefore only mention them in this Place. Thus we see how many ways Poetry addresses it self to the Imagination, as it has not only the whole Circle of Nature for its Province, but makes new Worlds of its own, shews us Persons who are not to be found in Being, and represents even the Faculties of the Soul, with her several Virtues and Vices, in a sensible Shape and Character.

I shall, in my two following Papers, consider in general, how other kinds of Writing are qualified to please the Imagination, with which I intend to conclude this Essay.

No. 420   Wednesday, July 2, 1712.   [Addison]

. . . Quocunque volent animum Auditoris agunto.[1]—Hor.

As the Writers in Poetry and Fiction borrow their several Materials from outward Objects, and join them together at their own Pleasure, there are others who are obliged to follow Nature more closely, and to take entire Scenes out of her. Such are Historians, natural Philosophers, Travellers, Geographers, and, in a Word, all who describe visible Objects of a real Existence.

It is the most agreeable Talent of an Historian to be able to draw up his Armies and fight his Battels in proper Expressions, to set before our Eyes the Divisions, Cabals, and Jealousies of Great Men, and to lead us Step by Step into the several Actions and Events of his History. We love to see the Subject unfolding it self by just Degrees, and breaking upon us insensibly, that so we may be kept in a pleasing Suspense, and have Time given us to raise our Expectations, and to side with one of the Parties concerned in the Relation. I confess this shews more the Art than the Veracity of the Historian, but I am only to speak of him as he is qualified to please the Imagination. And in this respect *Livy* has, perhaps, excelled all who went before him, or have written since his Time. He describes every thing in so lively a Manner, that his whole History is an admirable Picture, and touches on such proper Circumstances in every Story, that this Reader becomes a kind of Spectator, and feels in himself all the variety of Passions which are correspondent to the several Parts of the Relation.

---

[1] "They must lead the hearer's soul where they will."

But among this Sett of Writers, there are none who more gratifie and enlarge the Imagination, than the Authors of the new Philosophy, whether we consider their Theories of the Earth or Heavens, the Discoveries they have made by Glasses, or any other of their Contemplations on Nature. We are not a little pleased to find every green Leaf swarm with Millions of Animals, that at their largest Growth are not visible to the naked Eye. There is something very engaging to the Fancy, as well as to our Reason, in the Treatises of Metals, Minerals, Plants, and Meteors. But when we survey the whole Earth at once, and the several Planets that lye within its Neighbourhood, we are filled with a pleasing Astonishment, to see so many Worlds hanging one above another, and sliding round their Axles in such an amazing Pomp and Solemnity. If, after this, we contemplate those wide Fields of *Ether,* that reach in height as far as from *Saturn* to the fixt Stars, and run abroad almost to an infinitude, our Imagination finds it Capacity filled with so immense a Prospect, and puts it self upon the Stretch to comprehend it. But if we yet rise higher, and consider the fixt Stars as so many vast Oceans of Flame, that are each of them attended with a different Sett of Planets, and still discover new Firmaments and new Lights, that are sunk farther in those unfathomable Depths of *Ether,* so as not to be seen by the strongest of our Telescopes, we are lost in such a Labarynth of Suns and Worlds, and confounded with the Immensity and Magnificence of Nature.[2]

Nothing is more pleasant to the Fancy, than to enlarge it self, by Degrees, in its Contemplation of the various Proportions which its several Objects bear to each other, when it compares the Body of Man to the Bulk of the whole Earth, the Earth to the Circle it describes round the Sun, that Circle to the Sphere of the fixt Stars, the Sphere of the fixt Stars to the Circuit of the whole Creation, the whole Creation it self to the Infinite Space that is every where diffused about it; or when the

[2] Compare *The Spectator,* No. 465.

Imagination works downward, and considers the Bulk of a Human Body, in respect of an Animal a hundred times less than a Mite, the particular Limbs of such an animal, the different Springs which actuate the Limbs, the Spirits which set these Springs a going, and the proportionable Minuteness of these several Parts, before they have arrived at their full Growth and Perfection. But if, after all this, we take the least Particle of these Animal Spirits, and consider its Capacity of being wrought into a World, that shall contain within those narrow Dimensions a Heaven and Earth, Stars and Planets, and every different Species of living Creatures, in the same Analogy and Proportion they bear to each other in our own Universe; such a Speculation, by reason of its Nicety, appears ridiculous to those who have not turned their Thoughts that way, tho' at the same time, it is founded on no less than the Evidence of a Demonstration. Nay, we might yet carry it farther, and discover in the smallest Particle of this little World, a new inexhausted Fund of Matter, capable of being spun out into another Universe.

I have dwelt the longer on this Subject, because I think it may shew us the proper Limits, as well as the Defectiveness, of our Imagination; how it is confined to a very small Quantity of Space, and immediately stopt in its Operations, when it endeavours to take in any thing that is very great, or very little. Let a Man try to conceive the different Bulk of an Animal, which is twenty, from another which is a hundred times less than a Mite, or to compare, in his Thoughts, a length of a thousand Diameters of the Earth, with that of a Million, and he will quickly find that he has no different Measures in his Mind, adjusted to such extraordinary Degrees of Grandeur or Minuteness. The Understanding, indeed, opens an infinite Space on every side of us, but the Imagination, after a few faint Efforts, is immediately at a stand, and finds her self swallowed up in the Immensity of the Void that surrounds it: Our Reason can pursue a Particle of Matter through an infinite variety of Divisions, but the Fancy soon loses sight of it, and feels in it self a kind of Chasm, that wants to be filled with Matter of a more sensible Bulk. We can neither widen nor contract the Faculty to the Dimensions of either Extreme: The Object is too big for our Capacity, when we would comprehend the Circumference of a World, and dwindles into nothing, when we endeavour after the Idea of an Atome.

It is possible this Defect of Imagination may not be in the Soul it self, but as it acts in Conjunction with the Body. Perhaps there may not be room in the Brain for such a variety of Impressions, or the Animal Spirits may be incapable of figuring them in such a manner, as is necessary to excite so very large or very minute Ideas. However it be, we may well suppose that Beings of a higher Nature very much excel us in this respect, as it is probable the Soul of Man will be infinitely more perfect hereafter in this Faculty, as well as in all the rest; insomuch that, perhaps, the Imagination will be able to keep Pace with the Understanding, and to form in it self distinct Ideas of all the different Modes and Quantities of Space.

No. 421   Thursday, July 3, 1712.   [Addison]

Ignotis errare locis, ignota videre
Flumina gaudebat; studio minuente laborem. [1] —Ov.

The Pleasures of the Imagination are not wholly confined
to such particular Authors as are conversant in material Objects, but are often to be met with among the Polite Masters
of Morality, Criticism, and other Speculations abstracted from
Matter, who, tho' they do not directly treat of the visible Parts
of Nature, often draw from them their Similitudes, Metaphors,
and Allegories. By these Allusions a Truth in the Understanding is as it were reflected by the Imagination; we are able to
see something like Colour and Shape in a Notion, and to discover a Scheme of Thoughts traced out upon Matter. And
here the Mind receives a great deal of Satisfaction, and has
two of its Faculties gratified at the same time, while the Fancy is busie in copying after the Understanding, and transcribing Ideas out of the Intellectual World into the Material.

The Great Art of a Writer shews it self in the Choice of
pleasing Allusions, which are generally to be taken from the
great or *beautiful* Works of Art or Nature; for though whatever is New or Uncommon is apt to delight the Imagination,
the chief Design of an Allusion being to illustrate and explain
the Passages of an Author, it should be always borrowed from
what is more known and common, than the Passages which
are to be explained.

Allegories, when well chosen, are like so many Tracks

---

[1] "He delighted in wandering in unknown places and seeing unknown rivers;
his enthusiasm making it very little trouble."

of Light in a Discourse, that make every thing about them clear and beautiful. A noble Metaphor, when it is placed to an Advantage, casts a kind of Glory round it, and darts a Lustre through a whole Sentence: These different Kinds of Allusion are but so many different Manners of Similitude, and, that they may please the Imagination, the Likeness ought to be very exact, or very agreeable, as we love to see a Picture where the Resemblance is just, or the Posture and Air graceful. But we often find eminent Writers very faulty in this respect; great Scholars are apt to fetch their Comparisons and Allusions from the Sciences in which they are most conversant, so that a Man may see the Compass of their Learning in a Treatise on the most indifferent Subject. I have read a Discourse upon Love, which none but a profound Chymist could understand, and have heard many a Sermon that should only have been preached before a Congregation of *Cartesians*. On the contrary, your Men of Business usually have recourse to such Instances as are too mean and familiar. They are for drawing the Reader into a Game of Chess or Tennis, or for leading him from Shop to Shop, in the Cant of particular Trades and Employments. It is certain, there may be found an infinite Variety of very agreeable Allusions in both these kinds, but, for the generality, the most entertaining ones lie in the Works of Nature, which are obvious to all Capacities, and more delightful than what is to be found in Arts and Sciences.

It is this Talent of affecting the Imagination, that gives an Embellishment to good Sense, and makes one Man's Compositions more agreeable than another's. It setts off all Writings in general, but is the very Life and highest Perfection of Poetry. Where it shines in an Eminent Degree, it has preserved several Poems for many Ages, that have nothing else to recommend them; and where all the other Beauties are present, the Work appears dry and insipid, if this single one be wanting. It has something in it like Creation; It bestows a kind of Existence, and draws up to the Reader's View several Objects which are not to be found in Being. It makes Additions to Nature, and gives a greater Variety to God's Works. In a word, it is able to beautifie and adorn the most illustrious Scenes in the Universe, or to fill the Mind with more glorious Shows and Apparitions, than can be found in any Part of it.

We have now discovered the several Originals of those Pleasures that gratifie the Fancy; and here, perhaps, it would not be very difficult to cast under their proper Heads those contrary Objects, which are apt to fill it with Distaste and Terrour; for the Imagination is as liable to Pain as Pleasure. When the Brain is hurt by any Accident, or the Mind disordered by Dreams or Sickness, the Fancy is over-run with wild dismal Ideas, and terrified with a thousand hideous Monsters of its own framing.

> *Eumenidum veluti demens videt Agmina Pantheus,*
> *Et solem geminum, & duplices se ostendere Thebas.*
> *Aut Agamemnonius scenis agitatus Orestes,*
> *Armatam facibus matrem & serpentibus atris*
> *Cum videt, ultricesque sedent in limine Diræ.*[2] — Virg.

There is not a Sight in Nature so mortifying as that of a Distracted Person, when his Imagination is troubled, and his whole Soul disordered and confused. *Babylon* in Ruins is not so melancholy a Spectacle. But to quit so disagreeable a Subject, I shall only consider, by way of Conclusion, what an infinite Advantage this Faculty gives an Almighty Being over the Soul of Man, and how great a measure of Happiness or Misery we are capable of Receiving from the Imagination only.

We have already seen the Influence that one Man has

---

[2] "Like Pentheus, when, distracted with his fear,
He saw two suns, and double Thebes, appear;
Or mad Orestes, when his mother's ghost
Full in his face infernal torches toss'd,
And shook her snaky locks: he shuns the sight,
Flies o'er the stage, surpris'd with mortal fright;
The Furies guard the door and intercept his flight."

—Dryden's translation.

over the Fancy of another, and with what Ease he conveys into it a Variety of Imagery; how great a Power then may we suppose lodged in him, who knows all the ways of affecting the Imagination, who can infuse what Ideas he pleases, and fill those Ideas with Terrour and Delight to what Degree he thinks fit? He can excite Images in the Mind, without the help of Words, and make Scenes rise up before us and seem present to the Eye, without the Assistance of Bodies or Exterior Objects. He can transport the Imagination with such beautiful and glorious Visions as cannot possibly enter into our present Conceptions, or haunt it with such ghastly Spectres and Apparitions as would make us hope for Annihilation, and think Existence no better than a Curse. In short, he can so exquisitely ravish or torture the Soul through this single Faculty, as might suffice to make up the whole Heaven or Hell of any finite Being.

This Essay on the Pleasures of the Imagination having been published in separate Papers, I shall conclude it with a Table of the principal Contents in each Paper.

The CONTENTS.

PAPER I.

PAPER II.

Survey of outward Objects. How what is Great *pleases the Imagination. How what is* New *pleases the Imagination. How what is* Beautiful, *in our own Species, pleases the Imagination. How what is* Beautiful *in general pleases the Imagination. What other Accidental Causes may contribute to the* heightening *of these Pleasures.*

PAPER III.

Why the Necessary Cause *of our being pleased with what is* Great, New, *or Beautiful, unknown. Why the* Final Cause *more known and more useful. The Final Cause of our being pleased with what is* Great. *The Final Cause of our being pleased with what is* New. *The Final Cause of our being pleased with what is* Beautiful in our own Species. *The Final Cause of our being pleased with what is* Beautiful in general.

PAPER IV.

The Works of Nature *more pleasant to the Imagination than those of* Art. *The Works of Nature still more pleasant, the more they* resemble *those of Art. The Works of Art more pleasant, the more they* resemble *those of Nature. Our* English Plantations *and* Gardens *considered in the foregoing Light.*

PAPER V.

Of Architecture *as it affects the Imagination.* Greatness *in Architecture relates either to the* Bulk *or to the* Manner. *Greatness of Bulk in the* Ancient Oriental Buildings. *The ancient Accounts of these Buildings confirm'd,* 1. *From the Advantages, for raising such Works, in the first Ages of the World and in the Eastern Climates:* 2. *From several of them which are still Extant. Instances how* Greatness of Manner *affects the Imagination. A* French *Author's Observation on this Subject.*

Why Concave and Convex Figures give a Greatness of Manner to Works of Architecture. Every thing that pleases the Imagination in Architecture is either Great, Beautiful, or New.

PAPER VI.

The Secondary *Pleasures of the Imagination. The several Sources of these Pleasures* (Statuary, Painting, Description and Musick) *compared together. The* Final Cause *of our receiving Pleasure from these several Sources. Of* Descriptions *in Particular. The Power of* Words *over the Imagination. Why one Reader is* more pleased *with Descriptions than another.*

PAPER VII.

How a whole Set of Ideas Hang together, &c. *A Natural Cause assigned for it. How to* perfect *the Imagination of a Writer. Who among the* Ancient Poets *had this Faculty in its greatest Perfection.* Homer *excelled in Imagining what is Great;* Virgil *in Imagining what is Beautiful;* Ovid *in Imagining what is New. Our own Country-Man* Milton, *very perfect in all three respects.*

PAPER VIII.

Why any thing that is unpleasant *to behold, pleases the Imagination when well Described. Why the Imagination receives a more Exquisite Pleasure from the Description of what is* Great, New, *or* Beautiful. *The Pleasure still heightned, if what is described raises* Passion *in the Mind.* Disagreeable *Passions pleasing when raised by apt Descriptions. Why* Terrour *and* Grief *are pleasing to the Mind, when excited by Descriptions. A particular Advantage the Writers in Poetry and Fiction have to please the Imagination. What Liberties are allowed them.*

PAPER IX.

Of that kind of Poetry which Mr. Dryden *calls the* Fairy-way of Writing. *How a Poet should be* Qualified *for it. The* Pleasures *of the Imagination that arise from it. In this respect, why the* Moderns *excell the* Ancients. *Why the* English *excell the* Moderns. *Who the Best among the* English. *Of* Emblematical *Persons.*

PAPER X

What Authors please the Imagination who have nothing to do with Fiction. *How* History *pleases the Imagination. How the* Authors of the New Philosophy *please the Imagination. The* Bounds *and* Defects *of the Imagination. Whether these Defects are* Essential *to the Imagination.*

PAPER XI.

How those please the Imagination who treat of Subjects abstracted from Matter, *by Allusions taken from it. What* Allusions *most pleasing to the Imagination. Great Writers how* Faulty *in this respect. Of the Art of* Imagining *in General. The Imagination capable of* Pain *as well as Pleasure.* In what Degree *the Imagination is capable either of Pain or Pleasure.*

No. 465   Saturday, August 23, 1712.   [Addison]

Qua ratione queas traducere leniter ævum:
Ne te semper inops agitet vexetque cupido;
Ne pavor & rerum mediocriter utilium Spes.[1]—Hor.

Having endeavoured in my last *Saturday's* Paper to shew the great Excellency of Faith, I shall here consider what are the proper Means of strengthning and confirming it in the Mind of Man. Those who delight in reading Books of Controversie, which are written on both sides of the Question in Points of Faith, do very seldom arrive at a fixed and settled Habit of it. They are one Day entirely convinced of its important Truths, and the next meet with something that shakes and disturbs them. The Doubt which was laid revives again, and shews it self in new Difficulties, and that generally for this Reason, because the Mind which is perpetually tost in Controversies and Disputes, is apt to forget the Reasons which had once set it at rest, and to be disquieted with any former Perplexity, when it appears in a new Shape, or is started by a different Hand. As nothing is more laudable than an Enquiry after Truth, so nothing is more irrational than to pass away our whole Lives, without determining our selves one way or other in those Points which are of the last Importance to us. There are indeed many things from which we may with-hold our Assent; but in Cases by which we are to regulate our Lives, it is the greatest Absurdity to be wavering and unsettled, without closing with that Side which appears the most safe and the most probable. The first

[1] "How you may be able to pass your days in tranquillity. Is greed, ever penniless, to drive and harrass you, or fears and hopes about things that profit little?"

Rule therefore which I shall lay down is this, that when by Reading or Discourse we find ourselves thoroughly convinced of the Truth of any Article, and of the Reasonableness of our Belief in it, we should never after suffer ourselves to call it into question. We may perhaps forget the Arguments which occasioned our Conviction, but we ought to remember the Strength they had with us, and therefore still to retain the Conviction which they once produced. This is no more than what we do in every common Art or Science, nor its it possible to act otherwise, considering the Weakness and Limitation of our intellectual Faculties. It was thus, that *Latimer,* one of the glorious Army of Martyrs who introduced the Reformation in *England,* behaved himself in that great Conference which was managed between the most Learned among the Protestants and Papists in the Reign of Queen *Mary.* This venerable old Man knowing how his Abilities were impaired by Age, and that it was impossible for him to recollect all those Reasons which had directed him in the Choice of his Religion, left his Companions who were in the full Possession of their Parts and Learning, to baffle and confound their Antagonists by the Force of Reason. As for himself he only repeated to his Adversaries the Articles in which he firmly believed, and in the Profession of which he was determined to die. It is in this manner that the Mathematician proceeds upon Propositions which he has once demonstrated, and though the Demonstration may have slipt out of his Memory, he builds upon the Truth, because he knows it was demonstrated. This Rule is absolutely necessary for weaker Minds, and in some measure for Men of the greatest Abilities; but to these last I would propose, in the second place, that they should lay up in their Memories, and always keep by them in a readiness, those Arguments which appear to them of the greatest Strength, and which cannot be got over by all the Doubts and Cavils of Infidelity.

But, in the third place, there is nothing which strengthens Faith more than Morality. Faith and Morality naturally produce each other. A Man is quickly convinced of the Truth of Religion, who finds it is not against his Interest that it should be true. The Pleasure he receives at present, and the Happiness which he promises himself from it hereafter, will both dispose him very powerfully to give Credit to it, according to the ordinary Observation that *we are easie to believe what we wish*. It is very certain, that a Man of sound Reason cannot forbear closing with Religion upon an impartial Examination of it; but at the same time it is as certain, that Faith is kept alive in us, and gathers Strength from Practice more than from Speculation.

There is still another Method which is more Persuasive than any of the former, and that is an habitual Adoration of the Supreme Being, as well in constant Acts of Mental Worship, as in outward Forms. The Devout Man does not only believe but feels there is a Deity. He has actual Sensations of him; his Experience concurs with his Reason; he sees him more and more in all his Intercorses with him, and even in this Life almost loses his Faith in Conviction.

The last Method which I shall mention for the giving Life to a Man's Faith, is frequent Retirement from the World, accompanied with religious Meditation. When a Man thinks of any thing in the Darkness of the Night, whatever deep Impressions it may make in his Mind, they are apt to vanish as soon as the Day breaks about him. The Light and Noise of the Day, which are perpetually solliciting his Senses, and calling off his Attention, wear out of his Mind the Thoughts that imprinted themselves in it, with so much Strength, during the Silence and Darkness of the Night. A Man finds the same difference as to himself in a Crowd and in a Solitude; the Mind is stunned and dazzled amidst that variety of Objects which press upon her in a great City: She cannot apply her self to the Consideration of those things which are of the utmost Concern to her. The Cares or Pleasures of the World strike in with every Thought, and a Multitude of vicious Examples give a kind of Justification to our Folly. In our Retirements every thing disposes us to be serious. In Courts and Cities we are entertained with the Works of Men, in the Country with those of God. One is the Province of Art, the other of Nature. Faith and Devotion naturally grow in the Mind of every reasonable Man, who sees the Impressions of Divine Power and Wisdom in every Object on which he casts his Eye. The Supream Being has made the best Arguments for his own Existence, in the Formation of the Heavens and the Earth, and these are Arguments which a Man of Sense cannot forbear attending to, who is out of the Noise and Hurry of human Affairs. *Aristotle* says, that should a Man live under Ground, and there converse with Works of Art and Mechanism, and should afterwards be brought up into the open Day, and see the several Glories of the Heav'n and Earth, he would immediately pronounce them the Works of such a Being as we define God to be. The Psalmist has very beautiful Strokes of Poetry to this purpose, in that exalted Strain, *The Heavens declare the Glory of God: And the Firmament sheweth his handy Work. One Day telleth another: And one Night certifieth another. There is neither Speech nor Language: But their Voices are heard among them. Their Sound is gone out into all Lands: And their Words into the Ends of the World.* [2] As such a bold and sublime Manner of Thinking furnishes very noble Matter for an Ode, the Reader may see it wrought into the following one.

I.

> *The Spacious Firmament on high,*
> *With all the blue Etherial Sky,*
> *And spangled Heav'ns, a Shining Frame,*
> *Their great Original proclaim:*
> *Th' unwearied Sun, from Day to Day,*
> *Does his Creator's Power display,*
> *And publishes to every Land*
> *The Work of an Almighty Hand.*

[2] Psalm 19.

II.

Soon as the Evening Shades prevail,
The Moon takes up the wondrous Tale,
And nightly to the listning Earth
Repeats the Story of her Birth:
Whilst all the Stars that round her burn,
And all the Planets, in their turn,
Confirm the Tidings as they rowl,
And spread the Truth from Pole to Pole.

III.

What though, in solemn Silence, all
Move round the dark terrestrial Ball?
What tho' nor real Voice nor Sound
Amid their radiant Orbs be found?
In Reason's Ear they all rejoice,
And utter forth a glorious Voice,
For ever singing, as they shine,
'The Hand that made us is Divine.'

No. 499   Thursday, October 2, 1712.   [Addison]

> . . . . *nimis uncis*
> *Naribus indulges . . .* [1]—Pers.

My Friend WILL HONYCOMB has told me, for above this half Year, that he had a great Mind to try his Hand at a *Spectator,* and that he would fain have one of his Writing in my Works. This Morning I receiv'd from him the following Letter, which, after having rectified some little orthographical Mistakes, I shall make a Present of to the Publick.

Dear SPEC,

I was, about two Nights ago, in Company with very agreeable young People of both Sexes, where talking of some of your Papers which are written on conjugal Love, there arose a Dispute among us, whether there were not more bad Husbands in the World than bad Wives. A Gentleman, who was Advocate for the Ladies, took this Occasion to tell us the Story of a famous Siege in *Germany,* which I have since found related in my Historical Dictionary, after the following Manner. When the Emperor *Conrade* the Third had besieged *Guelphus,* Duke of *Bavaria,* in the City of *Hensberg,* the Women finding that the Town could not possibly hold out long, petitioned the Emperor that they might depart out of it, with so much as each of them could carry. The Emperor, knowing they could not convey away many of their Effects, granted them their Petition: When the Women, to his great Surprise, came out of the Place with every one her Husband upon her Back. The Em-

---

[1] "You take too much freedom in turning up your nose."
426

peror was so moved at the Sight, that he burst into Tears, and after having very much extolled the Women for their conjugal Affection, gave the Men to their Wives, and received the Duke into his Favour.

The Ladies did not a little triumph at this Story, asking us, at the same Time, whether in our Consciences we believed that the Men of any Town in *Great Britain* would, upon the same Offer, and at the same Conjuncture, have loaden themselves with their Wives; or rather, whether they would not have been glad of such an Opportunity to get rid of them? To this my very good Friend *Tom Dapperwit,* who took upon him to be the Mouth of our Sex, replied, that they would be very much to blame if they wou'd not do the same good Office for the Women, considering that their Strength would be greater, and their Burdens lighter. As we were amusing our selves with Discourses of this Nature, in order to pass away the Evening, which now begins to grow tedious, we fell into that laudable and primitive Diversion of Questions and Commands. I was no sooner vested with the regal Authority, but I enjoined all the Ladies, under Pain of my Displeasure, to tell the Company ingenuously, in Case they had been in the Siege abovementioned, and had the same Offers made them as the good Women of that Place, what every one of them would have brought off with her, and have thought most worth the Saving? There were several merry Answers made to my Question, which entertained us 'till Bed-time. This filled my Mind with such an Huddle of Ideas, that upon my going to sleep I fell into the following Dream.

I saw a Town of this Island, which shall be nameless, invested on every Side; and the Inhabitants of it so streightned as to cry for Quarter. The General refused any other Terms than those granted to the abovementioned Town of *Hensberg,* namely, that the married Women might come out with what they could bring along with them. Immediately the City Gates flew open, and a Female Procession appeared, Multitudes of the Sex following one another in a Row, and staggering under their respective Burdens. I took my Stand upon an Eminence in the Enemies Camp, which was appointed for the general Rendezvous of these female Carriers, being very desirous to look into their several Ladings. The first of them had an huge Sack upon her Shoulders, which she set down with great Care: Upon the opening of it, when I expected to have seen her Husband shot out of it, I found it was filled with China-Ware. The next appeared in a more decent Figure, carrying an handsome young Fellow upon her Back: I could not forbear commending the young Woman for her conjugal Affection, when, to my great Surprise, I found that she had left the good Man at home, and brought away her Gallant. I saw the third at some Distance with a little withered Face peeping over her Shoulder, whom I could not suspect for any but her Spouse, 'till upon her setting him down I heard her call him dear Pugg, and found him to be her favourite Monkey. A fourth brought a huge Bale of Cards along with her; and the fifth a *Bolonia* Lap-dog, for her Husband it seems being a very burly Man, she thought it would be less Trouble for her to bring away little *Cupid*. The next was the Wife of a rich Usurer, loaden with a Bag of Gold; she told us that her Spouse was very old, and by the Course of Nature could not expect to live long, and that to shew her tender Regards for him she had saved that which the poor Man loved better than his Life. The next came towards us with her Son upon her Back, who, we were told, was the greatest Rake in the Place, but so much the Mother's Darling that she left her Husband behind, with a large Family of hopeful Sons and Daughters, for the Sake of this graceless Youth.

It would be endless to mention the several Persons, with their several Loads, that appeared to me in this strange Vision. All the Place about me was covered with Packs of Ribbands, Brocades, Embroidery, and Ten Thousand other Materials, sufficient to have furnish'd whole Street of Toy-Shops. One of the Women, having an Husband who was none of the heaviest, was bringing him off upon her Shoulders, at the same Time that she carried a great Bundle of *Flanders-Lace* under her Arm; but finding her self so overloaden that she could not save both of them, she dropp'd the good Man, and brought away the Bundle. In short, I found but one Husband among this great Mountain of Baggage, who was a lively Cobler, that kicked and spurr'd all the While his Wife was carrying him on, and, as it was said, had scarce passed a Day in his Life without giving her the Discipline of the Strap.

I cannot conclude my Letter, Dear SPEC, without telling thee one very odd Whim in this my Dream. I saw, methoughts, a dozen Women employed in bringing off one Man; I could not guess who it should be, 'till upon his nearer Approach I discovered thy short Phiz. The Women all declared that it was for the Sake of thy Works, and not thy Person, that they brought thee off, and that it was on Condition that thou shouldst continue the *Spectator*. If thou thinkest this Dream will make a tolerable one, it is at thy Service, from,

Dear SPEC,

Thine, Sleeping and Waking,

WILL. HONYCOMB.

The Ladies will see, by this Letter, what I have often told them, that WILL is one of those old-fashioned Men of Wit and Pleasure of the Town, that shews his Parts by Raillery on Marriage, and one who has often tryed his Fortune that Way without Success. I cannot however dismiss his Letter, without observing, that the true Story on which it is built does Honour to the Sex, and that in Order to abuse them, the Writer is obliged to have Recourse to Dream and Fiction.

No. 517   Thursday, October 23, 1712. [Addison]

Heu pietas! heu prisca fides! . . .[1] — Virg.

We last Night received a Piece of ill News at our Club, which very sensibly afflicted every one of us. I question not but my Readers themselves will be troubled at the hearing of it. To keep them no longer in Suspense, Sir ROGER DE COVERLY *is dead.*[2] He departed this Life at his House in the Country, after a few Weeks Sickness. Sir ANDREW FREEPORT has a Letter from one of his Correspondents in those Parts, that informs him the old Man caught a Cold at the County Sessions, as he was very warmly promoting an Address of his own penning, in which he succeeded according to his Wishes. But this Particular comes from a Whig Justice of Peace, who was always Sir ROGER'S Enemy and Antagonist. I have Letters both from the Chaplain and Captain *Sentry* which mention Nothing of it, but are filled with many Particulars to the Honour of the good old Man. I have likewise a Letter from the Butler, who took so much Care of me last Summer when I was at the Knight's House. As my Friend the Butler mentions, in the Simplicity of his Heart, several Circumstances the others have passed over in Silence, I shall give my Reader a Copy of his Letter, without any Alteration of Diminution.

[1] "Alas for goodness, alas for old-world honor!"
[2] Announcing the death of Sir Roger was a step toward bringing *The Spectator* to a close. No. 513 had been devoted to a letter, made up of reflections on death, by the clerical member of Mr. Spectator's club, who reported himself to be seriously ill. No. 530 announced the marriage of Will Honeycomb, and in No. 541 appeared the Templar's farewell to his poetical studies. Captain Sentry's retirement to the country in No. 544 and Sir Andrew Freeport's removal to his estate in No. 549 complete the breakup of the society.

'Honoured Sir,

Knowing that you was my old Master's good Friend, I could not forbear sending you the melancholy News of his Death, which has afflicted the whole Country, as well as his poor Servants, who loved him, I may say, better than we did our Lives. I am afraid he caught his Death the last County Sessions, where he would go to see Justice done to a poor Widow Woman, and her Fatherless Children that had been wronged by a Neighbouring Gentleman; for you know, Sir, my good Master was always the poor Man's Friend. Upon his coming home, the first Complaint he made was, that he had lost his Roast-Beef Stomach, not being able to touch a Sirloin, which was served up according to Custom; and you know he used to take great Delight in it. From that Time forward he grew worse and worse, but still kept a good Heart to the last. Indeed we were once in great Hope of his Recovery, upon a kind Message that was sent him from the Widow Lady whom he had made Love to the forty last Years of his Life; but this only proved a Light'ning before Death. He has bequeathed to this Lady, as a Token of his Love, a great Pearl Necklace and a Couple of Silver Bracelets set with Jewels, which belonged to my good old Lady his Mother: He has bequeathed the fine white Guelding, that he used to ride a hunting upon, to his Chaplain, because he thought he would be kind to him, and has left you all his Books. He has, moreover, bequeathed to the Chaplain a very pretty Tenement with good Lands about it. It being a very cold Day when he made his Will, he left for Mourning, to every Man in the Parish, a great Frize Coat, and to every Woman a black Riding-hood. It was a most moving Sight to see him take Leave of his poor Servants, commending us all for our Fidelity, whilst we were not able to speak a Word for weeping. As we most of us are grown grayheaded in our Dear Master's Service, he has left us Pensions and Legacies, which we may live very comfortably upon, the remaining Part of our Days. He has bequeathed a great Deal more in Charity, which is not yet come to my Knowledge, and it is peremptorily said in the Parish, that he has left Money to build a Steeple to the Church; for he was heard to say some Time ago, that if he lived two Years longer *Coverly* Church should have a Steeple to it. The Chaplain tells every Body that he made a very good End, and never speaks of him without Tears. He was buried, according to his own Directions, among the Family of the *Coverly's,* on the left Hand of his Father Sir *Arthur.* The Coffin was carried by Six of his Tenants, and the Pall held up by Six of the *Quorum:* The whole Parish followed the Corps with heavy Hearts, and in their Mourning-Suits, the Men in Frize, and the Women in Riding-hoods. Captain *Sentry,* my Master's Nephew, has taken Possession of the Hall-House, and the whole Estate. When my old Master saw him a little before his Death, he shook him by the Hand, and wished him Joy of the Estate which was falling to him, desiring him only to make a good Use of it, and to pay the several Legacies, and the Gifts of Charity which he told him he had left as Quit-rents upon the Estate. The Captain truly seems a courteous Man, though he says but little. He makes much of those whom my Master loved, and shews great Kindness to the old House-dog, that you know my poor Master was so fond of. It wou'd have gone to your Heart to have heard the Moans the dumb Creature made on the Day of my Master's Death. He has ne'er joyed himself since; no more has any of us. 'Twas the melancholiest Day for the poor People that ever happened in *Worcestershire.* This being all from,

> Honoured Sir,
>   *Your most sorrowful Servant,*
>   Edward Biscuit.

P.S. My Master desired, some Weeks before he died, that a Book which comes up to you by the Carrier should be given to Sir *Andrew Freeport,* in his Name.'

This Letter, notwithstanding the poor Butler's Manner of Writing it, gave us such an Idea of our good old Friend, that upon the Reading of it there was not a dry Eye in the Club.

Sir *Andrew* opening the Book found it to be a Collection of Acts of Parliament. There was in Particular the Act of Uniformity,[3] with some Passages in it marked by Sir *Roger's* own Hand. Sir *Andrew* found that they related to two or three Points, which he had disputed with Sir *Roger* the last Time he appeared at the Club. Sir *Andrew,* who would have been merry at such an Incident on another Occasion, at the Sight of the old Man's Hand-writing burst into Tears, and put the Book into his Pocket. Captain *Sentry* informs me, that the Knight has left Rings and Mourning for every one in the Club.

[3] An act of 1662 designed to guarantee that no dissenting preachers should occupy Anglican pulpits. As a Whig merchant Sir Andrew was presumably more tolerant of dissenters than the Tory squire Sir Roger.

No. 519   Saturday, October 25, 1712.   [Addison]

Inde hominum, pecudumque genus, vitæque volantum,
Et quæ marmoreo fert monstra sub æquore pontus [1]—Virg.

Though there is a great deal of Pleasure in contemplating the
Material World, by which I mean that System of Bodies into
which Nature has so curiously wrought the Mass of dead Matter, with the several Relations which those bodies bear to one
another; there is still, methinks, something more wonderful
and surprizing in Contemplations on the World of Life, by
which I mean all those Animals with which every Part of the
Universe is furnished. The Material World is only the Shell
of the Universe: The World of Life are its Inhabitants.

If we consider those Parts of the Material World which
lie the nearest to us, and are therefore subject to our Observations and Enquiries, it is amazing to consider the Infinity
of Animals with which it is stocked. Every part of Matter is
peopled: Every green Leaf swarms with Inhabitants. There
is scarce a single Humour in the Body of a Man, or of any other
Animal, in which our Glasses do not discover Myriads of living Creatures. The Surface of Animals is also covered with
other Animals, which are in the same manner the Basis of other
Animals that live upon it; nay, we find in the most solid Bodies, as in Marble it self, innumerable Cells and Cavities that
are crouded with such imperceptible Inhabitants, as are too
little for the naked Eye to discover. On the other Hand, if we
look into the more bulky Parts of Nature, we see the Seas, Lakes

[1] "Thence the race of man and beast, the life of winged things, and the strange
shapes ocean bears beneath his glossy floor."
434

and Rivers teeming with numberless Kinds of living Creatures: We find every Mountain and Marsh, Wilderness and Wood, plentifully stocked with Birds and Beasts, and every part of Matter affording proper Necessaries and Conveniences for the Livelihood of Multitudes which inhabit it.

The Author of the *Plurality of Worlds*[2] draws a very good Argument from this Consideration, for the *peopling* of every Planet, as indeed it seems very probable from the Analogy of Reason, that if no part of Matter, which we are acquainted with, lies waste and useless, those great Bodies which are at such a Distance from us should not be desart and unpeopled, but rather that they should be furnished with Beings adapted to their respective Situations.

Existence is a Blessing to those Beings only which are endowed with Perception, and is, in a manner, thrown away upon dead Matter, any further than as it is subservient to Beings which are conscious of their Existence. Accordingly we find, from the Bodies which lie under our Observation, that Matter is only made as the Basis and Support of Animals, and that there is no more of the one, than what is necessary for the Existence of the other.

Infinite Goodness is of so communicative a Nature, that it seems to delight in the conferring of Existence upon every degree of Perceptive Being. As this is a Speculation which I have often pursued with great Pleasure to my self, I shall enlarge farther upon it, by considering that part of the Scale of Beings which comes within our Knowledge.

There are some living Creatures which are raised but just above dead Matter. To mention only that Species of Shellfish, which are formed in the Fashion of a Cone, that grow to the Surface of several Rocks, and immediately die upon their being severed from the Place where they grow. There are many other Creatures but one Remove from these, which have no other Sense besides that of Feeling and Taste. Others have still an

[2] Bernard LeBovier de Fontenelle (1657-1757).

additional one of Hearing; others of Smell, and others of Sight. It is wonderful to observe, by what a gradual Progress the World of Life advances through a prodigious Variety of Species, before a Creature is formed that is compleat in all its Senses, and even among these there is such a different degree of Perfection in the Sense, which one Animal enjoys beyond what appears in another, that though the Sense in different Animals be distinguished by the same common Denomination, it seems almost of a different Nature. If after this we look into the several inward Perfections of Cunning and Sagacity, or what we generally call Instinct, we find them rising after the same manner, imperceptibly one above another, and receiving additional Improvements, according to the Species in which they are implanted. This Progress in Nature is so very gradual, that the most perfect of an inferior Species comes very near to the most imperfect of that which is immediately above it.

The exuberant and overflowing Goodness of the Supream Being, whose Mercy extends to all his Works, is plainly seen, as I have before hinted, from his having made so very little Matter, at least what falls within our Knowledge, that does not Swarm with Life: Nor is his Goodness less seen in the Diversity than in the Multitude of living Creatures. Had he only made one Species of Animals, none of the rest would have enjoyed the Happiness of Existence; he has, therefore, *specified* in his Creation every degree of Life, every Capacity of Being. The whole Chasm in Nature, from a Plant to a Man, is filled up with diverse Kinds of Creatures, rising one over another, by such a gentle and easie Ascent, that the little Transitions and Deviations from one Species to another, are almost insensible. This intermediate Space is so well husbanded and managed, that there is scarce a degree of Perception which does not appear in some one part of the World of Life. Is the Goodness or Wisdom of the Divine Being, more manifested in this his Proceeding?

There is a Consequence, besides those I have already mentioned, which seems very naturally deducible from the foregoing Considerations. If the Scale of Being rises by such a regular Progress, so high as Man, we may by a Parity of Reason suppose that it still proceeds gradually through those beings which are of a Superior Nature to him, since there is an infinitely greater Space and Room for different Degrees of Perfection, between the Supream Being and Man, than between Man and the most despicable Insect. This Consequence of so great a Variety of Beings which are superior to us, from that Variety which is inferior to us, is made by Mr. *Lock*, in a Passage[3] which I shall here set down, after having premised, that notwithstanding there is such infinite room between Man and his Maker for the Creative Power to exert it self in, it is impossible that it should ever be filled up, since there will be still an infinite Gap or Distance between the highest created Being, and the Power which produced him.

That there should be more Species *of intelligent Creatures above us, than there are of sensible and material below us, is probable to me from hence; That in all the visible corporeal World, we see no Chasms, or no Gaps. All quite down from us, the descent is by easie steps, and a continued series of things, that in each remove, differ very little one from the other. There are Fishes that have Wings, and are not Strangers to the airy Region; and there are some Birds, that are Inhabitants of the Water; whose Blood is cold as Fishes, and their Flesh so like in Taste, that the scrupulous are allowed them on Fish-days. There are Animals so near of kin both to Birds and Beasts, that they are in the middle between both: Amphibious Animals link the Terrestrial and Aquatique together; Seals live at Land and at Sea, and Porpoises have the warm Blood and Entrails of a Hog, not to mention what is confidently reported of Mermaids, or Sea-men. There are some Brutes, that seem to have as much Knowledge and Reason, as some that are called Men; and the Animal and Vegetable Kingdoms are so nearly joyn'd, that if you will take the low-*

---

[3] *An Essay Concerning Human Understanding,* III, vi, 12.

est of one, and the highest of the other, there will scarce be perceived any great difference between them; and so on till we come to the lowest and the most inorganical parts of Matter, we shall find every where that the several Species *are linked together, and differ but in almost insensible degrees. And when we consider the infinite Power and Wisdom of the Maker, we have reason to think, that it is suitable to the magnificent Harmony of the Universe, and the great Design and infinite Goodness of the Architect, that the* Species *of Creatures should also, by gentle degrees, Ascend upward from us toward his infinite Perfection, as we see they gradually descend from us downward: Which if it be probable, we have reason then to be persuaded, that there are far more* Species *of Creatures above us, than there are beneath; we being in degrees of perfection much more remote from the infinite Being of God, than we are from the lowest state of Being, and that which approaches nearest to nothing. And yet of all those distinct* Species, *we have no clear distinct* Ideas.

In this System of Being, there is no Creature so wonderful in its Nature, and which so much deserves our particular Attention, as Man, who fills up the middle Space between the Animal and Intellectual Nature, the visible and invisible World, and is that Link in the Chain of Beings which has been often termed the *nexus utriusque mundi.* So that he, who in one Respect is associated with Angels and Arch-Angels, may look upon a Being of infinite Perfection as his Father, and the highest Order of Spirits as his Brethren, and may in another Respect say to *Corruption, thou art my Father, and to the Worm, thou art my Mother and my Sister.*[4]

---

[4] Job, 17:14

No. 530   Friday, November 7, 1712.   [Addison]

Sic visum Veneri; cui placet impares
Formas atque animos sub juga ahenea
Sævo mittere cum joco. [1] — Hor.

It is very usual for those who have been severe upon Marriage, in some part or other of their Lives to enter into the Fraternity which they have ridiculed, and to see their Raillery return upon their own Heads. I scarce ever knew a Woman-hater that did not, sooner or later, pay for it. Marriage, which is a Blessing to another Man, falls upon such an one as a Judgment. Mr. *Congreve's Old Batchelor* is set forth to us with much Wit and Humour, as an Example of this kind. In short, those who have most distinguished themselves by Railing at the Sex in general, very often make an honourable Amends, by chusing one of the most worthless Persons of it, for a Companion and Yoke-fellow. *Hymen* takes his Revenge in kind, on those who turn his Mysteries into Ricicule.

My Friend *Will. Honeycomb,* who was so unmercifully witty upon the Women, in a couple of Letters, which I lately communicated to the Publick, has given the Ladies ample Satisfaction by marrying a Farmer's Daughter; a piece of News which came to our Club by the last Post. The *Templer* is very positive that he has married a Dairy-maid: But *Will,* in his Letter to me on this Occasion, sets the best Face upon the Matter that he can, and gives a more tollerable account of his Spouse. I must confess I suspected something more than ordi-

[1] "Such the decree of Venus, whose delight it is in the cruel sport to force beneath her brazen yoke bodies and hearts ill-mated."

nary, when upon opening the Letter I found that *Will* was fallen off from his former Gayety, having changed *Dear Spec.* which was his usual Salute at the Beginning of the Letter, into *My Worthy Friend,* and subscribed himself at the latter End of it at full length *William Honeycomb.* In short, the gay, the loud, the vain *Will Honeycomb,* who had made Love to every great Fortune that has appeared in Town for above thirty Years together, and boasted of Favours from Ladies whom he had never seen, is at length wedded to a plain Country Girl.

His Letter gives us the Picture of a converted Rake. The sober Character of the Husband is dashed with the Man of the Town, and enlivened with those little Cant-phrases which have made my Friend *Will* often thought very pretty Company. But let us hear what he says for himself.

'*My Worthy Friend,*

I question not but you, and the rest of my Acquaintance, wonder that I, who have lived in the Smoak and Gallantries of the Town for thirty Years together, should all on a sudden grow fond of a Country-life. Had not my Dog of a Steward run away as he did, without making up his Accounts, I had still been immersed in Sin and Sea-Coal. But since my late forced Visit to my Estate, I am so pleased with it, that I am re-solved to live and die upon it. I am every Day abroad among my Acres, and can scarce forbear filling my Letter with Breezes, Shades, Flowers, Meadows, and purling Streams. The Simplici-ty of Manners, which I have heard you so often speak of, and which appears here in Perfection, charms me wonderfully. As an Instance of it, I must acquaint you, and by your means the whole Club, that I have lately married one of my Tenants Daughters. She is born of honest Parents, and tho' she has no Portion she has a great deal of Virtue. The natural Sweetness and Innocence of her Behaviour, the Freshness of her Complec-tion, the unaffected Turn of her Shape and Person, shot me through and through every time I saw her, and did more Exe-cution upon me in Grogram, than the greatest Beauty in Town or Court had ever done in Brocade. In short, she is such an one as promises me a good Heir to my Estate, and if by her means I cannot leave to my Children what are falsely called the Gifts of Birth; high Titles and Alliances: I hope to convey to them the more real and valuable Gifts of Birth; strong Bodies and Healthy Constitutions. As for your fine Women, I need not tell thee that I know them. I have had my share in their Graces, but no more of that. It shall be my Business hereafter to live the Life of an honest Man, and to act as becomes the Master of a Family. I question not but I shall draw upon me the Raillery of the Town, and be treated to the Tune of *the Marriage-Hater matched;* but I am prepared for it. I have been as witty upon others in my time. To tell thee truly, I saw such a Tribe of Fashionable young fluttering Coxcombs shot up, that I did not think my Post of an *homme de ruelle*[2] any longer tenable. I felt a certain Stiffness in my Limbs, which entirely destroyed that Jauntyness of Air I was once Master of. Besides, for I may now confess my Age to thee, I have been eight and forty above these twelve Years. Since my Retirement into the Country will make a Vacancy in the Club, I could wish you would fill up my Place with my Friend *Tom Dapperwitt.* He has an infinite deal of Fire, and knows the Town. For my own part, as I have said before, I shall endeavour to live hereafter suitable to a Man in my Station, as a prudent Head of a Family, a good Husband, a careful Father (when it shall so happen), and as

> *Your most Sincere Friend*
> *and Humble Servant,*
> WILLIAM HONEYCOMB.'

[2] A frequenter of levees.

No. 549   Saturday, November 29, 1712. [Addison]

Quamvis digressu veteris confusus amici,
Laudo tamen . . .[1]—Juv.

I believe most People begin the World with a Resolution to
withdraw from it into a serious kind of Solitude or Retirement,
when they have made themselves easie in it. Our Unhappiness
is, that we find out some Excuse or other for deferring such
our good Resolutions till our intended Retreat is cut off by
Death. But among all kinds of People there are none who are
so hard to part with the World, as those who are grown old
in the heaping up of Riches. Their Minds are so warped with
their constant Attention to Gain, that it is very difficult for
them to give their Souls another Bent, and convert them towards those Objects, which, though they are proper for every
Stage of Life, are so more especially for the last. *Horace* describes an old Usurer as so charmed with the Pleasures of a
Country Life, that in order to make a Purchase he called in
all his Mony; but what was the event of it? Why in a very few
Days after he put it out again. I am engaged in this Series of
Thought by a Discourse which I had last Week with my worthy Friend Sir ANDREW FREEPORT, a Man of so much natural
Eloquence, good Sense, and Probity of Mind, that I always
hear him with a particular Pleasure. As we were sitting together, being the sole remaining Members of our Club, Sir ANDREW
gave me an Account of the many busie Scenes of Life in which
he had been engaged, and at the same time reckoned up to

[1] "Though troubled by the departure of my old friend, I must still commend
him."

me abundance of those lucky Hits, which at another time he would have called pieces of good Fortune; but in the Temper of Mind he was then, he termed them Mercies, Favours of Providence, and Blessings upon an honest Industry. Now, says he, you must know, my good Friend, I am so used to consider my self as Creditor and Debtor, that I often state my Accounts after the same manner, with regard to Heaven and my own Soul. In this case, when I look upon the Debtor-side, I find such innumerable Articles, that I want Arithmetick to cast them up; but when I look upon the Creditor-side, I find little more than blank Paper. Now tho' I am very well satisfied that it is not in my Power to ballance Accounts with my Maker, I am resolved however to turn all my future Endeavours that way. You must not therefore be surprized, my Friend, if you hear that I am betaking my self to a more thoughtful kind of Life, and if I meet you no more in this Place.

I could not but approve so good a Resolution, notwithstanding the Loss I shall suffer by it. Sir ANDREW has since explained himself to me more at large in the following Letter, which is just come to my Hands.

Good Mr. SPECTATOR,

Notwithstanding my Friends at the Club have always rallied me, when I have talked of retiring from Business, and repeated to me one of my own Sayings, *that a Merchant has never enough till he has got a little more,* I can now inform you that there is one in the World who thinks he has enough, and is determined to pass the Remainder of his Life in the Enjoyment of what he has. You know me so well, that I need not tell you, I mean, by the Enjoyment of my Possessions, the making of them useful to the Publick. As the greatest Part of my Estate has been hitherto of an unsteady and volatile Nature, either tost upon Seas or flucuating in Funds; it is now fixt and settled in Substantial Acres and Tenements. I have removed it from the Uncertainty of Stocks, Winds and Waves, and disposed of it in a considerable Purchase. This will give me great

Opportunity of being charitable in my way, that is in setting my poor Neighbours to Work, and giving them a comfortable Subsistence out of their own Industry. My Gardens, my Fish-ponds, my Arable and Pasture Grounds shall be my several Hospitals, or rather Work-houses, in which I propose to maintain a great many indigent Persons, who are now starving in my Neighbourhood. I have got a fine Spread of improveable Lands, and in my own Thoughts am already plowing up some of them, fencing others; planting Woods, and draining Marshes. In fine, as I have my Share in the Surface of this Island, I am resolved to make it as beautiful a Spot as any in Her Majesty's Dominions; at least there is not an Inch of it which shall not be cultivated to the best Advantage, and do its utmost for its Owner. As in my Mercantile Employment, I so disposed of my Affairs, that from whatever Corner of the Compass the Wind blew, it was bringing home one or other of my Ships; I hope, as a Husband-man, to contrive it so, that not a Shower of Rain, or a Glimpse of Sunshine, shall fall upon my Estate without bettering some part of it, and contributing to the Products of the Season. You know it has been hitherto my Opinion of Life, that it is thrown away when it is not some way useful to others. But when I am riding out by my self, in the fresh Air on the open Heath that lies by my House, I find several other Thoughts growing up in me. I am now of Opinion, that a Man of my Age may find Business enough on himself, by setting his Mind in order, preparing it for another World, and reconciling it to the Thoughts of Death. I must, therefore, acquaint you, that besides those usual Methods of Charity, of which I have before spoken, I am at this very Instant finding out a convenient Place where I may build an Alms-house, which I intend to endow very handsomly, for a Dozen superannuated Husbandmen. It will be a great Pleasure to me to say my Prayers twice a Day with Men of my own Years, who all of them, as well as my self, may have their Thoughts taken up how they shall die, rather than how they shall live. I remember an excellent Saying that I learned at School, *Finis coronat opus.* You know best whether it be in *Virgil* or in *Horace,* it is my business to apply it. If your Affairs will permit you to take the Country Air with me sometimes, you shall find an Apartment fitted up for you, and shall be every Day entertained with Beef or Mutton of my own feeding; Fish out of my own Ponds; and Fruit out of my own Gardens. You shall have free Egress and Regress about my House, without having any Questions asked you, and in a Word such an hearty Welcome as you may expect from

> *Your most Sincere Friend*
> *and humble Servant,*
> ANDREW FREEPORT.

The Club of which I am a Member being entirely dispersed, I shall consult my Reader next Week, upon a Project relating to the Institution of a new one.

No. 555   Saturday, December 6, 1712.   [Steele]

Respue quod non es . . .[1]—Pers.

All the Members of the Imaginary Society, which were described in my First Papers, having disappeared one after another, it is high time for the *Spectator* himself to go off the Stage. But, now I am to take my Leave I am under much greater Anxiety than I have known for the Work of any Day since I undertook this Province. It is much more difficult to converse with the World in a real than a personated Character. That might pass for Humour, in the *Spectator,* which would look like Arrogance in a Writer who sets his Name to his Work. The Fictitious Person might contemn those who disapproved him, and extoll his own Performances, without giving Offence. He might assume a Mock-Authority; without being looked upon as vain and conceited. The Praises or Censures of himself fall only upon the Creature of his Imagination, and if any one finds fault with him, the Author may reply with the Philosopher of old, *Thou dost but beat the Case of* Anaxarchus. When I speak in my own private Sentiments, I cannot but address my self to my Readers in a more submissive manner, and with a just Gratitude, for the kind Reception which they have given to these Daily Papers that have been published for almost the space of Two Years last past.

I hope the Apology I have made as to the Licence allowable to a feigned Character, may excuse any thing which has been said in these Discourses of the *Spectator* and his Works; but the Imputation of the grossest Vanity would still dwell

[1] "Cast off everything that is not yourself."

upon me, if I did not give some Account by what Means I was enabled to keep up the Spirit of so long and approved a Performance. All the Papers marked with a C, an L, an I, or an O, that is to say, all the Papers which I have distinguished by any Letter in the Name of the Muse CLIO, were given me by the Gentleman, of whose Assistance I formerly boasted in the Preface and concluding Leaf of my *Tatlers*. I am indeed much more proud of his long continued Friendship, than I should be of the Fame of being thought the Author of any Writings which he himself is capable of producing. I remember when I finished the *Tender Husband,* I told him there was nothing I so ardently wished, as that we might some time or other publish a Work written by us both, which should bear the Name of *the Monument,* in Memory of our Friendship. I heartily wish what I have done here, were as Honorary to that Sacred Name, as Learning, Wit and Humanity render those Pieces which I have taught the Reader how to distinguish for his. When the Play abovementioned was last Acted, there were so many applauded Stroaks in it which I had from the same Hand, that I thought very meanly of my self that I had never publickly acknowledged them. After I have put other Friends upon importuning him to publish Dramatick, as well as other Writings he has by him, I shall end what I think I am obliged to say on this Head, by giving my Reader this Hint for the better judging of my Productions, that the best Comment upon them would be an Account when the Patron to the *Tender Husband* was in *England,* or Abroad.

The Reader will also find some Papers which are marked with the Letter X, for which he is obliged to the ingenious Gentleman[2] who diverted the Town with the Epilogue to the *Distressed Mother.* I might have owned these several Papers with the free Consent of these Gentlemen, who did not write them with a design of being known for the Authors. But as a can-

[2] Eustace Budgell (1686-1737), a cousin of Addison, who contributed to the revival of *The Spectator* in 1714.

did and sincere Behaviour ought to be preferred to all other Considerations, I would not let my Heart reproach me with a Consciousness of having acquired a Praise which is not my Right.

The other Assistances which I have had have been conveyed by Letter, sometimes by whole Papers, and other times by short Hints by unknown Hands. I have not been able to trace Favours of this kind, with any Certainty, but to the following Names, which I place in the Order wherein I received the Obligation, tho' the first I am going to Name can hardly be mentioned in a List wherein he would not deserve the Precedence. The Persons to whom I am to make these acknowledgments are Mr. *Henry Martin*, Mr. *Pope*, Mr. *Hughs*, Mr. *Carey* of *New-College* in *Oxford*, Mr. *Tickell* of *Queen's* in the same University, Mr. *Parnelle*, and Mr. *Eusden* of *Trinity* in *Cambridge*. Thus to speak in the Language of my late Friend Sir ANDREW FREEPORT, I have Ballanced my Accounts with all my Creditors for Wit and Learning. But as these Excellent Performances would not have seen the Light without the means of this Paper, I may still arrogate to my self the Merit of their being communicated to the Publick.

I have nothing more to add, but having swelled this Work to Five hundred and fifty five Papers, they will be disposed into seven Volumes, four of which are already published, and the three others in the Press. It will not be demanded of me why I now leave off, tho' I must own my self obliged to give an Account to the Town of my Time hereafter, since I retire when their Partiality to me is so great, that an Edition of the former Volumes of *Spectators* of above Nine thousand each Book is already sold off, and the Tax on each half Sheet has brought into the Stamp-Office one Week with another above 20*l.* a Week arising from this single Paper, notwithstanding it at first reduced it to less than half the Number that was usually Printed before this Tax was laid.

I humbly beseech the Continuance of this Inclination to favour what I may hereafter produce, and hope I have in many Occurrences of Life tasted so deeply of Pain and Sorrow, that I am Proof against much more prosperous Circumstances than any Advantages to which my own Industry can possibly exalt me.

> I am,
>> My Good-natured Reader,
>>> Your most Obedient,
>>>> Most Obliged Humble Servant,
>>>>> Richard Steele.
> Vos valete & plaudite. — Ter.

The following Letter regards an ingenious Sett of Gentlemen, who have done me the Honour to make me one of their Society.

'Mr. SPECTATOR,   Dec. 4. 1712.

The Academy of *Painting*, lately established in *London*,[3] having done you, and themselves, the Honour to chuse you one of their Directors, that Noble and Lovely Art, which before was entitled to your Regards, as a *Spectator*, has an additional Claim to you, and you seem to be under a double Obligation to take some care of her Interests.

The Honour of our Country is also concerned in the Matter I am going to lay before you; we (and perhaps other Nations as well as we) have a National false Humility as well as a National Vain-Glory; and tho' we boast our selves to excell all the World in things wherein we are out-done abroad; in other things we attribute to others a Superiority which we our selves possess. This is what is done, particularly, in the Art of *Portrait* or *Face-Painting*.

Painting is an Art of vast Extent, too great by much for any mortal Man to be in full Possession of, in all its Parts; 'tis

---

[3] By Sir Godfrey Kneller (1646-1723) in 1711. Sir Godfrey, the ablest portrait painter of the day, was a member of the Kit-Cat Club, to which Addison and Steele belonged, and did a series of portraits of the entire membership.

enough if any one succeed in painting Faces, History, Battels, Landscapes, Sea-pieces, Fruit, Flowers, or Drolls, &c. Nay no Man ever was excellent in all the Branches (tho' many in Number) of these several Arts, for a distinct Art I take upon me to call every one of these several Kinds of Painting.

And as one Man may be a good Landscape-Painter, but unable to paint a Face or a History tollerably well, and so of the rest; one Nation may excell in some kinds of Painting, and other kinds may thrive better in other Climates.

Italy may have the Preference of all other Nations for History-Painting; *Holland* for Drolls, and a neat finished manner of Working; *France* for Gay, Janty, Fluttering Pictures; and *England* for Portraits; but to give the Honour of every one of these kinds of Painting to any one of those Nations on account of their Excellence in any of these parts of it, is like adjudging the Prize of Heroick, Dramatick, Lyrick or Burlesque Poetry, to him who has done well in any one of them.

Where there are the greatest Genius's, and most Helps and Encouragements, 'tis reasonable to suppose an Art will arrive to the greatest Perfection: By this Rule let us consider our own Country with respect to Face-Painting. No Nation in the World delights so much in having their own, or Friends or Relations Pictures; whether from their National Good-Nature, or having a Love to Painting, and not being encouraged in that great Article of Religious Pictures, which the Purity of our Worship refuses the free use of, or from whatever other Cause. Our Helps are not inferior to those of any other People, but rather they are greater; for what the Antique Statues and Bas-reliefs which *Italy* enjoys are to the History-Painters, the beautiful and noble Faces with which *England* is confessed to abound, are to Face-Painters; and besides, we have the greatest Number of the Works of the best Masters in that kind of any People, not without a competant Number of those of the most Excellent in every other Part of Painting. And for Encouragement, the Wealth and Generosity of the *English* Nation affords that in such a degree, as Artists have no reason to complain.

And accordingly in fact, Face-Painting is no where so well performed as in *England:* I know not whether it has lain in your way to observe it, but I have, and pretend to be a tolerable Judge. I have seen what is done Abroad, and can assure you that the Honour of that Branch of Painting is justly due to us. I appeal to the judicious Observers for the Truth of what I assert. If Foreigners have oftentimes, or even for the most part, excelled our Natives, it ought to be imputed to the Advantages they have met with *here,* join'd to their own Ingenuity and Industry, nor has any one Nation distinguished themselves so as to raise an Argument in favour of their Country; but 'tis to be observed, that neither *French* nor *Italians,* nor any one of either Nation, notwithstanding all our Prejudices in their Favour, have, or ever had, for any considerable time, any Character among us as Face-Painters.

This Honour is due to our own Country; and has been so for near an Age: So that instead of going to *Italy,* or elsewhere, one that designs for Portrait Painting ought to Study in *England.* Hither such should come from *Holland, France, Italy, Germany,* &c. as he that intends to Practise any other kinds of Painting, should go to those Parts where 'tis in greatest Perfection. 'Tis said the Blessed Virgin descended from Heaven to Sit to St. *Luke;* I dare venture to affirm, that if she should desire another *Madonna* to be Painted by the Life, she would come to *England;* and am of Opinion that your present President, Sir *Godfrey Kneller,* from his Improvement since he Arrived in this Kingdom, would perform that Office better than any Foreigner living. I am, with all possible Respect,

> Sir,
>
> > *Your most Humble, and*
> >
> > > *most Obedient Servant,* &c.'

The Ingenious Letters sign'd the Weather-Glass, *with several others, were receiv'd, but came too late.*

POSTSCRIPT.

It had not come to my Knowledge, when I left off the *Spectator,* that I owe several excellent Sentiments and agreeable Pieces in this Work to Mr. *Ince* of *Grey's-Inn.*

R. STEELE.

Rinehart Editions